African American Culture
and Legal Discourse

Previous Publications

Lovalerie King
James Baldwin and Toni Morrison: Comparative Critical and Theoretical Essays (2006; co-editor)
Race, Theft, and Ethics: Property Matters in African American Literature (2007)
New Essays on the African American Novel (2008; co-editor)
The Cambridge Introduction to Zora Neale Hurston (2008)

Richard Schur
Parodies of Ownership: Hip-Hop Aesthetics and Intellectual Property Law (2009)

African American Culture
and Legal Discourse

Edited by Lovalerie King and Richard Schur
with a Foreword by Gerald Horne

First published in 2009 by PALGRAVE MACMILLAN® in the United States—a
division of St. Martin's Press LLC, 175 Fifth Avenue, New York, NY 10010.

Where this book is distributed in the UK, Europe, and the rest of the world, this is
by Palgrave Macmillan, a division of Macmillan Publishers Limited, registered in
England, company number 785998, of Houndmills, Basingstoke, Hampshire RG21
6XS.

Palgrave Macmillan is the global academic imprint of the above companies and has
companies and representatives throughout the world.

Palgrave® and Macmillan® are registered trademarks in the United States, the United
Kingdom, Europe and other countries.

ISBN: 978-0-230-61988-3

Library of Congress Cataloging-in-Publication Data

   African American culture and legal discourse / edited by Lovalerie King and
Richard Schur, with foreword by Gerald Horne.
     p. cm.
   Includes bibliographical references and index.
   ISBN 978-0-230-61988-3 (alk. paper)
    1. African Americans—Intellectual life. 2. African Americans—Legal status, laws,
etc.—History. 3. Race discrimination—Law and legislation—United States—History.
4. Law—Social aspects—States—History. 5. Law and literature—United States—
History. 6. Literature and society—United States—History. 7. American literature—
African American authors—History and criticism—Theory, etc. I. King, Lovalerie II.
Schur, Richard L.
   E185.86A3316 2009
   342.7308'73—dc22   2009015664

A catalogue record of the book is available from the British Library.

Design by Scribe Inc.

First edition: December 2009

10 9 8 7 6 5 4 3 2 1

Printed in the United States of America.

Lovalerie would like to dedicate this book to her brothers, Freddy, Charles, Chris, Bobby, Billy, and Stevie King.

Richard would like to dedicate this book to Victor and Eileen Schur, who inspired his passion for justice.

Was this what so many places in America were going to be like until the law, *justice*, took off her goddamn blindfold and saw what she had been doing with it *on*?

—John A. Williams, *The Man Who Cried I Am*

Contents

Acknowledgments

We would first like to thank our families and friends for the love and support that keeps us going every day. We are indebted to Drury University and Pennsylvania State University as well as our many wonderful colleagues at both institutions whose support made this project possible. Marie Tracy (Drury) provided a wealth of help with editing and formatting the manuscript. Elizabeth Neyens and Aqsa Ahmad (both Pennsylvania State University) provided additional editing and proofreading assistance. Carla Mulford (Pennsylvania State University) provided space in her Working Papers program for early dialogue about the issues covered in the volume.

We especially acknowledge and appreciate our contributors' patience and hard work during the years it took to bring this project to fruition. Finally, we would like to thank Rachel of Twin Oaks Indexing for going far beyond the call of duty in creating our index.

Foreword

Gerald Horne

Not so long ago, the ties between law and art were considered to be as tenuous as those between chalk and cheese. This kind of thinking was part of a rigid binary, a dichotomy that divided intellectual life into separate spheres as impervious to penetration as the separate spheres that were said to characterize life along the gender line.[1] But in any case, the idea of the "male public sphere" and the "female private sphere" hardly applied to African Americans and, likewise, the supposed barrier separating law from art is equally inapplicable.

More than that, attempting to maintain such a "Great Wall" between law and literature in the realm of African American Studies can be not only misleading but also dangerous. Thus, when the phenomenon known as "gangsta rap" erupted some years ago, it was discussed almost exclusively in the light it supposedly shone on African Americans, with much blathering about our alleged "pathologies." Yet, few bothered to note that historically the entertainment industry in the United States—and, indeed, in other nations as well—has been suffused by the influence of organized crime; this has been notably true of Hollywood,[2] the synecdoche for movie-making—which just happens to be situated in Los Angeles,[3] the headquarters of "gangsta rap." In other words, discussing this turn in music as a "thing in itself," apart from a broader discussion of the political economy, would be as fallacious as discussing other trends within popular culture beyond the broader context.

Thus, as Akilah N. Folami points out cogently, trends within hip-hop—not least, the rise of "gangsta rap"—were influenced decisively by the Telecommunications Act of 1996, just as the grittiness of this music itself was shaped inexorably by its birthplace in the Bronx, New York, which was being squeezed by a kind of "planned shrinkage" that involved escalating unemployment, growing poverty, proliferating racism, and worse. This disturbing tendency reached an apogee during a national television broadcast of baseball's "World Series" in 1977, when the announcer of stentorian tones, Howard Cosell, informed a stunned viewing audience that had tuned in to the game unfolding in the Bronx's Yankee Stadium: "Ladies and Gentlemen, the Bronx is Burning."[4] The television cameras then panned from the pastoral green of the baseball diamond to the disturbing scene beyond the warning track, where buildings were ablaze, an outgrowth of a dastardly scheme by rapacious landlords to burn out tenants and reclaim property. It was in such an environment that hip-hop itself was born and, consequently, analyzing this cultural form without consideration of its origins would be akin to seeking to analyze American racism without consideration of the African slave trade[5] and Jim Crow. Similarly, discussing

"gangsta rap" without consideration of the Telecommunications Act is equally misleading. This legislation fed a concentration of ownership, particularly in the radio
business, that contributed to a reduction in alternative voices, ideas, news, and art
heard on the airwaves. This radio deregulation had as damaging an impact as its
counterparts in the airlines (poorer service, higher fares, fewer airlines, etc.) or Wall
Street (more scams, more bankruptcies, more layoffs, etc.). More to the point, rap
was reduced to the lowest common denominator in the logic of Gresham's law; arising from the rubble was "gangsta rap," and buried in the rubble was a more hopeful
"conscious" or more politicized rap.

Folami illuminates both law and rap by probing their intersection. D. Quentin
Miller performs a similar service in his scintillating analysis of James Baldwin's
signature work, *The Fire Next Time*. This trailblazing book is difficult to comprehend without engaging how the law defined enslaved Africans as chattel and then
substantiated Jim Crow. Indeed, as the author notes perceptively, the entire corpus
of African American fiction is grounded in law, insofar as it is compelled perforce
to grapple with this constructed status of inferiority. Police and imprisonment
are inescapable aspects of the black experience, which implicates the machina-
tions of criminal law. Like any stimulating piece of writing, Miller's work forces
the reader to consider weighty matters that soar beyond the meticulousness of his
finely honed prose. Thus, should not black intellectuals retrospectively withdraw
diplomatic recognition of the United States because of slavery and Jim Crow eras?
This legal maneuver would not only complement the force of Baldwin's brilliance
but it would also raise the profound question the legitimacy of the American Revolution and its progeny. It would also convey enhanced retrospective recognition
on those rebels who merit more honor, including Gabriel Prosser, Denmark Vesey,
Paul Robeson, Shirley Graham Du Bois,[6] and others.

D. Quentin Miller is not the only author, however, in this illuminating collection
who forces the reader to ponder profundities. I speak of Matthew L.M. Fletcher: in
limning the snares that have entangled the Cherokee Nation and their insistence
on sovereignty and African American leaders and their objection to stripping the
Black Freedmen of tribal membership (a putative violation of U.S. law), it does seem
that appeals to a third legal regime—beyond the Cherokees and the United States,
that is, international law—could be the sharp blade to slice this Gordian knot. Certainly, the author is correct in observing that the sovereignty of indigenes should
be contemplated more carefully by all those concerned with progress. Thus, those
desiring to preserve and extend affirmative action should examine more carefully
the legal basis of tribal sovereignty, which is grounded not on the "racial character"
of indigenes but, instead, on the "political relationship" between indigenes and the
government now based in Washington, DC. The latter basis strikes me as something
of particular significance for African Americans. Similarly, if reproductive rights are
circumscribed on territory administered by Austin or Albany, conceivably tribal sovereignty could wind up being a savior for women in particular. In a similar vein, Sharon Harris's exposition of the life of Lucy Terry, the first recorded African American
poet, reminds us once more that those designated as enemies by Washington are not
necessarily the enemies of those of African descent.

There may be no clearer connection between art and the law than the sordid
tale of how African Americans who developed ragtime, blues, and jazz—among

other art forms—found their copyrights divested and, through inequitable contracts, their earnings pilfered, a story told quite well by K. J. Greene. Complement-
ing this work quite nicely is Richard Schur's exploration of trademark law and its
intersection with Aunt Jemima and other racialized emblems that have descended
through the decades.

Unfortunately, space constraints do not allow for consideration of the other
gems that comprise this wonderful collection. Suffice it to say, however, that a real
treat awaits the reader who digs deeply into this enlightening text. For herein it
is not only justice that is unveiled but also the ineffable bonds that bind the presumed separate spheres that are law and art.

Notes

1. See Rosenberg, *Beyond Separate Spheres*, and Davidson and Hatcher, *No More Separate
   Spheres!*
2. See Horne, *Class Struggle in Hollywood*, and Horne, *The Final Victim of the Blacklist*.
3. See Horne, *Fire This Time*.
4. See Mahler, *Ladies and Gentlemen, the Bronx is Burning*.
5. See Horne, *The Deepest South*.
6. See Horne, *Race Woman*.

Bibliography

Davidson, Cathy N., and Jessamyn Hatcher. *No More Separate Spheres!* Durham, NC: Duke
    University Press, 1982.
Horne, Gerald. *Class Struggle in Hollywood, 1930–1950: Moguls, Mobsters, Stars, Reds and
    Trade Unionists*. Austin, TX: University of Texas Press, 2001
———. *The Deepest South: The United States, Brazil, and the African Slave Trade*. New York:
    New York University Press, 2007.
———. *The Final Victim of the Blacklist: John Howard Lawson, Dean of the Hollywood Ten*.
    Berkeley, CA: University of California Press, 2005.
———. *Fire This Time: The Watts Uprising and the 1960s*. Charlottesville, VA: University of
    Virginia Press, 1995.
———. *Race Woman: The Lives of Shirley Graham Du Bois*. New York: New York University
    Press, 2000.
Mahler, Jonathan. *Ladies and Gentlemen, the Bronx is Burning: 1977, Baseball, Politics, and
    the Battle for the Soul of a City.*, New York: Farrar, Straus, and Giroux, 2005.
Rosenberg, Rosalind. *Beyond Separate Spheres: The Intellectual Roots of Modern Feminism*.
    New Haven, CT: Yale University Press, 1982.

Introduction

"Justice Unveiled"

Lovalerie King and Richard Schur

The ancient Greeks imagined justice in the form of the goddess Themis. Artists typically depicted her holding a scale in one hand and a sword in the other, her eyes covered with a veil. Her veiled eyes suggested that she viewed controversies impartially. The identities of the parties involved did not affect her insight, knowledge, or judgment. Modern American democracy, with its putative emphasis on equality before the law, has adopted this image for its judicial system. It has become commonplace to assert that "justice is blind," meaning that courts should not decide cases based on favoritism or bias. The veiled figure thus represents the highest ideals of neutrality. In contemporary Anglo-American social and political philosophy, John Rawls transformed this metaphor into a bedrock philosophical principle. In his *A Theory of Justice* (published after the height of the civil rights movement and during the early stages of the Black Arts Movement), Rawls reasserted the claim that society can only achieve consensus on society's just founding principles if its members adopt a veil of ignorance. This veil allows people to select the best rules for structuring society rather than simply adopting those rules that will most enrich them.[1] This blend of classical ideals and neo-Kantian ethics has led many to conclude that veiling legal decision makers creates the conditions for more just decisions.[2]

While dominant legal discourse has overwhelmingly affirmed the veil of ignorance, African and African American culture has a lengthy history of questioning the neutrality and objectivity offered by such veils. Ma'at, the Egyptian precursor of Themis, was frequently depicted with a scale but not a veil. For most ancient Egyptians as well as the ancient Greeks, balance—not blindness—was the primary metaphor for justice. In its classical origins, which were likely affected by Egyptian and other African concepts, justice was a relational and contextual concept in which bodies and political affiliations mattered. In his *The Souls of Black Folk*, W. E. B. Du Bois posits that a veil separates African Americans from whites and distorts the self-consciousness of African Americans. In an oft-quoted passage, he writes the following: "The Negro is a sort of seventh son, born with a veil, and gifted with second-sight in this world, a world which yields him no true self-consciousness, but only lets him see himself through the revelation of the other world. It is a peculiar sensation this double-consciousness, this sense of always looking at one's self through the eyes of others, measuring one's soul by the tape of a world that looks on in amused contempt and pity."[3] For Du Bois, veils connote both a second sight and a second-class form of citizenship rooted in legal, social, and economic inequalities. A common misreading of this passage emphasizes the psychological dissonance experienced by African Americans due to the demands placed on them by white Americans.[4] However, within the context of his critique of Booker T. Washington's accommodationist rhetoric, Du Bois's demand for social, political, and educational equality shows little evidence of this disenabling tension. Rather, the book clearly but forcefully provides sociological, historical, literary, and autobiographical evidence to support his claim that legal discourse must rip off the veil, acknowledge the fundamental humanity of African Americans, and recognize their basic rights.[5]

This volume collects essays that seek to dismantle the veil of ignorance about the experiences of African Americans under the law. Borrowing from Toni Morrison's efforts to reveal the Africanist presence in American literature, the essays focus on how race and racism haunt legal thinking and decision making via narratives and metaphors. In order for the legal system to make just decisions, it must be cognizant of the racial and racist implications of existing legal doctrines and metaphors. A variety of texts—from Du Bois's *The Souls of Black Folks* to gangsta rap—constitute products of a legal culture that has the power to affect artists' lives and to shape cultural production and dissemination. Unveiling justice requires that we chart the effects of race on law and African American culture in order to facilitate reform of the literary and legal imagination that will assist in achieving the Constitutional promise of freedom and equality.

The essays collected in this volume offer a wide-ranging analysis of African American culture's relationship with legal discourse. Eschewing a singular vision of law and moving between novels, poetry, music, visual culture, and autobiographical writings, the essays present race as a significant factor shaping the interaction between legal discourse and specific texts.[6] The collection seeks to examine African American culture as a powerful intertext that shapes American legal and literary discourses prior to any specific encounters in the contemporary law and literature movement.[7] In other words, the experience of African Americans frequently constitutes a necessary context for understanding the overlap, intersection, or tension between law and literature in American culture. These essays uncover the hidden layers of meaning within the veil metaphor as deployed by Rawls and Du Bois and as a general symbol for justice within the Western world. Readers will discover four aspects to the veil metaphor in this collection. At the first level, a veil is a cover that masks reality. The veil obscures both the vision of the person who wears it and that of the person who views the veiled figure. For Du Bois, this image makes it clear that there is an asymmetry between the vision of African Americans and whites. In this spirit, the essays offer strategies to clarify the vision of people on both sides of the veil. A second level of meaning, also suggested by Du Bois, is related to the use of the veil in the marriage ceremony. The veil is a prelude toward the ultimate union of marriage. In Du Bois's account, marriage functions as a metaphor for racial integration, especially in contrast to the social segregation endorsed by Booker T. Washington. These essays ultimately suggest that racial justice requires a deeper commitment to integration on a level that is even more foundational than earlier scholarly projects, which were designed to rid legal and literary discourse of racism, may have suggested.

The concept of "justice unveiled" also pushes against or challenges Du Bois's (and Rawls's) use of the veil metaphor. The third layer of meaning engages with the veil as a gendered metaphor, suggesting that racial justice, by design, must reveal inequalities resulting from gender. Unveiling justice thus signifies a concern with how legal violence against African Americans frequently affects men and women differently. A number of essays herein specifically examine justice as a gendered phenomenon and offer strategies to incorporate gender analysis within race-based criticism of legal and literary discourse.

Veils also invoke a sexual subject and thus a fourth meaning of unveiling justice speaks to the use of veils to denote a sexual purity and innocence. Rawls implicitly references this sexual aspect of the veil by using it to signify a general lack of knowledge and desire, which he terms the "original position." For Rawls, it is this lack that creates the necessary precondition for ethical decision making and justice. Du Bois makes it clear that any veiled figure possesses desire, albeit a frequently desexualized desire. In our usage, unveiling justice suggests that any efforts to create justice must engage with knowing and desiring subjects; understanding how race has shaped desire is a necessary prelude for any effort at fostering justice. Moreover, unveiling justice suggests that claims of racial purity or innocence, especially those attending claims of colorblindness, obfuscate the very way legal discourse is deeply implicated in existing racial inequalities. Assertions of innocence and efforts to desexualize justice create hiding spaces for racism's remnants. The innocence-guilt binary also offers an interesting angle from which to criticize some efforts at interdisciplinary research in this area. Scholars seem to alternate between assigning disciplinary "innocence" to literature or law and positing the other discipline as somehow guiltier, more infected by racism and racialized thinking. By contrast, the essays collected in this volume reflect African Americans' wariness of both law and literature, suggesting that any effort to rely on either discourse uncritically and ahistorically will neglect these discourses' frequent complicity with racism and racialization.

Last but not least, framing justice as unveiled is our attempt to further recent efforts to move law, literature, and cultural studies beyond the written text. The emphasis on unveiling obviously refers to increased attention to the power of visual images. Several essays examine visual culture and the very act of looking itself as key elements in the quest for social justice. In addition, several essays on music and the law call attention to the importance of sound in relation to social justice. Legal discourse has not only been blind to numerous instances of racial injustice but it has also been deaf to the power of music and sound for shaping cultural and legal relations. We hope that removing the blindfold from Lady Justice will have the added effect of uncovering her ears so that America will hear, and thus respond to, the call for justice contained in blues, jazz, and hip-hop music.

As Du Bois's deployment of the metaphor suggests, the veil and the attempts to demolish it have profoundly shaped both the content and the form of African American music, literature, and art. Despite the many periods and styles that have ebbed and flowed in popularity, African American textual producers have continually used their various texts to challenge racism and its manifestations in the law. Such an engagement has, in turn, affected the kinds of narratives and images that they created as they sought to illustrate how American law failed to realize its own lofty ideals. Time and again, these textual producers have demonstrated the worth of African Americans, have exposed logical contradictions, have uncovered racist stereotypes hidden within legal doctrines, and have revealed how law has privileged and continues to implicitly favor the white majority.

The legal impediments to freedom and equality over the past four hundred years have impelled African Americans to exert control—sometimes successfully and sometimes not—over the social, political, economic, and legal narratives that governed their lives. African Americans have exhibited sophisticated strategies and theories for explicating the complex relationship between African American culture and American legal discourse. While American colonialists revolted against England, African Americans made note of the contradiction in the legal arguments put forward by the founding fathers and the paradoxical marriage between slavery and freedom. The very arguments that necessitated revolution also could be, and were, deployed by enslaved African Americans against their white owners. Nevertheless, state and federal legislative bodies continued to enact and enforce laws supporting the institution of slavery until the Civil War period.

Following the Civil War and Reconstruction, the South resurrected its states' rights rhetoric. Segregation statutes at both the state and local level worked to segregate African Americans and whites. The United States Supreme Court ultimately federalized Jim Crow segregation in *Plessy v. Ferguson* (1896). The Court's ruling that separate facilities did not violate the Constitution so long as they were equal echoed Booker T. Washington's Atlanta Exposition speech of the previous year in which he endorsed racial segregation with his infamous hand metaphor. In economics, African Americans and whites would be together like a fist, but separation or segregation (i.e., the open hand with spread fingers) would rule in all things social. In *Plessy*, the Court translated Washington's hand imagery into the governing interpretation of the Constitution. This doctrine was easily co-opted in the service of white supremacy and remained the law of the land until the 1950s.

In addition to enacting and enforcing Jim Crow laws, supporters of white supremacy embraced lynching as a strategy for instilling fear and terror among the black population and generally dissuading most blacks from attempting to exercise the rights and privileges that came with citizenship. While it was an extralegal practice, lynching nonetheless constituted a key feature of segregation law. In particular, lynching and the fear of lynching impeded many African Americans from having any meaningful access to formal legal procedures to redress a wide range of harms or injustices. Indeed, historian and pan-Africanist Rayford Logan described the period between 1890 and 1915 as the *nadir* for African Americans because of the social and political damage they suffered during the nation's systematic betrayal of them. Incidences of lynching peaked around 1893, but, as a terror tactic meant to dissuade black Americans from enjoying full citizenship rights, lynching continued well into the first half of the twentieth century—with the occasional cases making news in the present.

Because law and politics failed to provide a solution to lynching,[8] African Americans relied on cultural texts to articulate claims for racial justice. In literary terms, Paul Laurence Dunbar's "We Wear the Mask" (1896) expressed the frustration of being forced to wear a racial mask in order to negotiate the terms of existence in segregated America. The plots, central metaphors, and narrative voices of novels from this period serve double duty: they tell a story about African Americans, and they challenge existing racial injustices against African Americans caused by the failure of American law. Even the Harlem Renaissance in the 1920s, probably the most famous movement of this period, is intertwined with legal discourse. The Harlem Renaissance constitutes a response to the relative failure of African American literature to effectively challenge Jim Crow segregation and lynching. The law's relative explicit absence from texts produced during the Harlem Renaissance may reflect the considerable skepticism about law as a possible venue for reform; however, that skepticism did not lessen calls for racial justice. For Alain Locke, the New Negro Movement would inaugurate a new era of mutual understanding—which, in turn, would "call for less charity but more justice, less help but infinitely closer understanding."[9]

Still, justice remained a key word in the conversation about African American literature, and optimism about legal reform reemerged during Roosevelt's New Deal. Several key events during the 1950s helped to dismantle legal segregation. In 1951 a group of parents in Topeka, Kansas, filed a class action lawsuit against the board of education that resulted in the 1954 landmark school-desegregation decision in *Brown v. Board of Education*. In 1952 the United States Army disbanded its all-black regiments, and in 1953 Blacks in Baton Rouge, Louisiana, staged a successful bus boycott. The 1955 lynching of Emmett Till in Money, Mississippi, sparked national outrage among African Americans.[10] Later that same year, long-time NAACP member and activist Rosa Parks (1913–2005) helped to spark the Montgomery bus boycott. The boycott, which lasted over a year, catapulted Martin Luther King, Jr., (1929–68) into national prominence and resulted in the Supreme Court's affirmation of a June 1956 federal district court ruling that race-based separation on city buses was unconstitutional.[11] The Montgomery bus boycott is often credited with being the inaugural event of the civil rights movement of the mid-twentieth century, though clearly the Baton Rouge bus boycott preceded it. Montgomery gave the civil rights movement a major boost in momentum that lasted over a decade. The combined effects of the *Brown* decision, organized protest, and the Civil Rights Act of 1964 effectively obliterated the legal effect of *Plessy*.

Since 1975, African Americans have been integrating into the legal academy and gaining access to the highest levels of the academy. Just as earlier generations of African American lawyers and litigants challenged legal discrimination since the colonial era, this new cohort of scholars and intellectuals sought to examine how race affected the operation of legal discourse. They helped create critical race theory (CRT), and, though CRT never achieved universal agreement on a single method or approach for reconstructing legal discourse, its proponents did share several assumptions:

1. "Racism is ordinary, not aberrational."
2. Racism and racialization serve important material and psychological functions within American culture.
3. "Race and races are products of social thought and relations."[12]

CRT, as a result, began its analysis with the lived experiences of ordinary African Americans under a racialized legal discourse.

CRT and its examination of the unconscious ways that race shapes legal thinking deeply influences the methods and theories employed in this collection. The scholarship collected herein examines historical patterns of racism; it also demonstrates how legal discourse's recent return to market-based metaphors for explaining human behavior effectively promotes and endorses unconscious racism and racially disparate effects. Through their use of CRT concepts and methods—such as the interest-convergence thesis, storytelling, the black-white binary, intersectionality, representation, and legal subjectivity—these essays explore how African American cultural texts have long articulated legal criticism and provide an alternative conceptualization of the interrelationship between law and culture. Collectively, they reveal how justice cannot be achieved by veiling itself to the operation of race in American culture. Rather, they suggest, law must engage in a more thorough engagement with race, racialization, and racism to eradicate remaining injustices.

*   *   *

African American Culture and Legal Discourse brings together the work of humanists and legal scholars to illustrate that justice has rarely been colorblind in the United States. While several essays reveal the perspective on legal discourse presented in specific literary texts, others consider legal doctrines and decisions from the perspective of African American cultural history, thereby reading law against the grain and engaging in what I. Bennett Capers terms "reading back, reading black" (Chapter 1). These genuine engagements with legal and literary discourses have resulted in essays that adopt a fairly diverse range of linguistic, scholarly, and organizational approaches. In part because there is tension between how lawyers write and how humanities faculty write, the volume has been edited to incorporate the range of disciplinary writing styles. *African American Culture and Legal Discourse* also provides significant support for the fairly well-known claim that African American texts have been deployed as weapons in the fight for social justice. Most commentators identify slavery, Jim Crow segregation, or a fairly general racial bias within legal discourse as the primary focus of African American cultural texts. The essays contained here go further to consider how specific areas of American law— including copyright, trademark, federal Indian law, property law, communications law, the right to privacy, criminal procedure, and affirmative action—contain the remnants of race-based thinking.

The collection is divided into three parts: "Rights and Sovereignty," "(Il)Legal Violence," and "Owning Culture." The first part, "Rights and Sovereignty," examines rights discourse and the question of political sovereignty. Most accounts consider rights as an essential building block of the rule of law, and these essays consider how rights discourse in American culture has historically relied on racial distinctions as an unspoken foundation. Because rights discourse can elide how racial hierarchy operates to marginalize racial minorities, the concept of rights is paired with the vibrant debates about political sovereignty as applied to African Americans and Native Americans. This contrast suggests that rights discourse alone may be insufficient to remedy how racism has shaped our social, political, economic, and legal structures.

Part I opens with "Reading Back, Reading Black, and *Buck v. Bell*" by I. Bennett Capers. Building on postcolonial theory and black literary theory, Capers asks how a reading of rights discourse grounded in the experiences of African Americans will shape our understanding of the law's approach to rights. His analysis of *Buck v. Bell* reveals that the court's anxiety about ordering the sterilization of Carrie Buck, a white woman, resulted from the inherent contradiction of applying a policy supported by the eugenics movement against a white person, thus destabilizing the very racial order they were promoting. Next, in "W. E. B. Du Bois and the Right to Privacy," Karla Holloway contrasts Du Bois's use of the autobiographical voice in *The Souls of Black Folks* against the initial formulation of the right to privacy, published just a few years earlier by two Harvard law professors. For Holloway, the right to privacy seeks legal recognition for wealthy white men's expectations about the boundary between their personal lives and the public sphere. Privacy, as a right, gains coherence, Holloway argues, when placed against the violability of black bodies for most of American history.

In Chapter 3, Rochelle Zuck examines how Martin Delany and other African American leaders deployed the rhetoric of sovereignty in their quest for justice. Zuck argues that during the 1850s African Americans, especially Delany, adopted and adapted the rhetoric of *imperium in imperio* so that African Americans could position themselves like Indian tribes to exert pressure on U.S. political and legal institutions and explore alternative visions of sovereignty and citizenship. These new articulations of divided sovereignty, according to Zuck, influenced the work of later writers such as Sutton Griggs, Rev. Benjamin Tanner, W. E. B. Du Bois, and Booker T. Washington. Matthew Fletcher, in "On Black Freedmen" (Chapter 4), explores how the conflict between rights and sovereignty played out in the Cherokee Nation of Oklahoma's recent decision to strip the black Freedmen of tribal membership. His analysis makes vividly clear that the black-white binary has become the dominant way of understanding race within legal discourse—even though the reality is more complicated—especially when some African Americans are also American Indians. The central principles of antidiscrimination law, according to Fletcher, conflict with the foundational elements of American Indian law: tribal sovereignty, the trust relationship, and measured separatism.

Chapter 5 examines contemporary iterations of rights discourse in the context of the affirmative action debates. William Gleason's "It Falls to You: Rawls, Bartleby, and the Ethics of Affirmative Action in Charles Johnson's "Executive Decision" demonstrates how Charles Johnson's approach to such debates in "Executive Decision" is influenced by both Melville and Rawls. Gleason shows that rights discourse is not enough to decide whom to hire; rather, logic must be supplemented by human experience and emotion. Gleason's analysis suggests that African Americans' claims for social justice are deeply grounded in a broader American framework even as he shows how the historical experiences of African Americans modify the application of Rawlsian notions of fairness.

The chapters in Part II, "(Il)Legal Violence," consider how racial violence has shaped African American experiences in understanding and thinking about law. Chapter 6, Sharon Harris's "Lucy Terry: A Life of Radical Resistance," investigates Terry's life to consider the relationship between property and freedom. By examining this extraordinary woman's life from both legal and literary perspectives, Harris reveals the ways in which Terry's ballad, "Bar's Fight," exposed the duplicitous nature of Massachusetts's emphasis on legal borders and how Terry's play with systems and language reflects the possibilities for a colonized person to "master" the dominant language in order to explode or expose the colonizer's position of power and, through the use of satire, the limitations of that power. In Chapter 7, D. Quentin Miller's "*The Fire Next Time* and the Law" explores how racial violence has affected the law's legitimacy in the eyes of many African Americans. Law was, for James Baldwin, nothing more than a legitimized use of force, which all too often operated to divide, control, and oppress African Americans. Despite his unyielding critique of the law's historical function, Baldwin retains his faith, according to Miller, that redemption is possible if America recognizes its racial guilt and sin in its treatment of African Americans.

Charlton Copeland, in his "Race, Gender, Violence, and the Reconstruction of the Word in Toni Morrison's *Jazz*" (Chapter 8), examines the law's relationship to violence against black bodies in general, and black, female bodies specifically. Morrison's narrative, Copeland argues, illustrates how black communities publicly challenge lawless violence committed by whites while leaving black women vulnerable to the violence committed by black men. For Copeland, this situation renders violence against black men a public problem to be remedied by the rule of law but frames violence against women as private and beyond the scope of legal discourse. Rebecca Wanzo follows with an examination of sexual violence against black women in Chapter 9 in her insightful reading of Gayl Jones's *Corregidora*, which also explores the limits of legal reparative remedies for racial slavery and segregation. For Wanzo, *Corregidora* challenges law as a mechanism for redressing black pain because legal rules about the admissibility of evidence, especially the multigenerational and historical nature of racial harms, tends to alienate African Americans from the legal process.

The collection concludes with Part III titled "Owning Culture," which considers how intellectual property and communications law confers and denies African American ownership claims over racial imagery. The essays in this section sketch out the important role that law plays in shaping cultural memory. K. J. Greene, in Chapter 10, uses the music of James Brown to examine copyright law's historical failure to provide African American musicians compensation for their innovations and to show how recent decisions about hip-hop sampling might be impeding further innovation within African American music.

In Chapter 11, "Legal Fictions: Trademark Discourse and Race," Richard Schur examines how trademark doctrines—including consumer confusion, false designation of origin, and dilution—have relied on a racialized set of assumptions in developing property rights in logos, symbols, and product names. Schur argues that trademark law continues to allow corporations to invest in racialized worldviews and promote the very kinds of stereotypes civil rights activists sought to challenge during the civil rights movement. Finally, Akilah Folami explores the effect of communications law on rap music, especially as a vehicle for political expression, in "The Telecommunications Act of 1996 and the Overdevelopment of Gangsta Rap." Rather than facilitating communication between a historically marginalized group (urban black and Latino male youth) and dominant mainstream society, Folami argues that the Telecommunications Act of 1996 has contributed to limiting discourse within the hip-hop community by increasing and solidifying corporate media conglomeration and control of the nation's radio airwaves. This conglomeration has been instrumental in creating the dominant gangsta image that has become, for the most part, the de facto voice of contemporary hip-hop culture.

By lifting the veil to reveal how race has shaped legal thinking, how law has influenced African American cultural production, and how African American cultural texts critique and criticize American law, the collected essays reimagine justice as a phenomenon that recognizes the subjectivity of historically marginalized groups, maximizes the autonomy of all individuals, balances communal and individual interests, addresses long-standing power inequalities, guards against the incorporation of stereotypes into legal doctrine, and views law as a possible venue for repairing the violence caused by racism. By tackling racism and its doctrinal remnants in its many manifestations, the authors blend legal critique with a sense of optimism that lawyers, judges, legislators, and scholars can create a more just legal system if they view racism as invidious, ubiquitous, and infecting the substance, procedure, enforcement, and administration of law.

Notes

1. Rawls, *A Theory of Justice*, 136–41.
2. Most mainstream judges, legal scholars, and critics argue for colorblindness as a prerequisite for achieving the Constitutional goals of due process and equal protection of the law. Neil Gotanda, however, has argued that the desire for colorblindness requires judges to ignore the lived experiences of historically marginalized people and force them to disembody and universalize their claims within ahistorical and decontextualized categories. Gotanda, "A Critique of Our Constitution is Color-blind," 16–21.
3. Du Bois, *The Souls of Black Folk*, 10–11.
4. See generally Allen, "Du Boisian Double Consciousness."
5. Ibid., 40–42.
6. Although some early law and literature texts viewed law almost as a transcendental signifier without temporal or spatial boundaries, others engaged in detailed analyses of particular historical junctures. See generally Cover, *Justice Accused*; Thomas, *Cross-Examinations of Law and Literature*; and Thomas, "*Plessy v. Ferguson* and the Literary Imagination." It should be noted that while many of these texts explored issues of race, they did so by primarily focusing on high-cultural sources and published legal decisions. This volume expands the focus to folk and popular-culture materials and also considers theories derived from African American perspectives rather than the putatively universal lens of most literary theory.
7. Julia Kristeva first developed the concept of the intertext, in *Desire in Language: A Semiotic Approach to Literature and Art*, to describe how language, and thus knowledge itself, cannot be reduced to a simple relationship between the signifier and the signified. For Kristeva and later Barthes, the concept of the intertext examined how any text or discourse necessarily relied on other texts and discourses to define its own meaning. See Barthes, "The Death of the Author," 3–7. Moreover, this theory posits that authors and readers rely on a range of cultural knowledge that exceeds what is clearly referenced or cited. In other words, texts are never hermetically sealed objects. Rather they necessarily evoke a wide range of extent or circulating metaphors, myths, and assumptions. This volume explores how race, racism, and racialization operate as intertexts for law and literature and constitute a matrix that structures the relationships between law and literature.

8. In 2005, the U.S. Congress issued an official apology for failing to enact a federal anti-lynching statute.

9. Locke, "The New Negro," 10.

10. Purportedly, Till was lynched after commenting on the attractiveness of a white woman. The woman's husband and an associate, both of whom had bragged about the murder, were subsequently acquitted by an all-white jury. For details surrounding this lynching, see Till-Mobley and Benson, *Death of Innocence*.

11. By the end of the 1950s, Martin Luther King, Jr., was a major leader in the blossoming civil rights movement and Malcolm X had risen to a position of prominence in the Nation of Islam, an organization that operated primarily in large urban areas. Malcolm X had become a member while he was imprisoned in Massachusetts.

12. Delgado and Stefancic, *Critical Race Theory*, 7.

Bibliography

Allen, Earnest, Jr. "Du Boisian Double Consciousness: The Unsustainable Argument." *Massachusetts Review* 43, no. 2 (Summer 2002): 215–53.

Barthes, Roland. "The Death of the Author." In *The Death and Resurrection of the Author?* edited by William Irwin, 3–7. Westport: Greenwood, 2002.

Brown v. the Topeka Board of Education. 347 U.S. 483 (1954).

Cover, Robert. *Justice Accused: Antislavery and the Judicial Process*. New Haven: Yale University Press, 1975.

Delgado, Richard, and Jean Stefancic. *Critical Race Theory: An Introduction*. New York: New York University, 2001.

Du Bois, W. E. B. *The Souls of Black Folk*. Norton Critical ed. New York: Norton, 1999.

Dunbar, Paul. "We Wear the Mask." In *Lyrics of Lowly Life*. 1896. Reprint, Secaucus, NJ: Carol Press, 1997.

Gotanda, Neil. "A Critique of Our Constitution is Color-blind." *Stanford Law Review* 44 (1991): 1–68.

Logan, Rayford. *The Betrayal of the Negro*. New York: Collier Books, 1965.

Locke, Alain. "The New Negro." In *The New Negro: Voices of the Harlem Renaissance*, First Touchstone ed., edited by Alain Locke, 3–18. New York: Simon & Schuster, 1997.

Plessy v. Ferguson, 163 U.S. 537 (1896).

Thomas, Brook. *Cross-Examinations of Law and Literature: Cooper, Hawthorne, Stowe, and Melville*. New York: Cambridge University Press, 1987.

Thomas, Brook. "*Plessy v Ferguson* and the Literary Imagination." *Cardozo Studies in Law and Literature* 9, no. 1 (Spring–Summer 1997): 45–65.

Till-Mobley, Mamie, and Christopher Benson. *Death of Innocence: The Story of the Hate Crime that Changed America*. New York: Random House, 2003.

Part I

Rights and Sovereignty

I

Reading Back, Reading Black, and *Buck v. Bell*

I. Bennett Capers

> All of us, readers and writers, are bereft when criticism remains too polite or too fearful to notice a disrupting darkness before its eyes.
>
> —Toni Morrison, *Playing in the Dark*

> To choose an attitude toward interpretation—and therefore toward language— these days is to choose more than just an attitude: it is to choose a *politics* of reading, it is to choose an *ethics* of reading.
>
> —Alice Jardine, "Opaque Texts and Transparent Contexts"

When I was in law school, the main task was to master the black letter law. It was only after law school, when I gained some distance, that I realized that there was also another type of law that was equally important, which I've come to think of as "white letter law."[1] Unlike black letter law—which brings to mind statutory law, written law, the easily discernible law set forth as black letters on a white page—"white letter law" suggests societal and normative laws that stand side by side and often undergird black letter law but, as if inscribed in white ink on white paper, remain invisible to the naked eye.[2] Still later, I realized that part of what I was bringing to the law was a different type of reading, a reading that was both counterhegemonic and attuned to the frequencies and registers of race—a reading practice I described in an essay titled *Reading Back, Reading Black*.[3]

In this essay, I'd like to apply this reading practice to a difficult, troubling, embarrassing case: *Buck v. Bell*.[4] But before I describe this case and my reading of it, it is useful to recount what motivated my thinking about "reading back, reading black." Part of the motivation came from the questions literary theorist Michael Awkward posed in his *Race, Gender, and the Politics of Reading*: "How does blackness direct, influence, or dictate the process of interpretation? Is there a politics of interpretation that is determined or controlled by race in ways that can be compared to the ideologically informed readings of, for example, feminist critics?"[5] Part of the motivation also came from my interest in the work of scholars such as Henry Louis Gates, Jr., who had edited two volumes of critical essays devoted to mapping the contours of black literary theory,[6] and Edward Said, who ushered in postcolonial theory, enjoining readers in his *Culture and Imperialism* to "read the great canonical texts, and perhaps also the entire archive of modern and pre-modern European and American culture, with an effort to draw out, extend, give emphasis and voice to what is silent or marginally present or ideologically represented . . . in such works."[7] And of course, I was influenced by Toni Morrison's seminal *Playing in the Dark: Whiteness and the Literary Imagination* in which she invited readers to see the "Africanist" presence in the works of Poe, Melville, Cather, and Hemingway.[8]

What interested me most, however, was developing the tools of this emerging black literary theory and applying these tools to the law. The questions I posed in my earlier essay *Reading Back, Reading Black*, I repeat here:

> If the reading of Western literature can be enriched by examining such texts through the lens of race, can a similar enrichment obtain from using a similar practice to read the law? And what would such a reading practice entail? Would it have its own methodology? Its own ideology? Would it be applicable to judicial texts that are not, ostensibly, about race? What are the implications of such a reading practice to a law that prides itself on its neutrality, its universality? And how, exactly, would such a reading practice enrich the study of law? Stanley Fish has argued that we each belong to interpretive communities, and that members of these communities are guided in their readings of texts by a common "consciousness," which produces interpretative "strategies [that] exist prior to the act of reading and therefore determine the shape of what is read."[9] If this is true, what does it mean for the study of law to have a community of black readers?[10]

What it means for the study of law, I argued, is a different type of reading—something I and other scholars had been engaged in without calling it such. For starters, it is a reading practice that by definition implies a type of reading back, a rereading that reads not only contextually but also critically. It suggests an independence, a certain "you've had your say now let me tell you what I think"—an attitude we associate with the temerity of "talking back" except this time without the sass. Second, it is a type of reading attuned not only to the often unheard registers of race that underlie many judicial opinions but also to class, gender, sexuality, and other hierarchical underpinnings. It is a type of reading that seeks to decode the coded, say the unsaid, and render visible the gaps, the fissures, and the solecisms. It is a reading that is counterdiscursive and counterhegemonic. And it is a reading with a difference, something akin to what Henry Louis Gates identifies as "signifyin(g)," or a trope of repetition and revision.[11] It is a reading practice that goes beyond interpretation of what a judicial opinion means to ask how these opinions function—the work they do and for whom.

What it does not mean is that one has to be black in order to read black or that being black by definition permits one to read black. Justice Thurgood Marshall, I believe, read black. So did Justice William Brennan. Justice Clarence Thomas, with one or two notable exceptions, generally does not.[12]

In my prior essay, I illustrated this reading practice by applying it to *The Queen v. Dudley & Stephens*, the famous nineteenth-century cannibalism case, and to

Muller v. Oregon, in which the Supreme Court addressed the constitutionality of an Oregon statute that limited the workday of females employed in any mechanical establishment, factory, or laundry, to ten hours a day. In this essay, I turn to another case that, on its face, would not appear to be involved in "race work" at all. That case is *Buck v. Bell*.

In *Buck v. Bell*, the Supreme Court considered a challenge to Virginia's law permitting the sterilization of "defective persons" in order to promote "the welfare of society."[13] At the center of the case was Carrie Buck, an inmate at the Virginia State Colony for Epileptics and the Feebleminded. According to state officials, Buck was the feebleminded daughter "of a feeble-minded mother in the institution, and the mother of an illegitimate feeble-minded child."[14] Pursuant to state law, officials had ordered her sterilized. Through her court-appointed guardian and friend, Buck challenged the law.

The Supreme Court, in a decision authored by Justice Oliver Wendell Holmes, summarily rejected Buck's challenge. Buck had been afforded due process, the Court concluded, since Buck had been ordered sterilized only after "scrupulous compliance with the statute"—which included notice, opportunity to be heard, and judicial review—"and after months of observation."[15] Similarly, Buck's substantive due process rights had not been infringed. The sterilization, the Court remarked, was after all based on a factual finding that Buck was "the probable potential parent of socially inadequate offspring, likewise afflicted, that she might be sexually sterilized without detriment to her general health, and that her welfare and that of society will be promoted by her sterilization."[16] Given these findings and the purpose of the legislation to promote societal welfare, sterilization was justified. Justice Holmes (in)famously concluded,

> We have seen more than once that the public welfare may call upon the best citizens for their lives. It would be strange if it could not call upon those who already sap the strength of the State for these lesser sacrifices, often not felt to be such by those concerned, in order to prevent our being swamped with incompetence. It is better for all the world if, instead of waiting to execute degenerate offspring for crime or to let them starve for imbecility, society can prevent those who are manifestly unfit from contributing to their kind. The principle that sustains compulsory vaccination is broad enough to cover cutting the Fallopian tubes . . . Three generations of imbecility are enough.[17]

This was the decision Virginia wanted, and on October 19, 1927, Carrie Buck, who at the time was only twenty-one years old, was sterilized.[18] However, the case was about more than Carrie Buck. Her case was a major victory in a eugenics movement that had begun decades earlier. Even prior to *Buck v. Bell*, Indiana had begun sterilizing "confirmed criminals, idiots, rapists, and imbeciles."[19] California, for its part, was doing the same, and by the time *Buck v. Bell* was decided, the State of California had already sterilized more than 2,500 "social undesirables."[20] But several lower courts had frowned on the practice, finding it unconstitutional. What the eugenics movement wanted was the Supreme Court's imprimatur, and, with *Buck v. Bell*, they received it. After the decision in *Buck v. Bell*, nearly half the states enacted legislation permitting some form of sterilization.[21] Other countries, looking at the eugenics movement in America, followed suit, including Canada,

Denmark, Finland, France, and Sweden.[22] Eventually, over 65,000 individuals would be sterilized.[23] It was only when eugenics was taken to its next step in Nazi Germany—with the mass extermination of homosexuals, Jews, and other perceived undesirables—that the eugenics movement in this country reconsidered its goals. And it was only then that the Supreme Court decided *Skinner v. Oklahoma*, in which the Court sheepishly retreated from *Buck v. Bell* by striking down Oklahoma's sterilization statute on the rather tepid ground that the statute drew irrational, unjustifiable distinctions. The holding was narrow, but the underlying message was clear: *Buck v. Bell* was a mistake.

This is *Buck v. Bell* then: a case about more than Carrie Buck, and yet it's Carrie Buck that I return to, in part, because of mounting evidence that Buck was not feebleminded at all, but merely poor and expendable, someone Virginia could use in an orchestrated test case to get the Supreme Court to approve sterilization.[24] But what really interests me, what really causes me to pause, to read again, is the Supreme Court's initial description of Carrie Buck: "Carrie Buck is a feeble-minded white woman who was committed to the State Colony above mentioned in due form."[25]

A feebleminded white woman: Why did it matter that Buck was white? Or female, for that matter? After all, it was her supposed feeblemindedness and projected fecundity that "justified" her sterilization, not her race. Allow me to ask the question again, and to this time add two more facts. Why did it matter that Carrie Buck was white, especially since her race was nowhere referred to in the opinion below? Why did it matter that Carrie Buck was white, especially since she could not have been anything but white? The State Colony for Epileptics and Feebleminded was, after all, for whites only.[26]

This is what I want to suggest: race was everything. To borrow from Cornel West, race mattered.[27] What I want to suggest is that this case makes sense, seems almost "sensible," when one considers the racial current that runs underneath the case. Consider this: The eugenics movement was concerned about weeding out the so-called feebleminded and the criminal, but who was deemed feebleminded and criminal was informed by race. The feebleminded and the criminal came from the lower races (i.e., the non-Anglo-Saxon immigrants and Negroes), and their numbers were increasing. Between 1890 and 1910, almost twelve million immigrants had arrived, mostly from the southern and eastern parts of Europe. For many Americans, what was at stake was nothing less than the purity of the superior "Nordic" race.[28] Tellingly, the two leading experts on eugenic sterilization were also leaders in the movement to stem the admission of immigrants into the country. Harry Laughlin testified before Congress about the "biological and eugenical aspects of immigration,"[29] namely, that immigrants had a higher rate of defective children and that these "women of the lower race [were] not, as a rule, adverse to intercourse with men of the higher," and as such the very purity of the "American" stock was in jeopardy.[30] Charles Davenport was even more specific: the Irish "brought alcoholism, considerable mental defectiveness and a tendency to tuberculosis;" Jews were overly sexual and, "with their intense individualism and ideals of gain at the cost of any interest," represented "the opposite extreme of the early English."[31] These sentiments were not unique. Madison Grant's *The Passing of the Great Race*, praising Nordic superiority and advocating strict racial segregation, immigration restrictions, forced sterilization, and essentially the elimination of all "lower races," was a bestseller.[32] Even Theodore Roosevelt was a believer and wrote to Davenport, "Some day we will realize that the prime duty, the inescapable duty, of the good citizen of the right type is to leave his or her blood behind him in the world; and that we have no business to permit the perpetuation of citizens of the wrong type."[33]

All of this, I think, informs the *Buck v. Bell* decision—but only up to a point. After all, there's nothing to suggest Carrie Buck was part of the foreign menace the eugenicists so feared. Her patronym, if anything, suggests the good "American stock" the eugenicists favored. And perhaps, this is where reading back, reading black comes in. *Carrie Buck is a feeble-minded white woman.* Could it be it wasn't only her supposed feeblemindedness that counted as a strike against her, but also her whiteness? Consider the contradiction. This was a time when America was claiming that the Nordic stock was superior and that the immigrant and Negro population was the bane of society. But here Carrie Buck stood in contradiction to this claim. If this were a trial on the supposed racial superiority of whites, Carrie Buck would be a defense exhibit. Her very presence, and the presence of her offspring, proved the claim of racial superiority to be a deeply flawed one. If whites were the superior race, they must *be* the superior race. But here was Carrie: white, poor, uneducated. Here was Carrie: a very challenge to the meaning of whiteness. Now, when I read Justice Holmes's description, I hear it too. "Carrie Buck is a feeble-minded white woman." This is what I hear: Embarrassment. Anger. Disgust.

Below the surface, below the empty talk about procedure being followed and the grounds justifying the result—below all the sophistry—this is *Buck v. Bell*. And this is my point about reading back, reading black. Far from diminishing these opinions—these grand narratives, these master texts—reading black reveals other layers, other meanings, and in the process deepens and widens our understanding not only of the holding of these opinions but also the how and why of them.

Postscript

As I write this essay—which I promised the editors would be about *Buck v. Bell*—the news is abuzz with Congress's efforts to secure a no-confidence vote with respect to Attorney General Alberto Gonzalez, with Paris Hilton's efforts to evade her forty-five-day jail sentence, and with the unanimous decision of the North Carolina State Bar Disciplinary Committee to disbar Michael Nifong, the District Attorney who withheld evidence and otherwise violated norms of professional conduct in his prosecution of three Duke University lacrosse players on charges that they raped a black stripper during a party. It is this last news item that grabs my attention and holds it. That raises other questions. That seems personal.

I recently wrote a law review article in which I noted that because of media attention—which too often translates into police attention—I could easily summon the names of white female victims:[34] Nicole Simpson Brown, Natalee Holloway, Elizabeth Smart, Laci Peterson, Chandra Levy. By contrast, the only black female victim that came to mind was someone later discredited as a nonvictim: Tawana Brawley. Now, another had been added to this list: the nonvictim in the lacrosse players case; never mind that black women are several times more likely to be victimized by crime.[35] Their victimization, as so often is the case, is simply not newsworthy. It remains invisible.

I think about visible nonvictims and invisible victims, but I also think about language. Some commentators were rightfully critical of the use of the term stripper—a salacious detail, something to titillate. But more than titillate, it called into question not only her credibility but also her capability. Underneath the description was a question, an uncertainty, a sneer, a wink—a raped stripper? Yeah, right. The wink becoming wider with "black" added to the description. Because we all know about black women, right? I mean, if black female basketball players could be described on national radio as "hoes," as radio host Don Imus did, then we all know about black women.

But my thoughts on language aren't limited to the words used to define the accuser. I'm also interested in the other side of the equation, the Duke lacrosse players. Because even after the players were indicted and became defendants, the media continued to refer to them as the Duke lacrosse players: Duke standing in for educated? Lacrosse standing in for privileged? Players standing in for "just playing?" Language does this to me. Even before the charges were dismissed and the defendants were defendants no more, the media, either intentionally or unintentionally, had managed to create a topsy-turvy world where the word "victim" could apply to no one, to anyone, to everyone.

Mostly, though, I find myself thinking about another infamous "rape" case. About nine male youths, ages thirteen to twenty, who hopped a ride aboard a freight train en route to Huntsville, Alabama back in 1931, got into an altercation with another group of youths and, in doing so, set off a chain of events that would scar this country. What happened was this: The second group of youths ran to the stationmaster and demanded that the stationmaster press charges against the first group of youths. The stationmaster, in turn, got the sheriff involved, and the sheriff, in turn, assembled an armed posse to go after the first group.[36] When the train stopped in Scottsboro, the sheriff and his posse boarded the freight car and found the youths. But here's the thing: they found two young women as well.[37] It is probably here that some racial designations are necessary, because this story only makes sense once race is known. The nine youths on the train were black. The youths they got into an altercation with, who later complained to the stationmaster, were white. Maybe this is obvious, since it is hard to imagine a group of black youths running to a stationmaster in Alabama in 1931 and demanding anything. The stationmaster, the sheriff, and the sheriff's posse were white, which, again, is perhaps obvious. And the two women were white. And this made all the difference in the world. Otherwise, the sheriff would not have turned to the women and wondered what the hell was going on. There would be no (in)famous Scottsboro Boys case. Race matters.

How did the two young women explain their presence in a freight car with nine black youths? Their explanation was simple. It fit in with an expected narrative of black men and sex and violence. The white women, Victoria Price and Ruby Bates, said they were raped. The rest, as they say, is history. Within days, the district attorney had indicted all nine youths on charges of rape (a capital offense in 1931), and, six days later, the district attorney tried the defendants before all-white juries, securing sentences of death against all of the defendants except one. (The case against the ninth defendant, the thirteen-year-old, resulted in a mistrial when seven of the jurors insisted on the death penalty, notwithstanding the fact that the district attorney had asked only for life imprisonment considering the defendant's youth.)[38] The convictions went all the way up to the Supreme Court, and were twice reversed in two landmark opinions: *Powell et al. v. Alabama* and *Norris v. Alabama*. Each time, the district attorney tried the defendants again and convicted them again. The district attorney was tenacious. It didn't matter that the two women were both prostitutes,[39] that Price's story was filled with contradictions,[40] that the medical evidence was inconsistent with rape or even recent sexual intercourse,[41] or that Bates had recanted her story and was now testifying for the defense. The district attorney was tenacious—by this I mean he stuck to his convictions. By 1950, when the last defendant was finally paroled, the nine defendants had served in aggregate more than a hundred years in jail.[42]

The parallels between the Scottsboro Boys case and the Duke lacrosse case, as they have both come to be known, are striking: the questionable medical evidence, the inconsistent stories of the accusers, the status of the accusers as workers in the sex industry, and the doggedness of the district attorney. The only difference, to my mind, is in the race of the accused and the accuser—and the public reaction. Despite all the evidence suggesting that the alleged rape in the Scottsboro Boy's case was an utter fabrication, southerners rallied to the defense of the two women, Victoria Price and Ruby Bates. As one newspaper put it during the first round of trials, when a mob of approximately eight thousand people gathered outside the courthouse, "mob spirit is whipped up to such a degree that it is common knowledge there will be a mass lynching of all nine if . . . a verdict [for the electric chair] is not speedily rendered."[43] That the two women were prostitutes was irrelevant. A townsperson put it this way: Price "might be a fallen woman, but by God she is a white woman."[44] In the Duke lacrosse case, by contrast, sentiment from day one seemed to be against the "black stripper" and with the accused boys, the Duke lacrosse players. Duke standing in for educated? Lacrosse standing in for privileged? Players standing in for "just playing"? So much sentiment that District Attorney Nifong withdrew from the case, and another prosecutor was put in charge. And on April 11, 2007, that prosecutor dismissed the charges.

Was I the only one who noticed that the new prosecutor dismissed the charges against the Duke lacrosse players the same day CBS announced it was firing Don Imus for referring to several black female players as "nappy-headed hoes"?

The Scottsboro Boy's case and the Duke Lacrosse case: In one, a public clamoring for a conviction. In another, a public clamoring for a dismissal of the charges. Maybe this is progress. Maybe three-quarters of a century later, we just have a better idea what justice looks like. Maybe the public would have reacted the same in the Duke lacrosse case had the accused been black men, and the accuser a white female. Maybe.

And now, an ethics committee has disbarred District Attorney Nifong, who is now officially former District Attorney Nifong. The *New York Times* headline reads, "Hearing Ends in Disbarment for Prosecutor in Duke Case."[45] The *Chicago Tribune* headline reads, "Prosecutor to be Disbarred for Duke Lacrosse Case 'Fiasco.'"[46] *USA Today* adds, "Disbarment May Not End Nifong's Troubles."[47]

So I think about the Scottsboro Boys case and other cases too. Like the youths wrongfully convicted in the Central Park jogging case. The prosecutors were tenacious: one even argued in summation that the hair found on the victim "matched" the hair of one of the defendants, an argument that was simply not true.[48] It would take thirteen years before the real rapist would be apprehended and the convictions vacated. In fact, it seems that every time I open a newspaper or turn on the news there is another story about a wrongful conviction come to light, more often than not against men of color. Men who actually got time, served time, lost time, lost their youth, and lost their prime because prosecutors were tenacious—because prosecutors refused to see the contradictions and inconsistencies in their cases. And I wonder: is anyone demanding that those prosecutors be disbarred?

This is what justice looks like.

This is what justice looks like from where I'm standing.

This, too, is reading back, reading black.

Notes

1. See Capers, "The Trial of Bigger Thomas," 4–5.
2. Ibid., 5.
3. Capers, "Reading Back, Reading Black."
4. See *Buck v. Bell*, 200.
5. Awkward, "Race, Gender, and the Politics of Reading," 5–6.
6. See Gates, *"Race," Writing, and Difference*; Gates, *Black Literature and Literary Theory*.
7. Said, *Culture and Imperialism*, 66.
8. Morrison, *Playing in the Dark*.
9. Fish, *Is There a Text in this Class?* 14.
10. Capers, "Reading Back, Reading Black," 10–11.
11. Gates, "The Blackness of Blackness," 285–86.
12. Two exceptions come immediately to mind. One, Justice Thomas's statements during oral argument in *Virginia v. Black*, which involved a First Amendment challenge to a Virginia statute criminalizing the burning of crosses. During the argument, Justice Thomas transformed the legal debate to a personal one by describing what cross burning means to blacks. See Mauro, "Remarks by Thomas Alter Argument," 7.
13. *Virginia v. Black*, 205.
14. *Buck v. Bell*, 205.
15. Ibid., 206–7.
16. Ibid., 207.
17. Ibid.
18. Bruinus, *Better for All the World*, 3.
19. Indiana—Act of March 9, 1907, ch. 215, 1907 Ind. Laws 377.
20. Ibid., 10.
21. Ibid., 72.
22. Ibid., 10.
23. Ibid., 9.
24. See Lombardo, "Three Generations, No Imbeciles," 30; and Bruinus, *Better for All the World*, 50–77.
25. *Buck v. Bell*, 205.
26. Ibid., 40.
27. West, *Race Matters*.

28. Bruinus, *Better for All the World*, 17.
29. Ibid., 255.
30. Ibid., 258–59.
31. Ibid., 167.
32. Grant, *The Passing of the Great Race.*
33. Bruinus, *Better for All the World*, 191 (citing Charles B. Davenport Papers, American Philosophical Society Library, "Theodore Roosevelt" file).
34. Capers, "Crime, Legitimacy, and Testilying."
35. Bureau of Justice Statistics, *Sourcebook of Criminal Justice Statistics*, 191, table 3.4.
36. Carter, *Scottsboro*, 5.
37. Ibid., 5.
38. Ibid., 48.
39. Carter, *Scottsboro*, 81–84.
40. Ibid., 206–13.
41. One of the state's medical examiners testified that the amount of semen found in Price's vagina was small, and therefore inconsistent with her claim that she had been raped by several youths. In addition, the semen was nonmotile, indicating that it had been present at least twelve hours prior to Price boarding the train. Ibid., 213.
42. For more on the Scottsboro case generally, see Carter, *Scottsboro.*
43. "Nine Negro Workers Face Lynch Mob in Ala. as Trial Opens on Horse Swapping, Fair Day," *The Daily Worker*, April 7, 1931, p. 1.
44. Bruinus, *Better for All the World*, 210.
45. Wilson, "Hearing Ends in Disbarment for Prosecutor in Duke Case," sec. A.
46. Beard, "Prosecutor to be Disbarred for Duke Lacrosse Case 'Fiasco,'" sec. A.
47. Parker, "Disbarment May Not End Nifong's Troubles," sec. A. In fact, Nifong's troubles did not end. Later he would be convicted of criminal contempt and sentenced to one day in jail.
48. Dwyer and Saulny, "Hair Evidence in Jogger Case Is Discredited," sec. A.

Bibliography

Awkward, Michael. "Race, Gender, and the Politics of Reading." *Black American Literature Forum* 22, no. 1 (Spring 1988): 5–6.

Beard, Aaron. "Prosecutor to be Disbarred for Duke Lacrosse Case 'Fiasco.'" *Chicago Tribune*, June 17, 2007, sec. A.

Bruinus, Harry. *Better for All the World: The Secret History of Forced Sterilization and America's Quest for Racial Purity*. New York: Knopf, 2006.

Buck v. Bell, 274 U.S. 200 (1927).

Bureau of Justice Statistics. *Sourcebook of Criminal Justice Statistics*. Washington, DC: U.S. Department of Justice, 2002.

Capers, I. Bennett. "Crime, Legitimacy, and Testilying." *Indiana Law Journal* 83, no. 3 (2008): 835–80.

———. "Reading Back, Reading Black." *Hofstra Law Review* 35, no. 1 (2006): 9–22.

———. "The Trial of Bigger Thomas: Race, Gender, and Trespass." *NYU Review of Law and Social Change* 31, no. 1 (2006): 1–49.

Carter, Dan T. *Scottsboro: A Tragedy of the American South*. Baton Rouge: Louisiana State University Press, 1969.

Dwyer, Jim, and Susan Saulny. "Hair Evidence in Jogger Case is Discredited." *New York Times*, October 25, 2002, sec. A.

Fish, Stanley. *Is There a Text in this Class?* Cambridge, MA: Harvard, 1980.

Gates, Henry Louis, Jr. "The Blackness of Blackness: A Critique of the Sign and the Signifying Monkey." In *Black Literature and Literary Theory*, edited by Henry Louis Gates, Jr., 285–86. New York: Routledge, 1990.

———, ed. *"Race," Writing, and Difference.* Chicago: University of Chicago Press, 1985.

Grant, Madison. *The Passing of the Great Race.* New York: C. Scribner's Sons, 1916.

Jardine, Alice. "Opaque Texts and Transparent Contexts." In *The Poetics of Gender*, edited by Nancy K. Miller, 96–97. New York: Columbia University Press, 1986.

Lombardo, Paul A. "Three Generations, No Imbeciles: New Light on *Buck v. Bell*." *NYU Law Review* 30, no. 1 (1985): 30–62.

Mauro, Tony. "Remarks by Thomas Alter Argument." *Legal Times*, December 16, 2002, p. 7.

Morrison, Toni. *Playing in the Dark: Whiteness and the Literary Imagination.* New York: Vintage, 1992.

Muller v. Oregon, 208 U.S. 412 (1908).

Norris v. Alabama, 294 U.S. 587 (1934).

Parker, Lauer. "Disbarment May Not End Nifong's Troubles." *USA Today*, June 18, 2007, sec. A.

Powell et al. v. Alabama, 287 U.S. 45 (1932)

The Queen v. Dudley & Stephens, 14 Q.B.D. 273 (1884).

Said, Edward W. *Culture and Imperialism.* New York: Vintage, 1993.

Skinner v. Oklahoma, 316 U.S. 535 (1942).

Virginia v. Black, 538 U.S. 343 (2003).

West, Cornel. *Race Matters.* Boston: Beacon, 1993.

Wilson, Duff. "Hearing Ends in Disbarment for Prosecutor in Duke Case." *New York Times*, June 17, 2007, sec. A.

2

W. E. B. Du Bois and the Right to Privacy

Karla F. C. Holloway

Negotiating the Perp Walk: Executive Whiteness

A recent surge in "executive perp walks" has featured accused white collar criminals in designer suits and handcuffs. Whether the accused wrongdoer is wearing a sweatshirt over his head or an Armani suit on his back, we suspect that perp walks are broadcast by networks and reprinted in newspapers at least in part for their entertainment value . . . At the same time, we are cognizant that the characteristics of the perp walk that serve legitimate government purposes also implicate the accused's privacy interests.

—*Caldarola v. County of Westchester* (2003)

The construction of this event—the "perp walk"—is necessarily specular. The public's gaze is its mediator: the camerafolk, the newscasters with microphones, and the alleged "perpetrators" of whatever misfortune brings them to this space between the camera's gaze and our own populate the scene. It is also a subtextually racialized moment in its bodies as well as with its language. Although the accused have been walked into police stations and courthouses handcuffed—sometimes shackled—innumerable times before the event of the walk itself gained juridical review, it was not until the spectacle was used by policemen for white folks of a certain class—the "executive perp walks" referenced in *Caldarola*—that our national attention was turned to wonder at these accused. Labeled with the shortened verbiage that law enforcement has historically used for perpetrators and forced into the space more often occupied by those wearing "a sweatshirt over their head," the appearance of executive whiteness ("Armani suits") has focused our notice on these moments. Prior to this they were a visual sideswipe—barely detectable in our peripheral vision. Our familiarity with these moments and these folk was a reliable stand-in for the labor of a sustained glance, our mind's eye easily recollecting the vignettes: men's bodies paraded in a certain way—shackled sometimes, certainly handcuffed, the finale of the performance coming with an (often) white hand shoving a (usually) black head into the back of a police car.

But in 1999 these visual memories were disrupted by the vitality of a new scenario. This time, when a white corrections officer found himself caught in his own profession's performative ritual, he balked—suing the county, the county executive, and the county commissioner of the department of corrections; alleging violation of his fourth amendment rights; and arguing that the event constituted an unreasonable seizure. The United States Court of Appeals for the Second Circuit took up the case on plaintiff's appeal. The opinion rendered in *Caldarola v. County of Westchester* (that eventually affirmed the district court's grant of summary judgment in favor of the defendants) recalled that this was not the first time they had considered an event like this. In the *Caldarola* opinion, the court recalled the context of the first time such a case had come to it and its deliberations in a case, *Lauro v. Charles*, that might best be described as legal theatre: "Approximately two hours after Lauro was arrested and brought to the police station, a police detective staged a perp walk in response to media interest in the arrest. A detective handcuffed Lauro, escorted him outside of the police station, drove him around the block in a police car, and then escorted him from the car back into the station. A television crew filmed the staged walk from the car back into the station."[1] In that case, ruling for the plaintiff, the court concluded that "legitimate state interest in accurate reporting of police activity . . . is not well served by an *inherently fictional dramatization* of an event that transpired hours earlier."[2] Notably, it was a fiction that earned the court's judgment for the plaintiff rather than a judgment on the spectacle inherent in that performance of the state's "legitimate interest."

Nevertheless, it is important not to displace the observation that this event's review was not unattached to the privilege of the men suddenly positioned into these scenes. Terry Eagleton's reminder of the "privileged positions" earned by "certain meanings [that] are elevated by social ideologies" and the ways in which they become "centers around which other meanings are forced to turn" is helpful to our understanding of the nexus of intimate relationships between class, positionality, and the language attached to these moments.[3] A perp walk, both in the linguistic informality and familiarity invoked in its casual abbreviation—as well as in its current specular effort to embrace bodies other than those it has historically claimed—has a meaning that social ideology elevates. Bodies in this captive position were already framed as a national ideogram. Although there had certainly been the grumbling of civil libertarians about these events that make folk "look," a certain way, especially those that make folk "look guilty," it has been largely *sotto voce*. But the force of its turn towards incorporating a privileged, executive whiteness into the ideography of spectacle contained a trespass too egregious to ignore. The second-generation outrage (the first had provoked little public notice) led to a juridical presentation of an argument regarding the social ideology of privacy. Even though the black bodies these moments had historically claimed had no such consideration (their communal and public habitation of "perp" had become socially normative), its "elevation" to incorporate a privileged whiteness when white men—especially those of a certain and "remarkable" class—found themselves on parade was problematic in its displacement of the communal insularity of an unnamed and unremarked racialized specularity.[4] The white men's names, remarkability, and individuation had had the protections of a privileged presumption of privacy, or, at the very least, they had a practiced control over these dimensions of their lives. However, once shoved into that iconically black and public space of the perp walk, those privileges negotiated through whiteness vanished.

The signifiers "black" and "public" locate the sociocultural exceptionalism of whiteness. The vulnerability of privileged white maleness to those all too readily available spaces haunted with the bodies, "made possible (and plausible) through stereo[type]," is "a process of subjectification" that Bhabha, correctly I think, indicates as a contagion of location.[5] Perhaps only a white male like Bill Clinton finds such an irony of place bearable.[6] In *Constructing the Black Masculine*, Maurice Wallace recalls this stereotype hypothesis of Bhabba's and writes persuasively from this perspective regarding the "public struggle to reconcile the nation's anxieties on black male bodies" and calling our attention to the angst in "the private will to survive the visually inflected problematics of race and manhood in American culture."[7] Although Wallace makes this argument with specific reference to Richard Wright's *Native Son*, I want to suggest that his critical notice of the "national" boundaries in this anxiety precisely articulates the space where the problematic visual schematic of something like a perp walk might trap white male privilege as well—at least and especially within its urge to adjudicate or to produce this particular kind of exposition and then to want to, or expect to, step aside. But the "national" is a bordered land from within *and* without, and the vulnerability of the master to his own creations is the stuff of legends. The potential permeability, if not outright leakiness, of national boundaries becomes evident as the perp walk evolves to entrap whiteness in its own public architecture—a sphere constructed to maintain the visual economies of class and racial exclusivity. Once vulnerable to enclosure there, literally bound and figuratively fixed into that synecdochic space created between the camera's eye and the long arm of the law, the private exceptionality of class and whiteness goes public. Negotiating that space of the perp walk foregoes the private enclosures assured in liberal personhood. What piece of that Armani suit might be raised up to act as a shield? How low might its lapels allow one's head to sink in a desperate effort to reclaim the buffer of the private?

Property, Person, and Privacy

> It could be done only on principles of private justice, moral fitness and public convenience, which, when applied to a new subject, make common law without a precedent; much more when received and approved by usage.
>
> —*Millar v. Taylor* (1769)[8]

For decades it has been surmised, argued, and asserted that the impetus for the famous *Harvard Law Review* essay on "The Right to Privacy" resulted from the Samuel L. Warren clan's outrage when *The Saturday Evening Gazette* exhausted the patience of the family with their attempt to crash a "lavish breakfast party" given to celebrate the wedding of the daughter of Samuel Warren.[9] The *Gazette* of the 1880s and 1890s was certainly known for its gossipy coverage of upper-crust affairs. Later scholarship indicates, however, that this annoyance could not have been the motive, as Warren's daughter was just six years old at the time of the essay's publication. Still, there is good reason for speculation about the motives of the coauthors to "The Right to Privacy." It is nearly strident in its outrage over the gossip published in the press (calling it an "evil invasion") and rigorously defensive regarding the line crossed with this inquiry and interest into personal affairs—especially those family affairs of the well-heeled. Warren, and his law partner Louis D. Brandeis (later to become U.S. Supreme Court Justice Brandeis), fuming over this presumptive violation of their classed protectionism, collaborated to write what became a pathbreaking article for the *Harvard Law Review* that was credited with beginning a new chapter of American jurisprudence. Warren and Brandeis wrote that this "intrusion upon the domestic circle" was crudely occasioned by "gossip . . . no longer the resource of the ideal and of the vicious, but . . . a trade, which is pursued with industry as well as effrontery."[10] This oft-cited excerpt suggests the alleged impetus for the piece. But, in addition to the one carved out of journalism's invasions of the sanctity of upper-crust domesticity, the context claims an additional landscape.

Warren and Brandeis's defense also discloses the ways in which the material constructedness of class is foundational to the impetus, to the architecture, and to the argument of the piece. It was, after all, some insult or effrontery that the well-heeled "lawyer-socialite" Warren (or Brandeis) took as a violation to the insularities earned, or at least anticipated, from their class membership that occasioned their focused attention on a right to privacy. They claimed an authorial interest here that extended from a subject position that had become uncomfortably vulnerable. Intimately understanding that "subject position is everything," Patricia Williams exposes the consequence of the "tyranny of what we call the private," arguing in *The Alchemy of Race and Rights* that there are different inhabitations of a choice between exposure and hiding.[11] But this might only be a choice—and I suspect that Williams would agree—primarily reserved for those who occupy positions of privilege. The righteous indignation Warren and Brandeis claimed seemed then, and now, a precious, proscriptive luxury born of class and the license to presume a protected individualism. (One wonders at the fate of this essay had it been penned by a lawyer graduated from and working in a less privileged space.)[12]

Warren and Brandeis begin the law review essay with a pronouncement in the form of a recollection: "That the individual shall have full protection in person and in property is a principle as old as the common law." Their argument is generated from this history as they note that "the development of the law [from these principles of protection of person and property] was inevitable," writing that "the intense intellectual and emotional life, and the heightening of sensations which came with the advance of civilization, made it clear to men that . . . the right to privacy . . . must soon come before our courts for consideration."[13] Although my ellipses here bridge several lines of text, they highlight the rhetorical link between the advance of civilizations and the emergence of this new right. The generative "new subject" of Warren and Brandeis's concern is not only the material space of privacy, but it becomes the person who is the privileged inheritor of that evolution of legal principles from property to person to privacy.

In their argument, the advances of civilization and culture have an inherent relationship to the emergent sanctity of the individual. The law partners note that "the intensity and complexity of life, attendant upon advancing civilization, have rendered necessary some retreat from the world, and man, under the refining influence of culture, has become more sensitive to publicity so that solitude and privacy have become more essential to the individual."[14] The consequence of this construction is that the essay's rhetorical structure grows increasingly dependent on a conceptual binary: some bodies are the subject of this vicious gossip, while other bodies—the "indolent" consumers who become, in this essay, an undifferentiated multitude contaminated by this lowering of social standards and of morality—read about it. The rhetorical binary that finally binds the essay finds its impetus in protecting an apparent privilege of class. The narrow patriarchal positionality of the essay is apparent—race and gender both explicitly complicate the insularities implicit in this privilege.

If we consider the Boston of 1890 when "The Right to Privacy" was published, it was certainly a city where the distinctions between privilege and power were apparent. This was not only true in terms of the property lines that divided race and social classes but true as well in the body of one small, black man who had come to Harvard College two years before the essay's appearance, certain of his individual distinctiveness and sure in his developing self importance. His eminent biographer David Levering Lewis tells us that many years later, when W. E. B. Du Bois was ninety-two, he wrote for *The Massachusetts Review* that Harvard was "an endured experience charged with frivolity, snobbishness, and conservatism—merely adequate to the intellectual needs of a sojourner preoccupied with the predestined part he was to play in the larger world."[15] He anticipated that his experience at Harvard would allow him "to enlarge my grasp of the meaning of the universe." Lewis further notes his claim that he had his "island within." Du Bois wrote that "he was 'in Harvard but not of it."[16]

Inviolate Personhood

The principle . . . is in reality not the principle of private property, but that of an inviolate personality.

—Samuel L. Warren and William Brandeis, "Right to Privacy"

Many people think that grief is privatizing, that it returns us to a solitary situation and is, in that sense, depoliticizing. But I think it furnishes a sense of political community of a complex order.

—Judith Butler, *Precarious Life*

Whatever the offenses of or challenges to class and privilege that contributed to Warren and Brandeis's path-breaking essay, they were in absolute circulation during Du Bois's Harvard graduate and undergraduate years. Additionally, law's new "chapter" (whether in the legacy of law or in the certain endowments of social privilege) was likely a subject of discussion among the professoriate and within wealthy Bostonian drawing rooms. During the years following its publication, the essay drew consistent and considerable attention.[17]

Du Bois arrived at Harvard and enrolled, in 1888, as an undergraduate.[18] David Levering Lewis writes that despite Du Bois's subsequent revisionist versions of an "inflated" Harvard experience, those Harvard years were for him "uneven" and he sometimes "faltered." "It took," Lewis writes, "time and considerable effort to become himself."[19] He received his undergraduate degree from Harvard in June of 1890—six months before the famous piece on privacy that appeared in the *Harvard Law Review*'s December issue—but he was surely steeped enough in the cultural intrigues of the upper classes to appreciate the complexities inherent in his proximity to privilege. His Harvard years would not go unremarked regarding these matters of class. One could even argue that he was preoccupied with it. His attention to dress and to the benefits of a certain social network was readily apparent. Lewis writes of the way he cultivated these aspirations, becoming, by the time he completed a graduate degree in 1892, willing and grateful for his easy circulation among the presumptively privileged "Charles Street Circle"—those affluent black Bostonians where he "felt release from the pressures and challenges to seek more than marginal social presence in white Cambridge."[20] Racially, he was obviously distinct from those other students who traversed the grounds of Harvard Yard, and that difference surely contributed to at least one measure of his considered response where his bearing and dress labored to assume the well-cultivated demeanor of a certain class. We see, throughout his oeuvre, residue of his presumptions to upper class distinctiveness not only in the attentions to his own body and garb but also in the cultivated rhetoric that expressed his philosophies—the exclusivity defined in his conceptualization of the "Talented Tenth" being one notable example.[21] But we see this preoccupation with class and personhood especially, and for the first time in sustained manner, in *The Souls of Black Folk* where—likely by coincidence rather than by intent—he substantively engages the constitutive elements of the Warren and Brandeis discourse on the right to privacy.

The social and class issues that emerged during his Harvard tenure, and in the years immediately preceding the publication of *The Souls of Black Folk*, were, at their core, a matter of his negotiations of privacy. His own personhood resides curiously between the folk and his presumptive residence among the elite, as if, in some manner, he is always renegotiating that Harvard experience of being "in but not of." Hazel Carby recalls a telling journal entry in February of 1893 that reveals this ambivalence: "I am firmly convinced that my own best development is not one and the same with the best development of the world . . . I . . . work for the rise of the Negro people, taking for granted that their best development means the best development of the world."[22] He seems, even at age twenty-five, not quite one of the folk here nor is he one of the "world." Instead, he claims a privileged and arguably distant individualism here—a private persona that allows him to dip down to help ("the rise of the Negro people") while at the same time claiming to be not "one and the same" with these worldly folk. This journal entry exposes Du Bois's anxious and oblique engagement with the complex web of issues regarding race and class that was to emerge again and again in the decade of individual essays that eventually contributed to that book. But as determined as he was to raise these issues of the "folk," they circulate as aggressively in frustrated negotiations about his own personhood and its relationship to the "world." Despite what seems his global reach, I believe that at its core his argument has, essentially, the national locus articulated in Hazel Carby's vital study, *Race Men*.[23]

Carby, with reference to Etienne Balibar, perceptively explores the "ideological contradictions" of the essays in *Souls*, noting that the text "exposes and exploits the tension that exists between the internal egalitarian impulse inherent in the concept of nation and the relations of domination and subordination that are embodied in a racially encoded social hierarchy."[24] We cannot escape the passive agency implicit in Carby's analysis. Neither imperialism nor nation building might be accomplished without machination—they are impulses that must finally be operationalized by someone or something. In a note, Carby reinforces this argument with an important reference to Benedict Anderson, citing his perspective from *Imagined Communities*, that the "nation is conceived as a deep, horizontal comradeship"—implicating the shadowy agency at work in the process of nation building.[25] Although "domination and subordination" happen in public, whoever has the agency to formulate these conceptions also has the resident protection of a veneer of privacy.

The essays in *The Souls of Black Folk* evidence a struggle with public and private contexts. Although a black community of "souls" constitutes the book's central congregants, it is Du Bois's labored interaction with these folk that constructs its complexity. His yearning for an acknowledged individuation juxtaposed against a wistful engagement with the private is consistent. Indeed, his prescient extrapolation of this complex construction of life in America for black folk begins on page one in what he titles the "Forethought" with the first cautionary words of the book proper: "Herein Lie buried many things."[26] It seems to me the first warning of a dark interiority—that it is his own body secreted within these pages. "Forethought" concludes with a cautionary reminder that places Du Bois into the community of the folk who are his subject. But then he completes the corporeal frame of the chapter with another embodied image, this time as inquiry: "Need I add that I who speak here am bone of the bone and flesh of the flesh of them that live within the Veil?"[27] It is notable in its clear claim of his body's inescapable presence, but at the same time, wrapped in this fleshly imagery, it is protective and silent in the regard of what he brings to the text: his intellect. The interrogative structures a strategic rhetorical device that allows him this disidentificatory gesture.

I focus on this particular passage because it both signals and exemplifies the interior, self-centeredness of *Souls* that emerges more fully with each chapter. His first chapter, "Of Our Spiritual Strivings," unambiguously pronounces his "subject position" and those that differ from his own. With the rhetorical flourish of the forethought still in our memory, his readers are encouraged to appreciate and to respect the difference when he writes, "between me and the other world there is ever an unasked question . . . How does it feel to be a problem?" Du Bois then labors in the chapter to cast himself not only outside of whiteness, dramatically revealing his distinction when "it dawned upon me that I was different from the [white] others; or like, mayhap in heart and life and longing, but shut out from their world by a vast veil."[28] But even as he laments this visible loss of an acknowledged sameness ("the worlds I longed for, and all the dazzling opportunities, were theirs, not mine"), he also struggles to claim that otherwise invisible difference from his own race, explaining how for "*other* black boys the strife was not so fiercely sunny: their youth shrunk into tasteless sycophancy, or into silent hatred of the pale world about them and mocking distrust of everything white . . . Why did God make me an outcast and a stranger in mine own house?"[29] His query would be plaintive if it were not so strategic a claim to a critical intellectual exceptionality from black folk. His world—contemplative, interior, personal, and private—was not theirs.

From this lens, I view an implicit and racialized version of the right to privacy as an essential argument yet one less attended to in *The Souls of Black Folk*. In the book's second chapter, a "study of the period of history from 1861 to 1872 so far as it relates to the American Negro," Du Bois himself is fully absent until its concluding paragraph where his "I" finally reappears as a distant overseer: "I have seen a land right merry with the sun, where children sing, and rolling hills lie like passioned women wanton with harvest."[30] Who is this "I," and where was he in the rest of that chapter? Certainly, as his tourist's perspective reveals, he was not located among those "American Negroes" whose history he has just summarized. Instead, his remove, enabled by a prose David Lewis labels as "mythic" and "threnodic," leads him to a vaulted oversight.[31] By the time his narrative returns to the famous lines of the chapter's opening, Du Bois is positioned as a commentator, removed once again from the folk and able to theorize the subject he has distanced from himself. When it comes time to repeat for conclusion and effect that provocative assertion in the chapter's opening—that "the problem of the twentieth century" is "the problem of the color line"—his reader has no idea whose problem this might be.[32]

That Du Bois was finally uncomfortable with the insular prophetic space cultivated in that second chapter standing as the narrative space that serves the rest of the text is displayed in the nimble narrative shifts later chapters accomplish between large communities of folk, exemplars of these folk, and his own omniscient perspectives. These discursive segments are variously constructed through the memory of his youth, his travels, or through the "profoundly mystical" conceptualization of a divided self.[33] His own voice and person negotiate these spaces with tricksterlike linguistic dexterity. The much-commented-upon veil that shapes his sight in *Souls* and the "second sight" of the African American (a gift of the folk that he does claim as befits an omniscient narrator) is not only a radical notion of racial twoness but also a concept that preserves, protects, and claims a precious interiority that the exterior responsibilities of his talent would otherwise have obviated as he shouldered the mantle of "race man." It is a positionality that critically maintains the narrative agility that allows, and indeed encourages, his metaphysical flexibility.[34] How might he acknowledge that space that seems the ultimate appropriation of privilege if he were to be "of" the folk? The challenge of his exceptionality becomes, of necessity, as much a claim to private personhood as it accomplishes the public work of announcing Negro potential.

Understanding implicitly, I think, the writerly legerdemain at work here, Hazel Carby seems appropriately suspicious of Du Bois's "attempts to fuse his own body with a racialized way of knowing the world" while he "also situates himself as an intellectual and a spiritual mediator between the world and his people."[35] This is a difficult terrain to negotiate, but Du Bois cultivated its tensions because it allowed him the exceptionalism that distinguishes him from his kinsfolk.

Whether or not Du Bois read the Warren and Brandeis law review article will likely remain an elusive historical footnote. But when these coauthors wrote that "the protection afforded to thoughts, sentiments, and emotions, expressed through the medium of writing or of the arts . . . is merely an instance of the enforcement of the more general right of the individual to be let alone," it was a conceptualization that may easily have intrigued the contemplative Du Bois and it seems, at the least, an arguable text of *Souls*. [36] His chapter titled "Of the Passing of the First Born" is exemplary of the way in which he both cultivated the private exceptionality of class and negotiated his members-only, privileged way through a racialized landscape. This juxtaposition, as instrumental as it was, forced a crisis when he found himself held captive by a public story of a private grief. "Of the Passing" captures that moment of crisis and Du Bois's poignant response.

Burghardt, the only son of Nina and William Du Bois was born on October 2, 1897, in Great Barrington, Massachusetts. Du Bois traveled from Atlanta to his wife and child upon the news of his son's birth, and later the three of them returned to Atlanta. Nearly nineteen months later, on May 24, 1899, Burghardt died of dysentery. His father had been unable to find a black doctor who was available, or a white doctor who was willing, to come.

It seems both necessary and appropriate to acknowledge here the racialized and gendered anguish this moment provoked. Du Bois, at this time, was already an accomplished "race man"—he had made "an international reputation as a social scientist and historian" and was contemplating the next stage of his career as an activist agent for social change.[37] But the impotence that must have raged in his inability to secure social change for one small, black baby—his own—must have been devastating to both his private personhood and the public manhood he cultivated—within the confines of his own marriage, within the black community, as well as in the white world whose gaze he cultivated. It is clearly a chapter that foregrounds *his* grief, to the displacement and near disregard of Nina Gomers's anguished motherloss.[38] The deeply textured symbolism of "Of the Passing of the First Born," a chapter that departs somewhat in style but not, importantly, from the substance of *Souls* testifies to this complex terrain of mourning, memory, and grief.

In *Precarious Life*, Judith Butler explores the ways in which some lives become "grief-worthy," noting that "each of us is constituted politically in part by virtue of the social vulnerability of our bodies—as a site of desire and physical vulnerability, *as a site of publicity at once assertive and exposed*."[39] Du Bois's public encounter surely began when he "rushed out in a futile search for one of the two or three black physicians living on the other side of town."[40] That this frantic moment tragically comes full circle when he and Nina both took to the streets again, some days later, walking behind the casket of their son. It was a damage that cannot go unremarked. This grief work was in part my own occupation in *Passed On: African American Mourning Stories*. It was there I first considered how that chapter in *Souls* was not the aberration that others have implied.[41] I suggest instead that "despite the anguish and deeply personal tones" of his rehearsal of Burghardt's death in *Souls*, "the issue in that chapter was [that it was] a *public* black story . . . Indeed, Du Bois may have been the first to characterize an 'African American mourning story,' selecting as he did a vocabulary to describe his son's death and dying that had its generation and was fully vested in the symbolic and racialized language of this nation's history of slavery and liberation . . . His accounting of his child's burial procession had the character of a public incident report."[42] In my analysis, the public space he constructed for that essay was both necessary and relevant to the negotiations of body and race within that text, in the chapters that preceded it, as well as in those that followed. I extend that analysis here, encouraged by the focus that Judith Butler has recently brought to my thinking on this matter in her deeply provocative consideration of the instrumentality of obituary:

> I think we have to ask, again and again, how the obituary functions as the instrument by which grievability is publicly distributed. It is the means by which a life becomes, or fails to become, a publicly grievable life, an icon for national self-recognition, the means by which a life becomes noteworthy. As a result, we have to consider the obituary as an act of nation-building. The matter is not a simple one, for, if a life is not grievable, it is not quite a life; it does not qualify as a life and is not worth a note ... It is not just that a death is poorly marked, but that it is unmarkable. Such a death vanishes, not into explicit discourse, but in the ellipses by which public discourse proceeds.[43]

In this public space of mourning, the text that would mark it emerges as stark and dangerous.[44] At that moment of conduct through Atlanta's streets, these parents are locked into the mourning ritual behind their child's casket on a "ghostly unreal day ... down the unknown street behind a little white bundle of posies that shrouded their child [with] the shadow of a song in their ears." But whatever that shade of song, what was plainly heard was a verbal assault when some who glanced their way as they passed called out "Niggers!"[45] This language and its memory construct what I argue here as the discursive assault that "Of the Passing" labors to displace. In making that publicly rehearsed response to black death a matter of record and for redress in *Souls*, wondering "where ... beneath thy broad blue sky shall my dark baby rest in peace,"[46] Du Bois restates the essential question of the book: where might a black life find bodily integrity without the invasive dismemberment of racism and despite the conferred burden of a presumptive problematic inferiority or the "heavy fact of color prejudice"? The ironic reversal here lies in the struggle of this essential obituary with the national work of public notice it must accomplish in this space and the local intimacy of its source when it forces a private grief into public.

It is the legal quandary that Brandeis and Warren articulate between privacy and public space, and it is the personal invasion in which those two privileged elites found themselves embroiled. But recall that Du Bois makes it quite clear that the public space of the racist verbal assault launched at that melancholic black family had already accomplished and arguably repeated the violence done to them in the manner of their son's loss. Du Bois's anguished effort in "Of the Passing" labors to mend the agony by restating the act and its language and then by reinscribing and renarrativizing that moment to displace the incident of public recognition with the ritual inscription of obituary. He accomplishes this through an instantiation of private grief, making his son and those other souls he pulls into the symbolic landscape into lives worthy of note—conferring back to them their personhood as he accomplishes the public ontological work of memorial. This enables, in a critically important way, the body work implicit in the title of the book that displaces the physical for the spiritual—for how can a body be without a soul? These bodies are his sites for theory.

In "The Right to Privacy," Warren and Brandeis argue a corporealized history for this protection of privacy, arguing, "It is like the right not to be assaulted or beaten, the right not to be imprisoned, the right not to be maliciously prosecuted, the right not to be defamed. In each of these rights . . . there inheres the quality of being owned or possessed—and (as that is the distinguishing attribute of property) there may be some propriety in speaking of those rights as property. But . . . the principle . . . is in reality not the principle of private property, but that of an inviolate personality."[47]

Herein lies the expansive landscape of *Souls*. The methodology of its sustained argument between public and private provides at least an unintended commentary on the matter of the Warren and Brandeis argument. The whole of *The Souls of Black Folk* and paradigmatically that chapter "Of the Passing" recover both a national and a personal experience with the reinscription of a *violable* black person. It is the work of memorial, this making of and writing the body. As with the impetus for that law review essay, but with a gravity absent from it, the violation of private personhood—racial and familial, mind and body—prompt this consideration of the assumptions of individuation and community—at bottom, a consideration of privacy. With intent only to suggest a sense of that violation, but not to minimize at all the deep anguish of that moment, I cannot help but to suspect the impulse of William Du Bois, race man, at that precarious moment of verbal assault was to turn and wonder where the Niggers might be. And with this injudicious speculation, I am brought back to the event of the perp walk.

Desire, Autonomy, and Authority

When Du Bois found himself trapped into that horrid epithet, we might read his experience into the discursive spaces of executive whiteness that explores the shock of discovery engendered in the vulnerability revealed in nurtured social insularity. Both instances find men who had considered themselves protected from public deconstruction but who eventually find themselves similar enough—in deed or in body—to change places with the "other" in a public spectacle. Du Bois's laborious and consuming effort to define the realm of the folk that was to have the subtextual, but nonetheless vital, consequence of distinguishing him from them was finally an unsustainable circumlocution. Rather than the authorial hand maintaining its control and instead of the social scientist's objective spyglass, he was left with the same result that finally assaults the accoutrements of executive whiteness and the privileges of prosperity.

A public's gaze is the ultimate mediator—its speculation is both judgmental and ready as it flings a cultivated reputation into a sound bite (or photo shoot), displacing private particularity with public generalization. There is little nuance in this gaze—intellect, character, and, yes, even the ineffable qualities of souls all collapse into a visual dynamic of what one's body most looks like when viewed within the boundaries of this socially constructed sphere and by the public. And such a turn of events is a particularly painful consequence, I suspect, when there has been effort like Du Bois's to assert and to sustain an alternative.[48]

The authorities we claim and those we desire meet in the negotiations of the body's politics, whether it is the reflection of one body back to the other, or membership within a community of souls in search of bodily integrity despite their exposure to the public's gaze, as in Du Bois's *Souls*. In *Private Matters: In Defense of a Personal Life*, psychotherapist Janna Malamud Smith writes that "perhaps the hardest dilemma of privacy is not just . . . the ways in which it must be balanced with communal needs, but its . . . fragility . . . how quickly it can be harmed by other, more predatory, human impulses."[49] I think that this is the correct way to understand the racialized complication of desire. Its simultaneous investment in both the public as well as the private is its essential juxtaposition. The stereotype predation in the public has a vigorous assertiveness, and the urged interiority in the private is needful. Although Du Bois does not claim privacy in the language of *Souls*, its juxtaposed longing seems nevertheless evident in both methodology and example. Desire provokes its mindfulness and its claim to a principled, differentiated authority that is sustained, I submit, from the imperatives that privacy assumes. The storied texts of *Souls* reflect Du Bois's desires for the race as intimately bound to his own longing for an autonomous and authoritative selfhood.

The writing of legal scholars and bioethicists is replete with examples that argue the relevance and implicit value of autonomy. It is a notion that is finally constructed, I suspect, to validate the intimacy of the private and to instantiate the authority of private personhood. A legal right to privacy became viable, at least as argument, following the Warren and Brandeis essay's focus on its basic principle—the autonomous "right to be let alone." But in the century of court cases that followed its publication, privacy—although engaged by the courts—has been increasingly viewed as a secondary claim to society's primary interests. In other words, the bodies politic that negotiate and interpret this right substantially find for the primacy and value of society's collective interest over individual desire. In that environment, the racialized landscape that Du Bois introduced to this claim of autonomy and authority adds critical substance to its history. Du Bois's claim of the stage of social science as the intellectual space to forward this scholarly authority strategically positioned his own body within the field's vision as well as within the field's work. Although his scholarship and positionality, as evidenced in *Souls*, was certainly and unabashedly self-serving, it constructed a text for a lifetime project of articulating the shape-shifting borders of national imaginaries as they "regarded" the private intimacies of bodies like his.

Notes

1. *Caldarola v. County of Westchester*, 6–22.
2. Ibid., 7–20; emphasis added. In *Caldarola*, Justice Parker, writing for the court but adopting the vernacular, recalled that the Court's "first foray into the constitutional implications of the perp walk" represented a question of the Fourth Amendment's constraints on seizure. In that first case (*Lauro v. Charles*), as noted in my text, the court decided for the plaintiff upholding that a "staged" walk violated rights to "unreasonable" seizure. Justice Parker notes that Lauro informed the analysis of *Caldarola*, although here, the Court concluded that "legitimate government purposes served by the County's actions outweigh . . . privacy interests" (21) and that the plaintiff "did not suffer any violation of his Fourth Amendment rights" (23).
3. Eagleton, *Literary Theory*, 131.
4. Current, highly visible scenarios of "the executive perp walk" include that of Ken Lay, former chief executive of Enron Corporation. Media lined up at the courthouse,

anticipating the public display, as they had done earlier in cases like the arrest of Adelphia Communication's chief, John Rigas.

5. Bhabha, *Location of Culture*, 95.

6. Nobel Laureate Toni Morrison proposed that President Clinton "white skin notwithstanding . . . is our first black president. Blacker than any actual black person who could ever be elected in our children's lifetime" (32). Morrison makes what is for this essay the essential point of connection in this assignation: it is, finally, a body politic that negotiates this claim. "The President's body, his privacy, his unpoliced sexuality became the focus of the persecution, when he was metaphorically seized and body-searched" (32).

7. Wallace, *Constructing the Black Masculine*, 44.

8. Warren and Brandeis use this *Millar v. Taylor* citation as their epigraph to "Right to Privacy."

9. The story seems to have started with Prosser's "Privacy, A Legal Analysis." More recent appearances of this rumor, although they abound in the scholarly literature, include Strum's "Privacy," Alderman and Kennedy's *The Right to Privacy*, and Smith's *Private Matters: In Defense of the Personal Life*. But Ken Gormley's "100 Years of Privacy" refers scholars to Alfred Lief's biography of Brandeis noting that Brandeis was unhappy when photographers took pictures of his daughter and turned to his friend with the notion of the article. Whatever the story, it is certainly not Warren's as has been reported by the distinguished scholars above whose work has perpetuated what seems now, at least, an exaggeration if not a total fiction. Gormley suggests the tale "appears as fatuous as the newspaper gossip which Warren and Brandeis chided" (1349).

10. Warren and Brandeis, "Right to Privacy," 196.

11. Williams, *The Alchemy of Race and Rights*, 1.

12. This is not as casual a speculation as it might seem. Edward Bloustein's "Privacy, Tort Law, and the Constitution: Is Warren and Brandeis' Tort Petty and Unconstitutional as Well?" suggests a similar sentiment, noting the concerns of Kalven's 1966 essay that there may well be some relationship between the impact of the Warren and Brandeis article and "the glamour of their names and the intellectually seductive character of their prose" (see Kalven, "Privacy in Tort Law: Were Warren and Brandeis Wrong?"). Bloustein suggests a "tone of personal prissiness that underlies their philosophic concern" (613).

13. Warren and Brandeis, "Right to Privacy," 194.

14. Ibid., 195.

15. Lewis, *W. E. B. Du Bois*, 80.

16. Du Bois, *Autobiography*, 136.

17. The *Harvard Law Review* is interesting and illustrative in this regard. Although "the right to privacy" appears neither in the index nor in the notes section of this journal prior to 1890, in the decade after its publication, citations and notes appear in at least seven volumes (from 1891–1900) including (among others) references to "a question of libel" (7:493); a "first attempt to make a careful presentation of the reasons against the right" (8:281); "a lawsuit where a child was operated on in the presence of the mother and medical students that argued the 'publicity of the operation' as well as publication of a pamphlet that was illustrated by photographs" (10:179); and a cigar manufacturer who used "the name and likeness of a deceased son" (13:415).

18. Lewis explains that Du Bois's baccalaureate from the historically black college, Fisk, received in 1888, gave him two years credit toward the same degree at Harvard.

19. Lewis, *W. E. B. Du Bois*, 81.

20. Ibid., 105.
21. Du Bois's concept that the top ten percent, the "exceptional men" among educated African Americans, might each reach down to the masses to develop in them, through education, redemptive social values. It was in part a response to Booker Washington's "bootstraps" and "buckets" notion of industrial education but also, notably, a profoundly classist and sexist assignment.
22. See Carby, *Race Men*, 9.
23. For a searing exposition of the narrow gendered space of *Souls*, see Carby, *Race Men*, "The Souls of Race Men," 9–44. It seems ironic, that as flexible and nimbly accomplished as his shifting between the mass and self that he might be, Du Bois's book is, finally, profoundly sexist. Women are instrumentalized, either as mythic and archaic reference (see "On the Wings of Atalanta"), or are summarily dismissed from the scenes with Du Bois's interpretive authority standing in for their presence (see especially, the chapters "Of the Passing of the First Born" and "Of the Coming of John"). They are silenced, secondary, and meager players in this text about black folk. Carby's book frames a necessary intervention in the understanding and rereading of *Souls*. See also Griffin, "Black Feminists and Du Bois," and James, *Transcending the Talented Tenth*.
24. Carby, *Race Men*, 27.
25. Ibid., 198n42.
26. Du Bois, *The Souls of Black Folk*, 1.
27. Ibid., 2.
28. Ibid., 4.
29. Ibid., 4–5; emphasis added.
30. Ibid., 35.
31. Lewis, *W. E. B. Du Bois*, 279.
32. Du Bois, *The Souls of Black Folk*, 15.
33. Lewis, *W. E. B. Du Bois*, 281.
34. See note 26.
35. Carby, *Race Men*, 24.
36. Warren and Brandeis, "Right to Privacy," 205.
37. Lewis, *W. E. B. Du Bois*, 225.
38. The loss of the mother in this chapter seems nearly an afterthought. Others (see Lewis, *W. E. B. Du Bois*; and Carby, *Race Men*) have also commented on the language and tone of this chapter. Lewis contends that a contemporary audience's response might read it as "bathos" (Lewis, *W. E. B. Du Bois*, 227) and suggests that it is overwritten. Carby calls attention to the loss of Nina Gomer's presence. Her absence is indeed notable and troublesome. I suspect, however, that it is yet another indication of the linguistic trickster at work and that Du Bois may be instantiating his voice in place of his wife's, taking on what might read (to him and perhaps his contemporary readers) as a more feminized prose of grief—a tactile, viscerally intense language of loss. I think that this stylistic choice is an additional indication of Du Bois's ego as he places himself into a language that might have been hers, and an example of his ability to control the visibility of his wife.
39. Butler, *Precarious Life*, 20; emphasis added.
40. Lewis, *W. E. B. Du Bois*, 227.
41. I had been perplexed over the presence of so personal a chapter in this book and especially fixed by my concern over the vulnerability and exposure at risk in this public space. It would be my own eventual experience with grief that led me to an intimate understanding of its labor. I discuss this chapter and that perspective in *Passed On: African American Mourning Stories—A Memorial*. There is an inconsolable loss of the

private in grief made public. The urge, following this moment, is to rewrite the narrative that a public space distorted—to reclaim—to reinscribe a body back to one's own and one's self through the language of what I read now, with grateful acknowledgment to Judith Butler, as obituary.

42. Ibid., 5–6.
43. Butler, *Precarious Life*, 34–35.
44. Du Bois's public space—the streets of Atlanta—scarred his child's body. Newsprint disembodied my child's. I think now that neither of us, as writers especially, could bear the public language having the final say, leaving its mark. Their bodies were ours to speak of and to memorialize.
45. Du Bois, *The Souls of Black Folk*, 173.
46. Ibid., 214.
47. Warren and Brandeis, "Right to Privacy," 205.
48. Du Bois's condition in *Souls* resembles the symbolic reversal of fortunes explored in Flannery O'Connor's short story, "Everything That Rises Must Converge." The story's dramatic narrative peaks at the moment a black woman boards a city bus and sits directly across from an elderly white woman bemoaning the loss of social stratifications that allowed white folks to have spaces "to ourselves" (276). Both women are wearing the same garish and expensive hat. The encounter in black and white constructs a dramatic vignette that is especially wounding to the white woman who has desperately held onto the distinction that the woman sitting across from her erases. She had had to talk herself into the purchase of the hat—something far more dear than her usual expenditures, finally deciding that "you only live once and paying a little more for it, I at least won't meet myself coming and going" (272). The irony, of course, is that she does exactly that. The encounter forces a collision of selves and the unrecoverable deconstruction of privatized racial zones of difference.
49. Smith, *Private Matters*, 17.

Bibliography

Alderman, Ellen, and Caroline Kennedy. *The Right to Privacy*. New York: Vintage, 1995.

Bhabha, Homi. *The Location of Culture*. New York: Routledge, 2004.

Bloustein, Edward. "Privacy, Tort Law, and the Constitution: Is Warren and Brandeis' Tort Petty and Unconstitutional as Well?" *Texas Law Review* 46, no. 5 (1968): 611–29.

Butler, Judith. *Precarious Life: The Powers of Mourning and Violence*. London: Verso, 2004.

Caldarola v. County of Westchester, No. 01-7457. U.S. Court of Appeals, 2d Cir (2003).

Carby, Hazel. *Race Men*. Cambridge, MA: Harvard University Press, 1998.

Du Bois, W. E. B. *The Souls of Black Folk*. 1903. Reprint, New York: Modern Library, 2003.

Du Bois, W. E. B. *Autobiography of W. E. B. Du Bois: A Soliloquy on Viewing My Life from the Last Decade of Its First Century*. New York: International, 1968.

Eagleton, Terry. *Literary Theory: An Introduction*. Minneapolis, MN: University of Minnesota Press, 1983.

Gormley, Ken. "100 Years of Privacy." *Wisconsin Law Review* (September/October 1992): 1335–49.

Griffin, Farah. "Black Feminists and Du Bois: Respectability, Protection and Beyond." *Annals of the American Academy* 568, no. 1 (March 2000): 28–40.

Holloway, Karla F. C. *Passed On: African American Mourning Stories—A Memorial*. Durham, NC: Duke University Press, 2002.

James, Joy. *Transcending the Talented Tenth: Black Leaders and American Intellectuals.* New York: Routledge, 1997.

Kalven, Harry. "Privacy in Tort Law: Were Warren and Brandeis Wrong?" *Law and Contemporary Problems* 31 (1966): 326–41.

Lauro v. Charles, 219 F.3d 202 (2d Cir. 2000).

Lewis, David Levering. *W. E. B. Du Bois: Biography of a Race.* New York: Henry Holt, 1993.

Millar v. Taylor, 4 Burr. 2303, 98 Eng. Rep. 201 (KB 1769).

Morrison, Toni. "Talk of the Town." *New Yorker,* October 5, 1998.

O'Connor, Flannery. "Everything that Rises Must Converge." In *Collected Works,* 481–696. New York: Literary Classics of the United States, Library of America, 1988.

Prosser, William L. "Privacy, A Legal Analysis." *California Law Review* 48 (1960): 338–423.

Smith, Janna Malamud. *Private Matters: In Defense of the Personal Life.* Emeryville, CA: Seal, 1997.

Strum, Phillipa. "Privacy." In *The Oxford Companion to American Law,* edited by Kermit Hall, 637–39. New York: Oxford University Press, 2002.

Wallace, Maurice. *Constructing the Black Masculine: Identity and Ideality in African American Men's Literature and Culture, 1775–1995.* Durham, NC: Duke University Press, 2002.

Warren, Samuel L., and William Brandeis. "Right to Privacy." *Harvard Law Review* 4 (1890): 193–220.

Williams, Patricia Williams. *The Alchemy of Race and Rights.* Cambridge, MA: Harvard University Press, 1991.

3

Martin R. Delany and Rhetorics of Divided Sovereignty

Rochelle Raineri Zuck

Martin Robison Delany's engagement with the American legal system extended far beyond the pages of his first and only novel, *Blake; or, The Huts of America* (published serially 1859, 1861–62). While perhaps best known today for his fictional interventions into the cultural and legal milieu of the 1850s, Delany had a lifelong interest in the law. He believed that African Americans had to be well versed in the law in order to make effective arguments against slavery and racism. Delany himself was familiar with statutory law and British and American common law. He drew on his knowledge of jurisprudence while debating the meaning of the Constitution with Frederick Douglass in the pages of *The North Star*.[1] Furthermore, he was part of a larger literary community in which African American writers challenged white readings of the Constitution and judicial decisions regarding African American citizenship, personal freedom, and property in the pages of the periodical press. The contributions of Delany and other African American writers to American legal thought often have been overlooked because many were not practicing attorneys. Instead, a great deal of critical attention has focused on African Americans as subject to American law rather than agents of its production.

The work of critical race theorists such as Derrick Bell, Alan Freeman, Kimberlé Crenshaw, Patricia Williams, and Richard Delgado, however, provides not only the impetus to explore the racist assumptions that undergird much of American jurisprudence but also offers ways to read the stories which people of color have used to interpret and challenge dominant group interpretations of the law.[2] This scholarship, along with that of feminist scholars and postmodern theorists, invites further consideration of the interplay between power, race, and the law and the ways in which African Americans themselves strategically exploited the fissures in U.S. legal and social institutions.

To continue the study of nineteenth-century African Americans' involvement with the law requires broadening our understanding of what it meant to "practice" law to include more than just admittance to the bar. Scholars cite the 1840s as the decade that produced the first African American lawyers, but African

Americans had been using the genre of the petition, or "memorial," since the 1780s to articulate their concerns to state and federal authorities. Fraternal and religious organizations such as the Black Freemasons, the African Methodist Episcopal (AME) Church, and Philadelphia's Free African Society (led by AME Bishop Richard Allen) provided fellowship, material assistance, and informal networks that worked to improve the legal status of members.[3] The life and work of Martin Delany—nineteenth-century novelist, editor, medical doctor, U.S. Army officer, Freedman's Bureau employee, and African explorer—provide an example of one way in which African Americans fused the "practice" of law and the composition of literary texts. Delany turned to law, rather than other readily available discourses such as Christianity or sentimentality, to make his case against slavery and foster a consolidated African American community. Delany's work reveals not only the depth of African American use of American common law but also the transatlantic dimensions of African American legal thought.

This essay argues that for Delany, British common law provided a vocabulary for rearticulating the position of African Americans vis-à-vis the American government. In particular the concept of divided sovereignty, derived from Blackstone's commentaries, provided one way to assert African Americans' political subjectivity and think broadly about new kinds of political and legal formations in America or in an as yet to be created African American colony. Using the idea of divided sovereignty allowed Delany to explore the possibility of alternative forms of sovereignty, which were departures from ideas of liberal self-government and exclusive possession of a particular space espoused by white Americans. Delany argued for a kind of ethnic sovereignty that would be uniquely available to African Americans and, for his white readers, raises the specter of revolution from within.[4] While the shifting legal and cultural situation of the post-Civil War United States would complicate visions of divided sovereignty, later African Americans such as Booker T. Washington and Sutton Griggs would continue to invoke the idea of African Americans as a nation within a nation. Ultimately, this essay suggests that the concept of divided sovereignty, which had its roots in British common law, described on a larger scale in what Du Bois would later characterize as "double consciousness." As such, it served as a way to think about the "veil" between the U.S. nation and the African American community within its borders.

*   *   *

Despite the antislavery legislation passed by Great Britain (most notably the Somersett decision), the question remains: why would Delany draw from British common law to formulate his critiques of racial oppression?[5] At times, Delany himself despaired that the conditions of African Americans could be improved by legal means. He was aware that the laws passed by Great Britain did little to erase the racial oppression and violence in colonies such as Jamaica. However, British common law was historically seen as the law of the people and not that of the religious or secular elite. As such, it provided an intellectual framework for the discussions of property issues and personal freedom raised by debates over slavery. Moreover, because American common law was based largely on the British model, British common law was a cherished part of the American national consciousness. Couching his arguments in legal terms resonated with white audiences and provided Delany a way to circulate what he viewed as an important body of knowledge among African American readers. As he argued in *Blake, The Condition, Elevation, Emigration, and Destiny of the Colored People of the United States* (1852) and other writings, knowledge of the law was key to the development and politicization of the African American community.

During the eighteenth and nineteenth centuries, common law was part of a larger constellation of ideologies—including classical republicanism, liberalism, and Christianity—that informed the way white Americans and people of color thought about their relationship to judicial, executive, and legislative powers and to other individuals.[6] Common law originated in England as the law of the people and was comprised of those cases that were not of interest to the king or the church. Examples might include estate issues and criminal complaints. There was no formal written code, so judges consulted the written records of previous cases when making their decisions. They were expected not only to memorize important cases but also to understand the logic or reason behind the decisions rendered. The process of adjudication was seen as an art, blending history, philosophy, and classical rhetoric. Common law, along with the unwritten English constitution that it informed, was thought to preserve the liberty of the people, providing for the appointment of judges and the jury system. As James R. Stoner has noted, the liberal theory that was first articulated by Thomas Hobbes arose in opposition to British common law. In his *Commentaries on the Laws of England (1765–1769)*, Blackstone reworked many of the precepts of common law to reflect the growing prominence of liberal and Enlightenment ideologies.[7] It is Blackstone's version of common law that American colonists looked to in creating their own legal culture. They appealed to common law to argue against what they saw as British tyranny, and, with some notable exceptions, the colonies adopted the major tenets of common law as part of their state and federal legal systems.

From Blackstone's writings and from their own readings in history and political theory, Americans gained an understanding of the concept of divided sovereignty, generally defined as two separate authorities existing within the same political structure. Blackstone's work articulated cultural anxieties about the rise of Roman Catholic power in Protestant Britain. From ancient Roman law, Blackstone derived the idea that a republic must have a supreme authority. There had to be, as Blackstone put it, "a supreme, irresistible, absolute, uncontrolled authority in which the *jura summa imperii*, or the rights of sovereignty, resides."[8] In his own particular historical moment, Blackstone feared the introduction of a "foreign power" into England and asserted that Roman Catholics would subvert the monarchy "by paying that obedience to papal process, which constitutionally belonged to the king alone."[9] The divided allegiance of Roman Catholic people, according to this line of argument, made them a threatening presence to the body politic. For Blackstone and many of his American readers, truly divided sovereignty was thought to be a political impossibility. Multiple sovereign powers would be like a two-headed monster, constantly fighting itself for power and authority.

Yet in the division of power between state and federal authorities, America's founding generations attempted to use the notion of divided sovereignty in order to safeguard the rights of the people and create a balance of power. This system was not without its detractors, as divided sovereignty was thought to weaken the power of the government and plant the seeds of internal conflict. Writing as "Publius" in Federalist No. 15, Alexander Hamilton expressed concern about giving too much power to the states, while John Adams took a much more optimistic view and claimed that America would be the first successful example of divided sovereignty.[10] A letter published in *The Atlantic Monthly* in 1825 reflected on the division of power between state and federal authorities and between the three branches of government and argued that this constituted a "qualified" form of divided sovereignty. The anonymous author, purportedly a visitor from France who was relaying his observations of the American political system to his father, claimed that "abstractly, this plan [divided sovereignty] is extremely difficult to comprehend," but that the American example of divided sovereignty had been "stripped of all of the fancied terrors it once possessed for rational lovers of freedom."[11] In the nineteenth century, however, the "terrors" associated with divided sovereignty were projected onto a variety of racial and ethnic groups who were perceived as threats to white sovereignty.

One of the earliest uses of the rhetoric of divided sovereignty was to describe the legal and political condition of African Americans within the United States. In an 1827 speech Samuel Knapp reflected on the formation of the American Colonization Society, attributing its origins to the fact that "we wanted no nation of blacks here."[12] The idea of an African American *imperium* was articulated much more explicitly by a writer for the *Christian Watchman* who claimed that if colonization was unsuccessful in its mission "we shall have an *imperium in imperio*, a nation within a nation, in the worst sense of the term." The author further asserted that there would be more than half a million people "not only distinguished by their complexion, but bound together by a feeling of nationality among themselves." They could never be American citizens, this writer maintained, because if given political power, they will always act "as Africans in America."[13] These statements implied that not only was an African American nation threatening, but it could never be assimilated into U.S. legal and political culture because physical differences and sentimental attachments would prevent African Americans from being seen as and seeing themselves as Americans. According to this line of argument, African Americans could never achieve the kind of disembodied and disinterested benevolence required of republican citizenship.

*   *   *

Adopting and adapting such discourses of divided sovereignty, Delany both played on white fears of internal strife and worked to envision a new form of sovereignty for African American people. This section will show how Delany's fictional and nonfictional writings evoked key elements of American and British common law to demonstrate the failure of the former to promote African American sovereignty. Delany sought to rearticulate the meaning of sovereignty as part of the larger project of refashioning African American identity, which he said had been "broken" as a result of slavery and racial oppression. His vision of sovereignty was based on ethnic identity, not property ownership, citizenship, or the exercise of particular political rights such as voting. As Delany's writings and political activities suggest, the concept of divided sovereignty could be invoked as a way for African Americans to explore the possibilities of a consolidated political position that was equal to, but distinct from, the U.S. government. Redefining sovereignty in terms of ethnic identity gave Delany a way to think beyond the two models of sovereignty that were rendered unavailable to African Americans by the American legal system: (1) individual sovereignty equated with white, masculine, liberal citizenship and (2) national sovereignty that was predicated on the ownership of a particular territory.

Delany's novel *Blake, or The Huts of America*, published serially between 1859 and 1862 in *The Anglo-African Magazine* and *The Weekly Anglo-African*, dramatized the revolutionary potential of divided sovereignty by detailing the formation of an African American "nation" within the United States and Cuba. The novel chronicles the life of Henrico Blackus (also known as Henry Holland and, later, Blake), a West Indian man who is abducted and sold into slavery in Louisiana. There he marries an enslaved woman, Maggie, who is later sold by her owner/father. At this point, Henry escapes and travels throughout the American South and Cuba spreading plans for revolution. In Cuba, he finds Maggie, buys her freedom, and transforms himself into Blake, general of a revolutionary army intending to overthrow the Cuban government and prevent an American takeover. This novel, considered by Robert Levine to be "a Pan-African vision of black nationalism that means to combat and expose the limits of the U.S. nationalism espoused by blacks aligned with [Frederick] Douglass," showed how the African American population could be mobilized and politicized through kinship ties and informal social networks.[14]

Blake explicitly mentioned landmark cases of the 1850s as part of its argument for a new vision of African American sovereignty.[15] There are references throughout the novel to the Fugitive Slave Law and *Dred Scott v. Sanford* (1857), cases that denied African American people sovereignty over their own person and participation in the sovereign nation. As Jeffrey Clymer has noted, "Delany has his most racist characters ventriloquize phrases from Chief Justice Roger B. Taney's decision" that African Americans have no rights that whites must respect.[16] Clymer also has suggested that *Blake* drew on another important case, *Lemmon v. People* (1852). In this case, which was tried in New York, Juliet Lemmon, who was moving from Virginia to Texas, made a brief stop in New York with eight enslaved people. According to New York state law, any slave who entered the state was considered to be free. Upon learning of the situation, a free African American named Louis Napoleon petitioned for a writ of habeas corpus on behalf of those held in bondage by Lemmon. Lemmon cited his right to transport property from one state to another, but a Superior Court judge declared the enslaved people to be free. For Clymer, this case resonated with the novel's discussion of Maggie's trip to Saratoga and may have inspired Delany's discussions of "property, liberty, slavery, and nationhood."[17]

While Delany demonstrates his knowledge of the law throughout *Blake*, the text suggests that not all whites are well versed in the American legal system. While leading a group of slaves, Henry meets a white man who demands to know "if them air black folks ye got wey yer am free, cause if they arn't, I be 'sponsible for 'em 'cording to the new law, called, I 'bleve the Nebrasky Complimize Fugintive Slave Act, made down at Califory, last year."[18] The man goes on to explain correctly the penalties that he will face if he does not comply with the law: "This are a law made by the Newnited States of Ameriky, an' I be 'bliged to fulfill it by ketchin' every fugintive that goes to cross this way, or I mus' pay a thousand dollars, and go to jail till the black folks is got, if that be's never. Yer see yez can't blame me, as I mus' 'bey the laws of Congress I'll swog it be's hardly a fair shake nuther, but I be 'bliged to 'bey the laws, yer know."[19] Henry demands to know why this man is serving the slaveholder's interests and not his own. This scene suggests that white people, particularly those who are not part of the social elite, also suffer under racist legislation such as the Fugitive Slave Law. They are forced to obey laws that they do not fully understand and that run counter to their own interests. The novel contends that just as African Americans are justified in violently rebelling against oppressive laws so too should the ferryman resist the Fugitive Slave Law rather than serve the slaveholders' cause.

In addition to its critique of particular cases, *Blake* suggests that the whole American legal system is flawed. When comparing the social, political, and economic prospects of several nations, Blake remarks that American jurisprudence is but a "sad reflection" of British law: "How sublime the spectacle of the colossal stature (compared with the puppet figure of the Judge of the American Supreme Court), of the Lord Chief Justice when standing up and declaring to the effect: that by the force of British intelligence, the purity of their morals, the splendor of their magnanimity, and aegis of the Magna Charta, the moment the foot of a slave touched British soil, he stood erect, disenthralled in the dignity of a freeman, by the irresistible genius of universal emancipation."[20] Despite the praise heaped on British jurisprudence, the novel is not naïve in its understanding of the obstacles that still faced African Americans living under British law. Earlier in the novel, the narrator had expressed doubts about the enactment of "universal emancipation" in Canada, noting that "according to fundamental British Law and constitutional rights, all persons are equal in the realm, yet by a systematic course of policy and artifice . . . [the African American] is excluded from the enjoyment and practical exercise of every right."[21] Thus, it is not enough simply to become a subject of British law, but rather, as Delany argued throughout the rest of his writings, African Americans must draw from British legal theory and create their own nation.

Specifically, in his articulation of African American sovereignty, Delany employed the rhetoric of divided sovereignty, or the concept of a nation within a nation. In *The Condition, Elevation, Emigration, and Destiny of the Colored People of the United States* (1852), Delany used this language to explain the legal and political situation of African Americans: "That there have in all ages, in almost every nation, existed a nation within a nation—a people who although forming a part and parcel of the population, yet were from force of circumstances, known by the peculiar position they occupied, forming in fact, by the deprivation of political equality with others, no part, and if any, but a restricted part of the body politic of such nations, is also true."[22] Here Delany draws on the concept of *imperium in imperio* but used the English translation to make it more accessible for his readers. This rhetoric allows him to convey the visual image of Africans and African-descended people as a nation "restricted" and even constricted by the American nation. By using this image, Delany avoids the language of vertical hierarchy that was often employed in discussions of African Americans' political position within the United States.

As a nation within a nation, African Americans' position was similar to many white ethnic populations, an argument that challenged discourses of racial inferiority. Delany compared the African American *imperium* to the conditions of "the Poles in Russia, the Hungarians in Austria, the Scotch, Irish, and Welsh in the United Kingdom, and . . . the Jews." These groups, he argued, are able to maintain their distinct ethnic sovereignty even without a direct connection to a specific territory. They are, he wrote, "scattered throughout not only the length and breadth of Europe, but almost the habitable globe, maintaining their national characteristics, and looking forward in high hopes of seeing the day when they may return to their former national position of self-government and independence, let that be in whatever part of the habitable world it may."[23] In this passage, Delany foreshadowed his argument for emigration by suggesting that the national identities of these groups, like that of Africans, can be recreated. Delany himself used the word "colored" so as not to distinguish between Africans in America and those who lived elsewhere. As opposed to dominant discourses of African Americans as a nation in the making—a nation that can only be actualized in Africa—Delany suggested that African nationhood constitutes a *return* rather than a creation and would be possible in any space of the "habitable world." He argued that while the African American nation was "broken" and "depriv[ed] of political equality," it was nonetheless a nation. What they needed, as he had concluded in *Blake*, was a "space for action."[24]

Delany's sense that an African American nation needed "space" suggests a blending of white American definitions of sovereignty as the sole ownership of territory and the ethnic definition of sovereignty in which he invested so much revolutionary power. And here is where some interesting tensions in Delany's political thought surfaced. In *The Condition . . . of the Colored People of the United States*, he asserted that African Americans are American citizens based on their birth: "We are Americans, having a birthright citizenship—natural claims upon the country—claims common to all others of our fellow citizens—natural rights, which may, by virtue of unjust laws, be obstructed, but never can be annulled. Upon these do we place ourselves, as immovably fixed as the decrees of the living God."[25] When considering this passage within the context of Delany's larger project, the question becomes how can he argue that African Americans are "immovably fixed" with birthright citizenship in America and, within the same work, promote emigration.[26] Taking a closer look at Delany's belief in both African Americans' "birthright" and the need for emigration reveals the limitations of discourses of ethnic sovereignty and nations within nations.

To reconcile his belief that America was the most appropriate place for an African American nation with his desire that black people should leave the United States, Delany rhetorically expanded "America" to include what we would now consider the Americas (North, Central, and South America as well as the Caribbean). He ultimately rejected Canada as a possible location for an African American nation because black people could never form a majority there, and he believed that a black majority was necessary to the enactment of African American sovereignty. Instead he looked to Central and South America because of his belief in the climatalogical flexibility of African Americans and because of the common features that they shared with the indigenous Americans who inhabited these locations. He thought that Central and South America would provide an opportunity for the formation of a "colored" (i.e., African American and American Indian) American nation.

African Americans would be able to make this move, Delany claimed, because they are uniquely able to flourish in almost any climate. Using language that was somewhat reminiscent of the rhetoric of American exceptionalism, Delany proclaimed that God created black people to be "denizens of *every soil*" and the "*lords of terrestrial creation*." He continued,

> There is one great physiological fact in regard to the colored race—which, while it may not apply to all colored persons, is true of those having black skins—that they can bear *more different* climates than the white race. They bear *all* the temperates and extremes, while the other can only bear the termperates and *one* of the extremes. The black race is endowed with natural properties, that adapt and fit them for temperate, cold, and hot climates; while the white race is only endowed with properties that adapt them to temperate and cold climates; being unable to stand the warm climates; in them, the white race cannot work, but become perfectly indolent, requiring somebody to work for them—and these, are always people of the black race.[27]

Here Delany reversed racist depictions of African-descended peoples as "indolent" and unwilling to work and instead applied this language to whites. Moreover, he drew on languages of African American hardiness, often used to justify their enslavement, and instead made this a qualification for their freedom: they are fit to live anywhere and so should not stay in the United States where they will continue to be oppressed.

South America would provide a particularly hospitable environment, Delany argued, because there the African American will be able to "unite and make common cause in elevation, with our similarly oppressed brother, the Indian."[28] African- and American Indian-descended peoples, he contended, were linked by blood ties and their lived experiences of oppression and thus could form one ethnic nation. "The aboriginee of the continent," Delany wrote, "is more closely allied to us in consanguinity, than to the European—being descended from the Asiatic, whose alliance in matrimony with the African is very common—therefore, we have even greater claims to this continent on that account."[29] In a somewhat problematic move, Delany touted the links between African Americans and American Indians as proof of a valid connection to the land. His language here was not unlike that of white Europeans as they celebrated the marriage of Pocahontas and John Rolfe as proof of English dominion over Powhatan lands. In creating a fantasy of political collectivity and shared ethnic solidarity, Delany glossed over any cultural differences that exist between African Americans and indigenous Americans.

Delany assumed that the indigenous Americans would welcome black emigrants. His beliefs about Indian and black relations were first presented in *Blake* in a scene where Henry visits Chickasaw and Choctaw peoples in Arkansas. Mr. Culver, an aging chief, explains that while they hold slaves, they work alongside those slaves and that within their nation, black people and Indian people intermarry freely and have peaceful relations. Delany expanded his sense of the possibilities for a "colored" American nation made up of American Indians and African Americans in *The Condition . . . of the Colored People of the United States*. He wrote, "No—go when we will, and where we may, we shall hold ourselves amenable to defend and protect any country that embraces us. We are fully able to defend our-selves, once concentrated, against any odds—and by the help of God, we will do it. We do not go, without counting the cost, cost what it may; all that it may cost, it is worth to be free."[30] This passage reflected Delany's understandings of a nation as a bounded territory in which a people can be "concentrated" and that they can defend against outside invaders. The idea of a geographically bounded homeland marked a departure from earlier discourses of African American nationalism that likened black people to the Israelites, an ethnic nation with a common culture and ties to an as yet to be realized homeland. For Delany, the African American *imperium*, which has been consolidated through conditions of oppression within the United States, should go to a more "welcoming" environment where his vision of sovereignty could be realized.

Yet Delany later explored the possibility of forming an *imperium* within the United States. His vision of an African American *imperium* was mobilized at the "Chatham meeting" that took place in Chatham, Canada on May 8, 1858. At this meeting, John Brown, Delany, and several supporters met to discuss the situation in Kansas. Jean Fagan Yellin noted, in her book *The Intricate Knot: Black Figures in American Literature, 1776–1863* (1972), that the group took an oath of secrecy at Delany's request, created a provisional Constitution, and elected officers. John Brown himself was named commander-in-chief.[31] Delany's first biographer, Frances Rollin (who published under the name Frank A. Rollin), quoted Delany as saying,

> The whole matter had been well considered, and at first a state government had been proposed, and in accordance a constitution prepared. This was presented to the convention; and here a difficulty presented itself to the minds of some present, that according to American jurisprudence, negroes, having no rights respected by white men, consequently could have no right to petition, and none to sovereignty.
>
> Therefore it would be a mockery to set up a claim as a fundamental right, which in itself was null and void.
>
> To obviate this, and avoid the charge against them as lawless and unorganized, existing without government, it was proposed that an independent community be established within and under the government of the United States, but without the state sovereignty of the compact, similar to the Cherokee nation of Indians, or the Mormons.[32]

This plan was designed to "test, on the soil of the United States territory, whether or not the right to freedom would be maintained where no municipal power had organized."[33] While this plan was never put into action, it was intended to be an *imperium in imperio*—a sovereign power within the United States that would allow African Americans to elide American jurisdiction and establish their own form of sovereignty.

Delany's constructions of sovereignty, which drew on discourses of an African American *imperium*, spoke to the double-edged nature of discourses of a nation within a nation and the challenges of imagining alternatives to the nineteenth-century nation-state. White Americans who used the discourse of *imperium in imperio* to construct African Americans as a threat to the body politic saw this same language used to mobilize African American communal identity. Yet, as Delany's political philosophies demonstrate, characterizing African Americans as an *imperium* risked replicating the nationalist terms that he sought to avoid. Moreover, shifts in the legal situation of African Americans during the late-nineteenth century rendered this language increasingly problematic because to argue for an African American *imperium* resonated with the "separate but equal" ideology of the Jim Crow laws.

*   *   *

It is difficult to say with certainty whether particular individuals read Delany's writings and self-consciously engaged his use of divided sovereignty. What is clear, however, is that the kind of rhetorical moves Delany made were revived by later writers as part of their arguments for African American rights. Within the legal milieu of postbellum America, some African Americans challenged the efficacy of framing themselves as a nation within the United States. Others, even social conservatives such as Booker T. Washington, recalled the threatening implications suggested by Blackstone. By 1899, this particular trope had become so significant in discussions of African Americans and the U.S. nation that Sutton Griggs titled his first novel *Imperium in Imperio*. This novel brought together the radicalism of Delany and the conservatism of Washington and introduced new ways of thinking about the dividedness of the African American experience.

Later uses of the concept of an African American *imperium* did not always acknowledge the revolutionary potential of this rhetorical construction. According to one writer, African American institutions, specifically "colored" newspapers such as *The Anglo-African*, were contributing to the formation of an African American *imperium* and should be disbanded. Identifying himself only as a "colored man," this writer argued in an 1863 letter to the editor of *The Independent*, "The distinction between the white and colored inhabitants of this country has been so long and so harshly maintained, that there has grown up a nation within a nation, a social organization entirely independent of the great mass of the American people. It is as the representatives of this social and religious life of colored people that such papers have right to live."[34] He argued that "colored" newspapers did nothing to help the situation of African Americans because white people would not read them. The formation of separate institutions was not furthering the political and legal advancement of black people but instead reaffirming their disfranchisement.

There were similar concerns expressed by religious leaders about African American religious institutions. *The Christian Recorder*, published in Philadelphia, Pennsylvania, by the AME Church, featured an 1875 article in which the author claimed that "the ultimatum of the white American people to us, is that two [*sic*] be an *imperium* in *imperio;* and as anomalous as such a state is, there remains for us, but to take up the gauntlet, and begin the work."[35] In 1882, the same publication included an article regarding the separation that existed between the Methodist Church and the AME Church. Founded by Bishop Richard Allen in 1816, the AME Church had split from St. George Methodist Church in Philadelphia over issues of racial prejudice. Written more than sixty years after the founding of the AME Church, this 1882 article regarded the formation of separate religious groups for black and white people with skepticism. The author contended that

African Americans would soon be denounced by the American public for forming an *imperium in imperio* if they continued to distinguish themselves from white religious institutions.[36] Both authors understood divided sovereignty as a form of segregation in which African American people were positioned as outside of mainstream American legal, social, and religious institutions.

With the adoption of Jim Crow laws, which codified segregationist practices in many parts of the South, more writers expressed concern about the framing of African Americans as an *imperium*. As Dr. Marshall Taylor, delegate for the Methodist Episcopal General Conference, wrote in 1882,

> If the Chinese are to be kept out by reason of the fear that they may, by their clannishness, build up an imperium in imperio, we may rest assured that the time is not far distant when an attempt on our part to do the same will meet with the same public disapproval. The nation is to be unified. Its peoples are eventually to be one. The blood of Shem, Ham and Hapheth are to flow together on the American continent, where is to grow up a race like to that that was at first, before the Dispersion. Whether the whites like it or the blacks like it, the result is to be the same.[37]

Delany's vision of an African American *imperium* was one in which their sovereign status served to connect them, not only with other oppressed groups, but also with other nations. However, the above quotation suggests that, in the post-Reconstruction era, Dr. Taylor viewed this rhetoric as problematic because it divided African Americans from white culture and linked them instead with immigrant groups such as the Chinese. In the wake of the Chinese Exclusion Act (1882), which placed limitations on immigration from China, associations with the Chinese were thought to further the disfranchisement of African Americans. Considering the political situation from an explicitly Christian standpoint, Dr. Taylor saw the racial and cultural mixture of black and white people as the key to unification.

Despite the skepticism of some writers, Delany's brand of rhetorical brinksmanship, achieved by his invocations of divided sovereignty and revolution from within, found new life in some unlikely sources. At an 1896 Presbyterian Home Mission Rally at Carnegie Hall in New York City, Booker T. Washington warned his listeners:

> Within the next two decades it will be decided whether the negro, by discarding antebellum ideas and methods of labor, by putting brains and skill into the common occupations that lie at his door, will be able to lift up labor out of toil, drudgery and degradation into that which is dignified, beautiful and glorified. Further it will be decided during this time whether he is to be replaced, crushed out as a helpful industrial factor, by the fast spreading trade unions and thousands of foreign skilled laborers that even now tread fast and hard upon his heels and begin to press him unto death. This question is for your Christian church to help decide. And in deciding, remember that you are deciding, not alone for the negro, but whether you will have eight millions of people in this country, or a race nearly as large as Mexico, a nation within a nation that will be a burden, a menace to your civilization, that will be continually threatening and degrading your institutions, or whether you will make him a potent, emphatic factor in your civilization and commercial life.[38]

At first glance, this passage reveals the assimilationist ideology often associated with Washington as well as the concern that native-born African Americans were threatened by the presence of immigrant workers. Perhaps more interesting, given traditional readings of Washington, is his mention of divided sovereignty. He contended that unless white Christians did something to improve the material lives of African Americans, they would become a threatening presence within the United States. By using words like "menace," "threatening," and "degrading," Washington evoked traditional associations of divided sovereignty with political strife and violent revolution.

Unlike Delany, Washington claimed that emigration—even the exodus of African Americans from the southern states—would not solve the social problems facing black people living in the United States. While Delany argued that since African American people already comprised a separate nation, they could easily remove and reestablish that nation in a more welcoming location. For Washington, the sheer size of the African American "nation" made such a move impossible:

> We have almost a nation within a nation. The Negro population in the United States lacks but two millions of being as large as the whole population of Mexico. It is nearly twice as large as the population of the Dominion of Canada. Our black population is equal to the combined populations of Switzerland, Greece, Honduras, Nicaragua, Cuba, Uraguay, Santo Domingo, Paraguay, and Costa Rica. When we consider, in connection with these facts, that the race has doubled itself since its freedom, and is still increasing, it hardly seems possible for any one to consider seriously any scheme of emigration from America as a method of solution.[39]

As in his previous quote, Washington equated sovereignty and nationhood with population; African Americans are "almost a nation within a nation" by virtue of their number. Whereas Delany promoted emigration to a place where African American could outnumber whites, Washington felt that the African American *imperium* could not be so easily relocated. Emphasizing the sheer number of African Americans living within the United States also forced white readers and listeners to take seriously the conditions of black people and hinted at the possibility of threats from within. Washington's use of the concept of divided sovereignty was part of his larger argument for assimilation and racial uplift. Nevertheless, he retained traces of the kind of rhetorical brinksmanship practiced by Delany.

The same year, Baptist minister Sutton Griggs published a novel entitled *Imperium in Imperio*, which he distributed himself among his African American parishioners. This novel dramatized the revolutionary potential of divided sovereignty, tracing the formation of an African American nation in Texas with its capital at Waco. This government is led first by Belton, who represents "the spirit of conservatism in the Negro race," and later by Bernard, "a man to be feared."[40] The narrator revealed the threat that the *Imperium* posed to the United States:

> With Belton gone and this man at our head, our well-organized, thoroughly equipped Imperium was a serious menace to the peace of the world. A chance spark might at any time cause a conflagration, which, unchecked, would spread destruction, devastation and death all around.

I felt that beneath the South a mine had been dug and filled with dynamite, and that lighted fuses were lying around in careless profusion, where any irresponsible hand might reach them and ignite the dynamite. I fancied that I saw a man do this very thing in a sudden fit of uncontrollable rage. There was a dull roar as of distant rumbling thunder. Suddenly there was a terrific explosion and houses, fences, trees, pavement, stores, and all things on earth were hurled high into the air to come back a mass of ruins such as man never before had seen. The only sound to be heard was a universal groan; those who had not been killed were too badly wounded to cry out.

Such were the thoughts that passed through my mind. I was determined to remove the possibility of such a catastrophe. I decided to prove traitor and reveal the existence of the Imperium that it might be broken up or watched.[41]

Here the narrator alluded to the imperialistic and violent possibilities of the *Imperium* with Bernard as its leader. Although the narrator ultimately revealed the existence of the *Imperium*, so as to prevent racial warfare, the novel clearly articulated the connection between divided sovereignty and revolution from within. Aimed primarily at African American readers, the novel used the concept of divided sovereignty—the division between state and federal powers; the divisions between the United States and the *Imperium*; and the division between the two leaders, Belton and Bernard—to consider the legal and political situation of African Americans at the turn of the century.

Like Delany's work, *Imperium in Imperio* imagined a kind of ethnic sovereignty, which would challenge that promulgated by white Americans. Yet, when read alongside broader debates about divided sovereignty, these texts revealed the double-edged nature of discourses of a nation within a nation and the challenges of imagining alternatives to territorial forms of sovereignty. White Americans who used the discourse of *imperium in imperio* to isolate and regulate racial and ethnic populations were faced with the unintended consequence of this same language being used to consolidate and mobilize African American communities. Yet, as Delany, Washington, Griggs, and others suggested, characterizing African Americans as an *imperium* risked replicating the features of U.S. sovereignty that they sought to avoid. Moreover, within the context of the Jim Crow legislation, such language may have also resonated with segregationist ideologies. Yet, despite these limitations, rhetoric of ethnic nationalism and *imperium in imperio* continued to prove useful in exerting pressure on the U.S. nation and imagining alternative political futures.

*　　*　　*

The concept of divided sovereignty, derived from British common law, was adopted and adapted by a variety of African American writers in the latter half of the nineteenth century as a means to expose and challenge the racist features of American legal and political culture. This rhetorical trope also was used, in fictional and nonfictional writings alike, as a vehicle for imagining alternative forms of sovereignty. Ultimately, the importance of this concept may lie not only in the way that it circulated within the nineteenth century but also in the ways in which it anticipated twentieth-century notions of African American individual consciousness. In *The Souls of Black Folk*, W. E. B. Du Bois articulated his now famous theory of "double-consciousness." He wrote,

> After the Egyptian and Indian, the Greek and Roman, the Teuton and Mongolian, the Negro is a sort of seventh son, born with a veil, and gifted with second-sight in this American world,—a world which yields him no true self-consciousness, but only lets him see himself through the revelation of the other world. It is a peculiar sensation, this double-consciousness, this sense of always looking at one's self through the eyes of others, of measuring one's soul by the tape of a world that looks on in amused contempt and pity. One ever feels his two-ness,—an American, a Negro; two souls, two thoughts, two unreconciled strivings; two warring ideals in one dark body, whose dogged strength alone keeps it from being torn asunder.[42]

Du Bois here argued for the African American body as the site of a kind of divided sovereignty, in which blackness and Americanness constituted "two warring ideals in one dark body," threatening to tear the individual apart from within. For Du Bois, "the history of the American Negro is the history of this strife,—this longing to attain self-conscious manhood, to merge his double self into a better and truer self."[43]

Legal rhetoric not only was the means by which the dividedness of African American communities and individuals was enacted and enforced but, as this essay has tried to suggest, it also provided the means by which to question such divisions. Many African Americans who did not practice law professionally adopted legal language as a way to combat racist ideologies and practices during the nineteenth and early twentieth centuries. The writings of Martin Delany reveal the growing prominence of a particular legal trope—that of African Americans as a nation within a nation—in African American writings and speeches. Later writers, while they may not have read Delany, nonetheless engaged this language for their own legal, political, and social ends. And, while Delany has often been discussed alongside Frederick Douglass—his contemporary and, as scholars have argued, sometime rival—his participation in rhetorics of divided sovereignty might link him to later writers such as Washington, Griggs, and Du Bois. Focusing on the legal elements of Delany's writings not only offers new ways of seeing him as an author but perhaps also new stories to tell about the literary history of the nineteenth century.

Notes

1. For more, see Levine, "Delany and Douglass on Samuel R. Ward."
2. While it is not possible to detail all of the scholarship on critical race theory, representative examples include Bell, "Serving Two Masters"; Bell, *And We Are Not Saved*; Crenshaw et al., eds., *Critical Race Theory*; Delgado and Stefancic, *Critical Race Theory*; Freeman, "Truth and Mystification in Legal Scholarship"; and Williams, *The Alchemy of Race and Rights*. Recent scholarship that addresses African Americans' use of law includes King, *Race, Theft, and Ethics*, which focuses on African Americans' fictional treatments of U.S. property laws and the stereotypical figure of the black thief, and Suggs, *Whispered Consolations*.
3. For more on fraternal organizations, see Trotter, "African American Fraternal Organizations"; Liazos and Ganz, "Duty to the Race"; and Brooks, "Prince Hall, Freemasonry,

and Genealogy." Later organizations were much more explicit in their legal aims. The Brotherhood of Liberty, which included several African American lawyers, was founded in 1885 in Baltimore, Maryland. They published a treatise titled *Justice and Jurisprudence: An Inquiry Concerning the Constitutional Limitations of the Thirteenth, Fourteenth, and Fifteenth Amendments* (1889; repr. 1969), which focused on "the Positive Law of the Fourteenth Amendment" and revealed "the transparent veils of legal fiction under cover of which the civil rights of all races are being slowly undermined" (preface, i). For more, see "Not Only the Judges' Robes Were Black." Following the second national convention for African Americans in 1853, Hezekiah Grice (who was involved with organizing the first convention) founded the Legal Rights Association in Baltimore "for the purpose of ascertaining the legal status of the colored man in the United States." For more, see "The First Colored Convention," 309.

4. My understanding of "ethnic" sovereignty is derived from the work of Anthony D. Smith, who differentiated between "ethnic" and "territorial" nations. Ethnic nations are those based on kinship and ideas of descent, common public culture, language, religion, connection to an ancestral homeland that may or may not be occupied, and citizenship/membership based on blood ties. For more, see Smith, *The Ethnic Origins of Nations.*

5. In contrast to article 1 of the U.S. Constitution, the common law of Great Britain, as articulated by Blackstone, explicitly condemned slavery: "Upon these principles of the law, England abhors, and will not endure the existence of, slavery within this nation: so that when an attempt was made to introduce it, by statute 1 Edw. VI. c. 3. which ordained, that all idle vagabonds should be made slaves, and fed upon bread, water, or small drink, and refuse meat; should wear a ring of iron round their necks, arms, or legs; and should be compelled by beating, chaining, or otherwise, to perform the work assigned them, were it never so vile; the spirit of the nation could not brook this condition, even in the most abandoned rogues; and therefore this statute was repealed in two years afterwards. And now it is laid down, that a slave or negro, the instant he lands in England, becomes a freeman; that is, the law will protect him in the enjoyment of his person, his liberty, and his property." William Blackstone, "The Rights of Persons."

6. While modern American jurists speak of common law, they generally refer to the concept as it was articulated by Oliver Wendell Holmes, Jr., Justice of the Supreme Court from 1902 to 1932 and author of *The Common Law* (1881). Common law is understood as "'judge-made law,' devised in cases, extended by precedent, and limited only by the consensus of the bench and bar or by legislative intervention." This definition of the law, popularized by Holmes, based legal decisions not on "logic" or reason but "experience" and precedent and erased earlier notions of the concept that would have been more familiar to earlier generations of Americans. For a brief discussion of the ways in which early Americans cited Puritan theologians alongside figures such as Rousseau, Plutarch, and Blackstone, see Wood, *The Creation of the American Republic,* 7. See also Stoner, *Common-Law Liberty,* 10.

7. For a succinct summary of the development of British common law, see Stoner, 10–12.

8. Blackstone, "On Praemunire," 114.

9. Ibid., 114.

10. Alexander Hamilton, Federalist No. 15, in *The Federalist Papers,* 147. Madison wrote to Jefferson that the Constitution "involve[d] the evil of imperium in imperio." Madison, "Letter to Thomas Jefferson," 206–14.

11. "Letter from V. du C—— to his Father," 293.

12. "Annual Meeting of the Colonization Society," 11.

13. "Colonization and Anti-Slavery Societies," 122.

14. Levine, *Martin Delany, Frederick Douglass, and the Politics of Representative Identity*, 190. In terms of its publication history, *Blake* was partially serialized in 1859 and reprinted between 1861 and 1862. Floyd Miller, in his introduction to the first book-length edition (printed in 1970), suggested that Delany might have begun the novel as early as 1852, although we can only speculate about the precise chronology of Delany's composition (xix). Levine noted that Miller's edition, the only book-length reprint, shortened the novel's original title, *Blake; or the Huts of America: A Tale of the Mississippi Valley, the Southern United States, and Cuba*, which more fully demonstrates its transnational concerns (Levine, 191, 290). For more on *Blake* and transnationalism, see Clymer, "Martin Delany's *Blake*."

15. In "Martin Delany's *Blake* and the Transnational Politics of Property," Clymer focuses on how the novel "negotiates cultural and legal ideas concerning different forms of property—whether taking the form of land, moveable items, or persons—within his view of the antebellum international political economy" (710).

16. Clymer, "Martin Delany's *Blake* and the Transnational Politics of Property," 713.

17. Ibid., 714.

18. Delany, *Blake*, 139–40.

19. Ibid., 140.

20. Ibid., 263.

21. Ibid., 152–53.

22. Delany, *The Condition . . . of the Colored People*, 12.

23. Ibid., 13.

24. Delany, *Blake*, 197.

25. Delany, *The Condition . . . of the Colored People of the United States*, 49.

26. By "emigration," Delany referred to African American efforts to find a suitable national space within the Western hemisphere, as contrasted with white colonization efforts to transport African Americans to Liberia.

27. Delany, *The Condition . . . of the Colored People of the United States*, 214.

28. Ibid., 173.

29. Ibid., 173.

30. Ibid., 187.

31. Yellin, *The Intricate Knot*, 193. For more on this meeting, see Rollin, *Life and Public Service of Martin R. Delany*, 83–90.

32. Rollin, *Life and Public Service of Martin R. Delany*, 89.

33. Ibid., 89.

34. PHC, "Colored Men's Newspapers," 2.

35. "The Sunday School Convention."

36. "Dr. Taylor's Letter."

37. Ibid.

38. Washington, "Address of Booker T. Washington," 350.

39. Washington, "The Colored People in the South," 835.

40. Griggs, *Imperium in Imperio*, 262–3.

41. Ibid., 263–65.

42. Du Bois, *The Souls of Black Folk*, 3.

43. Ibid., 4.

Bibliography

Annual Meeting of the Colonization Society. *The African Repository* 2, no. 11 (January 1827): 11. American Periodicals Series Online, 1740–1900, ProQuest Information and Learning Company. http://www.il.proquest.com (accessed May 1, 2007).

Bell, Derrick. *And We Are Not Saved: The Elusive Quest for Racial Justice*. New York: Basic Books, 1987.

———. "'Serving Two Masters': Integration Ideals and Client Interests in School Desegregation Litigation." *Yale Law Journal* 85, no. 4 (1976): 470–516.

Blackstone, William. "On Praemunire." *Commentaries on the Laws of England (1765–1769)*, 114. Project Avalon, Yale University. http://www.yale.edu/lawweb/avalon/blackstone/bk4ch8.htm (accessed June 6, 2008).

———. "The Rights of Persons." *Commentaries on the Laws of England (1765–1769)*, 412. Project Avalon, Yale University. http://www.yale.edu/lawweb/avalon/blackstone/bk1ch14.htm (accessed June 6, 2008).

Brooks, Joanna. "Prince Hall, Freemasonry, and Genealogy." *African American Review* 34, no. 2 (2000): 197–216.

Clymer, Jeffrey. "Martin Delany's *Blake* and the Transnational Politics of Property." *American Literary History* 15, no. 4 (2003): 709–31.

"Colonization and Anti-Slavery Societies." *The Christian Watchman* 14, no. 31 (1833): 122. American Periodicals Series Online, 1740–1900, ProQuest Information and Learning Company. http://www.il.proquest.com (accessed May 12, 2007).

Crenshaw, Kimberlé, Kendall Thomas, and Gary Peller, eds. *Critical Race Theory: The Key Writings That Formed the Movement*. New York: New Press, 1995.

Delany, Martin R. *Blake; or, the Huts of America*. Edited by Floyd Miller. Boston, Beacon, 1970.

———. *The Condition, Elevation, Emigration, and Destiny of the Colored People of the United States*. New York: Arno, 1968.

Delgado, Richard, and Jean Stefancic, eds. *Critical Race Theory: The Cutting Edge*. 2nd ed. Philadelphia: Temple University Press, 2000.

"Dr. Taylor's Letter." *The Christian Recorder*, March 16, 1882. Accessible Archives. http://www.accessible.com/accessible/ (accessed June 7, 2008).

Du Bois, W. E. B. *The Souls of Black Folk: Essays and Sketches*. 3rd ed. Chicago: A. C. McClurgh, 1903.

The Federalist Papers. Edited by Isaac Kramnick. New York: Penguin, 1987.

Finkelman, Paul. "Not Only the Judges' Robes Were Black: African-American Lawyers as Social Engineers." *Stanford Law Review* 47, no.1 (1994): 161–209.

"The First Colored Convention." *Anglo-African Magazine* 1, no. 10 (1859): 309.

Freeman, Alan D. "Truth and Mystification in Legal Scholarship." *Yale Law Journal* 90, no. 5 (1981): 1229–37.

Griggs, Sutton E. *Imperium in Imperio*. New York: Arno, 1969.

Justice and Jurisprudence: An Inquiry Concerning the Constitutional Limitations of the Thirteenth, Fourteenth, and Fifteenth Amendments. Philadelphia: J. B. Lippencott, 1889.

King, Lovalerie. *Race, Theft, and Ethics: Property Matters in African American Literature*. Baton Rouge: Louisiana State University Press, 2007.

Lemmon v. People, 20 N.Y. 562. N.Y. Ct. of App. 1860.

"Letter from V. du C—— to his Father." *Atlantic Monthly* 2, no. 10 (February 1, 1825): 293. American Periodicals Series Online, 1740–1900, ProQuest Information and Learning Company. http://www.il.proquest.com (accessed June 4, 2008).

Levine, Robert S. "Delany and Douglass on Samuel R. Ward." In *Martin R. Delany: A Documentary Reader*, edited by Robert S. Levine, 174–79. Chapel Hill: University of North Carolina Press, 2003.

———. *Martin Delany, Frederick Douglass, and the Politics of Representative Identity*. Chapel Hill: University of North Carolina Press, 1997.

Liazos, Ariane, and Marshall Ganz. "Duty to the Race: African American Fraternal Organizations and the Legal Defense of the Right to Organize." *Social Science History* 28, no. 3 (2004): 485–534.

Madison, James. "Letter to Thomas Jefferson." In *Papers of James Madison*, vol. 10., 206–14, October 24, 1787.

Miller, Floyd. Introduction. In *Blake; or, The Huts of America*, by Martin R. Delany, xi–xxix. Boston: Beacon, 1970.

PHC. "Colored Men's Newspapers." *The Independent* 15, no. 769 (27 August 1863): 2. American Periodicals Series Online, 1740–1900, ProQuest Information and Learning Company. http://www.il.proquest.com (accessed May 1, 2007).

Rollin, Frank A. *The Life and Public Services of Martin R. Delany*. New York: Arno, 1969.

Smith, Anthony D. *The Ethnic Origins of Nations*. Malden, MA: Blackwell, 1988.

Stoner, James R., Jr. *Common-Law Liberty: Rethinking American Constitutionalism*. Lawrence: University Press of Kansas, 2003.

Suggs, Jon-Christian. *Whispered Consolations: Law and Narrative in African American Life*. Ann Arbor: University of Michigan Press, 2000.

"The Sunday School Convention." *The Christian Recorder*, October 28, 1875. Accessible Archives. http://www.accessible.com/accessible/ (accessed June 7, 2008).

Trotter, Joe W. "African American Fraternal Organizations in American History: An Introduction." *Social Science History* 28, no. 3 (2004): 355–66.

Washington, Booker T. "Address of Booker T. Washington." Quoted in "Presbyterian Home Mission Rally." *New York Observer and Chronicle* 74, no. 11 (March 12, 1896): 347–51. APS Online.

———. "The Colored People in the South." *Friends Intelligencer* 56, no. 44 (November 4, 1899): 835. APS Online.

Williams, Patricia J. *The Alchemy of Race and Rights*. Cambridge, MA: Harvard University Press, 1991.

Wood, Gordon. *The Creation of the American Republic, 1776–1787*. Chapel Hill: University of North Carolina Press, 1969.

Yellin, Jean Fagan. *The Intricate Knot: Black Figures in American Literature. 1776–1863*. New York: New York University Press, 1972.

4

On Black Freedmen in Indian Country

Matthew L. M. Fletcher

Most critical race theorists assume that the racial playing field in America is federal and state law and ignore the rising importance of American Indian law or the law of American Indian tribes. When questions of race discrimination arise, advocates for the victims of race discrimination turn *exclusively* to the Constitution or federal and state civil rights statutes. Even where the alleged perpetrators of discrimination are Indian tribes, advocates still turn to the Constitution and federal or state law. These advocates ignore or are unaware of the advantages of seeking relief from the proper sovereign—in this case, Indian tribes—because they fail to recognize the racial hierarchies in question. For the purposes of this chapter, most discussions of race identify rights as the central paradigm, metaphor, or fiction for challenging white supremacy because they posit the black-white binary and its handmaiden, antidiscrimination law, as *the* framework for understanding racial hierarchy. This chapter offers a different fiction, through the example of the black Freedmen, to ground a different role for law for promoting freedom and equality.

The tools for analyzing these questions are already in place. Derrick Bell's interest-convergence theory offers an important insight. The reduction of race discrimination had "value to whites, [especially] those whites in policymaking positions able to see the economic and political advances at home and abroad that would follow."[1] But where the persons in power are American Indians and the sovereign interest at stake is tribal, invoking federal and state law for a remedy against race discrimination is a request to the wrong sovereign. Worse, the appeal to federal and state law threatens tribal sovereignty. Still worse, resorting to federal and state law creates opportunities for "those whites in policymaking positions" to make determinations about the value of abrogating tribal sovereignty and to exercise the power to uphold or destroy tribal authority. The principal beneficiaries of those determinations are not the victims of race discrimination but white policymakers. This exemplifies Bell's interest-convergence thesis in that dominant interests use race law primarily to further their own interests by extending and strengthening the place of the black-white binary in legal discourse. Furthermore, the application of race law wrongly identifies tribal communities as responsible for discrimination against African Americans.

Compare Vine Deloria, Jr.'s indictment of "unthoughtful Johnny-come lately liberals," people that Deloria alleged "prefer[red] to place all people with darker skin in the same category of basic goals, then develop their programs to fit these preconceived ideas."[2] It was Deloria who presaged Derrick Bell's famous theory when he wrote, "Recently, blacks and some Indians have defined racial problems as having one focal point—the White Man. This concept is a vast oversimplification of the real problem, as it centers on a racial theme rather than specific facts. And it is simply the reversal of the old prejudicial attitude of the white who continues to define minority problems of his—that is, Indian problem, Negro problem, and so on."[3] Deloria rightly argues that federal law has consistently viewed race as a binary construct when, in fact, race has operated as a complicated hierarchical system. This hierarchy does not simply include "victims" and "victimizers" but a range of positions, some of which cannot be easily sorted into either category.

This chapter focuses on the "specific facts" of race discrimination and Indian tribal sovereignty. I begin by considering the problem as exemplified in the following fact patterns:

- An Indian tribe based in the Deep South adopts an amendment to the tribal constitution that excludes from membership the large majority of Nation members who are also African American. The amendment defines eligibility for membership in the Nation as excluding persons whose ancestors' names appeared on the "Freedmen" roll (or list) of members, while including the persons whose ancestors' names appeared on the "Blood" roll. All persons whose ancestors' names appeared on the Freedmen roll are African American.
- An African American woman marries an Indian man and moves with him to an Indian reservation. The woman is hired by the tribe's gaming enterprise to serve as a "slot tech," a person who performs basic maintenance on slot machines, in the tribe's casino. After two years of employment with a stellar performance record, the African American woman applies for a promotion. A member of the tribe without any experience in the casino, but who is otherwise equally qualified for the position, gets the job. The African American woman suspects race discrimination. When the African American woman asks why she was not promoted over the tribal member, her supervisors explain that they were obligated by the tribe's "Indian preference in employment" law to hire the tribal member.
- An Indian child who is eligible for membership in a Michigan Indian tribe but born and residing in Detroit, far from the tribe, is removed from her family at the age of five. The state social workers claims the child suffered from "neglect," a legal term defined by state statutes, regulations, case law, and practice. The child is sent to a non-Indian family in the Detroit area. Eventually, the state petitions for a court order terminating parental rights. Shortly thereafter, the child's foster family, with the blessings of the state, petitions the state to adopt the Indian child. The Indian tribe in which the child is eligible for membership intervenes in the matter and successfully petitions the state court to remove the case to the tribe's court in upper Michigan.

Each of these circumstances involves a critical area of American Indian law. "American Indian law" includes, for these purposes, "federal Indian law," the law that controls the relationship between the federal government, Indian tribes, and states, and "tribal law," or the law of Indian tribes. Assuming no complicating factors, the outcome to the disputes would be known and predictable—although the outcomes can be litigated or negotiated away. In the first case, the so-called Freedmen would have little or no remedy under federal Indian law. Congress and the U.S. Supreme Court have long recognized that Indian tribes have the inherent authority to make their own laws and be governed by them.[4] One of the most fundamental authorities Indian tribes have is the right to decide questions of membership.[5] Federal civil rights statutes and other constitutional guarantees do not apply to Indian tribes, so that avenue is foreclosed.[6] Even the 1968 Indian Civil Rights Act, enacted by Congress for the purpose of applying the Bill of Rights to Indian tribal governments, can only be enforced in tribal court subject to tribal remedies and sovereign immunity.[7] Perhaps the only way to restore redress for the hypothetical Freedmen's membership status is through the tribal political process.[8] American Indian law offers no other legal remedy.

In the second hypothetical, the African American woman denied the job promotion at the casino because of the preference for tribal members would face a similar situation. Congress expressly excluded Indian tribal employers from Title VII of the 1964 Civil Rights Act.[9] Federal statutes also authorize Indian tribes to adopt statutes that require nontribal employers on or near the reservation to apply an Indian preference in employment and contracting.[10] Even assuming the African American woman could prove race discrimination and that the invocation of the tribal Indian preference rule was invalid, she would have to bring her claim in tribal court and might have to face the tribe's sovereign immunity.[11] However, to be fair, many tribes have waived their immunity from suit in these kinds of claims.[12] As with the disenrolled Freedmen in the first fact pattern, federal Indian law offers no clear remedy, while tribal law may or may not allow for relief.

American Indian law leads to a predictable result in one direction, but if federal civil rights statutes, regulations, and case law were applied to these two fact patterns, the results might differ. On a superficial level, it would appear that these circumstances would be strong (if not slam-dunk) cases of race discrimination. The existence of tribal sovereignty not only places a bar to remedying these seeming cases of discrimination but in fact changes the very character of the cases so that there is no race discrimination at all. In these instances, the concept of sovereignty enables tribes to protect and promote their interests much more effectively than rights discourse, with its focus on the individual, would.

The third hypothetical offers a clue as to the myriad reasons why. This is a rote rendition of a classic Indian Child Welfare Act (ICWA) case.[13] This case differs from the other examples because it does not involve claims of race discrimination against African Americans, although they sometimes do involve claims of equal protection and race discrimination. The Act was intended to allow Indian tribes to intervene in state court proceedings where Indian child custody and parental rights are at issue, to transfer the case to tribal court in some circumstances, and to guarantee the jurisdiction of the tribal courts where the child is domiciled in Indian Country.[14] Congress enacted ICWA as a means to stem the flow of Indian children out of Indian Country, a situation created in many states by overzealous state social services workers and state court judges who saw Indian Country as a bad place for anyone to grow up.[15] In that regard, Congress created a preference for Indian children. However, in some circumstances, the Indian children (or their parents) are prejudiced by this statute—for example, by the delays involved or in circumstances where tribal services are not as extensive or helpful as state services. Yet the Act, with all its flaws, is considered one of the greatest and most helpful statutes ever enacted by Congress for Indian people and tribes.

The key element of the ICWA, for our purposes here, is that this statute is not a race-based statute even though the plain and clear qualification for its application to children is their *Indianness*. Unlike the standards used to determine racial categories such as "black" or "Asian" or "Latino/a" or any other immutable characteristic, ICWA uses something else—the political relationship between the child and an Indian tribe (and to a lesser but necessary extent, the federal government).[16] ICWA will apply to an Indian child only if that child is a member, or eligible to be a member, in a federally recognized Indian tribe.[17] Congress did not enact ICWA under its Reconstruction Amendment authority or its Interstate Commerce Clause authority as it has enacted other statutes related to race. Instead, Congress enacted ICWA in accordance with its authority under the Indian Commerce Clause and "other constitutional authority."[18] This source of constitutional authority distinguishes the statute from other race-based statutes and removes American Indian law from the realm of race law and its concomitant constitutional and political baggage.

One important question is whether Indian tribes that exclude or discriminate against African Americans are engaging in unconstitutional race discrimination. The hypothetical situations identified above certainly illustrate the possible conflicts between American Indian law and federal antidiscrimination law and I hope to answer that question. In addition, I also seek to examine how our existing racial discourse fosters this conflict between African Americans and Indian tribes as part of the dominant culture's effort to maintain an unspoken but all too real racial hierarchy.

The Divergent Legal Histories of American Indians and African Americans

As any scholar of American constitutional history is aware, the Framers' treatment of American Indians and African Americans left something to be desired. The Framers consigned African Americans to slavery with the infamous "euphemisms."[19] According to Chief Justice Taney's originalist interpretation of the Constitution in *Dred Scott v. Sanford* (1856), not even free blacks could become citizens. The Framers dealt with American Indian voting rights in a similar manner but with an important twist. While three-fifths of African American slaves would be counted in the census for purposes of representation in Congress, no American Indians would be counted, identified in the Constitution as "Indians not taxed."[20] In the *Dred Scott* case, Taney explained this phrase implied that there existed the theoretical possibility that Indians who were "taxed"—in other words, citizens—could become citizens and count for purposes of representation.[21] Scholars have suggested that some American Indians who had abandoned their tribal relations, such as those Indians in the so-called Massachusetts praying towns, could have counted as "Indians taxed," but it is doubtful that they ever acquired the benefits and protections of citizenship.[22] Regardless, in the strange and wicked racial hierarchy of the Constitution as written by the Framers, these Indians rested somewhere above blacks, while tribal Indians remained outside of the Constitution altogether. Consequently, it would be inaccurate to view the Constitution as creating a black-white binary. Rather, it relied on a more complex racial hierarchy.

Indian tribes located within and (especially) outside of the boundaries of the original thirteen colonies maintained a political existence with military and economic strength. The Framers, particularly James Madison and John Marshall, recognized their existence as being a true threat to the nascent United States.[23] Only a few decades before the Revolution, thousands of American Indians from the Great Lakes region banded together under the leadership of a charismatic Odawa Indian named Pontiac. He had choreographed a sophisticated and well-timed war on British outposts throughout Michigan and into Ohio that almost succeeded in driving the world's largest empire from the Great Lakes region. The founding generation was all too aware that another war on a similar scale could be disastrous for the United States in its weakened and debt-ridden, post-Revolution condition. As a result, the Framers, with Madison's prodding, had no choice but to acknowledge the presence of Indian tribes on the frontier.[24] The Indian Commerce Clause, which replaced a similar clause in the Articles of Confederation, served to place authority to deal with Indian tribes in the hands of Congress.[25] Presumably, the "Indians not taxed" mentioned in the Constitution included the members of these Indian tribes.

The Reconstruction Amendments after the Civil War shifted the relative legal rights and status of both African Americans and American Indians. The Fourteenth Amendment extended citizenship to every person born inside the boundaries of the United States *except* "Indians not taxed."[26] By doing so, the Framers of the Fourteenth Amendment expressly excluded Indians from the protections of the Constitution.[27] Again presumably, they retained the same status post-Civil War as they did pre-Civil War—Indians who abandoned their tribal relations could (in theory) become citizens, but tribal Indians could not. Indians, at that point, fell behind African Americans in the racial hierarchy of the Constitution. But Indian tribes and their members also remained (in theory) outside of the Constitution. In the changes to federal Indian law following the "closing" of the American frontier (and the placement of all Indian tribes *within* the United States), all American Indians have been transformed, for all practical purposes, into "Indians taxed." Although there will be a few dissenters from this opinion perhaps,[28] there are no longer any "Indians not taxed." The Constitution no longer cares whether Indians have abandoned their tribal relations or not. By 1924, Congress had extended American citizenship to all American Indians whether they liked it or not.[29]

The critical legal question now is whether the United States recognizes the sovereignty of an Indian tribe and thus maintains a political relationship with its members.[30] In other words, members of federally recognized Indian tribes are what I have termed "political Indians." These Indians, in general, are eligible for federal and state services created for Indian people.[31] However, there are a significant number of American Indians who are not eligible for membership in any Indian tribe (for a myriad of possible reasons often related to the vagaries of federal Indian law), but who retain status as what I have termed "racial Indians." These Indians are eligible for a lesser array of federal and state services or programs assuming they meet blood quantum or other requirements.[32] The key element of the IWCA, for our purposes here, is that this statute is not a race-based statute even though the plain and clear qualification for its application to children is their Indianness. These political Indians, who have been adopted into some tribal communities, have the unique status of not actually being racial Indians. A classic example of this later category of Indians is the Freedmen citizenry of the Cherokee Nation of Oklahoma, the Seminole Tribe of Florida, and the Muscogee (Creek) Nation.[33]

There are two important relevant consequences to these divergent legal histories. First, Constitutional protections and federal civil rights laws do not apply to tribal governments.[34] Unlike the federal and state governments, Indian tribes—governments that predated the United States—were not invited to the Constitutional convention or the debates on the Reconstruction Amendments and therefore did not ratify these rules and prohibitions. Tribal law, tribal courts, and tribal politics are the sole means with which to rectify discrimination or other manifestations of a tribal government denial of equal protection. Although there is a perception that the United States can control the activities of Indian tribes, thereby changing tribal action into federal or state action (a misperception created during the heyday of civil rights actions in the 1960s and early 1970s), this simply isn't true.[35] Second, federal (and to a lesser extent, state) government actions regarding Indian tribes and individual Indians that either create a benefit or a detriment for other Indians or tribes are not violations of equal protection. As Justice Blackmun theorized in *Morton v. Mancari* (1974), federal actions that benefit Indians do so not on the basis of the racial character of Indian people but on the basis of political relationship between Indians and the United States.[36]

The Gradual Intrusion of Race Law in American Indian Law

The "measured separatism"[37] of Indian tribes from the American political and legal system means that each of the more than 560 Indian tribes recognized as sovereign by the United States have some freedom to decide for themselves how to govern.[38] Tribal governments, assuming limited or no interference from the United States and its agents,[39] make their own laws and their own policies about how to deal with discrimination. In most instances, Indian tribes comply with the Indian Civil Rights Act and its guarantee of equal protection and due process.[40] But what worries some observers, including former Supreme Court Justice David Souter, is the right of Indian tribes to decide for themselves the exact contours of "equal protection" and "due process."[41] Congress intended all along for Indian tribes to interpret these Anglo-American legal terms in light of each tribe's customs and traditions.[42] Some cynical commentators take this aspect of American Indian law to mean that Indian tribes have a "license to discriminate."[43]

And there is anecdotal evidence aplenty to support the view that Indian tribes are abusing their constitutional status as the "other," free from the constraints of American civil rights law, to run roughshod over individual rights. An Indian tribe in Maine—arguably subject to state civil rights laws, unlike most tribes—faced criticism for applying an Indian preference in employment policy to the exclusion of white employees and job candidates.[44] Indian tribes operating casinos face ongoing challenges to their exemption from federal civil rights laws.[45] One Indian tribe that banned women from participating in a four-day horse ride through tribal lands faced sex discrimination suits.[46] Newspaper headlines trumpeting the exemption of Indian tribes from federal civil rights laws sell newspapers.

But the anecdotal evidence is insignificant compared to the tens of thousands of jobs created by Indian tribes that are filled annually by non-Indians where no such jobs existed before.[47] Federal and tribal money that feeds tribal governmental services creates jobs for non-Indians. Economic development projects (typically gaming related but not always) that are made possible because of tribal sovereignty create jobs for non-Indians. Tribal government and tribal businesses sometimes create a local economy where nothing existed prior to their creation. But this often does not prevent tribes from facing undue criticism. Non-Indians on or near Indian Country often complain that tribal governments should not have regulatory authority over them while, at the same time, they benefit directly from the presence of that same tribal government. A particularly egregious example is a woman who worked for the Indian Health Service dental clinic near the Port Madison Reservation in Washington state, home of the Suquamish Tribe, and she participated as a named plaintiff in a case designed to eradicate the sovereignty of the tribe.[48] In other words, even people like this woman, whose livelihoods depend on tribal governments and Indian sovereignty, will fight tribal governments. Indian tribes struggle *mightily* and in good faith to balance the need to raise revenue for tribal government services through for-profit business enterprises and to treat their employees fairly,[49] and it appears they succeed more often than not. Preliminary empirical and theoretical research indicates that non-Indians fare no worse in tribal courts than do tribal members.[50]

But this chapter is not intended to defend the practice of some tribal governments—often in employment contexts—that do discriminate on the basis of race or sex. Those tribes that do practice race- or gender-based prejudice have no moral defense despite much rationalizing, and they should stop. But the real—and, perhaps, the most important—question for the immediate future of Indian tribes is what legal remedy individuals can use to make them stop.

Federal civil rights laws have long been the favored method to remedy tribal government violations of equal protection. After the enactment of the Indian Civil Rights Act, numerous federal courts implied a federal court cause of action against tribal courts to enforce the Act.[51] In 1978, Justice Marshall's opinion in *Santa Clara Pueblo v. Martinez* (1978) ended that practice, holding that the Act did not create a federal cause of action and, even if it did, tribal governments retain immunity from suits in federal courts. Advocates of applying federal civil rights to Indian tribes often do not seem to realize that it was one of the greatest crusaders for civil rights—Thurgood Marshall—who recognized definitively that Indian tribes have the right to develop their own means and traditions of equal protection. Justice Marshall again noted in *National Farmers Union Insurance Companies v. Crow Tribe of Indians* (1985) that tribal courts and other available tribal forums exist to interpret tribal laws.[52] Despite recent cases suggesting that Section 1981 serves to remedy private discrimination by tribal business employers,[53] federal courts have been remarkably consistent in recognizing that federal courts and federal statutes are not available to remedy tribal civil rights violations.[54] Moreover, Congress has long resisted calls from former Senator Slade Gorton and others to force Indian tribes to comply with federal civil rights statutes.[55] Ironically, many who seek to require Indian tribes to comply with these statues have criticized these same laws for granting special rights for racial minorities, suggesting that it is not either rights- or sovereignty-based frameworks that trouble these opponents but rather the use of legal discourse by historically marginalized groups to remedy the consequences of white supremacy.

Tribal sovereignty in the modern era means the right and authority of Indian tribes to make their own laws and be governed by them.[56] But Indian tribes do not operate in a vacuum—and they know this fact. Some tribal communities are located near major metropolitan areas and do not envision restarting a traditional tribal community in that setting. Some tribes are located far from non-Indian population centers and retain much of their traditional forms of government. Most tribes are somewhere in the middle, and all are along a vast spectrum of experience. My own tribe, the Grand Traverse Band of Ottawa and Chippewa Indians, is located in a rural resort community in northwest, lower Michigan. Some of our members still speak the language, and they are hard at work attempting to pass it down to the children of the community. Many members follow traditional *Midewewin* teachings and most members act and think like "Indians."[57] The Band operates two casinos (only one of which is profitable) and an elite resort and is governed by what is known as a "model-IRA" style constitution, carbon copy documents imposed on tribal governments by federal bureaucrats after the enactment of the Indian Reorganization Act.[58] We are not the traditional tribal government of 1675, or even the governance structure of treaty times, but we are not carbon copies of federal, state, or municipal governments either. The Band has about four thousand members, most of whom live within a six-county area centered around Peshawbestown, Michigan in Leelanau County. This territory is in the heart of the Grand Traverse Reservation, which was created by the 1855 Treaty of Detroit.[59] The Band has a chairman who is the head of a seven-member tribal council, a tribal court, and a large bureaucracy of government workers who provide education, housing, health care, social services, public safety, and other government services to tribal members, nonmember Indians, and, to a lesser extent, non-Indians. The Band has a small land base, including clusters of parcels in Peshawbestown, with additional parcels in Benzie, Charlevoix, Antrim, and Grand Traverse Counties. Several in-house lawyers and at least two law firms work for the Band on numerous matters. On legal and political matters, the Band has been very successful in litigating and negotiating treaty hunting and fishing rights,[60] gaming rights,[61] land claims settlements,[62] and tax questions.[63]

It is important to consider the typical tribal government because few people know much, if anything, about modern tribal government. In fact, few people know much about how Indian people live in the twenty-first century, in large part because the black-white binary has dominated discussions of race and multiculuralism. Nonexpert observers of Indian Country law, politics, and society offer wide variations of perspectives on Indian Country, ranging from a perception that

Indian people still live off the land entirely to a perception that Indian people are exactly like non-Indian people except for their skin color. But not all Indians are alike. There are over 560 federally recognized nations (and perhaps hundreds more not recognized), each with their own experiences, circumstances, and cultures. There is no essential, pan-Indian experience on this level, but there are some common circumstances that each tribe must face as a result of two hundred years invested in the development of a pan-Indian federal Indian law and policy. As a result, strange and unique conflicts arise. For example, the Indian Civil Rights Act requires Indian tribes to apply Anglo-American notions of "equal protection" and "due process," but the Act leaves it to the tribes to decide what those terms mean for each tribe. In most places in Indian Country, tribes follow federal (and sometimes state) law in deciding how to interpret the Indian Civil Rights Act,[64] but, sometimes, they don't. The reason for the lack of a federal remedy to tribal civil rights violations has long been that the imposition of Anglo-American values of "due process" and "equal protection" through the application of civil rights statutes (race law) to Indian tribes would cause the destruction of tribal cultures. Of course, nothing is quite that simple. There are nuances and pitfalls in the argument that do not appear in the civil rights cases.

Race Law and the Cherokee Freedmen Problem

Randall Kennedy, a persistent critic of critical race theory, offered a stinging indictment of the ICWA. The law's purpose is to remedy historical patterns of removing American Indian children from their homes and tribes by placing them with American Indian parents or institutions. Kennedy's main argument is that American Indian children are no different *legally* than African American children when it comes to adoption or foster home placement. Or, put another way, American Indians are not different at all and there should be no separate law applying to American Indians. Kennedy's thesis has a sort of superficial appeal to it. If African American children are no different than Latino, Asian, or white children, then how can American Indian children be different?[65] He believes the act requires officials to reach for a kind of "racialist communalism," a "dubious" result in his mind,[66] but one that is very consistent with the "measured separatism" that American Indian law and policy has always sought.[67] In effect, Kennedy argues that Indian cultures and, by extension, Indian law must adapt via a form of assimilation in order to create the conditions for the survival of Indian people in "the modern world."

This position is similar to the criticisms of the Cherokee Nation of Oklahoma's (like other, similarly situated tribes) vote to disenroll the Cherokee Freedmen.[68] Adherents of this position want to force Indian tribes to comply with the Reconstruction Amendments, with the Bill of Rights, and with other federal civil rights statutes. Underlying these arguments is the premise that Indian tribes must be brought into "the modern world" where legally sanctioned racial prejudice is unacceptable. A world where Indian tribes can freely violate the American Constitution is unacceptable. Randall Kennedy would agree wholeheartedly.

But what would be lost if Indian tribes were brought into "compliance" with federal (and/or state) civil rights laws, laws designed to remedy the problem of official government (and, to a lesser extent, private) discrimination against persons of color? Indian tribes are, at this moment, in a remarkable position in American constitutional history. To bring Indian tribes into compliance with civil rights law is to force tribes to comply with laws that they had no real voice in forming. It is also essential to remember that Indians are a tiny demographic minority. Placing Indian tribes in the controlling hands of an American or even a statewide electorate is to eviscerate tribal legal and political identities. Difference (and the benefits of uniqueness) would be replaced with sameness—destructive assimilation advocated by commentators like Randall Kennedy. What specifically would be lost? Indian tribes, such as the Haudenosaunee in New York State or the Pueblos in New Mexico that have matriarchal or patriarchal governance traditions that have been successful for centuries, would be forced to comply with an American-style, gender-neutral governance tradition developed to remedy centuries of Anglo-American male supremacy over women.[69] Indian tribes without a tradition or experience in coercive police-investigation practices would be forced to comply with a rigorous American-style criminal procedure that could undermine critical social support networks, and, in some tribal communities, this could create an antagonistic division between tribal members and tribal government.[70] Forcing Indian tribes to comply with American law forces Indian tribes to live under a legal regime created as a response to Anglo-American legal and political problems. In so many instances, Indian tribes do not need these rules to survive, and the application of these rules is destructive to fragile and developing tribal communities.

Imagine a scenario where the United States amends its constitution to ban same-sex marriage, to ban all abortions, to ban stem-cell research, or even to establish a national religion.[71] Indian Country, because it derives its sovereign authority from its own constitutions, stands outside of the American constitutional structure and would be arguably exempt from these amendments. As such, Indian tribes and the persons within their jurisdictions would be free to experiment with same-sex marriage and abortion laws as well as stem-cell research. Indian and non-Indian people could practice their own religion (theoretically) free from government interference. All of these *positive* aspects of American Indian legal separatism would be foreclosed forever if a broad rule forcing tribes to comply with American law was created.

A Simple Proposal

As is the case with any people forced to deal with an overbearing hegemony attempting to impose foreign rules on indigenous legal structures, Indian tribes will resist legal assimilation. The events following the Cherokee Nation's vote to disenroll the Freedmen—defiance in the face of national political pressure from both the federal government and influential African American political leaders— are unsurprising. In the end, sovereignty is all Indian tribes believe they have. Tribes will not give up sovereignty any more than the United States would give it up to Mexico.

However, there is a very simple solution to the Cherokee Freedmen problem—one that few have considered. Most commentators have offered "solutions" that offer carrot-and-stick style proposals: punish the Cherokee Nation with denial of federal funds, or apply the Reconstruction Amendments and trample on the sovereignty of Indian tribes. None of these address the fundamental problem, but instead they are designed to address the symptoms of a bigger problem within the Cherokee nation. These solutions do not consider the federal origins of this problem. It was the federal government that forced the Cherokee Nation to sign an 1866 treaty—a treaty of punishment because the Nation signed on to the Confederacy during the Civil War—that placed the Freedmen on the Cherokee rolls. And, later, it was the federal government's Dawes Commission that divided the Nation into Indian and black, using racist and arbitrary rules to create "Blood" and "Freedmen" rolls.[72] The Cherokee Nation's problem may require a federal solution—and it's a simple one: the United States must recognize the Freedmen as an Indian tribe. The Cherokee Nation has exercised its sovereign right to exclude the Freedmen. These Freedmen are Indians, a discreet grouping of people that have significant blood quantum and a continuing manifestation of tribal culture. Why would this not work?

Conclusion: Converging Black and Indian Interests

Many African Americans are also American Indians, either due to historical family or political relationships or more recent intermarriage between urban Indians and other people of color in major metropolitan areas, such as southern California. The reality of the parallel legal and political structures governing these relationships is that African Americans who are also Indians may be forced to choose one legal remedy at the expense of the other to remedy alleged civil rights violations by Indian tribes. A greater understanding of American constitutional history and tribal cultures is necessary to grasp the reasons for this seeming anomaly.

Interest-convergence theory teaches us that fundamental race discrimination likely will not be remedied unless "those whites in policymaking positions" recognize the "value" of these remedies. While victims of race discrimination benefit from the recognition of the importance of these remedies, so, too, do whites. Take Randall Kennedy's view of the ICWA. His view that the Act encourages Indian tribes to become kidnapping racists (my phrasing) presupposes that tribal law is invalid in some way. His view is that the only source of power is in the "white policymakers"—they are the cause of *and* solution to all these racial problems. In Kennedy's world, resorting to another sovereign—Indian tribes—is a joke because they are not American entities, they are poor, and they are underqualified to make decisions about real people and real problems. Whether or not Indian tribes are qualified and capable of adjudicating or remedying race discrimination is the most important question here. Who will make this determination? Randall Kennedy would have the U.S. or state governments—"those white policymakers"—choose. Interest-convergence theory says those policymakers will choose a solution *that best suits those white policymakers.*

In the event that Indian tribes appear to engage in race discrimination in employment, citizenship, or elsewhere, those victims of race discrimination are sorely tempted to seek relief from a familiar source: American constitutional law as interpreted and implemented by the U.S. or state governments—and these victims might or might not receive the relief they request. In either event, it is ironic that antidiscrimination law has become one way that the federal government exerts increasing power over Indian tribes.

These victims of race discrimination can also turn to the sovereigns that have made these decisions and work within them to effect change. The Freedmen in some of the other Five Civilized Tribes have been more successful,[73] it is true, than the Cherokee Freedmen, but the template for reform is there. By investing in these governments, African Americans can help American Indians subvert the interests of "those white policymakers" and challenge the black-white binary within American legal culture.

Notes

The author of this chapter would like to thank Jeannine Bell, Richard Delgado, Myriam Jaïdi, Richard Schur, Wenona Singel, and Rose Villazor for their help and support in writing this chapter.

1. Bell, "*Brown v. Board of Education*," 524.
2. Deloria, *Custer Died for Your Sins*, 170.
3. Ibid., 171.
4. See *Williams v. Lee* (1959) and *Worcester v. Georgia* (1832).
5. See *Santa Clara Pueblo v. Martinez* (1978).
6. See *Talton v. Mayes* (1896).
7. 25 U.S.C. §§ 1301–3.
8. See *Santa Clara Pueblo v. Martinez* and Swentzell, "Testimony of a Santa Clara Woman," 97–104.
9. See 42 U.S.C. § 2000e(b) and Buffalo and Wadzinski, "Application of Federal and State Labor and Employment Laws to Indian Tribal Employers," 1367–76.
10. See 42 U.S.C. § 2000e-2(i) and Buffalo and Wadzinski, "Application of Federal and State Labor and Employment Laws to Indian Tribal Employers," 1367, 1371–76.
11. For examples of tribal court employment cases dismissed on the grounds that the tribal employer did not consent to suit, see *One Hundred Eight Employees of the Crow Tribe of Indians v. Crow Tribe of Indians* (2001); *Colville Tribal Enterprise Corp. v. Orr* (1998); and *Baca v. Puyallup Tribe of Indians* (2002).
12. For examples, see Grand Traverse Band Code, and Haddock and Miller, "Can a Sovereign Protect Investors from Itself?" 194–95.
13. 25 U.S.C. §§ 1901 et seq.
14. 25 U.S.C. § 1911.
15. See generally *Mississippi Band of Choctaw Indians v. Holyfield* and "Establishing Standards for the Placement of Indian Children in Foster or Adoptive Homes."
16. For a broader explanation of the "political status" of Indians and Indian tribes with the United States, see generally Fletcher, "The Original Understanding of the Political Status of Indian Tribes."
17. 25 U.S.C. § 1903(4).
18. 25 U.S.C. §§ 1901 (1)–(2).
19. See Bell, "Foreword" 6–7.
20. See "United States Constitution," art. I, § 2, cl. 3

21. See *Scott v. Sanford* (1856), 404.

22. See generally Clinton, "Sovereignty and the Native American Nation."

23. Ibid., 1098. See also Clinton, "There Is No Federal Supremacy Clause for Indian Tribe."

24. Madison, "Federalist No. 42." See also Prucha, *American Indian Policy in the Formative*, 30–31.

25. See United States Constitution, art. I, § 8, cl. 3; and Articles of Confederation, art. IX(4). See generally Fletcher, "Preconstitutional Federal Power."

26. United States Constitution, amend. XIV, §§ 1–2.

27. See generally Beck, "The Fourteenth Amendment as Related to Tribal Indian," and the United States Senate Committee on the Judiciary, "Effect of Fourteenth Amendment Upon Indian Tribes."

28. Porter, "The Demise of the Ongwehoweh and the Rise of the Native Americans," 126–28.

29. The Act of June 2, 1924 was codified at 8 U.S.C. § 1401(b).

30. Newton et al., *Cohen's Handbook of Federal Indian Law*, 138–40. See also Fletcher, "Politics, History, and Semantics," 487–518.

31. Ibid., 177–81.

32. For example, the Indian Health Care Improvement Act of 1976 authorizes some federal services for Indians who are two generations removed from a tribal member ancestor. 25 U.S.C. § 1603. See also Newton et al., *Cohen's Handbook of Federal Indian Law*, 181.

33. I am cognizant that a significant portion of the Freedmen citizens have intermarried with "racial Indians" so that many (perhaps a large majority) actually are "racial Indians," too. See generally Marilyn Vann, "Loss of Cherokee National Citizenship."

34. See *Talton v. Mayes* and *Native American Church of North America v. Navajo Tribal Council* (1959). See also Angela R. Riley, "Good (Native) Governance," 1049–1125.

35. See *Seneca Constitutional Rights Organization v. George* (1972).

36. *Morton v. Mancari*, 553n24. See also *Washington v. Washington Commercial Passenger Fishing Vessel Assn* (1979).

37. Charles Wilkinson coined the phrase "measured separatism" to describe the theory shaping treaty negotiations between Indian tribes and the United States. Wilkinson, *American Indians, Time, and the Law*, 14–19.

38. See *Williams v. Lee*.

39. This is a significant assumption, given that tribal-federal relations historically have been based on an imposition of law by the United States onto Indian communities. See generally Fletcher, "The Insidious Colonialism of the Conqueror," and Joranko and Van Norman, "Indian Self-Determination at Bay."

40. 25 U.S.C. § 1302(8).

41. *Nevada v. Hicks* (2001), 384.

42. See *Santa Clara Pueblo v. Martinez*, 71.

43. For example, see Danahy, "License to Discriminate." Of course, the author finds a great deal of irony in the law review of Florida State University—home of the "Seminoles" sports teams—in published arguments suggesting that Indian tribes discriminate against non-Indians.

44. See Meara, "MHRC to hear complaint against Micmacs Unity College."

45. David Shaffer, "Casinos Claiming Immunity from Basic Labor Laws," 1A.

46. Tom Philip, "No Women, No Ride, Says Civil Rights Law," B7.

47. See generally Fletcher, "Bringing Balance to Indian Gaming"; Fletcher, "In Pursuit of Tribal Economic Development as a Substitute for Reservation Tax Revenue"; and Riley, "Good (Native) Governance."

48. Fletcher, "Sawnawgezewog," 36.
49. See generally Fletcher, "Tribal Employment Separation."
50. See generally Berger, "Justice and the Outsider," and Fletcher, "Toward a Theory of Intertribal and Intratribal Common Law."
51. See *Necklace v. Tribal Court of the Three Affiliated Tribes of Fort Berthold Reservation* (1977).
52. *National Farmers Union Ins. Cos. v. Crow Tribe of Indians* (1985), 857.
53. See *Aleman v. Chugash Support Services, Inc.* (2007) and *Burrell v. Armijo* (2006).
54. See *Sac & Fox Tribe of the Mississippi in Iowa Election Board v. Bureau of Indian Affairs* (2006).
55. See generally Fletcher, "The Supreme Court and Federal Indian Policy" and Schlosser, "Sovereign Immunity: Should the Sovereign Control the Purse?"
56. *Williams v. Lee*, 221.
57. See generally Benton-Benai, *The Mishomis Book: The Voice of the Ojibway*; and Fletcher, "Stick Houses in Peshawbestown."
58. See generally Weeks, *Mem-Ka-Weh: Dawning of the Grand Traverse Band of Ottawa and Chippewa Indians*; and *Grand Traverse Band of Ottawa and Chippewa Indians v. United States Attorney for the Western District of Michigan* (2004).
59. "Treaty with the Ottowas and Chippewas," *Statutes at Large and Treaties* 621–29.
60. *Grand Traverse Band of Ottawa and Chippewa Indians v. Director, Michigan Department of Natural Resources*, 141 F.3d 635.
61. *Grand Traverse Band of Ottawa and Chippewa Indians v. United States Attorney for the Western District of Michigan*, 360 F.3d 920.
62. Michigan Indian Land Claims Settlement Act, 2652–66.
63. See "Tax Agreement between the Grand Traverse Band of Ottawa and Chippewa Indians and the State of Michigan" (May 27, 2004); and Fletcher, "The Power to Tax, the Power to Destroy, and the Michigan Tribal-State Tax Agreements."
64. See generally Fletcher, "Toward a Theory of Intertribal and Intratribal Common Law" and Fletcher, "Rethinking the Role of Custom in Tribal Court Jurisprudence." At least one Indian tribal court has left open the question of whether the Indian Civil Rights Act applies to them. See *Hopi Tribe v. Huma* (1995). It was Congress, after all, not Indian tribes, that enacted the statute. No tribe got a chance to vote on whether it applies unlike in the case of the Indian Reorganization Act.
65. Professor Kennedy goes on to argue that there are three serious problems with ICWA. First, Congressional fact finding leading up to the enactment of the statute that the Indian child welfare crisis was caused by race discrimination was incorrect. Second, Congressional fact finding about the impact of placing Indian children in non-Indian homes was incorrect. And, third, state court judges make bad decisions in ICWA cases in order to avoid ICWA's effects. Kennedy, *Interracial Intimacies*, 488. For a fuller rebuttal to Kennedy's arguments, see Fletcher and Singel, *The Indian Child Welfare Act at 30*.
66. Kennedy, *Interracial Intimacies*, 488.
67. Wilkinson, *American Indians, Time, and the Law*, 14–19.
68. Kennedy, *Interracial Intimacies*, 480–518.
69. See generally Riley, "(Tribal) Sovereignty and Illiberalism."
70. See generally Goldberg, "Individual Rights and Tribal Revitalization."
71. See generally Fletcher, "Same-Sex Marriage, Indian Tribes, and the Constitution," and Allen, "Conducting Embryonic Stem Cell Research on Native Lands in Michigan."
72. Newton et al., eds., *Cohen's Handbook of Federal Indian Law* § 4.07(1)(a).
73. *Graham v. Muscogee (Creek) Nation Citizenship* (2006).

Bibliography

8 U.S.C. § 1401(b).

25 U.S.C. §§ 1301–1303.

25 U.S.C. § 1603.

25 U.S.C. §§ 1901–1911

42 U.S.C. § 2000.

Aleman v. Chugash Support Services, Inc., 485 F.3d 286 (4th Cir. 2007).

Allen, Jake. "Conducting Embryonic Stem Cell Research on Native Lands in Michigan." *Journal of Law & Medicine* 11 (2007): 395–445.

Baca v. Puyallup Tribe of Indians, No. CV 01-278 (Puyallup Tribal Court, February 25, 2002).

Beck, George. "The Fourteenth Amendment as Related to Tribal Indians." *American Indian Culture and Research Journal* 28 (2004): 37–68.

Bell, Derrick, Jr. "*Brown v. Board of Education* and the Interest Convergence Dilemma." *Harvard Law Review* 93 (1980): 518–33.

———. "Foreword: The Civil Rights Chronicles." *Harvard Law Review* 99 (1985): 4–82.

Benton-Benai, Edward. *The Mishomis Book: The Voice of the Ojibway.* St. Paul, MN: Indian Country, 1979.

Berger, Bethany. "Justice and the Outsider: Jurisdiction over Nonmembers in Tribal Legal Systems." *Arizona State Law Journal* 37 (2005): 1047–1125.

Buffalo, William, and Kevin J. Wadzinski. "Application of Federal and State Labor and Employment Laws to Indian Tribal Employers." *University of Memphis Law Review* 25 (1995): 1365–99.

Burrell v. Armijo, 456 F. 3d 1159 (10th Cir. 2006).

Clinton, Robert. "Sovereignty and the Native American Nation: The Dormant Indian Commerce Clause." *Connecticut Law Review* 27 (1994): 1055–1147.

———. "There Is No Federal Supremacy Clause for Indian Tribe." *Arizona State Law Journal* 34 (2002): 113–260.

Colville Tribal Enterprise Corp. v. Orr, No. AP98-008 (Colville Confederated Tribes Court of Appeals, December 4, 1998).

Constitution of the Grand Traverse Band of Ottawa and Chippewa Indians. http://thorpe.ou.edu/constitution/GTBcons3.html.

Danahy, Scott. "License to Discriminate: The Application of Sovereign Immunity to Employment Discrimination Claims Brought by Non-Native American Employees of Tribally Owned Businesses." *Florida State University Law Review* 25 (1998): 679–703.

Deloria, Vine, Jr. *Custer Died for Your Sins: An Indian Manifesto.* 1969. Reprint, Norman: University of Oklahoma Press, 1988.

"Establishing Standards for the Placement of Indian Children in Foster or Adoptive Homes, To Prevent the Breakup of Indian Families, and for Other Purposes." H.R. Rep. 95-1386. July 24, 1978.

Fletcher, Matthew L. M. "Bringing Balance to Indian Gaming." *Harvard Journal on Legislation* 44 (2006): 39–95.

———. "ICWA and the Commerce Clause." In *The Indian Child Welfare Act at 30: Facing the Future*, edited by Matthew L. M. Fletcher, Wenona T. Singel, and Kathryn E. Fort. East Lansing, MI: Michigan State University Press, forthcoming.

———. "Indian Bill of Rights." In *Encyclopedia of American Civil Liberties*, vol. 2. Edited by Paul Finkelman, 806–10. New York: Routledge, 2006.

———. "The Insidious Colonialism of the Conqueror." *Washington University Journal of Law & Policy* 19 (2005): 273–311.

————. "The Original Understanding of the Political Status of Indian Tribes." *St. John's Law Review* 82 (2008): 153–81.

————. "Politics, History, and Semantics: The Federal Recognition of Indian Tribes." *North Dakota Law Review* 82 (2006): 487–518.

————. "Preconstitutional Federal Power." *Tulane Law Review* 82 (2007): 509–64.

————. "In Pursuit of Tribal Economic Development as a Substitute for Reservation Tax Revenue." *North Dakota Law Review* 80 (2004): 759–807.

————. "Rethinking the Role of Custom in Tribal Court Jurisprudence." *Michigan Journal of Race & Law* 13 (2007): 57–98.

————. "Same-Sex Marriage, Indian Tribes, and the Constitution." *University of Miami Law Review* 61 (2006): 53–85.

————. "Sawnawgezewog: 'The Indian Problem' and the Lost Art of Survival." *American Indian Law Review* 28 (2003–2004): 35–105.

————. "Stick Houses in Peshawbestown." *Cardozo Public Law, Policy, and Ethics Journal* 2 (2004): 189–287.

————. "The Supreme Court and Federal Indian Policy." *Nebraska Law Review* 85 (2006): 121–85.

————."Toward a Theory of Intertribal and Intratribal Common Law." *Houston Law Review* 43 (2006): 701–41.

————."Tribal Employment Separation: Tribal Law Enigma, Tribal Governance Paradox, and Tribal Court Conundrum." *University of Michigan Journal of Law Reform* 38 (2005): 273–343.

Goldberg, Carole. "Individual Rights and Tribal Revitalization." *Arizona State Law Journal* 35 (2003): 889–938.

Graham v. Muscogee (Creek) Nation Citizenship, No. 2003-53 (District Court of the Muscogee [Creek] Nation, March 16, 2006).

Grand Traverse Band Code, vol. 6, § 104(c).

Grand Traverse Band of Ottawa and Chippewa Indians v. United States Attorney for the Western District of Michigan, 360 F.3d 920 (6th Cir. 2004).

Haddock, David, and Robert Miller. "Can a Sovereign Protect Investors from Itself? Tribal Institutions to Spur Reservation Investment." *Journal of Small and Emerging Business Law* 8 (2004): 173–224.

Hopi Tribe v. Huma, No. AP-004-92 (Hopi Court of Appeals, January 13, 1995).

In re Bridget R. 49 Cal. Rptr. 2d 507 (Cal. App. 1996).

In re Santos Y. 112 Cal Rptr. 2d 692 (Cal. App. 2001).

Joranko, Timothy, and Mark C. Van Norman. "Indian Self-Determination at Bay: Secretarial Authority to Disapprove Tribal Constitutional Amendments." *Gonzaga Law Review* 29 (1993–1994): 81–104.

Kennedy, Randall. *Interracial Intimacies: Sex, Marriage, Identity, and Adoption.* New York: Pantheon Books, 2003.

Kiowa Tribe of Oklahoma v. Manufacturing Technologies, Inc., 523 U.S. 751 (1998).

Madison, James. "Federalist No. 42." *The Federalist Papers* (1788). http://www.foundingfathers.info/federalistpapers/.

McNickle, D'Arcy. "Indian and European: Indian-White Relations from Discovery to 1887." *Annals of the American Academy of Political and Social Science* 311 (1957): 1–11.

Meara, Emmet. "MHRC to hear complaint against Micmacs Unity College." *Bangor Daily News.* June 16, 1998.

Michigan Indian Land Claims Settlement Act, Public Law 105–43, *United States Statutes at Large* 111. Washington, DC: United States Government Printing Office, 1997.

Mississippi Band of Choctaw Indians v. Holyfield, 490 U.S. 30 (1989).

Morton v. Mancari, 417 U.S. 535, 553 n. 24 (1974).

National Farmers Union Ins. Cos. v. Crow Tribe of Indians, 471 U.S. 845, 857 (1985).

Native American Church of North America v. Navajo Tribal Council, 272 F.2d 131 (10th Cir. 1959).

Necklace v. Tribal Court of the Three Affiliated Tribes of Fort Berthold Reservation, 554 F.2d 845 (8th Cir. 1977).

Nevada v. Hicks, 533 U.S. 353 (2001).

Newton, Nell Jessup et al., eds. *Cohen's Handbook of Federal Indian Law*. Newark, NJ: LexisNexis, 2005.

One Hundred Eight Employees of the Crow Tribe of Indians v. Crow Tribe of Indians, No. 89-320 (Crow Court of Appeals, November 21, 2001).

Philip, Tom. "No Women, No Ride, Says Civil Rights Law." *Sacramento Bee*. November 5, 1994, B7.

Porter, Robert. "The Demise of the Ongwehoweh and the Rise of the Native Americans: Redressing the Genocidal Act of Forcing American Indian Citizenship upon Indigenous Peoples." *Harvard Black Letter Law Journal* 15 (1999): 107–82.

Prucha, Francis Paul. *American Indian Policy in the Formative Years: The Indian Trade and Intercourse Acts, 1790–1834*. Lincoln: University of Nebraska Press, 1962.

Riley, Angela. "Good (Native) Governance." *Columbia Law Review* 107 (2007): 1049–1125.

Riley, Angela. "(Tribal) Sovereignty and Illiberalism." *California Law Review* 95 (2007): 799–848.

Sac & Fox Tribe of the Mississippi in Iowa Election Board v. Bureau of Indian Affairs, 439 F. 3d 832 (8th Cir. 2006).

Santa Clara Pueblo v. Martinez, 436 U.S. 49 (1978).

Schlosser, Thomas. "Sovereign Immunity: Should the Sovereign Control the Purse?" *American Indian Law Review* 24 (2000): 309–55.

Shaffer, David. "Casinos Claiming Immunity from Basic Labor Laws, Status of Tribes Leaves Workers Unprotected." *St. Paul Pioneer Press*, October 31, 1993, 1A.

Scott v. Sanford, 60 U.S. 393 (1856).

Seneca Constitutional Rights Organization v. George, 348 F. Supp. 51 (W.D. N.Y. 1972).

Swentzell, Rina. "Testimony of a Santa Clara Woman." *Kansas Journal of Law & Public Policy* 14 (2004): 97–104.

Talton v. Mayes, 163 U.S. 376 (1896).

Treaty with the Ottowas and Chippewas, *Statutes at Large and Treaties*. vol. 11, 621–29. Boston: Little, Brown and Company, 1859.

United States Senate Committee on the Judiciary, *Effect of Fourteenth Amendment Upon Indian Tribes*, S. Rep. No. 268, 41st Congress, 3d Session (December 1870).

Vann, Marilyn. "Loss of Cherokee National citizenship." *Indianz.com* (accessed March 21, 2007).

Washington v. Washington Commercial Passenger Fishing Vessel Assn., 443 U.S. 658 (1979).

Weeks, George. *Mem-Ka-Weh: Dawning of the Grand Traverse Band of Ottawa and Chippewa Indians*. Peshawbestown, MI: Grand Traverse Band of Ottawa and Chippewa Indians, 1992.

Wilkinson, Charles. *American Indians, Time, and the Law: Native Societies in a Modern Constitutional Democracy*. New Haven, CT: Yale University Press, 1987.

Williams v. Lee, 358 U.S. 217 (1959).

Worcester v. Georgia, 31 U.S. 515 (1832).

5

It Falls to You

Rawls, Bartleby, and the Ethics of Affirmative Action in Charles Johnson's "Executive Decision"

William Gleason

Whatever affects one directly, affects all indirectly.

—Martin Luther King, Jr., "Letter from Birmingham Jail"

Although affirmative action remains one of the most divisive controversies within American law and Western ethics, literary fiction has by and large remained on the sidelines of this contentious debate with one striking exception: Charles Johnson's 1997 short story "Executive Decision." Johnson's tale not only dramatizes the vexing question at the heart of every affirmative action workplace decision—between equally qualified candidates, should an employer give special preference to an applicant from an historically underprivileged group?—but it also explores the roles of moral and political philosophy in framing the relevant issues at stake. In this chapter I will focus on two crucial and interrelated aspects of Johnson's story: its ultimate embrace of the social contract theory of John Rawls and its canny invocation of American literature's most puzzling tale of preference, Herman Melville's "Bartleby, the Scrivener." I will suggest that while "Executive Decision" makes a case, through fiction, for the appropriateness of affirmative action as a workplace remedy against ongoing employment discrimination, Johnson's story is no mere polemic. Instead it offers a thoughtful meditation—one that Johnson would also undertake in *Dreamer*, his 1998 novel on the life of Martin Luther King, Jr.—on a concept central to Rawls's theory of justice as fairness: the profound responsibility, in a just society, that human beings have toward the least fortunate—or, one might say, toward the Bartlebys—among them.

Indeed the pairing of Rawls and "Bartleby" in "Executive Decision" does more than merely mark a fortuitous combination of Johnson's longstanding interest in philosophy and his well-known regard for Melville. Rather it makes possible a fascinating revisioning of Melville's classic workplace tale through the lens of

Rawlsian ethics. Melville's story is, of course, not itself a study of affirmative action—if anything, it is a study of affirmative *in*action, embodied in Bartleby's demurring refrain, "I prefer not to." But in Johnson's hands, "Bartleby" reemerges as a fundamentally Rawlsian tale about the obligations that "men of unequal circumstances," as one character puts it, have to one another, a tale that provocatively asks, to what extent do we share one another's fate?[1] This is, after all, the central conundrum facing Melville's narrator-lawyer, a prudent man whose "eminently *safe*" world is upended by Bartleby's unfathomable intransigence. And the questions that confound that narrator in his relations with his employee—"What shall I do? what ought I to do? what does conscience say I *should* do?"[2]—are precisely those that trouble the hiring dilemma at the core of "Executive Decision." Of course Rawls's *A Theory of Justice* is no more a study of affirmative action than Melville's tale. Rawls never commented specifically on the role of racial preferences in his writings, nor is it immediately clear how his conception of justice would apply to contemporary affirmative action debates.[3] Nevertheless, "Executive Decision" not only draws Rawls's principles into the story's debate; in the end it endorses them.

In so doing, this tale might surprise a reader familiar with Johnson's wider body of work. Although his most acclaimed writings focus on central aspects of African American history, including slavery (e.g., *Oxherding Tale*, *Middle Passage*) and civil rights (e.g., *Dreamer*), Johnson has long maintained that race itself is an illusion, and as such he has strenuously avoided writing what one might call political fiction about racial topics. Taking a position on affirmative action—even in fiction and even framed explicitly in philosophical terms—might seem an unusual choice for such a writer. And yet in a 1998 interview, Johnson acknowledged writing "Executive Decision" in part "to clarify [his] feelings" on this controversial topic.[4] That is not to say he simply shaped the tale to prove a point; Johnson's writing always foregrounds process and discovery (including his own as a writer) over foregone conclusions.[5] Instead, in clarifying his thoughts about affirmative action, Johnson has imaginatively appropriated and transposed Melville's law-office story to a new time and place, moving it from the claustrophobic enclosures of mid-nineteenth-century Wall Street to the "breathtaking view[s]" of contemporary Seattle.[6] In the process, "Executive Decision" serves up a provocative new version of "Bartleby," one in which the refusal to copy—symbolized in Johnson's story by the narrator's rejection of his company's traditional hiring patterns—leads not to immobility and death, as in Melville's tale, but rather to integration and renewal.

"Your Task is Impossible"

Most readers of Johnson's story know it as the fifth of eight tales in his 2005 collection, *Dr. King's Refrigerator and Other Bedtime Stories*; but it was first published eight years earlier in Susan Shreve's anthology of reflections on the American legal system, *Outside the Law: Narratives on Justice in America*. In its original context, the tale's philosophical and ethical concerns emerge with special clarity. The tale is preceded, for example, by an epigraph from Kant's *Fundamental Principles of the Metaphysic of Morals*—more specifically, by Kant's first formulation of the categorical imperative: "Act as if the principle of thy action were to become by thy will a universal law of nature." Although Linda Seltzer has made us aware of the ways Johnson has used Kant elsewhere as a marker of a sterile rational formalism,[7] in this case Kant's imperative is an apt and unironic frame for Johnson's story, which depicts the struggle of its protagonist—a corporate CEO choosing between two finalists for a high-level opening in his company—not merely to make the best decision but to make the ethically appropriate one as well. Indeed, the epigraph does more than frame the tale. It also shapes the narrative point of view, whose unusual second-person voice, which places the reader in the CEO's shoes ("There are two names shortlisted for the position your company has advertised . . . If you delay the decision any longer, you will lose them to a competitor"), may be said to elaborate the direct address of Kant's imperative ("Act as if the principle of thy action . . ."). The opening of the story, however, suggests that acting as Kant's imperative demands will be anything but easy. "Put simply," the first sentence announces, "your task is impossible."[8] The burden of the tale is to discover how this may not be so.

For most of the story, the narrator cannot find his way to this result. No matter how closely he studies the files of the two finalists, he cannot uncover the "one fact or feeling" that might tilt the scales in either candidate's favor. They appear equally qualified—"or, if not exactly matched," the narrator observes, "what you see as deficiencies in one are balanced by a strength the other does not possess." Compounding this perplexity—and raising the stakes from a mere hiring decision to something the CEO comes to regard as a "paradox of justice"—is that, for all their apparent equality (and "except before the law, and in the eyes of God," the CEO wonders, "are *any* two people truly equal?"), the two finalists are also "antimonies": one is a white woman and the other a black man. In a company with no African Americans in the executive wing—a fact about which the firm's more junior black employees have begun to complain—does the African American candidate deserve preferential treatment even if the narrator feels more personally comfortable with the white candidate? Does his company—does any company, the story implicitly asks—have social obligations that extend beyond its office walls?[9]

Several factors would seem to tilt the field in favor of the white candidate. After all, Claire Bennett already has much in common with the CEO and the two chief executives who help him conduct the interviews. Not only are all three interviewers white but also, like the CEO, Bennett grew up in the Pacific Northwest in a family of privilege, and like all three she went to college in the northeast. The interview is chatty and comfortable. "It was as if you'd known her all your life," the CEO marvels. On the other hand, the African American finalist, Eddie Childs—who grew up in the South and was the first in his family even to go to college, also in the South—has virtually nothing in common with the three interviewers, making their interactions far more awkward. "Even after two interview sessions," recalls the CEO, Childs seemed "formal, guarded, and . . . opaque."[10]

Nonetheless, each candidate has a vocal supporter. The interviewer whose pending retirement has necessitated the new hire in the first place strongly favors Bennett. "Why discuss this any further?" this executive asks, after both finalists have had their last interviews. "I think she can weather any crisis that comes along, make us a lot of money, and keep the stockholders happy. That's all *I* need to know." The other chief executive, however, just as strongly favors Childs. Impressed in particular by his "strategies for improving diversity in personnel and ideas for better marketing the firm's products to minorities"—a crucial step for the coming century, he argues, when racial minorities in the United States will outnumber whites—this second executive votes (in, one might say, a Kantian sense) "categorically" for Childs. When the first executive refuses to budge on Bennett, the second poses a question that shifts the discussion away from corporate profit to matters of ethics and justice. "But," he asks, "does Bennett *deserve* the job more than Childs?" This question, asked at roughly the midpoint of "Executive Decision," finally brings the debate over affirmative action center stage. What it does not bring, however, is resolution. For although these two executives elaborate for the CEO (and the reader) the salient ethical and philosophical arguments on each side of the larger question, at the end of the evening the pair "[stagger] out together, carrying their disagreement into the hallway and elevator, neither of them willing to support the other's candidate for the job"—and leave the CEO, who has listened but not participated, to make the decision himself. "It falls to you," the tale instructs, "to break the tie."[11]

Justice as Fairness

The CEO's duty is not simply to decide which candidate to hire but also, in the spirit of Kant's imperative, to determine the principle on which to make that decision. The executives' debate models two very different approaches for the CEO to consider. On the one hand, the executive who prefers to hire the white candidate offers a libertarian defense of the freedom of contract, insisting that it should be within their rights, as a private company, to hire as they deem best without regard for broader questions of racial justice. When the second executive asks whether Bennett deserves the job more than Childs, for example, the first executive frowns in irritation: "How's that again—deserve, I heard you say? We have a job to offer, and it's ours to extend or withhold as we see fit. We may hire or fire the most qualified employee, as legal scholar Richard Epstein puts it, for good reason, bad reason, or no reason at all."[12] The first executive here alludes to arguments developed by University of Chicago law professor Richard Epstein in his controversial 1992 book, *Forbidden Grounds: The Case Against Employment Discrimination Laws*, in which he critiques "the entire complex of modern civil rights laws and their administration," specifically calling for the repeal of Title VII of the Civil Rights Act of 1964 as it applies to private employers. In Epstein's view, affirmative action and other antidiscrimination remedies exemplify an "unjustified limitation" on the freedom of "all persons to do business with whomever they please," a freedom rooted in the doctrine of employment at will as it developed in nineteenth-century American common law.[13] The first executive enthusiastically embraces Epstein's position that rational discrimination is not a problem to be regulated by the state but rather a natural human trait. "We *all* discriminate," the first executive insists. "Every moment of every day we choose one thing rather than another on the basis of our tastes, prejudices, and preferences. How *else* can we achieve life, liberty, and the pursuit of happiness?"[14]

The second executive, on the other hand, counters with the egalitarian liberalism of John Rawls, who in the story's imagined past had been the executives' instructor while they were undergraduates at Harvard. (Rawls taught at Harvard from 1962 through 1994; "Executive Decision" places the CEO and his two chief executives in Rawls's classroom in the mid-1960s, early in Rawls's career.) "Do you remember the class we took with John Rawls?" the second executive asks. "Vaguely, yes," replies the first. "I nearly flunked it. Had something to do with the state being like a joint-stock company. A lot of Hobbes and Locke rehashed, if I recall it rightly." The second executive refreshes the first's hazy memory with an account of one of Rawls's most central claims:

> There was more to it than that. [Rawls] said when justice is seen as fairness, men of unequal circumstances agree to share one another's fate. Social advantages and native endowments of any sort—whether they be inherited wealth, talent, beauty, or imagination—are undeserved. They are products of the arbitrariness of fortune. But Rawls did not say we must eradicate these inequities, only adjust them so that the least favored benefit too. If the fortunate do not share, then the least advantaged have every right to break the social contract that has so miserably failed to serve their needs. They riot. They rebel. Without the cooperation of the least favored, the social order collapses for *everyone*.[15]

As the second executive notes, Rawls's theory emphasizes the importance not of individual freedoms but of shared fates. For Rawls, life, liberty, and the pursuit of happiness are not, as is the case for Epstein, exclusively private goals but, instead, social ones. In a just society they are secured through two fundamental principles: first, that "each person is to have an equal right to the most extensive basic liberty compatible with a similar liberty for others"; and second, that "social and economic inequalities are to be arranged so that they are both (a) reasonably expected to be to everyone's advantage, and (b) attached to positions and offices open to all." The second executive is particularly concerned with Rawls's second principle, also known as the difference principle, that permits inequalities within a just society only when the arrangement of those inequalities ensures that everyone—from the most to the least favored—benefits from the way that society's "advantages" and "endowments" are distributed as a whole. The underlying ethic of the difference principle, as Rawls would eventually put it in A *Theory of Justice* (1971), is "mutual benefit."[16] The first executive professes to understand this ethic but doesn't see why it should apply beyond the company itself, especially when it comes to making a senior hire. When the second executive asks, "Then we have *no* greater social obligations?" the first replies, "My dear friend, . . . making the monthly payroll on time so employees and their families are not unduly inconvenienced is, in my humble opinion, social obligation enough. I am for the candidate who puts *that* first."[17]

The energetic staging of these two positions, as I have already suggested, does not immediately help the CEO make his decision. Long after the quarreling executives have staggered out, leaving the narrator to break the tie, he finds himself no closer to choosing either Bennett or Childs: "Come midnight, you are still torn, divided within as if you were two people, or perhaps three." Indeed, the very naming of the two executives—the Rawlsian is "Nips," the Epsteinian "Turk" (both are fraternity nicknames)—slyly suggests the debate itself is running neck and neck (i.e., "nip and tuck" ["nips and turk"]). And yet carefully laid clues hint that the Rawlsian view will prevail. For one, Johnson depicts Turk as something of a blowhard. Although his account of what Epstein calls rational discrimination at first seems perfectly reasonable—"I remember that *you*, back in our school days," he says to Nips, "never deigned to direct your affections toward women taller than yourself or, for that matter, toward men"—Turk quickly veers toward hyperbole: "Really man, be realistic. The Japanese don't spend a moment agonizing over things like this, and look how they trumped us in the eighties!" To the narrator, this is typical Turk, who, when "slightly in his cups, tilted toward the pomp and preachment of a Thrasymachus." Here Johnson has armed the narrator with a telling allusion, for Thrasymachus is none other than Socrates's Sophist foil in the first book of the *Republic*, infamous for impatiently insisting that justice is nothing but the advantage of the stronger over the weaker—or might makes right, a position the *Republic*, like Johnson's own tale, strenuously rejects. Nips, by contrast, though he is no saint (a night owl, he often arrives at work hungover), listens to Turk's rant with patience.[18]

A second clue lurks in the epigraph from Kant that opens the story, for it is Rawls's work, not Epstein's, that grounds itself in Kant's *Metaphysic of Morals*. Although commentators disagree on the aptness with which Rawls interprets Kant in *A Theory of Justice*,[19] Rawls understood his core principles of justice as themselves "categorical imperatives in Kant's sense." Indeed, of critical importance to Rawls is the difference between a hypothetical imperative and a categorical one. A hypothetical imperative seeks to satisfy a particular end or aim. A categorical imperative, however, Rawls notes, is "a principle of conduct that applies to a person in virtue of his nature as a free and equal rational being" without presupposing "a particular desire or aim." Thus "to act from the principles of justice is to act from categorical imperatives in the sense that they apply to us whatever in particular our aims are." In "Executive Decision," only Nips proposes a Kantian view of actions and ends. Rather than act according to our individual likes and dislikes, as Turk would have it, Nips recommends acting to advance the needs of all. Indeed, in urging that the fortunate share the benefits of their advantages and endowments with the least favored, only Nips may be said to endorse an ethic of mutual respect, which Rawls sees as the true basis of Kant's moral doctrine.[20]

On the morning after the CEO's long night's struggle to decide which finalist to choose—spoiler alert—he indeed finally picks Childs, affirming for himself the moral superiority of Rawls's neo-Kantian egalitarianism to Epstein's libertarian antidiscriminationism. In the process the CEO also discovers, and acts upon, a new respect for one of his existing employees—not an executive but a secretary. In order to understand the implications of both these discoveries, we need at last turn to Melville to parse the ways that "Bartleby, the Scrivener" serves as a fitting, if at first surprising, precursor text for Johnson's own.

Eminently Safe

Johnson's affinity for Melville is well documented, and in more than one interview he has noted that "Executive Decision" not only alludes to but is also "informed by" "Bartleby."[21] But in what specific ways and to what ends? The allusions are fairly easy to pin down. First, Johnson playfully appropriates most of the main characters from Melville's tale. The dueling executives Nips and Turk, for example, not only bring to mind the colloquial expression for a close contest, they are also reincarnations of Nippers and Turkey, the law copyists already employed in Melville's imaginary Wall Street firm when Bartleby arrives. There is more than name play involved here: Johnson borrows Melville's character templates and eccentric office dynamics as well. Turk, for example, Johnson's round-faced "dyspeptic" who is "notorious for being a morning person," is modeled after Turkey, the "short, pursy Englishman" who works productively before noon but turns reckless and injudicious after lunch. Nips, Johnson's compulsive rearranger (of his desk, of the world), channels not only Nippers's perpetual dissatisfaction but also his morning funk and afternoon placidity. (As in Melville's tale, one wonders whether the narrator should tolerate such dysfunction; but at least, as in "Bartleby," the slack times of these two key employees don't overlap.) Even Gladys McNeal, the narrator's efficient personal secretary in "Executive Decision," has a corresponding prototype from "Bartleby": Melville's "quick-witted" office helper, Ginger Nut, whose initials Gladys shares (Gladys McNeal, Ginger Nut). [22]

Other Melvillean details are sprinkled through the story. Johnson's narrator, like Melville's, has a "plaster-of-Paris bust of Cicero" in his office. The office itself is divided in much the same way as the premises in Melville's story: glass partitions separate the CEO from his employees, who work in "tiny, cluttered workstations" in contrast to his own "spacious chamber." And of course there is a Bartleby. When during the final round of interviews Turk invites Eddie Childs to his house to play in his weekly poker game, Childs declines in Bartleby's voice: "I would prefer not to." (All business, Childs doesn't play cards.) Though Childs also differs from Bartleby in significant ways, to the CEO he remains, like Bartleby (and quite unlike the thoroughly familiar Claire Bennett), deeply enigmatic. "He was," the CEO reflects, "what word do you want?—'different.' Sometimes you did not understand his humor. You certainly did not know his heart—*that* would come slowly, perhaps even painfully if you presumed to know too much about him, and it might be hard at first, a challenge, with you tripping lightly, walking on eggs around him until everyone in the office eased into familiarity. Was one candidate worth all that work?"[23] In having his narrator pose this last question—was one candidate worth all that work?—Johnson moves beyond the surface details of Melville's story toward one of its central philosophical preoccupations: how much understanding does one human being owe another? He also shifts the focus of the tale, much as one might argue Melville does, to the narrator himself, whose struggle to answer this question, and thus to calibrate his responsibility to a candidate like Childs, becomes the most important element of the story. In "Bartleby," of course, the lawyer's final answer to the particular version of this question that plagues him is no: Bartleby is not worth all that work. At first, disconcerted by Bartleby's intransigence, the lawyer decides to let the scrivener keep his position even though he refuses to compare his copies with the other clerks. But when Bartleby ceases copying altogether and his refusals threaten to ruin the lawyer's professional reputation, his patience runs dry. By the end of the story, Melville's narrator has all but abandoned Bartleby, although his conscience remains troubled by that decision. In Johnson's story, however, the answer turns out to be yes. Though never fully comfortable with Childs, the unnamed CEO narrator of "Executive Decision" ultimately decides Childs is worth "all that work" and is the right person to hire.

How does this happen? After all, at first glance Johnson's narrator looks like a fair copy of Melville's lawyer. In addition to the material similarities noted above (the plaster-of-Paris busts of Cicero, the hierarchical workspace of the offices), Johnson's CEO's opening self-introduction ("Imprimis: You are a man who, though radical in your youth . . .") mimes both the idiosyncratic phrasing of Melville's narrator's own address to the reader ("Imprimis: I am a man who, from his youth upwards . . .") and the lawyer's sense of his own character. Like his predecessor, who confides, "All who know me, consider me an eminently *safe* man," Johnson's narrator acknowledges, "Even [his] closest friends from college remark on how dull and safe . . . [he's] become." Prudence, in other words, is the watchword of both narrators. And yet Johnson's narrator differs in crucial ways from Melville's. Most strikingly, he has had what he calls a "radical" youth. At Harvard, he notes, he marched with civil rights workers and was twice arrested for taking part in campus demonstrations. Later, as a young executive in what was then his father's company, he urged the board, with moderate success, to recruit more women and minorities to the firm. Melville's narrator has no such radical past but has instead, "from his youth upwards," been "filled with a profound conviction that the easiest way of life is the best."[24] If Johnson's narrator now appears overly cautious, he at least recalls a time when he had thought it right to rock the boat for social justice.

It is reasonable to wonder whether Johnson isn't gently mocking his narrator when he has him describe his youth as "quite radical." Certainly Melville's narrator is prone to overestimating his own attributes. Indeed the gap between the lawyer's sense of his benevolence and the reader's is an important source of irony in Melville's story. And even if we are not meant to take the CEO's account of his past ironically, surely a radical past is no guarantee of a radical (or even liberal) future. But in "Executive Decision," the return to youthful origins is a recurrent trope and not an ironic one. In addition to the narrator's memories of his college activism and Nips's account of their course with Rawls, for example, the story rehearses the biographies of both Bennett and Childs, including brief descriptions of their childhoods. The story's denouement, moreover, is propelled in part by the narrator's memory of hiding in the closet of his father's office when he was a child. Even Childs's last name hints at this interest in origins—notably an interest that Melville's story shares but on which it cannot deliver. One of the chief frustrations of Melville's narrator is that he cannot write "a full and satisfactory biography" of Bartleby because Bartleby's past is all but unknown.[25] In "Executive Decision," however, the past is not only knowable but it also matters.

One past that matters deeply in Johnson's story—as it does in debates over affirmative action—is African American history itself. During his interview, Childs stuns the narrator into "respectful yet nervous silence" with an account of what he and his wife Leslie know about "this country's marginalized history—the contributions from people of color." Childs also describes, in minute detail, the impact of ongoing discrimination on black social and economic welfare. "You listened carefully to what he said," the CEO recalls.

> You learned that blacks suffered twice the unemployment rate of whites and earned only half as much (56 percent); that a decade ago they comprised 7 percent of professionals, 5 percent of managers, 8 percent of technicians, 11 percent of service workers, and 41 percent of domestic workers. There were, he told you, 620,912

black-owned businesses, but 47 percent of them had gross annual receipts of less than $5,000. For every 1,000 Arabs, 108 owned a business; for every 1,000 Asians, it was 96; for every 1,000 whites, 64, and for every 1,000 blacks, the number was 9. Worse, the typical black household had a net worth less than one-tenth that of white households. AIDS among black Americans was six times the rate it was for whites, and every four hours a young black male died from gunfire. Seventy percent of black children were born to single mothers; 57 percent were in fatherless homes, which was more than double the 21 percent for whites. This was the background of poverty and inequality Eddie and Leslie Childs had survived—a world in which black men in the early '90s accounted for half those murdered in America; they had less chance of reaching age sixty-five than men in Bangladesh. One out of three was in prison (the number was 827,440 in 1995) or on parole. It was a world where, as Childs put it, quoting Richard Pryor, justice was known simply as "just ice." Given these staggering obstacles, you are amazed this man is even alive.[26]

While it is not surprising to see a story of Johnson's veer toward a scene of instruction, I suspect that critics who have faulted "Executive Decision" for reading too much like a "civics lesson" may have in mind this passage, which on the surface reads more like an excerpt from a public policy brief or an op-ed piece than a short story.[27] But its function in the story, particularly when considered in light of Johnson's conscious adaptation of Melville, is more complex than this. In giving this speech to the story's Bartleby figure, for example, Johnson pointedly reverses Melville's original narrative dynamic, turning a garrulous narrator into a silent listener and his nearly mute employee into a purposeful lecturer. (Imagine how different Melville's story would be if Bartleby provided a detailed explanation of his motives and principles when the lawyer asks him why he has stopped copying, instead of merely replying, "indifferently," "Do you not see the reason for yourself.")[28] By having his own narrator both recall and rehearse Childs's speech so precisely, Johnson further suggests that his CEO, unlike Melville's lawyer, recognizes that multiple contexts, including the historical "background of poverty and inequality" Childs describes, might play a role in his eventual hiring decision.

This is one of the most important differences between Johnson's narrator and Melville's. As recent historicist interpretations of "Bartleby" have suggested, Melville's lawyer, though well meaning, is for the most part oblivious to (or has successfully repressed thoughts about) the economic, sociological, and even physical circumstances that might affect the labors of his employees.[29] His primary concern is that they do their work and "[reflect] credit" upon his business through their personal habits and appearance. Though aware that he provides Nippers and Turkey only "small . . . income" for their work, for example, he nonetheless resents Nippers's moonlighting (deriding it as "diseased ambition") and is appalled by Turkey's "execrable" wardrobe and his propensity to spend his wages on drink. When the lawyer's one attempt to help Turkey fails—he gives Turkey one of his own coats in the misguided hope that the grateful employee will turn teetotaler— the narrator blames the act of generosity itself. "I verily believe that buttoning himself up in so downy and blanket-like a coat had a pernicious effect upon him; upon the same principle that too much oats are bad for horses. In fact," the narrator reasons, "precisely as a rash, restive horse is said to feel his oats, so Turkey felt his coat. It made him insolent. He was a man whom prosperity harmed." It should come as no surprise that this same employer would not think twice about placing Bartleby's desk in a dim corner, looking out on a blank wall, behind a high folding screen—out of the lawyer's sight but not out of range of his voice—and then congratulate himself for an arrangement that conjoins "privacy and society."[30] Unlike Johnson's CEO, who at one time marched for the rights of others, Melville's narrator appears to have only a limited conception of what it might mean to act on the principle of mutual benefit; nearly all the lawyer's actions are calculated for his own gain, not his employees'. At the same time, in Johnson's story the CEO's readiness to absorb Childs's statistics does not in itself lead him to act in Childs's favor. After all, as Johnson is well aware, virtually the same statistics have been flourished by opponents of affirmative action as evidence of black failure rather than systemic discrimination.[31] It will take more than Childs's data, or the narrator's past, to convince the CEO that hiring Childs is the right course of action. It will require a chance encounter with a character who at first appears almost incidental to the story: Gladys McNeal, the firm's executive secretary.

Flicker-Flash

Much like Ginger Nut, her ostensible prototype in Melville's story, "old Gladys" inhabits the margins of Johnson's tale. Formerly the personal secretary of the CEO's father (and possibly, we are told, his lover), this "precise, never-married woman who could pass for actress Estelle Getty's sister" is efficient, reliable, and unobtrusive. She appears briefly at the beginning of the tale, as the narrator recalls that she supported his youthful efforts to diversify the company, but then largely disappears from view until the story's final scene when she arrives to open the office on the morning after the CEO's futile all-night struggle to decide which candidate to hire. Gladys's sudden appearance startles the CEO, who slips into his office bathroom to freshen his face and put on a new shirt from an adjacent closet. While changing, the CEO remembers how, as a boy, he sometimes hid in this same closet and listened to his father dictate letters to Gladys; he also remembers how "heartbreakingly beautiful" Gladys was, "a brunette with bee-stung lips and eyes so green, so light, you wondered if she could really see through them." And then a sudden sound stops the CEO "cold": "Someone is whistling a few bars from 'Uptown Downbeat,' an Ellington tune, one of your father's favorites. Walking to the bathroom's partly opened door, you see Gladys tidying up the files you left on the coffee table. Her hair, once obsidian and shiny, curls around her head in a cap of gray when she removes her rainbow-colored scarf. Believing herself to be alone in the office, she does a little dance step, snapping her fingers, shaking her hips, and for a flicker-flash instant she seems as young, as beautiful as Halle Berry. Different. Grasping for the same word he used to describe Childs, 'different'—a term whose repetition recalls Rawls's emphasis on the difference principle—the narrator is stunned to discover that, like Childs, Gladys is black. 'Or is she?' the CEO wonders, trying 'not to stare or seem too confounded' by this discovery. 'By all appearances, she is as white as you.'"[32]

But appearances can deceive. Finally understanding "why she looked away when the blacks in middle management complained that there were no Negroes in administration," the CEO is moved to ask Gladys her opinion of Bennett and Childs. And quietly but crucially she imparts the story's most important lesson:

> "Well, I liked them both, but—"
> "But what?"
> "Oh, it's nothing, just that Mr. Childs reminds me of Mr. Turk when he was hired. Neither was very much at ease. And I know your father never approved of Mr. Turk. His references weren't that good, if I remember, or his grades, but he got the job because he was your friend and you insisted. You acted on his behalf, and that was all right." She smiles and you see Halle Berry again; then, as the muscles around her mouth relax, Estelle Getty.[33]

This uncanny scene of resemblance and recognition—not only of Gladys as Halle Berry, but also of Childs as a version of Turk—finally tips the scales in Childs's favor and thus also in favor of acting, in Rawls's terms, on behalf of the "least favored"— something Melville's bewildered and overwhelmed narrator can never fully bring himself to do. Gladys frees Johnson's narrator, in other words, to act as a Rawlsian rather than an Epsteinian by reminding him that he has taken action on behalf of a less advantaged candidate before and that doing so was "all right." The parallels between the situations of Turk and Childs are of course not exact, and Turk may be said to have been "advantaged" in another sense by his relationship with the narrator. But that is, in part, the point. Gladys recognizes that Childs, like Turk, will need a compensatory advantage in order to be hired, and she helps the narrator see that acting in this way will be consistent with his own past actions. The fact that Gladys herself is black is a crucial part of the point here as well: by encouraging the CEO to act on behalf of Childs, she is also encouraging him to act on her behalf. As a black employee in a predominantly white company who has long endorsed the hiring of more African American employees but privately lamented their inability to break into senior management—a circumstance over which, as a secretary, she has no direct control—Gladys is encouraging the narrator to act as she would had she the power to redistribute the company's "advantages" as she believes would be most just. As the story's alternate Bartleby figure—"always the first employee to arrive and the last to leave," "always smiling ironically, as if she had a secret, Gladys never talked about herself, or her relations in New Orleans, or what she did away from the office," all of which adds "an element of mystery" to her—Gladys also redoubles Childs's role as a previously silenced character who now claims authority to speak and, indeed, to teach. [34]

Gladys's actions in the story's denouement thus do more than help the previously "safe" narrator make a temporarily "unsafe" (or "uncomfortable") decision by hiring Childs.[35] Her actions help the narrator break the cycle of unreflective hiring that has kept African Americans out of the firm's upper echelons. In this respect, "Executive Decision" not only crafts a fictional brief for affirmative action but also rings yet another canny change on "Bartleby, the Scrivener." The central function of the scriveners in Melville's law office, after all, is to produce copies, and Bartleby is, at first, the most enthusiastic of copyists, practically "gorg[ing]" himself on the lawyer's documents.[36] When Bartleby later expresses a preference not to compare his copies with the other clerks, however, and eventually refuses to copy at all, his story moves irrevocably toward stasis, death, and disintegration.

But in "Executive Decision," when the CEO elects to break the firm's traditional pattern by hiring Childs instead of Bennett, this proactive refusal to copy—a decisive revaluation of Bartleby's "I prefer not to"—leads not to stasis but to change, not to death but to renewal, and not to disintegration but to integration.

The CEO's decision to hire Childs is not the only action he takes at the end of the story. Just before asking Gladys to place a call to Childs so that he may offer him the position, the CEO makes one more resolution: to invite Gladys to lunch. "Your secretary has always taken her lunches alone," he reflects. "You know why, but today you will ask her to join you and Nips at Etta's, near the Pike Place Market."[37] This is a gesture not only of respect and inclusion but also perhaps equality, and it suggests that the narrator's decision to hire Childs may represent only the first of multiple actions intended to alter the company's usual divisions and hierarchies. It is also a decision most readers couldn't imagine Melville's narrator making— invite Bartleby to lunch?— so concerned is the lawyer with maintaining hierarchy and preserving his own best interests rather than those of the "least favored." And yet as Michael Colacurcio and others have suggested, in many ways Melville's narrator extends more generosity to Bartleby than readers are usually willing to give him credit for. However "underpowered" the lawyer's response to Bartleby may be, to the extent that the narrator is moved to act by Bartleby's condition—after all, he is by no means indifferent to the scrivener's fate—Melville's tale registers the possibility that its purpose is to take seriously the proposition that human beings should be judged by the aid they extend to the least fortunate in society. For some critics, as Colacurcio observes, this suggests that the story can be read as a "sort of oblique gloss on Matthew 25: 'whatever you do to the [forlornist] of mine, you do unto me.'"[38] I would suggest it also means Melville's tale can profitably be read in light of Rawls's theory of justice, particularly his difference principle. Or to put this another way: when we reread "Bartleby" through the lens of "Executive Decision," which explores Rawls's theory specifically by adapting Melville's story, the original text reappears, unexpectedly, as itself a kind of Rawlsian tale. Melville's lawyer is offered opportunities to act not merely according to Christian precepts but also, in a sense, according to Rawls's principles for a just society. This is not to argue for an anachronistic application of Rawls's theory to Melville's work, nor is it simply to endorse the links other scholars have seen between Rawls's work and Christian (or more broadly, Abrahamic) principles. Rather, it is to suggest that through its particular use of "Bartleby," "Executive Decision"—as a supplement to its own reflections on the Rawlsian justness of affirmative action—helps us recognize the extent to which similarly fundamental questions of justice and action are at stake in Melville's tale.[39]

Johnson's own embrace of Rawls's theory extends beyond its specific role in making the philosophical and ethical case for affirmative action in "Executive Decision." Indeed, in closing, I would suggest that "Executive Decision" helps us recognize Rawls's moral philosophy as a critical but underexamined influence on Johnson's recent writing.[40] For example, in his next major work after "Executive Decision," 1998's *Dreamer*, Johnson weaves Rawls's precepts into the very core of Martin Luther King, Jr.'s philosophy of political engagement. In an early chapter, Johnson imagines King in the early hours before dawn, unable to sleep and struggling to make sense of the innate ubiquity of inequality and to shape an appropriate ethical response to such a condition. As day finally breaks, King simultaneously intuits, almost verbatim, Rawls's difference principle. The echoes should, by now, be clear:

> The kitchen clock read 5:30. Sunlight yeasted into the kitchen, slowly brightening the room and his spirits as well. He lit a cigarette and thought: yes, inequality was stitched into the fabric of Being. No one deserved greater natural gifts than others. But despite the fortuitous differences in men, they could volunteer to share one another's fate. They could—in fact, should—rearrange the social world to redress the arbitrary whims of contingency, accident, and chance. If the fortunate did not help, rancor and bloodshed might never cease. The least advantaged had every right to break the social contract that had so miserably failed to meet their needs. They would rebel, riot as they were doing now in Chicago. For their own sake and survival, God's favored had to lift those on whom He'd turned His back.[41]

Though not a specific call for affirmative action, this scene is nonetheless reminiscent of the all-night struggle of the CEO in "Executive Decision." The principles King embraces are at once Rawlsian and Christian, and if they suggest the largely overlooked importance of Rawls's thought to Johnson's characterization of King, they also suggest the importance to Johnson of King—not merely as a civil rights activist but as a profound moral philosopher working, as did Rawls, to shape a more precise and effective concept of justice.[42] Turning back to "Executive Decision," we might thus also say that by imaginatively providing his CEO with not only the classroom instruction of Rawls but also the public example of King (the CEO's youthful radicalism, he recalls, blossomed "with the oratory of Martin Luther King Jr. . . . still echoing in [his] ears"),[43] Johnson equips his narrator with the kinds of tools we must all be called to employ—namely, the tools of moral philosophy—in striving together to make this world more truly just.

Notes

1. Johnson, "Executive Decision," 69.
2. Melville, "Bartleby," 635, 663.
3. Shortly after Rawls's death in 2002, Thomas Nagel recalled the philosopher expressing strong support for affirmative action in private conversations, even though he "never referred to it in his writings . . . except obliquely." See Nagel, "John Rawls and Affirmative Action," 82. This omission has not, of course, prevented scholars from enlisting Rawls's arguments—both pro and con—in discussions of affirmative action. See, for example, Goldman, *Justice and Reverse Discrimination*; Newell, "Affirmative Action and the Dilemmas of Liberalism"; Rosenfeld, *Affirmative Action and Justice*; and Sandel, *Liberalism and the Limits of Justice*.
4. Nash, "A Conversation with Charles Johnson," 221. Elsewhere Nash notes that Johnson also briefly explores affirmative action in his 1990 novel *Middle Passage*, though with a less "clearly defined sense" of his feelings than he would later express in "Executive Decision." See Nash, *Charles Johnson's Fiction*, 135.
5. As Johnson puts it, "[I see] the work of art as being like a laboratory. Instead of having test tubes and Bunsen burners, you have other tools—characters, plot, language's possibilities, the forms we inherit from the past—and you use those tools to test your

hypothesis. By the end of the process, your initial hypothesis may be confirmed, denied, or significantly modified. Whatever the case, you will have *learned* something about the phenomenon you were investigating and about yourself." Nash, "A Conversation with Charles Johnson," 224.

6. Johnson, "Executive Decision," 59.
7. See Seltzer, "The Genesis of Charles Johnson's Philosophical Fiction."
8. Johnson, "Executive Decision," 55.
9. Ibid., 59, 71, 59, 70.
10. Ibid., 59, 65.
11. Ibid., 66, 65, 66, 67, 70.
12. Ibid., 67.
13. Epstein, *Forbidden Grounds*, xii, 3.
14. Johnson, "Executive Decision," 67–68.
15. Ibid., 68–69.
16. Rawls, *A Theory of Justice*, 60, 102. Although Rawls later issued both a revised edition of *A Theory of Justice* (1999) and a shorter volume intended to clarify his main positions (*Justice as Fairness: A Restatement*), all quotations in this chapter come from the 1971 edition of *A Theory of Justice*. In Johnson's story the characters are specifically recalling formulations of Rawls's ideas from the 1960s when he was working on the 1971 edition.
17. Johnson, "Executive Decision," 69–70.
18. Ibid., 70, 68.
19. See, for example, Flickschuh, *Kant and Modern Political Philosophy*; and Kolm, *Modern Theories of Justice*.
20. Rawls, *A Theory of Justice*, 253. On Rawls's sense of "mutual respect" as the basis of Kant's moral doctrine, see *A Theory of Justice*, 256.
21. Nash, "A Conversation with Charles Johnson," 231. See also McWilliams, "An Interview with Charles Johnson," 276.
22. Johnson, "Executive Decision," 58, 66; Melville, "Bartleby," 637, 641.
23. Johnson, "Executive Decision," 58, 65.
24. Johnson, "Executive Decision," 56–57; Melville, "Bartleby," 635.
25. Melville, "Bartleby," 635.
26. Johnson, "Executive Decision," 63–64.
27. Moore, "Eight Easy Pieces," 7.
28. Melville, "Bartleby," 656.
29. See, for example, Post-Lauria, "Canonical Texts and Context"; Kuebrich, "Melville's Doctrine of Assumptions"; Foley, "From Wall Street to Astor Place"; and Reed, "The Specter of Wall Street."
30. Melville, "Bartleby," 639, 640, 639, 640, 642.
31. One such flourisher has been affirmative-action opponent Dinesh D'Souza, whose 1996 book *The End of Racism: Principles for a Multiracial Society* includes many of the same statistics cited by Childs. Johnson reviewed *The End of Racism* unfavorably not long before publishing "Executive Decision," specifically criticizing D'Souza's endorsement of Richard Epstein's view—later espoused by Turk in "Executive Decision"—that "people should be free to hire and fire others for good reason, bad reason or no reason at all." See Johnson, "Review of Dinesh D'Souza's *The End of Racism*," 191.
32. Johnson, "Executive Decision," 57, 72, 72–73. I do not have adequate space to discuss the erotic charge of the CEO's memory of Gladys's younger self, except to note that his attraction to Gladys (and her own role as his father's lover) radically personalizes the

CEO's discovery of both her race and, as I will discuss shortly, her principle for making the most just hire.

33. Johnson, "Executive Decision," 73, 74.

34. Ibid., 70, 72.

35. In an excellent analysis of Johnson's tale, Gary Storhoff argues that by opening his mind meditatively, the narrator is able to challenge his own "aversive racism," choosing to hire Childs even though such a decision will "make his environment temporarily 'unsafe' (that is, 'uncomfortable') for himself and his other employees." See Storhoff, "Opening the Hand of Thought."

36. Melville, "Bartleby," 642.

37. Johnson, "Executive Decision," 75.

38. Colacurcio, "Charity and Its Discontents," 63, 62–63. For another defense of Melville's narrator, see McCall, *The Silence of Bartleby*. The particular critic Colacurcio has in mind is H. Bruce Franklin.

39. On Rawls and Christian principles, see, for example, Dombrowski, *Rawls and Religion*. For two different treatments of the question of justice in "Bartleby," see Weinstock, "Doing Justice to Bartleby"; and Thomas, "The Legal Fictions of Herman Melville and Lemuel Shaw." For an ethical analysis of the roles of action and responsibility in "Bartleby," see Oehlschlaeger, "Toward a Christian Ethics of Reading."

40. To date no studies of Rawls's influence on Johnson's work exist.

41. Johnson, *Dreamer*, 49–50. Given the compositional proximity of "Executive Decision" and *Dreamer* and the Rawlsian influence on both, it is tempting to wonder whether, in selecting "Bartleby" as the antecedent literary form for "Executive Decision," Johnson was attracted not only by the focus of Melville's tale on preferences but also by its subtle depiction of the narrator and Bartleby as, at one point—when the narrator insists he is not responsible for Bartleby—figures for Cain and Abel, the central thematic and philosophical metaphor of *Dreamer*. For more on the Cain-Abel allusion in "Bartleby," see Kelley, *Melville's City*.

42. Although scholars disagree on the extent to which the philosophies of Rawls and King are fully compatible (e.g., see Schlueter, *One Dream or Two?*), when Johnson speaks of King's vision he often does so in terms that recall Rawls's emphasis on mutual respect and mutual benefit. "Underpinning [King's] belief in love's primacy," Johnson observed in 1996, "was the sense that our lives constitute an 'inescapable network of mutuality' that binds all people in a single 'garment of destiny'" ("The King We Left Behind," 198). For an analysis of the Buddhist elements of King's integrative vision, see Whalen-Bridge, "Waking Cain."

43. The specific passage the narrator recalls comes from King's August 1967 address to the Southern Christian Leadership Conference: "Power at its best is love implementing the demands of justice; justice at its best is love correcting everything that stands against love" ("Executive Decision," 57). For King's original address, see "Where Do We Go From Here?"

Bibliography

Byrd, Rudolph P., ed. *I Call Myself an Artist: Writings By and About Charles Johnson*. Bloomington, IN: Indiana University Press, 1999.

Colacurcio, Michael. "Charity and Its Discontents: Pity and Politics in Melville's Fiction." In *There Before Us: Religion, Literature, and Culture from Emerson to Wendell Berry*, edited by Roger Lundin, 49–79. Grand Rapids, MI: Wm. B. Eerdmans, 2007.

Conner, Marc C., and William R. Nash, eds. *Charles Johnson: The Novelist as Philosopher.* Jackson, MS: University Press of Mississippi, 2007.

D'Souza, Dinesh. *The End of Racism: Principles for a Multiracial Society.* New York: Simon and Schuster, 1996.

Dombrowski, Daniel A. *Rawls and Religion: The Case for Political Liberalism.* Albany, NY: State University of New York Press, 2001.

Epstein, Richard A. *Forbidden Grounds: The Case Against Employment Discrimination Laws.* Cambridge, MA: Harvard University Press, 1992.

Flickschuh, Katrin. *Kant and Modern Political Philosophy.* New York: Cambridge University Press, 2000.

Foley, Barbara. "From Wall Street to Astor Place: Historicizing Melville's 'Bartleby.'" *American Literature* 72, no. 1 (March 2000): 87–116.

Goldman, Alan. *Justice and Reverse Discrimination.* Princeton, NJ: Princeton University Press, 1979.

Johnson, Charles. *Dreamer.* New York: Simon and Schuster, 1998.

———. "Executive Decision." In *Dr. King's Refrigerator and Other Bedtime Stories,* by Charles Johnson, 55–75. New York: Scribner, 2005.

———. "The King We Left Behind." In *I Call Myself an Artist: Writings By and About Charles Johnson,* edited by Rudolph P. Byrd, 193–99. Bloomington, IN: Indiana University Press, 1999.

———. "Review of Dinesh D'Souza's *The End of Racism: Principles for a Multiracial Society.*" In *I Call Myself an Artist: Writings By and About Charles Johnson,* edited by Rudolph P. Byrd, 189–92. Bloomington, IN: Indiana University Press, 1999.

Kelley, Wyn. *Melville's City: Literary and Urban Form in Nineteenth-Century New York.* New York: Cambridge University Press, 1996.

King, Martin Luther, Jr. "Letter from Birmingham Jail." In *Why We Can't Wait,* 64–84. New York: Signet Classic, 2000.

———. "Where Do We Go From Here?" In *I Have a Dream: Writings and Speeches That Changed the World,* edited by James Melvin Washington, 169–79. New York: HarperCollins, 1992.

Kolm, Serge-Christophe. *Modern Theories of Justice.* Cambridge, MA: MIT Press, 2002.

Kuebrich, David. "Melville's Doctrine of Assumptions: The Hidden Ideology of Capitalist Production in 'Bartleby.'" *New England Quarterly* 69, no. 3 (September 1996): 381–405.

McCall, Dan. *The Silence of Bartleby.* Ithaca, NY: Cornell University Press, 1989.

McWilliams, Jim. "An Interview with Charles Johnson." In *Passing the Three Gates: Interviews with Charles Johnson,* 271–99. Seattle, WA: University of Washington Press, 2004.

———, ed. *Passing the Three Gates: Interviews with Charles Johnson.* Seattle, WA: University of Washington Press, 2004.

Melville, Herman. "Bartleby, the Scrivener: A Story of Wall Street." In *Pierre, Israel Potter, The Piazza Tales, The Confidence-Man, Billy Budd, Uncollected Prose,* edited by Harrison Hayford, 635–72. New York: Library of America, 1984.

Moore, Steven. "Eight Easy Pieces." Review of *Dr. King's Refrigerator,* by Charles Johnson. *Washington Post Book World,* February 20, 2005.

Nagel, Thomas. "John Rawls and Affirmative Action." *Journal of Blacks in Higher Education* 39 (Spring 2003): 82–84.

Nash, William R. "A Conversation with Charles Johnson." In *Passing the Three Gates: Interviews with Charles Johnson,* edited by Jim McWilliams, 214–35. Seattle, WA: University of Washington Press, 2004.

———. *Charles Johnson's Fiction.* Urbana, IL: University of Illinois Press, 2003.

Newell, W. R. "Affirmative Action and the Dilemmas of Liberalism." In *Affirmative Action: Theory, Analysis, and Prospects*, edited by Michael W. Cowles and John Gruhl, 44–60. Jefferson, NC: McFarland, 1986.

Oehlschlaeger, Fritz. "Toward a Christian Ethics of Reading. Or, Why We Cannot Be Done with Bartleby." In *Love and Good Reasons: Postliberal Approaches to Christian Ethics and Literature*, 49–82. Durham, NC: Duke University Press, 2003.

Post-Lauria, Sheila. "Canonical Text and Context: The Example of Herman Melville's 'Bartleby, the Scrivener: A Story of Wall Street.'" *College Literature* 20, no. 2 (June 1993): 196–205.

Rawls, John. *Justice as Fairness: A Restatement*. Edited by Erin Kelly. Cambridge, MA: Harvard University Press, 2001.

———. *A Theory of Justice*. Cambridge, MA: Harvard University Press, 1971.

Rosenfeld, Michael. *Affirmative Action and Justice: A Philosophical and Constitutional Inquiry*. New Haven, CT: Yale University Press, 1991.

Sandel, Michael J. *Liberalism and the Limits of Justice*, 2nd ed. New York: Cambridge University Press, 1998.

Schlueter, Nathan W. *One Dream or Two?: Justice in America and in the Thought of Martin Luther King, Jr.* Lanham, MD: Lexington Books, 2002.

Seltzer, Linda. "The Genesis of Charles Johnson's Philosophical Fiction." In *Charles Johnson: The Novelist as Philosopher*, edited by Marc C. Conner and William R. Nash, 1–19. Jackson, MS: University Press of Mississippi, 2007.

Shreve, Susan Richards, and Porter Shreve, eds. *Outside the Law: Narratives on Justice in America*. Boston: Beacon, 1997.

Weinstock, Jeffrey Andrew. "Doing Justice to Bartleby." *American Transcendental Quarterly* 17, no. 1 (March 2003): 23–42.

Storhoff, Gary. "'Opening the Hand of Thought': Eastern Meditation, Western Action in *Dr. King's Refrigerator and Other Stories*." Paper delivered at 42nd Western Literature Association Conference, Tacoma, WA, October 17–20, 2007.

Thomas, Brook. "The Legal Fictions of Herman Melville and Lemuel Shaw." *Critical Inquiry* 11, no. 1 (September 1984): 24–51.

Whalen-Bridge, John. "Waking Cain: The Poetics of Integration in Charles Johnson's *Dreamer*." *Callaloo* 26, no. 2 (Spring 2003): 504–21.

Part II

(II)Legal Violence

6

Lucy Terry

A Life of Radical Resistance

Sharon M. Harris

L ucy Terry (c. 1724–1821) is the first recorded African American poet in the United States. While her ballad "Bars Fight" was created to commemorate a battle in Deerfield, Massachusetts, during King George's War of 1744 to 1746, it should be read within multiple cultural contexts, including its place within African and American cultural traditions, its relation to Terry's longstanding engagement with colonial legal systems, and the popularity of political satire. By satirizing one of Euro-America's most popular genres—the Indian captivity narrative—Terry's poem stands at the forefront of a significant tradition in African American literary history, and it reveals one of the many ways in which enslaved peoples used coded language to challenge the system that enslaved them. To comprehend the complexities of "Bars Fight" in this context, we must examine the life that gave rise to the power to be one who critiques—to be one who, through bicultural play, turns the observers' gaze back on themselves—to be, perhaps, the subaltern who speaks.[1] As bell hooks has observed, the prevailing image of early African American female bodies is one of bondage and a lack of agency: "Rarely do we articulate a vision of resistance, of decolonizing that provides strategies for the construction of a liberatory black female body politics . . . Who among us when remembering 18th and 19th century representations of African American females can call to mind any visual representation of the body of a free black woman."[2] While Lucy Terry's physical likeness per se is unknown to us, her lifelong resistance to oppression may be a significant step toward reconfiguring our vision of black women's resistance.

Reinscribing Lucy Terry's Resistance

Knowledge of Lucy Terry's radical challenges to the dominant culture's devaluing of herself and her race expose and transgress eighteenth-century boundaries of domination and discourse. What becomes most evident is that Lucy Terry valued the power of voicing her opinions—of making her presence visible in a society that proscribed cultural invisibility for its enslaved members. Once freed, Terry repeatedly positioned herself—physically (bodily) as well as intellectually—in opposition to racist and sexist colonizing practices. An understanding of Terry's text will, therefore, be enhanced by first examining the personal and cultural contexts that figure her developing activism against contemporary racist practices.

Born in West Africa around 1724, Lucy Terry was kidnapped at a very young age and brought to Bristol, Rhode Island. Terry was first taken to Enfield, Connecticut, from Rhode Island, and her first master was Samuel Terry (1632–1730) of Enfield. With Samuel Terry's death in 1730, Lucy was apparently sold as part of the estate.[3] At the age of five or six, she became the property of a Deerfield slave master Ensign Ebenezer Wells (1691–1758), who held several civic positions in the town and a had high standing in the church. Being a slave owner increased rather than diminished Wells's standing in Deerfield, which, like all of Massachusetts Bay Colony's Puritan communities, relied largely upon property ownership for social and church status. During Lucy Terry's first years in Deerfield, the townspeople were actively involved in the Great Awakening revivals, and Lucy was baptized in Wells's church and, in 1744, became a member.[4] Later events suggest that one of Terry's greatest skills was using her religious training as a tool against the social and legal oppressions of the dominant culture.

On May 17, 1756, Terry married an older, property-owning, freed African American, Abijah Prince (1706–1794). Born in Wallingford, Connecticut, Abijah had been a slave to the Reverend Benjamin Doolittle; in 1717 he resettled in Northfield, Massachusetts, where Doolittle became the town's first minister. When Doolittle died in 1749, he apparently manumitted Abijah and willed to him some of his real estate rights.[5] While this grant may have been an act of kindness on the master's part, it was to a degree dictated by law. Throughout New England in the early eighteenth century, manumission had become a means of not having to support aging slaves. The practice became so common that most New England colonies passed laws requiring masters who manumitted a slave to prove that the slave could support himself or herself, and Massachusetts and Connecticut were the first colonies to do so, in 1703 and 1704, respectively. Two years after Doolittle's death, Abijah Prince was the owner of shares in three land divisions in the town. Although he apparently left Northfield for Deerfield around 1752, he retained his land there for the next thirty years.

For the first few years of their married life, the couple resided in Deerfield on land owned by Terry's master.[6] It is believed that Prince purchased Lucy Terry's freedom shortly after their marriage. In 1764, the Princes moved to Guilford, Vermont, where Abijah had inherited one hundred acres from Deacon Samuel Field, a friend and long-time supporter. Vermont was surely not an arbitrary choice of residence. The colony had long been recognized for an attitude of opposition to slavery. In the revolutionary years, it would be the first state to proclaim that all men were "entitled to life, liberty and happiness and that no person should serve another after he reaches maturity."[7] Abijah understood that property ownership was the primary means of maintaining his and his family's free status as well as the means of gaining recognition within the community. Therefore, in addition to owning the Northfield and Guildford properties, he petitioned King George III and the governor of New Hampshire to become one of the original grantees of Sunderland, Vermont. The request was granted, and he held equal shares with the other grantees in the divided lands,[8] with a total of three hundred acres in his name. Abijah thereby became one of the leading African American landowners in the colonies. Whereas extending property rights for African Americans was represented in Abijah's choices, Lucy chose the legal system as the landscape upon which she would manipulate the colonialist system on behalf of her family and her race.

Lucy Terry Prince had remarkable courage, and her oratorical talents served her particularly well in the social and legal disputes that subsequently arose. Three notable cases engaged her attention and demonstrate the means by which she sought to push the boundaries of rights for African Americans in New England during the early federal period. First, in 1785, Terry Prince spoke in a public forum, exposing white neighbors, Ormas and John Noyes, who destroyed the Princes' fences, set haystacks on fire, and threatened her family with violence in an attempt to remove Lucy and Abijah from their land. This was really Lucy's battle: Abijah was almost eighty years old and physically unable to take on the rigors of travel and court appearances. Lucy, however, was readily able. She traveled by horse across the state of Vermont to present her defense. Appearing before Governor Thomas Chittenden and his Council, Lucy Terry Prince asked for protection against racist persecution. On June 7, 1785—in spite of the Noyes family's wealth, leadership in the community, and racial advantage—the council ruled in Terry Prince's favor, ordering Guilford's selectmen to protect the Prince family and their property:

> On the Representation of Lucy Prince, wife of Abijah Prince, and others shewing that, the said Abijah, Lucy and Family, are greatly oppressed & injured by John and Ormas Noyce, in the possession and enjoyment of a certain farm or Piece of Land, on which the said Abijah and Lucy now Lives, the Council having Taken the same into consideration and made due enquiry, are of Opinion that the said Abijah and Lucy are much injured, and that unless the Town Take some due Methods to protect said Abijah, Lucy & family in the enjoyment of their possession, they must soon unavoidably fall upon the Charity of the Town.[9]

The Council therefore resolved that the town must "take some effectual Measures to protect the said Abijah, Lucy & Family, in the Possession of said Lands until the said dispute can be equally & equitably settled."[10] In this instance, it is clear the concern about having to support the black family if their land was usurped was as great a power in the Council's consideration as was Terry Prince's argument of injury by the Noyeses.

In 1793, Lucy Terry Prince again sought to push legal boundaries for African Americans. The Princes had six children, all of whom had been educated in Guilford's schools.[11] Terry Prince wanted her sons to have the same higher education opportunities as the other young men in the community. Thus, she applied for admission of her youngest son, Abijah, Jr., to Williams College in Williamstown, Massachusetts.[12] It was not a coincidence, surely, that Lucy Terry Prince chose Williams College for her son's application of admittance. The college was named in honor of Ephraim Williams, who had designated his estate for the founding of a liberal arts college. He was also second cousin of Rev. John Williams. Ephraim was captain of a company that had been raised in 1746 to invade Canada. Whether or not Abijah, Sr., was part of that specific company is unknown, but Ephraim

Williams's and Abijah Prince's names appear in the same military records during King George's War. Lucy Terry Prince might also have assumed that, because
her two eldest sons had served in the military during the American Revolution,
there was cause for consideration of her case, since many Euro-Americans used
military service as a basis for a variety of privileges after the war. When her son's
application was rejected, Terry Prince went before the college trustees, who had by
grant of the General Court the authority "to determine and prescribe the mode of
ascertaining the qualifications of the Students," and demanded the right to speak.[13]
One of the trustees was Elijah Williams, who had presided over the Princes' marriage in 1756; Terry Prince may well have expected support from her longtime
acquaintance. In an eloquent, three-hour speech, drawing on her knowledge of
law and scripture, Lucy Terry Prince argued on her son's behalf. She did not succeed in gaining admittance to Williams College for Abijah, Jr., but she did expose
the legal and religious hypocrisies of the community in a lengthy and articulate
public examination.

In her third public battle, in May 1796,[14] Lucy Terry Prince was successful. The
Princes' homestead was in the Batten Kill area of Sunderland, across a small creek
from the home of Colonel Ethan Allen, famous as the leader of the Green Mountain Boys and a Revolutionary War hero. One of their nearer neighbors, however,
was Colonel Eli Bronson, whose property abutted the Princes' land. Bronson had
attempted to steal a lot owned by the Princes, going so far as to extend his fences
around the disputed area. Over seventy years of age and widowed, Terry Prince
fought to retain the property, this time taking her case all the way to the U.S. Circuit Court for the District of Vermont. The Honorable Samuel Chase of Maryland
presided over the hearing at Bennington. Two leading Vermont attorneys, Stephen
R. Bradley and Royall Tyler (the playwright, who would become Vermont's Chief
Justice in 1807), defended Colonel Bronson. Although Terry Prince was advised by
Isaac Tichenor, a well-known lawyer and later a governor of Vermont, she chose to
argue the case on her own behalf.[15] Deciding in Terry Prince's favor, Judge Chase
observed of her defense that she had "made a better argument than he had heard
from any lawyer at the Vermont bar."[16]

While Terry's legal actions always reflected her commitment to property rights
for African Americans, the last case also reflects the complex situation of being a
widow if her property were seized and taken from her. Without property, women—
and especially women of color—were left in a precarious legal vacuum. Towns
were often unwilling to allow women to live in the community unless they owned
property or had evident financial support from male relatives. The act of "warning out" transients (i.e., warning them that they must leave a community or be
removed by local authorities) was well established by the time of Terry's court case.
But "transient" had a specific legal meaning in the eighteenth century: rather than
today's definition of homeless vagrants, "transient" in Lucy Terry's time meant "a
person who had been living in a town but had not become a legal inhabitant of
that town. Inhabitants had rights and privileges; transients, however, remained in
residence only by the permission of town leaders."[17] Terry's family had already seen
in their first legal battle the concerns of town leaders about having to support a
black family. In 1796, as a widow, her position was even more uncertain unless she
retained rights to her property, since "transient" did not allude only to people new

to a town. As Ruth Wallis Herndon has noted, however, "transient" also took on the connotation of "undesirable," and racial identity became a notable determiner in who was warned out in an era that saw a significant increase in the number of free African Americans due to processes of personal or state emancipations.[18] Whereas unmarried white women were those most often warned out, a woman of color often faced more harsh interpretations of her acceptability. Certainly many white citizens found Lucy Terry's continual outspokenness and legal challenges "disorderly" and "improper" for a black woman; thus, maintaining her property rights was a necessity for her survival.

Little is known about the remainder of Lucy Terry's life. Between 1757 and 1769, she had given birth to six children. Though they retained their Sunderland property, in later years Lucy and Abijah had returned to Guilford, where Abijah died in 1794. Lucy remained in Guilford until 1803, thereafter returning to Sunderland. Painful ironies reflect the increased opposition to racial equality in the early nineteenth century. In her late seventies, after almost a decade of struggling on her own to retain the family property and the rights she felt were inherent to *all* citizens of the new nation, Lucy Terry lost the farm which she and Abijah had established in 1764[19]—the purchasers were the Noyeses, whom she had defeated in their earlier legal battle over the land. Further, as William Loren Katz has observed, "It is one more of history's ironies that in 1821, the year of her death, the legislature of the state of Massachusetts established a committee to determine whether it ought to pass a law expelling black emigrants."[20]

Lucy Terry died in 1821 at the approximate age of ninety-seven. An obituary in *The Vermont Gazette* noted, "In this remarkable woman there was an assemblage of qualities rarely to be found among her sex. Her volubility was exceeded by none, and in general the fluency of her speech captivated all around her . . . All considered her a prodigy in conversation . . . Her knowledge of the scriptures was uncommonly great."[21] The obituary ended, appropriately, with a poem. Significantly, the poem's conclusion honors Lucy Terry by challenging the scientific racialism of the era:

> How long must Etheaopia's murder'd race
> Be doom'd by men to bondage & disgrace?
> And hear such taunting insolence from those
> "We have a fairer *skin* and *sharper nose*?"
> Their sable mother took her rapt'rous flight,
> High orb'd amidst the realms of endless flight:
> The haughty boaster sinks beneath her feet,
> Where vaunting tyrants & oppressors meet.[22]

Three major cultural contexts converge to explain how Lucy Terry came to produce her satirical poem about Euro-Americans being taken captive in a raid on Deerfield: first, the complicated history of colonialist and Native American relations in the Deerfield region; second, the popularity of Indian captivity narratives at the time of King George's War and especially in Deerfield, where one of the bestselling narratives had been written; and third, the system of slavery that supported the colonialists' plantations in Deerfield.

The First Cultural Context: Native and European Relations

In the precolonial period, the Pocumtuck Confederacy dominated the Connecticut Valley; their settlement encompassed the highly arable land at the conjunction of the Connecticut and Deerfield Rivers. For several decades after the arrival of European colonialists, relations between the various Native American and European groups in the area were relatively peaceful and productive. Although the Pocumtucks were trading corn with the colonialists as early as the mid-1630s, there were, even then, increasing restrictions made on trading that were intended to insure the settlers could best benefit from raising and selling corn. Relations became further strained with the outbreak of war. The Narragansetts, the Mohawks, and other tribal societies became increasingly involved in conflicts with the Pocumtucks, and colonialists' conflicts were often at the heart of seeming native disputes. Colonialists in the Deerfield region reneged on their friendly terms with the Pocumtucks as early as the 1660s. When the English gained the Dutch province of New Netherland in 1664, their negotiations with the Mohawks included assurances they would not assist the Abenakis or the Pocumtucks in any wars against the Mohawks. Thus, Deerfield settlers who had once been the Pocumtucks' business patrons and generally companionable neighbors refused to intervene when the Mohawks advanced upon the Deerfield clans in 1665. As one historian records, "After burning the fort and wigwams, and laying waste the cornfields of the Pocumtucks, the victors swept northward" to where the other clans of the Confederacy resided and enacted similar devastation there.[23] Colonialists recognized the opportunity in this moment of desolation and offered to buy the Pocumtucks' land.

By the 1740s, when Lucy Terry was enslaved in Deerfield, numerous battles had been fought between Native Americans and settlers in the region, not only during King Philip's War (1675–76), but also during the numerous "French and Indian" wars: King William's War (1688–97), with attacks on Deerfield every year from 1693 through 1696; Queen Anne's War (1702–1713), during which Rev. John Williams was taken captive; and "Father Rasle's" or "Grey Lock's War" in the 1720s. Although the 1746 attack during King George's War that Terry recounts in "Bars Fight" was the last of its kind, Deerfield had been the site of thirty battles between Native Americans and colonialists by that date. To understand the opposing communities and their reactions, we must understand the region as evolving within a war culture and a war mentality.

Like so many other conflicts in the colonies, King George's War was actually between European powers, but it was played out on New England soil. With the Austrian succession the focal point of English and Spanish hostilities, France sought this moment to engage her old nemesis, England, in war once again. The impact reverberated across the "New World" landscape, from Nova Scotia to the New England region. In preparation for war, mounts (tower lookouts) were built at several sites in Deerfield to defend against attacks from the French and their Native American allies. At a town meeting on May 21, 1744, the positioning of mounts was determined and included one such mount placed at the home of Lucy Terry's master. Scouting parties were under the charge of Captain Elijah Williams, son of Rev. John Williams and later the justice of the peace who married Lucy Terry and Abijah Prince, and Abijah was a member of the militia.

In 1746, a local militia from the region, led by Captain Ephraim Williams (who would become founder of Williams College), failed in an attempt to invade French Canada. Perhaps in retaliation or as already planned, a group of several hundred French, Mohawks, and Abenakis descended into the Connecticut Valley. Fort Massachusetts fell on August 19th. The community of Deerfield seems not to have heard of the fall of the fort, and that lack of information left them ill-prepared for the party of Native Americans that attacked Deerfield on August 25, 1746. It was this raid that Lucy Terry depicted in "Bars Fight."

The Second Cultural Context: The Captivity Narrative in Deerfield Local Mythology

Captivity narratives depended on national conflict, colonizers and resisters, and challenges to a dominant culture's values; they are cultural narratives shaped by and against which legal discourse was developed. To assert that Lucy Terry's "Bars Fight" is a satire of Euro-American captivity experiences requires evidence that she had access to the narratives of captivity that flourished in her era. There has been some debate as to whether or not Terry was literate, and my own belief is that she was.[24] No laws in Massachusetts forbade teaching slaves to read and write, and in an agrarian community, it is likely that slaves received at least the rudiments of a practical education. Even if she were nonliterate, however, Terry would easily have had access to the captivity narrative tradition. The long history of confrontations between Native Americans and the colonialists in Massachusetts from the 1690s through the mid-eighteenth century made captivity both a fact and a prominent fear among the early settlers. As Kathryn Zabelle Derounian-Stodola and James Levernier have documented, narratives about captivity were "interwoven into the fabric of early American culture."[25] Equally significant in relation to Lucy Terry is the fact that one of the most popular captivity narratives of the eighteenth century was written and published by a minister from Deerfield.

Rev. John Williams's *The Redeemed Captive, Returning to Zion* (1707) sold an estimated one thousand copies during its first week of publication and went through at least eleven editions.[26] Williams, most of his family, and several other residents of Deerfield had been taken captive in 1704. With the requisite graphic denouncement of surprise attacks, deaths, and kidnappings, Williams recounts the raid on Deerfield and admonishes watchmen who failed to see the oncoming attack of "the enemy . . . with painted faces and hideous exclamations."[27] The admonishment to the watchmen and the horrifying sense of invasion, coupled with graphic accounts of the murder of several residents (including Williams' spouse, Eunice Mather Williams, and two of their children) were also the bywords of numerous sermons delivered in the churches of Deerfield over several decades.[28] As a member of the Puritan church, Lucy Terry would have been exposed to many such sermons during her decade of attendance before the 1746 raid. John Williams died before Lucy was brought to Deerfield, but his legacy remained an integral element in the community's history, its sense of itself, and its mission. As an expansionist, he had profited highly from the colonialist incursion into Native American territories even after his captivity. On May 28, 1712, for instance, his petition requesting that the bounds of the town be extended nine miles westward was granted, which gave Williams and his heirs rights in perpetuity to rich farmland along the Connecticut River that had originally been the site of the Pocumtucks' village.[29]

The sermons of Williams's successor, the Rev. Jonathan Ashley, suggest that his attitudes toward Native Americans were compatible with those of Williams. What Lucy Terry heard in the sermons and captivity narratives was the colonialists' mythologizing of the Native American as savage and the inhabitants of the devil's domain.[30] The subject position taken by these Euro-Americans must have struck an intelligent woman like Terry as particularly ironic, considering her own history of being kidnapped and brought into slavery in a strange land.

The Third Cultural Context: Slavery in Deerfield

The first recorded account of slavery in Deerfield is found in John Williams's family register, where he noted the death of one of his slaves, Robert Tigo, on May 11, 1695.[31] At the time of the 1746 attack, the population of the town was about three hundred white settlers, and town records identify forty-seven African Americans who lived in Deerfield in the eighteenth century.[32] As in the South, field work was the primary labor of male slaves in Deerfield and, to large extent, of the white settlers as well since the community depended upon the productivity of the common fields for their survival. The women slaves worked in the fields, but they were also taught to spin and weave. Both Lucy Terry's and Abijah Prince's labor was used on occasion after their marriage to pay off accounts with the merchant Dr. Thomas Williams, and Abijah occasionally hired slave labor to work his farm.[33]

While slaves were baptized and admitted to fellowship in the church, there was no assertion that even converted African Americans were equal—legally, politically, or spiritually. The most notable account of Puritans' attitudes toward slaves is recorded by Terry's minister, Jonathan Ashley, in a 1749 lecture he delivered to African Americans in the community. While asserting that there were no human beings "too low and Dispicable for God to bestow salvation upon," Ashley made it clear that, for slaves, freedom was strictly a proposition for the next world. Basing his text on 1 Corinthians 7:22, he outlined his argument by first demonstrating "that Christianity allows of the relation of master & servants" and then declaring "that Such as are by Divine providence placed in the state of Servants are not excluded from salvation but may become the Lord's freemen."[34] Ashley may have chosen to give this sermon only days after preaching the funeral sermon for the Rev. Benjamin Doolittle because of the legal manumission of Abijah Prince upon Doolittle's death.[35] Clearly, Ashley sought to quell any thoughts of freedom in this life for the enslaved "servants" of Deerfield.[36]

Conjuring Subjectivity

The three cultural contexts detailed above, all of which are implicated in the legal and social colonizing practices of New England Puritans, are necessarily shaped by the patriarchal and androcentric nature of Puritanism itself. There were, however, two other major figures—each, if diversely, matriarchal and gynocentric—that offered themselves to Lucy Terry as models of resistance to the dominant culture.

One model was Eunice Williams, a Euro-American woman born into a privileged colonialist family in Deerfield; the other model was Jinny Cole, an African American enslaved woman whose position was culturally deprivileged. Each woman established a location of identity that allowed her to resist the oppressive nature of Puritanism. The Euro-American woman's resistance was, ironically, borne of the same acculturation process that the African American woman resisted, but Williams's acculturation was into a cultural site that the Puritans desperately sought to eradicate. In that uncommon alliance Eunice Williams and Jinny Cole each became touchstones for Lucy Terry's own evolving resistance.

Eunice Williams was seven years old when she was taken captive in the same raid as her father, Rev. John Williams. Her acceptance of Jesuit and Native American cultures presented a particularly threatening example of the possible "corruption" of the Puritan "errand in the wilderness." She was separated from her father and taken to the Mission de St. François Xavier du Sault St. Louis, a Kahnawake Mohawk fort. Within two years Eunice had become immersed in Kahnawake culture and forgotten her native language. The Kahnawake culture was a welcoming environment for females, as the society was matrilocal, matrilineal, and matrifocal.[37] Further, it was a culture renowned for its indulgence of children. Nothing could have been more different than Eunice's first seven years in a Puritan community where the raising of children was extremely strict and females were subservient to males. Eunice soon asserted that she did not want to return to her birth community. Certainly, religious and civic acculturation played a powerful role in her decision, but processes of acculturation speak powerfully about a community. For Eunice and dozens of other captives who followed similar patterns of remaining with their Native American captors and marrying into the community, it was a process of acceptance by the dominant culture. It was a strikingly different process than the Puritans' acculturation practices that demanded Native and African Americans accept positions of inferiority.

At the age of sixteen, Eunice married François Xavier Arosen, a Kahnawake Mohawk.[38] Shocked by the marriage, members of the Williams family journeyed several times to Canada and sought to encourage Eunice to return to Deerfield; in each instance, she refused. She further made her refusal explicit to her birth community by visiting the region three times in the 1740s, during which she set strict conditions that no one would detain her. The continual reappearance of Eunice Williams in the Deerfield community—while at the same time refusing to be reassimilated—made her a particularly visible reminder of the Puritans' failure. Of notable significance to Lucy Terry's perspective would have been Eunice's third visit from September 1743 through March 1744, two years before Terry produced "Bars Fight." Sermons preached during this visit explicitly linked slavery and captivity. One sermon, dedicated to Eunice who was in the audience, asserted, "When you think with Pity on the Slavery, Captivity, and mean State of this Person, whom you see here . . . remember that if you are without christ you are in a State of Slavery to sin."[39] If the Puritan community's sense of Williams was, as a memorial plaque asserts, that she "married a Savage and became one,"[40] "Bars Fight" reveals that Lucy Terry read the "text" of the community's conflation of slavery and captivity as ironic.

There was, however, an even greater influence on Lucy Terry than the actions of the masters. Within slave communities the sense of African pride and the valuing of African traditions endured through song, crafts, and terminologies that were assimilated into the customs of colonial America. In the case of Lucy Terry, however, she had the firsthand knowledge of an African woman, the enslaved Jinny Cole, as an example of the pride and customs that could be retained against the onslaught of oppression in the Puritan community.[41] Cole (c. 1723–1808) was born in Africa and lived there until she was nearly twelve years old, when she and several other children were kidnapped and brought to Boston to be auctioned into slavery. Her first owner is unknown, but in 1738 or 1739 she and her infant son, Cato, were purchased by Rev. Jonathan Ashley and brought to Deerfield. Jinny remained a slave for the Ashley family through at least three generations, covering a seventy-year period. She died on September 1, 1808, having broken her neck when she fell down the cellar stairs at a neighbor's house. Jinny Cole and Lucy Terry's lives in this small community overlapped for a twenty-year period.

Within the slave community, Jinny Cole was known as a powerful storyteller. She told of her early years in Guinea, of her position as the daughter of a king, and the richness of the culture in her homeland. Throughout her lifetime, Cole recounted the terrible wrongs that had been done to her and her people when they were kidnapped and brought into slavery. She insisted that one day (through her own actions or through death), she would be returned to Africa. In such an assertion, Cole reveals her familiarity with African folk–spiritual traditions that figure freedom from slavery as a return "home," whether that locale was Africa or heaven.[42]

Cole also amassed a collection of artifacts that seemed peculiar to her white neighbors. The historian George Sheldon, who knew Cole's son as a child, recounted that Jinny collected "all kinds of odds and ends, colored rags, bits of finery, peculiar shaped stones, shells, buttons, beads, *anything* she could *string*."[43] Though an abolitionist, Sheldon's assessment of this practice must be read within his colonizing lens of African "primitivism"; Cole's actions are, in fact, informed by African cultural practices, especially those that were enacted by the griot, or *dyeli*. The *dyeli* were a social group of particular West African peoples, recognized as professionals who specialized in music and oral traditions and were part of the larger *nyamakala*, professionals specializing in jewelry making, blacksmithing, music, and other artistries.[44] As a means of replicating former communal practices, Cole's gathering and stringing of colorful scraps conjures a site for memorializing her heritage as well as for mourning her cultural loss—the same results that are achieved in Lucy Terry's "piecing together" of the events of August 25th in order to dislocate the privileged status of white captivity. Jinny Cole represents a recognized component of the captive-exchange system that marks the economic basis of slavery and other forms of captivity. That is, she transcends her designated subordinate status by demonstrating unusual skills developed during the cross-cultural experience.[45] While exceptional carpentry, cooking, and other trade skills have long been understood as means by which slaves might transcend the usual brutalities of slave existence—sometimes even the means of attaining their freedom—Cole's (and later Terry's) storytelling skills were the means of exploiting the system to her own advantage, much as oratorical skills were, decades later, for Frederick Douglass.

Perhaps most important to Lucy Terry's own artistic development, Jinny Cole's stories repeatedly conveyed her horror and anger at having been kidnapped and brought to a strange country. She detailed the comfort and safety of her African home until the fateful day when she and several other children were playing near a well. Without warning, they were seized by white slave traders and immediately taken aboard the slave ship. Significantly, Jinny always concluded her story of being taken captive with the lament that the children never again saw their mothers. It is as much this image as that of "Young Samuel Allen" that impacts the conclusion of Lucy Terry's poem. Part of the discourse of imperialism is the assertion that colonization leads to assimilation and thus the perpetuation and expansion of the dominant culture. Certainly the experience of colonization necessarily alters the colonized (and the colonizers), but alteration is not always fully enacted as assimilation, and fractures of resistance are evident in any systemic representation of the imperialist/colonialist project. Jinny Cole represents one such fracture in the U.S. colonization of Africans. Her stories may well have acted as Lucy Terry's own restoration to knowledge about her West African traditions.[46]

"Bars Fight"

Once freed, Lucy Terry repeatedly and publicly positioned herself in opposition to racist colonizing practices, especially those maintained through the legal systems of colonial America. "Bars Fight" suggests that even while enslaved, Terry had begun her acts of resistance. The twenty-eight-line poem, stylized in the folk ballad tradition, acts as a satire of Euro-American colonialists' lamentations about "Indian captivity." Terry's insistence upon concluding rather than beginning the poem with "Young Samuel Allen" being carried away to Canada subverts the captivity narrative tradition. This technique and the satirical nature of the poem (which has heads rolling away from bodies and petticoats tripping up fleeing females), in fact, exposes, as all good satire does, a very serious theme: for African Americans, who had endured more than a century of enslavement by the time of the 1746 raid, there could be no *overt* narrative lamenting their captivity.

Folk ballads had a long history in African cultures, and in the eighteenth century they were becoming increasingly popular in the North American colonies. Folk ballads typically focused on one striking episode in a culture's history. With few exceptions, studies of the captivity narrative have excluded slave narratives. Each genre has emerged in recent scholarship as a highly codified, immensely popular, and culturally powerful genre, but to separate these genres risks the danger of erasing African Americans from both the discourse of captivity and from conceptions of historical identity. Whereas the captivity narrative is recognized as a community-binding and colonist-aggrandizing document, the slave narrative has often been represented as the achievements of an individual. In a discussion about neoslave narratives that holds significance for earlier narratives as well, John Edgar Wideman has argued that focusing on narratives that privilege one black individual removes that person from "the idea of a collective, intertwined fate," and thus "the mechanisms of class, race, and gender we have inherited are perpetuated ironically by a genre purporting to illustrate the possibility of breaking barriers and transcending the conditions into which one is born."[47] By positioning the two genres in relation to one another, we can begin to examine precisely those legal and cultural structures that support the status quo—and our own critical practices. This latter point is worth pursuing. Why, for instance, was there such a resurgence of interest in Euro-American captivity narratives in the 1990s? Certainly the best scholars of the genre are examining the displacement of the Native American through these narratives,[48] but the emphasis upon a genre that is largely produced by one race to oppress and justify the destruction of another deserves further interrogation. So, too, have scholars of slave narratives highlighted the necessity of Christian conversion and white authorization of these texts. Frances Smith Foster has recognized that "by assuming the role of historiographer without acknowledging this as an unusual position for one of her sex, race, and class, Terry is using silence to amplify her message" in "Bars Fight."[49] I would add that by recognizing the silenced story as part of the satirization of the dominant culture's popular genre, we can better understand the significance of Terry's poem. In part, the separation of the captivity narrative and slave narrative genres also reflects the shift that Foucault highlighted in his study of the political anatomy's move in the eighteenth century from an exercising of power through overt torture to the "discipline" of suppression. The effectiveness of this panoptic system relies upon its diffusion in a "multiple, polyvalent way throughout the whole social body."[50] The very "invisibility" of the slave system was rooted in its acceptance in early Euro-American culture, to the extent that slaveholders could lament the captivity of a white citizen without seeing a correlation between that event and their own political and social systems of slave captivity. Mary Louise Pratt reminds us that the critique of empire is not new; it was "coded ongoingly on the spot, in ceremony, dance, parody, philosophy, counterknowledge and counterhistory, in texts unwitnessed, [or] suppressed."[51] The satire of Lucy Terry's poem deserves witnessing.

Terry's intellect and courage served her well throughout her legal battles in the early federal period, but as Josiah Holland recorded in the nineteenth century, Terry was recognized especially "for her wit and shrewdness."[52] Eileen Southern has discerned that "After gaining her own freedom, [Terry] made her home a gathering place for slaves and freedmen of the community; a place where they could listen to tales and songs of old Africa."[53] As African American scholars have long noted, satiric wit is often misread by the white community as complacency or as the acceptance of the dominant culture's values. Captivity narratives were cultural scripts that reinforced white supremacy, patriarchal values, and cultural hegemony. Terry's poem, like her life, disrupts that script.

Even the title of the poem reflects contested cultural space. The usual gloss of "bars" is simply "meadows," but in Deerfield its meaning was much more specific. One of the most frequent issues of legislation created by the early settlers of Deerfield was the fencing of the meadow lands where their crops were produced, and both of Terry's later court cases centered on issues of the illegal fencing of property. Each family's section was fenced separately, and, in the 1660s, gates were built at all roads leading into the meadows, except in the South Meadows where a set of bars was placed. The bars soon became the local name for that particular section of the meadows. By Terry's time the southern part of the Bars had also come to be associated with colonialists' attitudes toward Native Americans with the use of diminishing terms for subsections such as "Indian Hole" and "Squaw Hill." Thus, the title of Terry's poem not only relates to the events of 1746 but recalls the long history of battles over contested cultural space in Deerfield and in the colonies.

Like many folk ballads, "Bars Fight" is rooted in factual events. The raid on Deerfield occurred within days after the fall of Fort Massachusetts. Unaware of that event, a party of haymakers set out for a day's work in the Bars on August 25th. Among the group were Samuel Allen (44), and his children Eunice (13), Caleb (9), and Samuel (8). Also included in the party were young Oliver (18) and Simeon (9) Amsden and three other men—John Saddler and Adonijah Gillett, soldiers whose job it was to guard the workers during wartime, and Eleazar Hawks, who was Samuel Allen's brother-in-law. Hawks made the fateful mistake of heading off for partridge hunting in a thicket that bordered the Bars, for it was there that the war party was hiding. Hawks was killed outright, Allen killed one Native American before he and Adonijah Gillett were slain. Oliver Amsden was killed, scalped, and decapitated; and Samuel Allen was indeed captured and taken to St. François, Quebec—notably the same site where Eunice Williams was taken in 1704. Only Caleb Amsden and John Saddler escaped without injury; Caleb hid in a corn field, and Saddler escaped across the river to a nearby island. Eunice Allen's fate is graphically rendered, in true captivity narrative tradition, by Sheldon: "Eunice was the last to be overtaken, but finally an Indian split her skull with his hatchet and left her for dead, not stopping, however, in his haste, to secure her scalp. Eunice survived the blow for seventy-two years, but she never fully recovered."[54]

For all of its attention to the "factual" details of the raid, the construction of Terry's poem relies less on the facts than on their impact. Most important, however, is Terry's double-voiced presence, as she speaks to the colonialists and African American audiences in decidedly different ways within a single poem. The first fourteen lines follow the traditional captivity narrative's lamentations over the violence of "Indian raids" and the heroic endeavors of the white citizenry under attack:

August 'twas the twenty-fifth,
Seventeen hundred forty-six;
The Indians did in ambush lay,
Some very valient men to slay,

The names of whom I'll not leave out.
Samuel Allen like a hero fout.
And though he was so brave and bold,
His face no more shall we behold.
Eleazar Hawks was killed outright,

Before he had time to fight,—
Before he did the Indians see,
Was shot and killed immediately.
Oliver Amsden he was slain,
Which caused his friends much grief and pain.

The seeming honor paid to colonists undoubtedly endeared the poem to the Euro-American residents of Deerfield over the next several generations. Yet, while the collective nature of community—so important in traditional captivity narratives to reestablishing the dominant power relations—is suggested in "His face no more shall *we* behold," the narrative "I" locates the unspoken third race in the poem—that is, the African American speaker. The noncollective sense of community responses is figured in line 14 when it is Oliver Amsden's *friends* (not the narrative "I" nor the collective "we") who lament his loss.

In the subsequent fourteen lines, Terry's double-voiced discourse, rendered through her wit, further jars the critical reader's participation in these lamentations with scenes that are grotesquely and uncomfortably comic, and the satire may explain why the poem was equally popular with generations of African Americans:

> Simeon Amsden they found dead,
> Not many rods distant from his head.
> Adonijah Gillett we do hear
> Did lose his life which was so dear.
> John Sadler fled across the water,
>
> And thus escaped the dreadful slaughter.
> Eunice Allen see the Indians coming,
> And hopes to save herself by running,
> And had not her petticoats stopped her,
> The awful creatures had not catched her,
>
> Nor tommy hawked her on her head,
> And left her on the ground for dead.
> Young Samuel Allen, Oh lack-a-day!
> Was taken and carried to Canada.

The reader or listener is apt to feel an impulse to laugh, however uncomfortably, at the grisly image of Simeon Amsden's head rolling away from his body; the rhythmic cadence and the poem's sudden shift to shock value invites such a response and immediately raises questions about the seriousness of the lamentation. This is true if one reads the poem with a satiric tone; if then read as a monody, the poem's dual possibilities of interpretation become more evident. In other words, audience and choice of tone create the ambiguity necessary to any slave's use of satire. In 1746, all residents of Deerfield would also have recognized the satiric jab taken at John Saddler, a soldier who was stationed there to protect the Deerfield residents but who, under attack, saved himself.

It is Terry's rendering of the tragic fate of Eunice Allen, emphasizing female clothing as what quite literally trips her up, that marks one of the sites in the poem where bicultural subterfuge is most brilliantly played out. Women's fashions have been a topic of cultural satire since the beginnings of early U.S. literature. Sewing and the preparation of clothing was a major part of women's work in Deerfield. One of the reasons fashion and clothing cannot be understood in a simple context of national identity, however, is that the very representations often exclude as much as they include. It is doubtful that Deerfield slaves were as scantily clothed as were many of their counterparts on southern plantations, but it is also unlikely they were afforded the same amount or quality of attire as their masters. Eunice Williams had also made clothing an issue during her 1743 return when she outraged the community by refusing to change from Kahnewake to Anglo clothing, even when attending church services. It has been asserted that clothing constitutes "the quintessential colonizing commodity,"[55] and, significantly, the reference to tripping on petticoats is the one nonfactual addition to the historical details that Terry makes in the poem. When subversive allusions are the only discursive option for the oppressed, what better means than to use the petticoats, which may well have been produced by slave labor, as a point of satire. Through her first name and by emphasizing clothing, Eunice Allen conjures Eunice Williams and the concluding sense of community failure rather than heroics.

Other elements of the poem are more subtle in their interpretive possibilities, but if we grant Terry the same consciousness of artistry that is typically afforded her Euro-American contemporaries and which is noted in every account of her by the people who knew her, there is much more bicultural play at work in the poem than has been acknowledged. For instance, it contains several references to water and passages across water. John Williams had used water similes to recount his captivity (e.g., "the enemy came in like a flood upon us"). "Bars," in one sense of the word, is specific to the Deerfield common-field system, but in a Puritan community, it may also have carried other implications. Many Deerfield residents had originally come from the seafaring coastal towns of the northeast, and the term may also reference the colloquial term for a submerged sand bank along a shoreline that often obstructs navigation and phrases such as "crossing the bar" have long been a part of maritime songs. This dual reading of "bars" is supported by the later reference to John Sadler's escape "across the water." While he escaped, unheroically, the others were barred from doing so by the attacking enemy. Several scholars have studied the impact on the early Puritans' collective consciousness of their treacherous passage across the Atlantic.[56] For people like Terry and Cole who had seen "the dreadful slaughter" of so many acquaintances brought to America via the Middle Passage slave trade, these images carried equally complex and enduring meanings.

So, too, is the act of an ambush emphasized by the reference to Eunice Allen's being "tommy hawked" by those lying in wait. But "tommy hawked" also implicates Eleazar *Hawks*, who wandered off into the thicket; he is left in poetic ambiguity as both the victim of his mistake and, ironically, the instigator of the attack. The "master" of events, the colonialist invader, is thereby implicated in the actions of his own making. Equally ambiguous is the narrator's reaction to the invaders of August 25th. As "awful creatures," they are both terrible in their horrific actions but, in good Puritan linguistic doubleness, "awe-ful" or creating a moment full of awe. What results in all of these moments of poetic ambiguity is an inability to identify who is guilty and who is victim. As William Andrews argues, in African American writing, "'simplicity' suggests a rhetorical technique open to black narrators of white-controlled texts—narrative diversion as a way of making an injustice tellable even when it is not correctable."[57] Like many slave songs that could be "read" by a white audience as harmless, the underlying meanings in "Bars Fight" dislocate significations and allow for multiple interpretations.

The most damning element of "Bars Fight," however, is the last couplet: "Young Samuel Allen, Oh lack-a-day! / Was taken and carried to Canada."[58] Euro-American women's narratives dominate the documented captivity experiences. Their narratives have one strikingly common element: they "stress that captivity's main metonymy was the dramatic and decisive fracturing of the original family unit."[59]

Terry's emphasis on the disintegration of the Allen family follows this pattern—with one significant difference. In Euro-American women's narratives the figure of the mother predominates. Mary Rowlandson emphasized her role as mother, carrying her wounded child, in the opening pages of her classic narrative. Even when the captive was male, he was often described in relation to his mother; for example, an account of the Deerfield captive John Catlin, age seventeen when he was captured, begins by describing him as "born in the 50th year of his mother's age."[60] Eunice Williams also made the issue of her mother one of the points of resistance to communicating with her father. After her marriage, while the surviving family members were still attempting to induce her to return, her spouse told their emissary, "had her father not Married again, She would have gone and Seen him long Ere this time."[61] Lucy Terry exploits this convention by focusing on the consequences of fractured families at the conclusion of her poem, but, significantly, she leaves the situation unresolved. The image of the child kidnapped and taken to a strange land not only recalls Samuel Allen's *and* Eunice Williams' fate but also replicates the conclusions of Jinny Cole's stories, which always ended with the lamentation that she and the other kidnapped African children never again saw their mothers.

Conclusion

Both Annette Kolodny and John Sekora have remarked on the fact that the first published African American slave narrative, Briton Hammon's 1760 text, was in fact an Indian captivity narrative that "dared not protest that most pernicious of captivities, chattel slavery."[62] Hammon's text, Kolodny asserts, "cries out against 'horrid cruelty and inhuman Barbarity,' even if its apparent target is a native tribe."[63] Produced fourteen years earlier, Terry's poem engages the same context. Again, John Saillant has astutely argued that Lemuel Haynes (who preached at Terry's funeral) also used the discursive elements of the Puritan captivity narrative in his text about two imprisoned men, *Mystery Developed* (1820). Haynes "merged the language of the captivity narrative with the language of slavery and emancipation" by inverting the "nature of the captors . . . in Haynes's captivity narrative the captors are representations of white society and executors of its laws."[64] Thus, reading Lucy Terry's poem not as an anachronism but as an appropriation of the Puritan captivity–narrative form in order to critique American slavery places her at the forefront of a significant tradition of resistance in African American literature and links her literary efforts to her challenges to the codification of racial difference in the colonial legal system.

These captivity texts by African Americans are best understood as autoethnographic expressions. In such expressions, the "colonized subjects undertake to represent themselves in ways that *engage with* the colonizer's own terms"; the autoethnographic text "involves partial collaboration with and appropriation of the idioms of the conqueror."[65] As a slave, Lucy Terry lacked the opportunity she would find when, during her freedom, she filed legal cases that remarked overtly upon her own condition; but as the "unspoken" third race in her text, African Americans and their enslavement are clearly marked within the cultural context of the poem. The third and perhaps most requisite stage of the traditional, Anglo-American captivity narrative was restoration: after the brutal moment of captivity and after having endured much hardship, religious captives inevitably asserted the necessity of faith and of adherence to a particular religion's tenets in their comments on restoration to their own communities. Equally important is the effect of the restoration scene that eclipses the sense of the loss of power that captivity has enacted on the community as a whole. John Williams's *Redeemed Captive* was intended to be as much a community restorative as it was to be an individual return. After Deerfield had "gained notoriety throughout New England" for its destruction in the Bloody Brook massacre of 1675 and again in the 1704 raid in which nearly three-fifths of the locals had been killed or captured,[66] Williams's narrative was a necessary antidote to communal defamation. Through the process of "describing and interpreting the experience of captivity, the [returned] captive reverses—after the fact—the 'national' power relations between 'savage' and 'civilized' that imprisonment has temporarily reversed."[67] The standard narrative-closure process of captivity narratives restores the power relations of white dominance.

In "Bars Fight," however, the Native American is not "captured" in the narrative and thus tamed by the dominant culture nor is the white captive restored to his position of racial and cultural dominance. By denying this traditional act of closure in her poetic account, Terry leaves the community as a whole in material and discursive disruption. What Terry's satire of colonialists' lamentations of captivity erases is any assertion that providential design can be read through the events of August 25th. Only the colonialists' own actions and reactions lead to rolling heads and disastrous entanglements with petticoats. The ending couplet of "Bars Fight" emphasizes the experience of being brutally abducted from one's homeland and taken to a strange environment. The "unspoken" subject position echoes throughout this abrupt conclusion: for the African American captive, there could be no requisite, climatic rendering of restoration. For well over a century, Africans had been enslaved in an alien environment with no hope of restoration and no praise for endurance. The bitingly understated "Oh lack-a-day!" culminates Terry's satirization of the white culture's genre of self-absorption—a self-absorption that allowed them to ignore the parallels between the fate of Young Samuel Allen and the hundreds of thousands of Africans enslaved in early America.

Lucy Terry's bicultural play with genre and diction is revolutionary in the sense in which Eric Cheyfitz uses the term. That is, a colonized person can "master" the dominant language in order to explode or expose the colonizer's position of power. "In the revolutionary situation," Cheyfitz argues, the colonized individual "does not so much master the master's language as take possession of it."[68] Terry's use of satire pushes the revolutionary gesture even further: she exposes not only the colonialists' power but also the limitations of that power. Against the discourse of scientific racialism, then, Terry posits the ability of African Americans to grasp the dominant culture's language and to use it to expose the masters' shortsightedness and, ironically, lack of reasoning. Lucy Terry's life of radical resistance through poetry and the courts needs to be acknowledged in our constructions of the struggle for cultural identities and resistance to the dominant culture's racism. After all, if the colonized person has greater knowledge than the colonizer—in this instance, a more complex understanding of captivity—who is captive and of what system?

Notes

This is a significantly revised version of a chapter that appeared in my book *Executing Race*.

1. African American feminist scholars have been the vanguard in rethinking early women's cultural contributions. The scholars whose work has most influenced my own thinking include Frances Smith Foster, Mary Helen Washington, Barbara Christian, Hazel Carby, Deborah McDowell, Valerie Smith, Nellie McKay, Hortense Spillers, Thadius Davis, Patricia J. Williams, Ann duCille, and Michele Wallace, among many others.
2. hooks, "Beyond a Politics of Shape," 26.
3. I am indebted to David Proper's study; while some of my conclusions may differ from his (he terms her poem "doggerel," for instance), his research has filled in several gaps in Lucy Terry's biography.
4. Records of the Church in Deerfield, 1731–1810 (Lucy Terry Papers).
5. Wesley, *In Freedom's Footsteps*, 73–75.
6. This fact may confirm the supposition that Ebenezer Wells did not free Lucy Terry Prince until his death.
7. Wesley, *In Freedom's Footsteps*, 103–4.
8. All of the other grantees, apparently, were Euro-Americans; only Abijah's name is followed by the designation "Negro." See Katz, *The Black West*, 60; and Martha Wright, "Bijah's Luce of Guilford, Vermont," 152.
9. *Records . . . Vermont*, 66.
10. Ibid.
11. Wright, "Bijah's Luce of Guilford, Vermont," 153.
12. In both the Noyes case and this one, few records remain extant. Ironically, Williams College was first established as the Free School, becoming Williams College in 1793. The information about these events is drawn from nineteenth-century histories (Sheldon; Holland), the authors of which interviewed residents or were themselves residents of the community.
13. *Laws . . . Massachusetts*, 2:599.
14. This date is based on the fact that Judge Samuel Chase presided over the trial; Chase served on the Supreme Court from 1796 to 1811, but he presided only one term—May 1796 in Bennington—over the U.S. Circuit Court in Vermont. Unfortunately, the Bennington County courthouse was leveled by fire three times after Lucy Terry Prince's case was heard. The records of Supreme Court cases heard in Bennington between 1790 and 1830 were destroyed in the various fires, thus later accounts are our only sources. See Potash and Hand, *Litigious Vermonters*, 18.
15. Terry Prince may have had good reason for doubting the efforts of her counsel. James Benjamin Wilbur has traced the relationship between Isaac Tichenor and Royall Tyler, who was the opponent's attorney in Terry's case. Wilbur describes Tyler as an "intimate friend" of Tichenor since the late 1780s and asserts that Tyler owed his appointment to the Vermont Supreme Court to Tichenor's influence (2:357).
16. Kaplan, *The Black Presence*, 211. It is impossible to know if this statement was actually uttered, but it has, like so many oral accounts, carried the weight of fact for two centuries in Deerfield history.
17. Herndon, "Women of 'No Particular Home,'" 270.
18. Ibid., 273. As Carol Wilson has observed, imprisonment was a tactic used not only for runaway slaves but also for free blacks as well: "Even if eventually found innocent of the crime of which they were charged, free blacks could become enslaved if they failed

to pay their fees. The majority of the black population often found payment of fees impossible" (46).

19. An obituary published upon Lucy Terry Prince's death asserts the land was lost "through inattention . . . which subjected her to penury" ("Lucy Terry Prince," 3). I have been unable to locate corroborating evidence for this assertion, and the suggestion of inattention would be highly uncharacteristic.

20. Katz, *The Black West*, 61.

21. "Lucy Terry Prince," 3.

22. Ibid.

23. Ibid., 68–69.

24. One scant piece of evidence exists to argue for Lucy Terry's literacy: a letter from Clarissa Ashley, sister of Lucy Terry's minister, to her brother Elihu, in which she asserts that her style may remind him of "old Luce's" style. In the middle of the first page of her letter, Clarissa writes, "I suppose you will scarcley read this however it will serve to put you in mind of old Luce for I begin at one corner of the paper and I have got all most down to the other" (qtd. in Proper, "Lucy Terry Prince," 193). Although it remains possible that she relied on her considerable intelligence and exceptional memory, her oratory skills and uses of the law and scripture suggest a significant level of literacy as well.

25. Derounian-Stodola and Levernier, *The Indian Captivity Narrative*, 8. More than a thousand titles may have been published in the genre. As John Sekora noted, "Because of the constant tension between settlers and tribes in the North and West, the captivities always possessed a timeliness. But that relevance was aggravated with each new quarrel. A new narrative or (more often) a new edition of a previous one appeared most years during the eighteenth century" (Sekora, "Red, White, and Black," 96).

26. Calloway, *North Country Captives*, 162.

27. Williams, *The Redeemed Captive*, 44.

28. Rev. Jonathan Ashley, minister during all of Lucy Terry's years in Deerfield, had preached many such sermons. In 1744 sermon, for example, he included the following call: "I know our days are determined in this world by God . . . but yet it is our duty to use means appointed for the lengthening out of our lives, and to defend ourselves against such as seek to take them away" (qtd. in Sheldon, *A History of Deerfield*, 1:536).

29. Holland, *History of Massachusetts*, 2:353.

30. Sheldon, *A History of Deerfield*, 1:536.

31. Sheldon, *A History of Deerfield*, 2:888–89.

32. Moon, "Master and Servant," 39–44.

33. Ibid., 19–23.

34. Lucy Terry Papers.

35. See Moon, "Master and Servant," 24–25; Proper, "Lucy Terry Prince," 194.

36. The Puritan tradition of using Christian rhetoric to support a proslavery stance was longstanding. In response to the heated debate between Samuel Sewell, who produced the first antislavery tract by a Puritan, *The Selling of Joseph* (1700), and John Saffin, a slave trader who responded with *A Brief and Candid Answer to . . . the Selling of Joseph* (1701), Cotton Mather published *The Negro Christianized* (1706) in which he asserted that baptizing slaves was a form of freeing them. Such ideas were predominant in the 1730s Great Awakening movement when Lucy Terry was baptized.

37. Demos, *The Unredeemed Captive*, 143ff; Foster, *Written by Herself*, 121–40.

38. François Xavier was his Catholic name; Arosen his Mohawk name (Demos, *The Unredeemed Captive*, 154).

39. Quoted in ibid., 204.

40. Quoted in Derounian-Stodola and Levernier, *The Indian Captivity Narrative*, 7.

41. The brief details of Jinny Cole's life are recounted by Sheldon, who as a child knew her son, Cato (*A History of Deerfield* 2:896–98).

42. These traditions have been recreated in some of the most powerful African American literature produced in the twentieth century, most notably Toni Morrison's *Song of Solomon*.

43. Sheldon, *A History of Deerfield*, 2:897.

44. "Griot" is a French designation; "dyeli" is West African (specifically Maninkan) in origin. See O'Toole, *Historical Dictionary of Guinea*, 71, 124.

45. Brooks, "This Evil Extends Especially," 281.

46. See below for a discussion of the significance of "restoration" in the white captivity–narrative tradition. My point here is that Terry's beliefs may have been as influenced by her African spiritual heritage as they were by Christianty.

47. Wideman, "Introduction," xxxi, xxxiii.

48. See Derounian-Stodola and Levernier, *The Indian Captivity Narrative*: "Whether negative or positive, stereotyping Indians ultimately served the same pragmatic racist purpose regarding the so-called Indian problem encountered by an essentially expansionistic, white, agrarian society that needed new territories as it grew in both size and military strength" (53).

49. Foster, *Written by Herself*, 25. Mae Gwendolyn Henderson, in "Speaking in Tongues," also remarked upon this tradition. African American women's writers, she notes, "have encoded oppression as a discursive dilemma, that is, their words have consistently raised the problem of the black woman's relationship to power and discourse. Silence is an important element of this code" (117).

50. Foucault, *Discipline and Punish*, 208–9.

51. Pratt, *Imperial Eyes*, 2.

52. Holland, *History of Massachusetts*, 2:359.

53. Southern, *The Music of Black Americans*, 55.

54. Sheldon, *A History of Deerfield*, 1:547.

55. Pratt, *Imperial Eyes*, 23.

56. See especially Patricia Caldwell's *The Puritan Conversion Narrative*.

57. Andrews, *To Tell a Free Story*, 38.

58. Like all folk ballads, different versions of "Bars Fight" have emerged. What has never been disputed, however, is the conclusion of "Bars Fight" in which the child Samuel Allen is abducted and taken to Canada.

59. Derounian-Stodola and Levernier, *The Indian Captivity Narrative*, 112.

60. Quoted in Sheldon, *A History of Deerfield*, 1:309.

61. Quoted in Demos, *The Unredeemed Captive*, 107–8.

62. Sekora, "Red, White, and Black," 94.

63. Kolodny, "Among the Indians," 29.

64. Saillant, "Slavery and Divine Providence," 123–24.

65. Pratt, *Imperial Eyes*, 7.

66. Melvoin, "New England Outpost," 281.

67. Derounian-Stodola and Levernier, *The Indian Captivity Narrative*, 7.

68. Cheyfitz, *The Poetics of Imperialism*, 152.

Bibliography

Andrews, William L. *To Tell a Free Story: The First Century of Afro-American Autobiography 1760–1865.* Urbana: University of Illinois Press, 1986.

Brooks, James F. "This Evil Extends Especially . . . To the Feminine Sex." *Feminist Studies* 22, no. 2 (1996): 279–309.

Calloway, Colin G. *North Country Captives: Narratives of Indian Captivity from Vermont, and New Hampshire.* Hanover, MA: University Press of New England, 1992.

Cheyfitz, Eric. *The Poetics of Imperialism: Translation and Colonization from "The Tempest" to "Tarzan."* New York: Oxford University Press, 1991.

Demos, John. *The Unredeemed Captive: A Family Story from Early America.* New York: Knopf, 1994.

Derounian-Stodola, Kathryn Zabelle, and James Arthur Levernier. *The Indian Captivity Narrative, 1550–1900.* New York: Twayne, 1993.

Foster, Frances Smith. *Written by Herself: Literary Production by African American Women, 1746–1892.* Bloomington: Indiana University Press, 1993.

Foucault, Michel. *Discipline and Punish: The Birth of the Prison.* Translated by Alan Sheridan. New York: Vintage, 1977.

Harris, Sharon M. *Executing Race: Early American Women's Narratives of Race, Society, and the Law.* Columbus: Ohio State University Press, 2005.

Hemenway, Abby Maria, collator. *Vermont Historical Gazetteer.* Vol. 5. Brandon, VT: Mrs. Carrie E. H. Page, 1891.

Henderson, Mae Gwendolyn. "Speaking in Tongues: Dialogics, Dialectics, and the Black Woman Writer's Literary Tradition." In *Reading Black, Reading Feminist: A Critical Anthology,* 116–42. New York: Meridian, 1990.

Herndon, Ruth Wallis. "Women of 'No Particular Home': Town Leaders and Female Transients in Rhode Island, 1750–1800." In *Women and Freedom in Early America,* edited by Larry D. Eldridge, 269–89. New York: New York University Press, 1997.

Holland, Josiah Gilbert. *History of Massachusetts.* 2 vols. Springfield, MA: Samuel Bowles, 1855.

hooks, bell. "Beyond a Politics of Shape: White Supremacy and the Black Female Body." *Z Magazine* (September 1995): 26–28.

Kaplan, Sidney. *The Black Presence in the Era of the American Revolution 1770–1800.* Washington, DC: New York Graphic Society, 1973.

Katz, William Loren. *The Black West.* Garden City, NY: Doubleday, 1971.

Kolodny, Annette. "Among the Indians: The Uses of Captivity." *New York Times Book Review,* January 2, 1993.

Lucy Terry Papers. Pocumtuck Valley Memorial Association Library, Deerfield, Massachusetts.

"Lucy Terry Prince." *Vermont Gazette Weekly,* August 1, 1821.

Melvoin, Richard I. "New England Outpost: War and Society in Colonial Frontier Deerfield, Massachusetts." Dissertation thesis, University of Michigan, 1983.

Moon, Jennifer. "Master and Servant." Lucy Terry Papers.

O'Toole, Thomas, and Ibrahima Bah-Lalya. *Historical Dictionary of Guinea.* 3rd ed. Lanham, MD: Scarecrow, 1995.

Potash, P. Jeffrey, and Samuel B. Hand. *Litigious Vermonters: Court Records to 1825.* Burlington: Center for Research on Vermont, 1979.

Pratt, Mary Louise. *Imperial Eyes: Travel Writing and Transculturation.* New York: Routledge, 1992.

Proper, David. "Lucy Terry Prince: 'Singer of History.'" *Contributions in Black Studies* 9 (1990–92): 187–214.

Salliant, John. "Slavery and Divine Providence in New England Calvinism: The New Divinity and a Black Protest, 1775–1805." *New England Quarterly* 68, no. 1 (March 1995): 584–608.

Sekora, John. "Red, White, and Black: Indian Captivities, Colonial Printers, and the Early African-American Narrative." In *A Mixed Race: Ethnicity in Early America*, edited by Frank Shuffleton, 92–104. New York: Oxford University Press, 1993.

Sheldon, George. *A History of Deerfield, Massachusetts*. 2 vols. Deerfield, MA: E. A. Hall, 1895.

Southern, Eileen. *The Music of Black Americans: A History*. New York: Norton, 1971.

Wesley, Charles. *In Freedom's Footsteps: From the African Background to the Civil War*. New York: Publishers Co., 1969.

Wideman, John Edgar. "Introduction." In *Life from Death Row*, edited by Mumia Abu-Jamal. Reading, MA: Addison-Wesley, 1995.

Wilbur, James Benjamin. *Ira Allen: Founder of Vermont*. 2 vols. Boston: Houghton Mifflin, 1928.

Williams, John. *The Redeemed Captive, Returning to Zion: A Faithful History of Remarkable Occurrences in the Captivity and Deliverance of Mr. John Williams*. Edited by Edward W. Clark. Amherst: University of Massachusetts Press, 1976.

Wright, Martha. "Bijah's Luce of Guilford, Vermont." *Negro History Bulletin* 28 (April 1965): 152–56.

7

The Fire Next Time and the Law

D. Quentin Miller

*T*he *Fire Next Time* (1963) is a pivotal work in James Baldwin's career. It consists of two essays: "My Dungeon Shook: A Letter to my Nephew on the One
Hundredth Anniversary of the Emancipation," originally published in *Progressive*,
and "Down at the Cross: Letter from a Region in My Mind," a lengthy, twenty-
thousand-word essay that first appeared in *The New Yorker*. Upon the publication
of the two essays as *The Fire Next Time*, readers couldn't help but pay attention
to the passionate intensity of this young writer who had burst onto the literary
scene a decade earlier with the publication of his bildungsroman, *Go Tell It on the
Mountain* (1953), and his manifesto, the essays collected in *Notes of a Native Son*
(1955). Baldwin remained in his first period of exile in Europe until 1957, when he
returned to a racially divided nation that was in desperate need of a spokesperson.
He stepped forward to fulfill that role, publishing "Down at the Cross" as a loud
wake-up call to his blissfully ignorant countrymen: biographer David Leeming
describes it as "his consideration of Western culture from the perspective of the
people oppressed by that culture."[1] The essay called attention not only to people
like Baldwin but also to Baldwin himself, as it involved elements of personal history, class, religion, and, of course, race. This widespread attention landed him on
the cover of *Time* magazine on May 17, 1963, and garnered him an invitation for
a personal audience with Attorney General Robert Kennedy the following week.
Moreover, it cemented his status as the intellectual leader of the civil rights movement, which was entering its most turbulent phase.

"Down at the Cross" integrates experience and observation in one of the most
rhetorically powerful essays of the civil rights era, earning Baldwin the title of
"prophet" so frequently used to describe his role in American life. This essay is
about the antithetical forces that contribute to the American conundrum: belong-
ing and exclusion, individuals and groups, black and white identity, Christianity
and Islam. It is a social critique in the broadest sense about a specific time period
("this difficult era"),[2] a nation ("an Anglo-Teutonic, antisexual country"),[3] and an
individual ("I was utterly drained and exhausted, and released, for the first time,
from all my guilty torment").[4] The force that connects these three perspectives
and that demonstrates so clearly the power relationship between them is the law.

Baldwin regards the law as a visible manifestation of power that, when mistreated, becomes a racially divisive force that systematically destroys the American dreams of unity, freedom, equality, and unmitigated respect for the individual.

An implicit critique of the American legal and judicial system is central to virtually all of Baldwin's works. For Baldwin, the law is not a benevolent force to maintain order in a civilized society; rather, it is a tool of oppression used by a paranoid and immoral majority to validate its worst impulses and to assert its power. The law is a complex and damaging force in Baldwin's writings: to resist it is to risk personal harm, wrongful imprisonment, and even death. Yet to shrink at the sight of the law's power is to resign oneself to defeat. In this chapter I will examine *The Fire Next Time* in the context of law ("the law"), broadly defined to include both the official history of policies and legal decisions that comprise the American legal system and the common perception of the law as a potentially menacing, regulatory force represented by police, corrections officers, judges, and prisons. All these facets of the law represent, for Baldwin, the potential for those in power to sustain their position of privilege while oppressing those who do not have it: the poor, the black, the immigrant, the homosexual, the artist, the drug addict—in short, the hero-victims of Baldwin's work. In *The Fire Next Time* we see Baldwin move from the law's power on the street (represented by the police) to the law's power on the national stage (represented by the Supreme Court) not only as a way of demonstrating its pervasiveness in his experience but also as a way of participating in the reshaping of American democracy through the advancement of a thorough critique.

In his study *Whispered Consolations*, Jon-Christian Suggs has broken important ground on the subject of African American literature and the law; he argues that "African American literature is universally grounded in law; in fact, all African American fiction carries the question of the legal status of blacks as its subtext."[5] Yet Suggs's study focuses on "a classical African American narrative whose chronological boundaries are roughly 1820 to 1954,"[6] stopping virtually at the beginning of Baldwin's career (Baldwin's first book was published in 1953). Gregg D. Crane's 2002 study *Race, Citizenship, and the Law in American Literature* similarly focuses on nineteenth- and early twentieth-century American literature.[7] The law and literature movement that developed in the early 1990s has become well established in the academy, but it has not impacted Baldwin studies in any meaningful way despite the resurgence of interest in Baldwin in the past decade. Baldwin's perception of the criminal justice system and its impact on society's power relations runs through nearly all of his work, and this perception is thus a fitting context for unifying and making sense of Baldwin's complete oeuvre. It has been noted by critics and biographers to varying degrees but has never been used to assess his legacy or to synthesize his entire career—a career that began virtually at the moment of the landmark *Brown v. the Topeka Board of Education* case (1954) and that reached its high-water mark, in terms of notoriety, virtually at the moment of the Civil Rights Acts of 1964 and the Voting Rights Acts of 1965, just after the publication of *The Fire Next Time*.

Because of the law's prominence in his writings, Baldwin is a crucial figure to focus on when extending the scope of Suggs's and Crane's studies: all of Baldwin's novels and plays have at their core a narrative of imprisonment, police brutality, police intimidation, or a rigged trial. These are also topics of his nonfiction, where he tends to meditate on the law as it is broadly defined, including in his inquiries into Supreme Court decisions and legal history. Prison is at the center of this web of associations connecting "the law." For Baldwin, imprisonment becomes the central metaphor not only of the African American experience but also of the broader restrictions that threaten to suffocate or alienate the disempowered individual, which is precisely the intent of imprisonment. Prison—like slavery, like legal decisions, like the police—exists for Baldwin as a means for society to compartmentalize, divide, control, and oppress. The law, in brief, is not a benevolent force, in Baldwin's eyes, but a way to exercise what he calls "a criminal power."[8] As a mechanism of order in society, the law is a flawed instrument. This is not to say that the law is completely malevolent or uniformly misguided in Baldwin's work, though. The idea that resurfaces in Baldwin's work—that black men are frequently imprisoned for crimes they did not commit and that racist institutions exist to keep black men down—is not merely one of powerless victimization, though that is certainly a large part of the idea. Rather, Baldwin's writing, across the span of his entire career, testifies to the way power is abused under the pretext of the law, resulting in a hypocrisy much deeper than even that exhibited by religious hypocrites such as Gabriel in *Go Tell It on the Mountain*, or Sister Margaret in *The Amen Corner*. Baldwin's unique contribution to American thought and to American literature is his analysis of the way power has manifested itself throughout history, disguised as a fair and equitable legal, judicial, and penal system and how this realization has shaped him and his literary imagination.

Critics pay attention to the personal and racial content of Baldwin's writings because they are described with such striking precision and honesty. Yet it is impossible to separate the personal and the racial from the legal in Baldwin's case. His complex definitions of equality and freedom in "Down at the Cross" are similarly inseparable from his complex definition of power. For Baldwin, there is nothing noble or fair about the legal system in America. Police for him always symbolize fear rather than protection; prisons always house the innocent or wrongfully accused (albeit not exclusively). Examples of these situations in the Baldwin oeuvre are numerous: Richard in *Go Tell It on the Mountain*, Caleb in *Tell Me How Long the Train's Been Gone* (1968), Fonny in *If Beale Street Could Talk* (1974), and Tony Maynard in *No Name in the Street* (1972) are some of the more familiar examples of fictional characters or real people imprisoned for crimes they did not commit. This recurrent motif stems from an event that I consider one of the formative moments in Baldwin's writing career: his incarceration in Paris for "receiving stolen goods" after a friend pilfered a sheet from a hotel and hid it in his room. This event was eventually laughed out of the French courts, but not until Baldwin had been imprisoned for eight days, as he describes in the 1955 essay "Equal in Paris."[9] While there, he sank into a pit of despair so deep that he attempted suicide, an attempt that Richard successfully repeats in *Go Tell It on the Mountain*. But the dominant note of "Down at the Cross" is not despair over the depraved state of the law in America; as Lawrie Balfour writes, "Does Baldwin's unsettling narrative recommend the abandonment of equality as a political principle? Not at all. In fact, Baldwin's critique is made in the name of the equal humanity of all persons, regardless of race, and of the equal entitlement of all Americans to the basic rights of citizenship."[10]

It is difficult to know how to rebel against the law's power other than to commit crimes, often more serious ones than stealing sheets. In "Down at the Cross," crime becomes one of the "gimmicks" that seems to offer a way out of the ghetto, but it is illusory as such. Baldwin observes, "One did not have to be very bright to realize how little one could do to change one's situation" and he recalls how a "cop in the middle of the street muttered as I passed him, 'Why don't you niggers stay uptown where you belong?'"[11] This quotation is evidence of a hard fact of Baldwin's upbringing: in Harlem, law-abiding citizens and criminals alike are literally kept in their place by the law. Ironically, American citizens pride themselves on their freedom of mobility, both literally in the sense that one can live where one chooses and metaphorically in such phrases as "class mobility." Here we see a law enforcement officer attempt to define a place for black people, an attempt that is, of course, the legacy of slavery and, later, of segregation. The police officer might argue that he was merely asking a question, but his question cannot be separated from his uniform, the symbol of power and often, in Baldwin, the mask of its abuse. At another point in the essay, Baldwin describes a young black robber being "carried off to jail,"[12] and it is obviously the police who are carrying him. This is another case of law enforcement officers "re-placing" the black citizen, putting him where they have decided he "belongs." Harlem as a whole is, by this association, itself a prison. Baldwin makes this association explicit in his 1971 essay "An Open Letter to my Sister, Angela Davis": "Black people were killing each other every Saturday night out on Lenox Avenue, when I was growing up; and no one explained to them, or to me, that it was *intended* that they should; that they were penned where they were."[13]

Moving outside of himself and his community and into history, Baldwin discusses the legacy of black servants robbing their white employers. Here he not only redefines crime, but he shows how it can be justified: "Negro servants have been smuggling odds and ends out of white homes for generations, and white people have been delighted to have them do it, because it has assuaged a dim guilt and testified to the intrinsic superiority of white people. Even the most doltish and servile Negro could scarcely fail to be impressed by the disparity between his situation and that of the people for whom he worked; Negroes who were neither doltish nor servile did not feel that they were doing anything wrong when they robbed white people."[14] Morality and legality are at odds with one another in this analysis. The act of robbery, officially a crime, is not considered a sin by either white or black people: the latter "did not feel that they were doing anything wrong" and the former were "delighted."[15] Both races see it as inevitable, but it is another version of the placement I describe above: the rich, white people feel superior, in Baldwin's eyes, which places them above their thieving servants. The law, in this case, is applied selectively, and is in the control of those in power. More important, though, the law can be interpreted historically, as Baldwin does here: "White people, who had robbed black people of their liberty and who profited by this theft every hour that they lived, had no moral ground on which to stand. They had the judges, the juries, the shotguns, the law—in a word, power. But it was a criminal power, to be feared but not respected, and to be outwitted in any way whatever."[16] The most striking facet of Baldwin's definition here is that power is defined exclusively as legal power, except in the case of firearms: power is "the judges, the juries . . . the law." This power is itself "criminal," though, and therefore does not garner respect. After all, there is "no moral ground" underneath it: it is simply force, which makes sense of the seemingly incongruous word "shotguns" in the middle of Baldwin's definition.

Those in power—wealthy, white people who have benefited historically from the legacy of slavery—are thus recast as the criminals of this society. Even more generally, "society" commits a crime by convincing the young Baldwin that he, too, "belongs" in jail, or back in Harlem: "The moral barriers that I had supposed to exist between me and the dangers of a criminal career were so tenuous as to be nearly nonexistent. I certainly could not discover any principled reason for not becoming a criminal, and it is not my poor, God-fearing parents who are to be indicted for the lack but this society."[17] By indicting his society, Baldwin is calling not only for an overhaul of the prejudiced attitudes that contribute to the racial divide but also for a reexamination of the legal system that upholds such attitudes. The racist comment of one police officer expands here to encompass legal power on all levels: "the judges, the juries, the shotguns, the law."

Baldwin's definition of power in terms of the law explains his identification with those who are subjugated by force and his initial interest in the Black Muslims, who represent a viable challenge to the law's power. If the law can take an innocent black man and intimidate him to the point of self-destruction, then it is a powerful force indeed. This realization is a kind of rite of initiation for Baldwin in "Down at the Cross" (not unlike his religious conversion) in which he describes "a fear that the child, in challenging the white world's assumptions, was putting himself in the path of destruction. A child cannot, thank Heaven, know how vast and how merciless is the nature of power, with what unbelievable cruelty people treat each other."[18] He realizes that "white people hold the power . . . and the world has innumerable ways of making this difference known and felt and feared."[19] The primary source of fear in Baldwin's personal history is the ubiquitous presence in Harlem of the police. The effect of their presence is an invisible barrier that separates the white world from the world where African Americans supposedly belong. "Down at the Cross" can be read as a meditation on legal power and the barriers it creates.

The first few pages of "Down at the Cross" are saturated with wall imagery. The essay begins with Baldwin's reflection on his discovery, as a teenager, of "God, His saints and angels, and his blazing Hell."[20] Beyond the obvious and stark distinction between acceptance and punishment, this God is also synonymous with safety, and Baldwin says, "I supposed Him to exist only within the walls of a church—in fact, of *our* church."[21] These walls separate good from evil and saints from sinners in the mind of the teenaged Baldwin, but for the mature Baldwin these walls are symbolic of the problem of modern society rather than its solution. "Safety" in Baldwin's work is always an illusion, or a force that consistently prevents individuals from giving themselves over to love.[22] Even the young Baldwin takes refuge in the church out of fear; he says, "I became . . . afraid of the evil within me and afraid of the evil without."[23] Religion becomes a way to purge the evil within and promise that punishment will come to the evildoers of the world, if it hasn't already. The walls of the church are meant to protect the saints from the sinners; yet the notion that evil or sin can be purged from the self and the notion that one can ever be in a truly safe place are both self-deceptive, and Baldwin astutely associates the church walls with other institutions that attempt to preserve societal power. The walls of the church here are replaced by prison walls later in the essay and throughout Baldwin's career.

Because the walls of the church and of the prison are associated with safety and goodness, they are sometimes invisible to those who are most affected by them—those who have been deemed a sinner or a criminal—often for no other reason than their blackness. These walls do little more than to divide a community. Part of Baldwin's fear of the evil in the world around him is the fate of his friends: "One found them in twos and threes and fours, in a hallway, sharing a jug of wine or a bottle of whiskey, talking, cursing, fighting, sometimes weeping: lost, and unable to say what it was that oppressed them, except that they knew it was 'the man'— the white man. And there seemed to be no way whatever to remove this cloud that stood between them and the sun, between them and love and life and power, between them and whatever it was that they wanted."[24] Here the barrier is some abstract notion of white power that is placed directly in the middle of a black man's life that separates himself from his aspirations. "The man" is also, of course, a euphemism for a police officer, as in Baldwin's most vitriolic short story "Going to Meet the Man" about a racist white sheriff who cannot become sexually aroused until he recalls or fantasizes about the castration of and lynching of a black victim. Baldwin foreshadows the publication of that story in "Down at the Cross" when he writes, "*Whoever debases others is debasing himself.* That is not a mystical statement but a most realistic one, which is proved by the eyes of any Alabama sheriff."[25]

This association with "the man" is foretold in "Down at the Cross" immediately after the quotation in which Baldwin recalls the policeman's comment, "Why don't you niggers stay uptown where you belong?" It relates an incident when he was ten: "Two policemen amused themselves with me by frisking me, making comic (and terrifying) speculations concerning my ancestry and probable sexual prowess, and for good measure, leaving me flat on my back in one of Harlem's empty lots."[26] This exercise of power becomes an example of "the evil without" from which the young Baldwin must take refuge. His world is a dangerous place, not necessarily because of the criminals who pervade it—"the whores and pimps and racketeers on the Avenue"[27]—but because the law that is supposed to protect him from those criminals reveals itself to be a criminal power. Referring to a remark by Allen Ginsberg, who said, "Don't call the cop a pig, call him a friend. If you call him a friend, he'll act like a friend," Baldwin remarked, "I know more about cops than that."[28] Keneth Kinnamon writes about this incident as though it were isolated: "[Baldwin] did suffer harassment from white policemen, including a terrifying incident at the age of ten mentioned in *The Fire Next Time* and treated at length in *Tell Me How Long the Train's Been Gone.* But for the most part white oppression was an abstract force, responsible somehow for the poverty and desperation which surrounded him, the invisible cause of a visible result."[29] Baldwin, however, describes police harassment as a repeated motif in his life, and anything but abstract; he writes later in the essay, "When a white man faces a black man, especially if the black man is helpless, terrible things are revealed. I know. I have been carried into precinct basements often enough."[30]

Baldwin's need to seek safety from such a criminal power is a real one, but one that damages his soul, for he realizes later in life, "To defend oneself against a fear is simply to insure that one will, one day, be conquered by it; fears must be faced."[31] To hide from the law, in other words, would be to acknowledge its power to intimidate and thus to sacrifice one's own power. Without blaming himself, Baldwin realizes the mistake he had made as a youth in supposing that there was a hiding place: "That summer," he says, "all the fears with which I had grown up, and which were now a part of me and controlled my vision of the world, rose up like a wall between the world and me, and drove me into the church."[32] Late in the essay, Baldwin completes the relationship between power, the legal system, and religion when he discusses the desire of the so-called American Negro to gain the sort of power and notoriety black men have in places like Africa: "As [American Negroes] watch black men elsewhere rise, the promise held out, at last, that they may walk the earth with the authority with which white men walk, protected by the power that white men shall have no longer, is enough, and more than enough, to empty prisons and pull God down from Heaven."[33] Baldwin's description of the revolt against a white God's power in terms of a prison riot solidifies the connection between religion and the law.

The walls of the early part of the essay are all associated with white power and with punishment, and it makes sense that the law gradually replaces the church in Baldwin's imagination. In the short prefatory essay in *The Fire Next Time*, "Letter to my Nephew," Baldwin makes the connection between a false sense of safety and wrongful imprisonment clear; he writes, "Those innocents who believed that your imprisonment made them safe are losing their grasp of reality."[34] He plays with the notion of innocence and crime throughout this brief essay: the "innocents" in this quotation are in fact *guilty*, in Baldwin's mind: they are the perpetrators of the crime of dooming their black brethren to the life of poverty and crime described at the beginning of "Down at the Cross." He writes, "I know what the world has done to my brother and how narrowly he has survived it. And I know, which is much worse, and this is the crime of which I accuse my country and my countrymen, and for which neither I nor time nor history will ever forgive them, that they have destroyed and are destroying hundreds of thousands of lives and do not know it and do not want to know it."[35] He goes on to equate criminality with innocence in the essay's most powerful rhetorical turn: "But it is not permissible that the authors of devastation should also be innocent. It is the innocence which constitutes the crime."[36] Here Baldwin redefines the very terms of the legal courtroom—crime and innocence—to prove his point: "innocence" is a close substitute for "ignorance" here, and igno-rance, as the saying goes, is no excuse for breaking a law. The crime he speaks of here is a crime against humanity, enabled through white Americans' willingness to erase history's impact on the present. This essay is, after all, occasioned by the one-hundredth anniversary of the Emancipation Proclamation. Baldwin disposes of the notion of "innocence" in a nation that has been historically guilty but that has never allowed itself to be tried for its crimes. In an atmosphere in which there appear to be victims of history but no acknowledged criminals, Baldwin has no choice but to criminalize the very notion of innocence.

In order for an individual to gain power against such a monolithic institution as the American legal system, he must resort to a new kind of rhetoric. In "Down at the Cross," Baldwin attempts to redefine the concept of "crime" and the meaning of "power" in order to combat the law's "criminal power." "Crime" is synonymous with "sin" in the early section of the essay, when he has run to the church for protection from both of these things. He sees "crime" as something nearly inevitable for the residents of Harlem: it figures into their destiny. He writes, "Crime became real, for example—for the first time—not as *a* possibility but as *the* possibility. One would never defeat one's circumstances by working and saving one's pennies; one would never, by working, acquire that many pennies, and, besides, the social treatment accorded even the most successful Negroes proved that one needed, in order to be free, something more than a bank account. One needed a handle, a lever, a means of inspiring fear. It was absolutely clear that the police would whip you and take you in as long as they could get away with it."[37] Crime here is a way out of the cycle of poverty and despair that trapped Harlem residents in the bleak 1930s. Ironically, the police do not respond to crime in this formulation: they cause it. The police, according to Baldwin, are predisposed to mistreat poor black Americans, so crime becomes a way—the only way—to claim one's identity.

Even though law enforcement officers are only the most visible evidence of the law's power, Baldwin regards them with the invective he generally reserves for church elders; he says, "All doormen, for example, and all policemen have by now, for me, become exactly the same, and my style with them is designed simply to intimidate them before they can intimidate me. No doubt I am guilty of some injustice here, but it is irreducible, since I cannot risk assuming that the humanity of these people is more real to them than their uniforms."[38] The word "injustice" plays on Baldwin's critique of the justice system, which is a much larger power than the police on the street. Baldwin's manipulation of words related to the law (such as "justice") is a consistent motif throughout the essay: his willingness to redefine the words that have been used to define his reality is, in fact, his attempt to secure power for himself. Every society defines crime as an illegal act, and this definition is intended as a line of demarcation indicating a society's moral beliefs. Yet when a society reflects widespread immorality, individuals must redefine crimes. For instance, Baldwin, describing his role as a Sunday School teacher, says, "I felt that I was committing a crime in talking about the gentle Jesus, in telling them to reconcile themselves to their misery on earth in order to gain the crown of eternal life."[39] This lesson is a "crime" in the adult Baldwin's eyes because it is not really the handle, lever, or means of inspiring fear that will allow Harlemites to survive on the street: crime itself is. Musing later on organized religion, he brings up the term "crime" again in a different context: "Whoever wishes to become a truly moral human being . . . must first divorce himself from all the prohibitions, crimes, and hypocrisies of the Christian church."[40] Crimes here are sins against humanity and thus act as evidence of the hypocrisy of a church that claims to profess love. Religion, in general, is a way to makes crimes holy; Baldwin later writes, "Legend and theology, which are designed to sanctify our fears, crimes, and aspirations, also reveal them for what they are."[41] In making this link, Baldwin seeks to disempower two institutions that have seized control of the definition of American morality: the Christian church and the legal system.

Elijah Muhammad uses the same word when talking about white immorality when he speaks about "the crimes of white people."[42] These "crimes"—not specified as Baldwin relates Elijah's words—are presumably the racist leftovers of the system of slavery. Baldwin and Elijah Muhammad agree that these are crimes worth examining and trying, but Baldwin chooses to focus more on the second word he seeks to redefine: power. In fact, Baldwin becomes interested in the Nation of Islam's speeches not because of their rhetoric, but because of their power to intimidate the police:

> Two things caused me to begin to listen to the speeches, and one was the behavior of the police. After all, I had seen men dragged from their platforms on this very corner for saying less virulent things, and I had seen many crowds dispersed by policemen, with clubs or on horseback. But the policemen were doing nothing now. Obviously, this was not because they had become more human but because they were under orders and because they were afraid. And indeed they were, and I was delighted to see it. There they stood, in twos and threes and fours, in their Cub Scout uniforms and with their Cub Scout faces, totally unprepared, as is the way with American he-men, for anything that could not be settled with a club or a fist or a gun. I might have pitied them if I had not found myself in their hands so often and discovered, through ugly experience, what they were like when *they* held the power and what they were like when *you* held the power.[43]

Baldwin finds the Black Muslims intriguing and impressive because they have a certain power over the police, who seem suddenly childish ("in their Cub Scout uniforms and with their Cub Scout faces") in Baldwin's mind. Although the police still have superior physical strength (symbolized here as clubs, fists, and guns), they now appear afraid and are rendered somewhat impotent in terms of the actual power they have. Still, though, Baldwin realizes the dangerous situation this creates: if the Black Muslims indeed have power over the police, then there is the potential that the police will act on their fear, overcompensating and transforming it into the use of excessive force. The power of intimidation that the Muslims exhibit is really no different from the criminal power of the police. This situation is parallel to what Baldwin concludes about Christianity and the Black Muslim movement: the latter is really no different from the former in terms of their willingness to separate the races and place one above the other; as Baldwin puts it, "The dream, the sentiment is old; only the color is new."[44]

Baldwin does not ultimately endorse the Black Muslim solution of gaining the power that has been denied them through revolt because, according to Baldwin, there is a higher force than raw power: love. Yet he acknowledges in this essay and elsewhere that it is sometimes difficult to resist the lure of power; he writes, "I knew the tension in me between love and power."[45] Resisting a facile opposition between these two terms, he seeks to define love as something tough that can, in fact, stand up to the type of power he has been describing throughout the essay: "I use the word 'love' here not merely in the personal sense but as a state of being, or a state of grace—not in the infantile American sense of being made happy but in the tough and universal sense of quest and daring and growth."[46] The love he describes is a commitment to the self-trust and self-knowledge described by American Transcendentalists such as Thoreau who believed that the individual conscience was the highest power and the one that all Americans should seek to develop apart from society's institutions; as Baldwin writes, "The person who distrusts himself has no touchstone for reality—for this touchstone can be only oneself."[47] And yet, Baldwin at least raises the question about his individualistic sense of social improvement weighed against the social improvement of the Black Muslims who had managed to teach so many young men to avoid the life of crime Baldwin once saw as a near inevitability; he sees himself as "perpetually attempting to choose the better rather than the worse. But this choice was a choice in terms of a personal, a private better (I was, after all, a writer); what was its relevance in terms of a social worse?"[48] As Lawrie Balfour concludes, "Baldwin rejects the sort of up-by-the-bootstraps individualism that is often associated with the term [personal responsibility]."[49]

If Baldwin believes that the solution to America's racial crisis does not take the form of ideological, social, religious, or race-based commitment such as that required by the Black Muslims, then one might assume that he would look toward legal avenues for social reform. Deak Nabers argues that Baldwin's essays of the 1960s, including "Down at the Cross," marked a "turn from social clarity to historical recognition . . . fueled by a growing skepticism that legislation could meaningfully address America's persistent civil rights problems."[50] He sees Baldwin's writings as part of a larger trend: "In turning from legal and social concerns to historical concerns he participated in a widespread re-articulation of the nature of American racial inequality as the Civil Rights movement scored its major national legislative successes. The trajectory of the Civil Rights movement in the 1960s increasingly took it away from the notion that racial disadvantage in the United States could be effectively addressed by something on the order of a legal strategy."[51] Although there is certainly a good argument to be made that Baldwin turned to "historical recognition," it does not necessarily come at the expense of a belief in the power of legislation, for at the end of "Down at the Cross," Baldwin repeatedly invokes the broadest manifestations of the law's power—Supreme Court decisions of both the past and the present—and he even begins to use the language of the courtroom in his essay.

Nabers is correct insofar as Baldwin is *skeptical* of legal solutions to social problems. Baldwin is wary, as was Dr. Martin Luther King in his "Letter from a Birmingham Jail," of the white liberals' calls for patience, and he thus defends Malcolm X's point that the willingness to fight, physically, for one's rights does not constitute "violence": "Malcolm's statement is *not* answered by references to the triumphs of the N.A.A.C.P., the more particularly since very few liberals have any notion of how long, how costly, and how heartbreaking a task it is to gather the evidence that one can carry into court, or how long such court battles take."[52] Nabers interprets this quotation as follows:

> It might seem here as though Baldwin is concerned about the strategic implications of legal responses to segregation. "Court battles" take too long, and exact too high a cost in human suffering, to count as effective instruments for achieving the social reform America needs. But Baldwin's objection to *Brown* is not simply that it was a very costly way of confronting school segregation; it is also that it was, in an important sense, beside the point of school segregation . . . If at first Baldwin implies that NAACP-style efforts at reform were inefficient, in terms of both time and human suffering, here he so downplays the force of those efforts as to make them seem virtually irrelevant, irrelevant not merely to the social conditions they might be thought to address but also to the legal results, like *Brown*, they seek to achieve.[53]

Nabers bases his conclusion on the following passage from "Down at the Cross":

> White Americans have contented themselves with gestures that are now described as "tokenism." For hard example, white Americans congratulate themselves on the 1954 Supreme Court decision outlawing segregation in the schools; they suppose, in spite of the mountain of evidence that has since accumulated to the contrary, that this was proof of a change of heart—or, as they like to say, progress. Perhaps. It all depends on how one reads the word "progress." Most of the Negroes I know do not believe that this immense concession would ever have been made if it had not been for the competition of the Cold war, and the fact that Africa was clearly liberating herself and therefore had, for political reasons, to be wooed by the descendants of her former masters. Had it been a matter of love or justice, the 1954 decision would surely have occurred sooner; were it not for the realities of power in this difficult era, it might very well not have occurred yet. This seems an extremely harsh way of stating the case—ungrateful, as it were—but the evidence that supports this way of stating it is not easily refuted. I myself do not think that it can be refuted at all.[54]

Geopolitics and the force of history do seem to overwhelm moral reasons (i.e., "love or justice") as the basis for legal reform in Baldwin's formulation and in Nabers's analysis of it. Yet the word "power" here must be connected to the "criminal power" Baldwin speaks of earlier in the essay if we are to make sense of the essay as a coherent whole. The "realities of power in this difficult era" involve *both* geopolitics *and* Supreme Court decisions *as well as* the criminal power of the police and of rich, white people that dominated the early part of the essay. In short, legal power in Baldwin's mind is still in the hands of the oppressors, and even if it is used for good—for "progress"—it is still not in the hands of the oppressed. He uses this observation as the basis for his indignation about the very basic premises of legal decisions: "There is absolutely no reason to suppose that white people are better equipped to frame the laws by which I am to be governed than I am. It is entirely unacceptable that I should have no voice in the political affairs of my own country, for I am not a ward of America; I am one of the first Americans to arrive on these shores."[55] The word "ward" is associated with imprisonment, which brings the discussion full circle: Baldwin is denying his status as someone being watched or guarded by the state and asserting his status as someone who has the right "to frame the laws" of his nation. He insists that he should have a "voice," which is precisely the instrument he uses to gain the power that has been used to oppress him.

In exercising his voice in order to gain power, Baldwin adopts the rhetoric of the courtroom in the latter half of the essay. His claim to power is his ability to argue in writing: to make a case. He is conscious of the connection between legal argument and rhetorical power from the moment he departs from the table of Elijah Muhammad and his followers: "And I looked around the table. I certainly had no evidence to give them that would outweigh Elijah's authority or the evidence of their own lives or the reality of the streets outside . . . All my evidence would be thrown out of court as irrelevant to the main body of the case."[56] Even this interaction with his Muslim brothers recognizes the importance of legal rhetoric to the shaping of their reality. Baldwin does not feel that he can persuade the Muslims to see things his way; the reason again is power, because for most people, "power is more real than love. And yet power *is* real, and many things, including, very often, love, cannot be achieved without it."[57] He overcomes this moment of despair at his inability to persuade anyone who is steeped in any kind of ideology or seduced by power in the conclusion of the essay when he reaffirms the ability of "the relatively conscious whites and the relatively conscious blacks, who must, like lovers, insist on, or create, the consciousness of the others."[58] There is finally affirmation in the essay that love can triumph over power—even legal power, even criminal power.

Toward the end of "Down at the Cross," Baldwin makes explicit the central difficulty of resolving America's racial woes; he says, "There is simply no possibility of a real change in the Negro's situation without the most radical and far-reaching changes in the American political and social structure."[59] The legal structure is in fact the intersection of the American political and social structures or, at the very least, the most tangible evidence of those structures. Baldwin was clearly aware of the relationship between the legal and the social/political: the preceding quotation appears in Baldwin's essay directly after a reference to the *Dred Scott* decision—the 1857 case that concluded that black people were not U.S. citizens—and immediately before a reference to "the 1954 decision"—that is, *Brown v. the Topeka Board of Education*—that ended the practice of segregation in public schools. Such examples from history and from Baldwin's lifetime demonstrate how the legal structure of the United States exerts a powerful influence over Baldwin's quest for identity and over his views of his nation's unfulfilled promise of justice for all of its citizens. As he says in a 1963 interview, "There are 20 million Negro people in this country, and you can't put them all in jail."[60] He states the same idea more obliquely in "Down at the Cross": "There is a limit to the number of people any government can put in prison."[61] The fact that black people make up roughly 12 percent of the U.S. population but over 50 percent of the U.S. prison population[62] suggests that the trend Baldwin noticed fifty years ago continues and indeed has increased. The "criminal power" to incarcerate, to harass, and to legislate decisions that continue to place minorities and other disenfranchised individuals where society believes they belong—in housing projects, in impoverished neighborhoods, and in jail—has not necessarily diminished since the publication of Baldwin's essay. In fact, the potential for abuse has arguably increased with such acts of Congress as the U.S.A. Patriot Act, which has allowed the U.S. government to detain terrorist suspects without charge at the military base in Guantanamo Bay, Cuba. Baldwin's fiery, prophetic conclusion to "Down at the Cross" should be enough to inspire Americans to monitor carefully the potential for abuse when such acts become the law.

Notes

1. Leeming, *James Baldwin*, 211.
2. Baldwin, *The Fire Next Time*, 87.
3. Ibid., 30.
4. Ibid., 31.
5. Suggs, *Whispered Consolations*, 8.
6. Ibid., 16.
7. Crane, *Race, Citizenship, and Law in American Literature*.

8. Baldwin, *The Fire Next Time*, 23.

9. In *Notes of a Native Son*, 138–58.

10. Balfour, *The Evidence of Things Not Said*, 125.

11. Baldwin, *The Fire Next Time*, 19.

12. Ibid., 20.

13. Baldwin, "An Open Letter to My Sister, Angela Davis," 15.

14. Baldwin, *The Fire Next Time*, 22.

15. Ibid.

16. Ibid., 23.

17. Ibid.

18. Ibid., 27

19. Ibid., 25–26.

20. Ibid., 16.

21. Ibid.

22. See especially Baldwin's second novel, *Giovanni's Room* (1956).

23. Baldwin, *The Fire Next Time*, 16.

24. Ibid., 19.

25. Ibid., 83.

26. Ibid., 19–20.

27. Ibid., 16.

28. Baldwin and Mead, *A Rap on Race*, 249.

29. Kinnamon, *James Baldwin*, 3.

30. Baldwin, *The Fire Next Time*, 53.

31. Ibid., 27.

32. Ibid.

33. Ibid., 77.

34. Ibid., 9.

35. Ibid., 5.

36. Ibid., 5–6.

37. Ibid., 21.

38. Ibid., 68.

39. Ibid., 39.

40. Ibid., 47.

41. Ibid., 70.

42. Ibid., 65.

43. Ibid., 48–49.

44. Ibid., 57.

45. Ibid., 60.

46. Ibid., 95.

47. Ibid., 43.

48. Ibid., 60–61.

49. Balfour, *The Evidence of Things Not Said*, 131.

50. Deak Nabers, "Past Using," 221

51. Ibid.

52. Baldwin, *The Fire Next Time*, 59.

53. Nabers, 227, 228.

54. Baldwin, *The Fire Next Time*, 87.

55. Ibid., 98.

56. Ibid., 72.

57. Ibid., 73.

58. Ibid., 105.
59. Ibid., 85.
60. Standley and Pratt, *Conversations with James Baldwin*, 41.
61. Baldwin, *The Fire Next Time*, 103.
62. Murty, Owens, and Vyas, *Voices from Prison*, 15.

Bibliography

Baldwin, James. *The Amen Corner*. New York: Dial, 1968.
———. "Down at the Cross: Letter from a Region in My Mind." *New Yorker*, November 17, 1962.
———. *The Fire Next Time*. 1963. Reprint, New York: Vintage, 1993.
———. "Going to Meet the Man." New York: Dial, 1968.
———. *Go Tell It on the Mountain*. 1953. Reprint, New York: Dell, 1985.
———. *If Beale Street Could Talk*. New York: Dial, 1974.
———. "My Dungeon Shook: A Letter to my Nephew on the One Hundredth Anniversary of the Emancipation." *Progressive* 26 (December 1962): 19–20.
———. *Notes of a Native Son*. 1955. Reprint, Boston: Beacon, 1984.
———. "An Open Letter to My Sister, Angela Davis." In *If They Come in the Morning: Voices of Resistance*, edited by Angela Davis, 13–18. New York: The Third Press, 1971.
———. *Tell Me How Long the Train's Been Gone*. New York: Dial, 1968.
Baldwin, James, and Margaret Mead. *A Rap on Race*. Philadelphia: J. B. Lippincott, 1971.
Balfour, Lawrie. *The Evidence of Things Not Said: James Baldwin and the Promise of American Democracy*. Ithaca: Cornell University Press, 2001.
Brown v. the Topeka Board of Education, 347 U.S. 483 (1954).
Crane, Gregg D. *Race, Citizenship, and Law in American Literature*. Cambridge: Cambridge University Press, 2002.
Dred Scott v. Sandford, 60 U.S. 393 (1857).
Kinnamon, Keneth. *James Baldwin: A Collection of Critical Essays*. Englewood Cliffs, NJ: Prentice Hall, 1974.
Leeming, David. *James Baldwin*. New York: Knopf, 1994.
Murty, Komanduri S., Angela M. Owens, and Ashwin G. Vyas. *Voices from Prison: An Ethnographic Study of Black Male Prisoners*. Dallas: University Press of America, 2004.
Nabers, Deak. "Past Using: James Baldwin and Civil Rights Law in the 1960s." *Yale Journal of Criticism* 18, no. 2 (2005): 221–42.
Standley, Fred, and Louise Pratt. *Conversations with James Baldwin*. Jackson: University Press of Mississippi, 1989.
Suggs, Jon-Christian. *Whispered Consolations: Law and Narrative in African American Life*. Ann Arbor: University of Michigan Press, 2000.

8

"Fists and the Voices of Sorrowful Women"

Race, Gender, Violence, and the Reconstruction of the Word in Toni Morrison's *Jazz*

Charlton Copeland

Toni Morrison's novel *Jazz* is an often overlooked novel, situated as it is between the remarkable triumph of *Beloved* and the harrowing narrative of *Paradise*.[1] *Jazz* is often depicted as a respite from the social questions raised in the other two novels. Twenty years after its publication, it is clear that *Beloved* has entered into the canon of literature addressed by the genre of law and literature, as it made a significant contribution to the enduring themes of slavery and its memory, personhood, violence and the state's authority.[2] *Jazz*, however, has been variously described as a novel about the black migration,[3] the black experience in the urban North,[4] and the soured romance between a husband and wife.[5] While these descriptions are accurate, they obscure the extent to which *Jazz* serves as a critique of the violence perpetrated against black bodies—often with the law's implicit and explicit sanction.[6] More particularly, *Jazz* is a critique of the failure of law to protect black women's bodies from violence against them from *within* the black community.

Jazz's narrative revolves around the murder of Dorcas, a young, black woman who migrated to New York City after the brutal murder of her parents in the East St. Louis race riots. Dorcas's killer was her much older lover, Joe Trace, who is trapped in what appears to be a passionless marriage to Violet Trace.[7] What connects Joe, Violet, and Dorcas is both their status as migrants to New York, and the underlying reasons for their sojourn—the violence that has driven them to leave their native homes. Beyond their troubled marriage, Joe and Violet Trace share a narrative in which they escaped their tragic and violent pasts as children "abandoned" by their mothers, who had lived under the constant threat of racialized terror in the South. These stories intertwine with that of Dorcas's aunt, Alice Manfred. Her perspective unifies the novel's critique of violence and law and helps imagine the possibility of reconstruction.[8]

Law and violence stand at the center of *Jazz*'s narrative. The novel examines the history of the violence endured by blacks in the American South and that follows them to urban centers, including East St. Louis and New York City. In the face of both organized, interracial violence and intimate, intraracial, gender violence, the law appears silent. By situating violence as endemic to the lives of the characters, the narrative represents how law naturalizes such violence through the construction of private domains into which it cannot reach that justifies its failure to respond. *Jazz* disrupts law's construction of private domains, and its corresponding naturalization of violence, by illustrating the racial and gendered dimension of its construction of privacy.

Section one of this chapter explores the narrative's depiction of both law and violence as pervasive within the lives of African Americans. In particular, the novel juxtaposes the violence against the black communal body with violence committed against black, female bodies.[9] Through this contrast, the narrative marks the gulf between the communal response to so-called racial violence and the differential response to the gendered violence experienced by black women in their intimate relationships.[10] As a result, the narrative calls attention to the way in which racial violence[11] is interpreted as public or political, while gender violence is interpreted as private and beyond the scope of political commentary.[12] *Jazz*'s narrative demonstrates how the public-private distinction effectively sanctioned racialized violence in the post-Reconstruction era; it disrupts any attempt to depict the separation of public and private domains as "natural," but rather a social construct that is implicated in, and perpetuates, gender and race hierarchies. Additionally, it enables a critique of how the construction of a public-private binary creates domains where unchecked racial and gender terror are possible.

The second section will examine the narrative's depiction of the black community as consistently vulnerable due to the failure of the law to protect it from a threatening outside world. Although *Jazz*'s narrative disturbs the public-private distinction, it simultaneously relies upon this distinction in its call for an autonomous domain for the protection and flourishing of the black community. This private domain is recognized as the site of potential violence and terror perpetrated against the less powerful even as privatization is also configured as the source of protection against invasions from a hostile, surrounding community. Thus, *Jazz*'s narrative attempts to redeploy privacy, in both its communal and individual dimensions, to serve the ends of protecting black individual and communal self-assertion. The narrative posits that this form of privacy serves to protect the dignity and integrity of oppressed communities; it also serves as the grounds for Morrison's critique of the wider society's unjust practices.[13] *Jazz* criticizes the social construction of privacy that denies public recognition for so-called private violence and limits privacy's privilege on the basis of race and gender. At the same time, the novel also celebrates the normative possibilities of privacy.

Finally, the third section will examine the narrative's implicit critique of law's capacity to create a more just social order. To the extent that the law's possibilities are bound to, and defined by, its textual articulations that are constrained by formalistic reasoning, rather than the lived experience of injustice, the texts, and the words that construct them, are shown to be inadequate to deal with the inequalities that create and shape the normative world of the characters in *Jazz*. Despite the fact that slavery is a distant memory and the U.S. Constitution includes an explicit textual commitment to the ideal of equality, black people's lives serve as a testament to the "failure" of the word and the impotence of law to live up to that ideal.[14] The law's failure is not limited to the novel's setting; rather, it is present in the continuing controversies about the duties of government to protect its citizens from the ravages of private violence. Concluding with a critique of the Supreme Court's decision in *Castle Rock v. Gonzalez* (2005), this section will articulate how "language" that is constructed in the private spheres of a racially segregated world provides the possibility for the reconstruction and revitalization of the "dead" language of the Constitution.

Law and "Private" Violence in *Jazz*

Throughout *Jazz*, racial violence is generally understood, by individual victims and the wider black community, as "public" or communal violence and that the occurrence of violence demands a communal reaction.[15] The difference between the forms of violence presented in *Jazz* forces the reader to confront the differential communal treatment of gender violence within the black community and make visible the invisibility that is typical of gender violence. The narrative impels the reader to conclude that lawlessness connects both racial and gender violence and makes each possible.

Violence is pervasive and everyday in the lives of Morrison's characters, and this culture of pervasive violence is presented as the setting in which black life takes place.[16] Morrison's use of a narrator to begin the story gives us something of the everyday, ordinary quality of violence. The narrator begins saying, "Sth, I know that woman."[17] This suggests that the dramatic violence that sits at the center of the novel falls into the category of mere gossip. It serves as a way of locating and describing certain "others" within the community. The central point of the narrator's "gossip" is not to express outrage at the killing of a young girl by her jilted lover. Rather, it is aimed at situating the characters for a more important story. Thus, Joe Trace's killing of Dorcas merely locates his wife, Violet, for the reader. Violet is further defined by references to violence when we are told of the attempted assault against the dead girl's corpse—that she tried "to cut [Dorcas's] dead face" in the middle of her funeral. We are not to be outraged by the violence, necessarily, but rather by the fact that it was aimed at something so inconsequential as a dead girl in the middle of her funeral. The violence, or rather the context of the violence, marks Violet as "crazy." At this point one hardly remembers what, or who, had actually killed Dorcas. That is beside the point. The violence against Dorcas's female body—in the form of murder—is unremarkable; in fact, it seems that it is only Violet's actions that make the story worthy of gossip at all.

The unremarkable nature of violence against black, female bodies is evidenced by its depiction as part of the scenery of Harlem in 1926. In describing the city's landscape, the narrator tells us about the interaction of the sunlight and the buildings. The narrator declares, "Below is shadow where any blasé thing takes place: clarinets and lovemaking, fists and the voices of sorrowful women."[18] For those—like Alice Manfred who reared Dorcas since her parents' death—who act as if the violence against black women is extraordinary, the world has a lesson for them. Manfred seeks to protect Dorcas from what she considers the life of the streets—a life of violence that exists "out there" in some other place. However, Manfred appears naïve when we are told by the narrator that she passes in and through a world in which violence is ever-present; from behind whose walls songs can be heard to say, "Hit me but don't quit me." Manfred is forced to recognize the close proximity of violence against black women's bodies when her niece is killed by Joe Trace, who, she believes, "killed her niece just because he could."[19] Dorcas's murder is incomprehensible for Manfred, who seems confused by the fact that Joe was "[a] nice neighborly, every-body-knows him man. The kind you let into your house because he is not dangerous . . . [and you] felt not only safe but kindly in his company . . . He knew wrong wasn't right and he did it anyway."[20] Manfred's confusion seems unjustified given what we learn about her experiences with violence, or at least the ever-present threat of violence, but Dorcas's death forces the violence against black women's bodies out of the background and into the foreground of Manfred's consciousness. Morrison writes,

> Alice Manfred had seen and borne much, had been scared all over the country, in every street of it. Only now did she feel truly unsafe because the brutalizing men and their brutal women were not just out there, they were in her block, her house . . . Every week since Dorcas' death, during the whole of January and February, a paper laid bare the bones of some broken woman. Man kills wife. Eight accused of rape dismissed. Woman and girl victims of. Woman commits suicide. White attackers indicted. Five women caught. Woman says man beat. In jealous rage man.[21]

While Manfred's response to her niece's murder opens her eyes to the pervasive nature of violence against black women at the hands of men, she, too, is willing to inflict pain on the black woman who stole her husband. Like Violet, Manfred's first reaction upon being abandoned by her husband is not to seek revenge against him, or anything more than "vicious, childish acts of violence to inconvenience him . . . but no blood." Rather, the act of bodily harm and physical violence is reserved for the woman for whom he has left her. Morrison writes,

> [Alice Manfred's] craving settled on the red liquid coursing through the other woman's veins. An ice pick stuck in and pulled up would get it. Would a clothesline rope circling her neck yanked with all Alice's strength make her spit it up? Her favorite, however, the dream that plumped her pillow at night was seeing herself mount a horse, then ride it and find the woman alone on a road and gallop till she ran her down under four iron hooves; then back again, and again, until there was nothing left but tormented road dirt signaling where the hussy had been.[22]

In this regard, Manfred is not very different from Violet, who had sought to disfigure Dorcas's already-dead body, even as Violet continued to cook dinner for the husband, who had both cheated with Dorcas and had killed her.[23] Here, Joe continues to be the recipient of wifely obligation, while Dorcas's corpse is the receptacle of Violet's expression of anger at having been betrayed. Black women's bodies, then, are not just undervalued and abused by men—black and white—they are abused (or seen as the appropriate sites of abuse) by black women as well as sites of revenge even as black men are forgiven.

While Morrison explicitly links the violence against the bodies of black women to their lives, their environment, and their present reality, the violence against black bodies in general is also pervasive and constitutes another background of *Jazz*'s narrative. The narrative depicts racial violence as less ordinary than gender violence, if only to the extent that its perpetration elicits some response.[24] That is to say, racial violence is countered by the black community's response to it—to march, to kill, and to run. The juxtaposition of the response (when there is one) to racial violence and the nonresponse to gender violence reveals the relative value placed on specific black bodies by both the black community and the dominant society.

Violence against black bodies is a part of the history of the black experience in the North, no less than it is in the South. Morrison includes in her description of Harlem the histories of people who have come there from other places "running from want and violence." Thus, while the "race" has been running from violence, or had the hope that violence could be outrun, black women—as women—have not been able to share that sense of hope.[25] No such communal effort, it seems, is ever made to "outrun" the violence against black women, which is never behind but always present.

The most poignant image of violence against black bodies is Alice Manfred's memory of how she came to rear Dorcas, whose parents, we are told previously, had died in a fire. What we are not told, at least until Manfred remembers it for us, is that they died, along with two hundred others, in the 1917 East St. Louis race riot. The violence against black bodies was explained as a white reaction to returning black servicemen "who had fought in all-colored units, were refused the services of the YMCA, over there and over here, and came home to white violence more intense than when they enlisted and the battles they fought in Europe." We are told that others thought it to be the result of white fears of black workers. But Manfred suggests to us that she "[knows] the truth better than everybody": "Her brother-in-law was not a veteran, and he had been living in East St. Louis since the War. Nor did he need a whiteman's job—he owned a pool hall. As a matter of fact, he wasn't even in the riot; he had no weapons, confronted nobody on the street. He was pulled off the streetcar and stomped to death, and Alice's sister had just got the news and had gone home to try to forget the color of his entrails, when her house was torched and she burned crispy in its flame."[26] Manfred does not offer for us any reason why the riot happened; she blames her sister and brother-in-law's horrific deaths on the disorderly music, the "dirty, get-on-down music," whose playing was like "violating the law."[27]

There is something strangely wrong (and indeed blind) about Manfred's explanation. While she resists the fall into sociopolitical explanations of the expectations of black veterans or the racism of white workers, she also resists her own prescient (and troubling) explanation regarding her niece's violent death. Through Manfred's confusion, either willed or not, we see the connection between the deaths of the parent and the child: the murderers of Manfred's sister and brother-in-law killed them for the same reasons that Joe Trace killed Dorcas—"just because [they] could." In this respect, Dorcas's death (at the hands of a black man) and her parents' deaths (at the hands of a white mob) are connected both by their defenselessness and by the impunity with which they could be perpetrated. Manfred's brother-in-law, like his daughter, was unarmed and unprepared for the violence of battle. For Morrison, violence against black bodies, in general, and black women's bodies, in particular, is always about the power to terrorize. Here one gets the novel's first juxtaposition of the violence aimed at the corporate, black body and that aimed at African American women.

The violence against the black community is linked, again, to violence against black women through the description of Violet's mother's suicide. Violet wonders what could have pushed her mother to voluntarily choose death by jumping down a well: "What was the thing . . . the final thing she had not been able to endure or repeat?" Among those things that Violet imagines might have "pushed" her mother to her death are two separate incidences of violence against the corporate, black body. Violet wonders, "Perhaps word had reached her about the four-day hangings in Rocky Mount: the men on Tuesday, the women two days later. Or had it been the news of the young tenor in the choir mutilated and tied to a log, his grandmother refusing to give up his waste-filled trousers."[28]

Morrison uses violence to structure the novel and the lives of her characters. Speaking about the multiple times that he has "changed himself," Joe Trace connects those changes to the violence that precipitates them. For example, Joe's third change coincides with the burning of a black community. Joe remembers, "Red fire doing fast what white sheets took too long to finish: canceling every deed; vacating each and every field; emptying us out of our places so fast we went running from one part of the county to another—or nowhere."[29] Joe's sixth change, after he has already moved north to New York, is related to the racial violence in East St. Louis, which killed Alice Manfred's sister and brother-in-law. He says, "Then long come a summer in 1917 and after those whitemen took that pipe from around my head, I was brand new for sure because they almost killed me. Along with many a more."[30]

What is significant about the acts of violence against the corporate, black body is the response that it engenders. The violence of the East St. Louis race riot engenders a march down Harlem's Fifth Avenue "to advertise their anger over two hundred dead [in the riots]."[31] This collective expression by "silent black men and women" represents how the black community in New York City saw its fate connected to the lives and well-being of those who lived hours away. This expression of outrage, while completely appropriate, only further distinguishes the violence aimed at the corporate, black body from the violence aimed at black, female bodies: the latter form of violence does not elicit a parade of angry men or women walking down the street.[32] The community's corporate body, in this regard, is defined by racial allegiance without regard to the violence committed within its community on the lines of other power hierarchies.

However, one way in which corporate and female violence are indistinguishable is in their relationship to the law. The very fact of violence, either against black women in particular or against blacks in general, evidences an absence of law and indicts it. Every race riot, every lynching, and every act of terror requires that we question the law's inability (or unwillingness) to eradicate such violence.[33] The acts of violence enacted against the black community, as presented by Morrison, are always public and serve the purpose of establishing a racialized social order. That blacks would collectively protest these acts of violence, including a mass migration from the south, provides evidence that this violence constituted a public act, which demanded a public response. The failure of the black community to contest violence aimed at black women's bodies in both their public and political dimension only exacerbates the failure of law.

This is not merely a historical failure but a present-day failure of black political discourse. Devon Carbado has argued that the "antiracist discourse" within black America has historically subordinated gender issues, including domestic violence.

Carbado argues that in antiracist discourse, "black male victimhood is privileged," and that the black antiracist discourse is predicated upon the construction of an essentialized black identity, which "is often structured, predominantly, or exclusively around Black male subordination."[34] The black community's political and intellectual attention, as a result of this feature of black antiracist discourse, has been largely galvanized around those issues that affect the interests of black men.[35] This has been discussed in the context of violence against women of color, most articulately, by Kimberlé Crenshaw, who argues that neither feminist nor antiracist discourses adequately address the issues raised by violence against women of color.

Both Crenshaw and Carbado argue that the political discourse of antiracism is usually aimed at protecting "the integrity of the community," which counsels against "airing" the dirty laundry of domestic abuse within the black family. Crenshaw illustrates this point by demonstrating the response to her attempt to collect statistics on the rate of domestic violence interventions by precinct. Minority communities opposed the release because "they were concerned . . . that the data would unfairly represent Black and Brown communities as unusually violent, potentially reinforcing stereotypes that might be used in attempts to justify oppressive police tactics and other discriminatory practices."[36] It is within this intersection that the violence against black women's bodies must be resisted.

The law has effectively "privatized" the violence aimed at blacks, as if the state's uninvolvement proved that the state was not an actor in the perpetration of such violence, which was hardly the case.[37] The characterization of particular acts as private, and therefore as occurring solely between individuals, serves to remove these acts from the Constitution's purview. Within the historical context of violence against black communities, the practice of lynching was characterized as private violence between individuals, a characterization that fundamentally undermined the political movement for antilynching legislation.[38] Morrison's construction of a narrative that gives voice to the political, social, and economic ramifications and responses to such "private" violence challenges the easy characterization of a public and private sphere as naturally occurring, rather than social constructions.[39] The "private" acts of lynch mobs and terror gangs in the South and the North are implicated in the history of black subordination and white supremacy.[40] To declare these acts immune from the control of the federal Constitution, particularly in the context of the racial dynamics of the American South during the post-Reconstruction era, was to condemn blacks to such violence and terror.[41] Morrison's critique of the privatization of violence against black bodies is consistent with criticisms that have been leveled by legal scholars who highlight the historical "under-enforcement" of the criminal law in black communities.[42] Such underenforcement was predicated upon an undervaluation of the lives of black people, no matter the race of the perpetrator.

Why does the black community appear to endorse the devaluation of black lives with its apparent indifference to Dorcas's murder? Why is Joe Trace allowed to roam freely after murdering his former lover? Why doesn't someone call the police, the quintessential embodiment of law in everyday life, to have Joe Trace arrested and prosecuted? The law's failure here, I would note, is not limited to the criminal law but includes blacks' interactions with public and private bodies in ways structured by the law. The answer to these questions comes early in the novel. The narrator tells us "there was never anyone to prosecute [Joe Trace] because nobody actually saw him do it, and the dead girl's aunt didn't want to throw money to helpless lawyers or laughing cops when she knew the expense wouldn't improve anything."[43] The law or, rather, the goals of the law seem unrealizable for Alice Manfred. Because of historical experience, Manfred believes that the law's promise will remain unrealized in her life specifically and in the lives of blacks more generally. Manfred is accustomed to the devaluation of black lives by the police. Later in the novel, we learn that she, in accordance with Prohibition laws, attempted to enlist the support of the police in ridding Harlem of liquor, but she found the police unhelpful at best.[44] Manfred articulates the unrealized presence of law in the lives of black victims of both intra- and interracial violence when we are told why she did not call the police on Joe Trace: "She would have called the police after both [Joe and Violet] if everything she knew about Negro life had made it even possible to consider. To actually volunteer to talk to one, black or white, to let him in her house, watch him adjust his hips in her chair to accommodate the blue steel that made him a man."[45]

The law's presence in the lives of blacks is not merely one of malign neglect but also of affirmative threat. For example, Felice, Dorcas's best friend, remembers a conversation with her father regarding the arrest of white police officers for killing "some Negroes": "Once I thought if I read the papers we'd saved I could argue with him. But I picked wrong. I read about the white policemen who were arrested for killing some Negroes and said, I was glad they were arrested, that it was about time . . . He looked at me and shouted, "The story hit the paper because it was news, girl, news!" . . . [My mother] explained to me what he meant: that for the everyday killings cops did of Negroes, nobody was arrested at all."[46] A history of underenforcement of criminality aimed at black bodies, whether committed by blacks or whites, underlies this conversation. Morrison calls for the law to take greater notice of the effects of criminality—both official and civilian—on the black community. However, the narrative's juxtaposition of the community's steady recognition of, and response to, racialized violence marks the stark contrast between this reaction and its silence in the face of the violence suffered by women in their intimate relationships. The narrative forces a confrontation with the ways in which forms of violence deemed private by others is challenged by the black community, while the community simultaneously remains silent in the face of a violence that appears to mark the landscape of communal life as directly. This disparity requires that we interrogate not simply the black community's response, but the configuration of privacy in ways that countenance terror.

Protecting Black Moral Autonomy

Alongside the call to make the violence against black bodies more public—and making perpetrators of such violence answerable to the law—lies the novel's seemingly contradictory desire to affirm the need for the privatization of the black community as a morally autonomous unit. *Jazz* criticizes the law's failure to protect certain private spheres from domination by others. The black communities that the novel describes are in desperate need of the protection that privacy ensures.[47] Any celebration of privacy, however, can only be understood in conjunction with *Jazz*'s critique of the silencing potentialities of privacy, which undermine black women's ability to make known the abuse suffered in their most intimate relationships. Beyond merely highlighting the narrative's simultaneous critique and celebration of privacy's silencing potential, this section explores the consequences of black moral autonomy, which is presented as privacy's by-product.[48]

Throughout *Jazz*, black musical production is as ubiquitous as violence. Black musical production, as a cultural form, is both the result of a cultural particularity that is made possible by a segregated world and evidence of the inability of even a rigid racial segregation to resist culture's dynamic tendency. Black musical expression offers an example of the kind of cultural production that is possible when black moral autonomy is protected. The novel's presentation of jazz and blues—amalgamations of European, African, and American cultural forms—resists the claims to separation and isolation of American legal thought at the height of the Jim Crow era. Further, the role that narrative plays in the text also disrupts the sacred/secular binary. To the extent that these musical forms borrow from religious musical traditions, they resist the strict separation that is made, often by the novel's leading characters, of the sinner and the saint.[49]

The black community's desire for an autonomy-supporting privacy is decidedly connected to the decision not to alert "outsiders" to intracommunity dangers and injustices. Alice Manfred's decision not to call the police is grounded in two impulses. The first—a distrust in "the law's" (in the form of police officers') ability to take the black community's concerns seriously, particularly when a black man kills his black female lover—was discussed in the first section. The second impulse lies in the desire to construct a private space for the protection of both Manfred's individual integrity and the integrity of the black community. *Jazz*'s narrative fluctuates between these two poles: (1) condemnation of the privatization of violence against the black body by whites and the privatization of violence against the black female body by the black community, and (2) the condemnation of the lack of respect or recognition accorded to the black community's privacy. To let the law into her house, Manfred must risk violating the black community's fragile independence.

The novel's rejection of the privatization of violence against black women's bodies places Morrison's critique within the mainstream of feminist criticism of the private domain. Traditional feminist critiques of domestic violence have been clear in connecting differing conceptions of privacy—marital privacy in particular—as essential parts in the problem of the subordination of women. The most striking example of this argument is articulated by Elizabeth Schneider, who argues that "concepts of privacy permit, encourage, and reinforce violence against women. The notion of marital privacy has been a source of oppression to battered women and has helped to perpetuate women's subordination within the family."[50] Further, Schneider contends that privacy has been read as a problem for feminist theorists because it "rests upon a division of public and private that has been oppressive to women and has supported male dominance in the family."[51] The public realm is the domain of law and politics, the domain of reason giving and state regulation, while the private realm is one whose legitimacy is based in affective attachments, which are beyond the abilities of the law to regulate or to control. Traditional feminist critiques have depicted privacy as involving vulnerability and danger for women and children, whose very lives are largely lived beyond the bounds of the law. Frances Olsen identifies the (gendered) power dynamics underlying the concept of privacy stating, "Privacy is most enjoyed by those with power. To the powerless, the private realm is frequently not a sphere of freedom but of uncertainty and insecurity."[52] In addition to highlighting this gendered dimension of the enjoyment of privacy, *Jazz* displaces the racial dimension of privacy's enjoyment and the conflicts that it creates for black women who stand as privacy's victims and the unequal beneficiaries of its virtues.

The calls for a "privatized" space to protect the black community's autonomy have been championed most vigorously by several black feminist scholars. For example, Patricia Williams has argued for privacy, saying,

> It is true that the constitutional foreground of rights was shaped by whites, parceled out to blacks in pieces, ordained from on high in small favors, random insulting gratuities. Perhaps the predominance of their imbalance obscures the fact that the recursive insistence of those rights is also a defined by a black desire for them—desire fueled not by the sop of minor enforcement of major statutory schemes like the Civil Rights Act, but by the knowledge of, and generations of existing in, a world without any meaningful boundaries—and "without boundary" for blacks has meant not untrammeled vistas of possibility, but the crushing weight of total—bodily and spiritual—*intrusion*.[53]

It is the "intrusion" upon the black community by those who have no respect for its boundaries that marks the black experience with the law as well. The law's pervasive presence beyond the respectable bounds of family and marriage within the domain of slavery has forced blacks to value the central meaning of the protections of privacy, particularly as they have been expressed in familial integrity.[54]

The call for privatization by the black community stems from the history of the law's racially disparate intrusions into black family life. As Reva Siegel has pointed out, the demise of the right of marital chastisement was aimed centrally at the denigration of black men, rather than the protection of women—black or white—from violence. Siegel has argued that the southern courts that initially denied men the right to chastise their wives "seem[ed] more interested in controlling African American men than in protecting their wives."[55] With this background in mind, it is certainly understandable why this narrative, along with black feminist legal scholars, seeks to construct a boundary around the black community that keeps certain others out.

The fragility of the black community's autonomy is depicted throughout *Jazz* in terms of both familial and bodily invasions. This is most vividly expressed in the novel's depiction of Joe Trace's family as they are evicted from their property: "Then I got a job laying rail for the Southern Sky. I was twenty-eight years old and used to changing now, so in 1901, when Booker T. had a sandwich in the President's house, I was bold enough to do it again: decided to buy me a piece of land. Like a fool I thought I'd keep it. They ran us off with two slips of paper I never saw nor signed."[56] Thus, the violations of blacks' property rights occur with impunity.[57]

The vulnerability of blacks to the actions of whites, and black women to the actions of men within the black community, is exemplified by the story of Golden Gray in *Jazz*. Gray is biracial, though he had been reared to believe that he was white. He has come to look for, and presumably kill, his black father whom he has never known. Upon arriving at the home of his father, we are told that he "makes no attempt to knock and the door is closed but not latched. He enters and looks about for a place to put his trunk." On the way to the house, he had rescued an unconscious black woman, who lies hurt along the road. Having placed her nearly naked body on a bed in the house, he notices, "Everything about her is violent, or seems so, but that is because she is exposed under that long coat, and there is nothing to prevent Golden Gray from believing that an exposed woman will explode in his arms, or worse, that he will, in hers."[58] The lack of control over black people's property and their persons, as depicted by the unlatched door and the black woman's body, respectively, are both the cause and symbol of black vulnerability to the whims of others, including those of the state authorities.[59] Reading *Jazz* within and against the rhetoric of privacy reveals the racialized and gendered nature of the public-private distinction.

The policing of black women's bodies bears the mark of slavery's denial of personal and communal autonomy. Control over black bodies, including their reproductive capacity, was the paradigmatic symbol of the lack of control blacks had over their own lives and fates.[60] Black women's sexuality, therefore, marks a site of battle to determine the fate of the black community. Winning the battle to control black women's sexuality and reproduction is a significant element in creating an autonomous black community.[61] In *Jazz*, Alice Manfred's experience with her body has been as the battlefield upon which the black community has fought for its respectability and autonomy against a world that sought to deny it.[62] It has been a fight against the always-public, always-accessible aspects of her black, female body and sexuality. Manfred's parents were preoccupied with her burgeoning sexuality, which might result in "pregnancy without marriageability."[63] Alice's sexuality opened the possibility for the continued violation of black communal autonomy; hence it had to be controlled. Ironically, the battle for Alice's sexuality would never end in the recognition that it belonged to her alone. Her sexuality, it seems, was always the public property of another. Manfred remembers that "the moment she got breasts they were bound and resented, a resentment that increased to outright hatred of her pregnant possibilities and never stopped until she married Louis Manfred."[64] Manfred's reaction to Dorcas's sexuality is no different: "She hid [Dorcas's] hair in braids tucked under, lest whitemen see it raining round her shoulders and push dollar-wrapped fingers toward her . . . Taught her to crawl along the walls of buildings, disappear into doorways, cut across corners in choked traffic—how to do anything, move anywhere to avoid a whiteboy over the age of eleven. Much of this she could effect with her dress, but as the girl grew older more elaborate specifications had to be put in place."[65] Being a black woman raised the stakes in cross-racial interactions, because they heightened the likelihood that Dorcas might suffer invasions that could not be controlled by the black community. Indeed, the narrative itself declares, "Alice Manfred had worked hard to *privatize* her niece."[66] Such privatization represents the erection of a barrier against an outside world that would despoil Dorcas's supposed sexual innocence. Such innocence is a prized commodity in an economy that values marriage as the ultimate goal, and marriage is prized because it carries with it the possibility of privacy.

Jazz's narrative frames privacy as multidimensional. It has both negative and positive aspects—simultaneously keeping dangerous "others" out and allowing what is preserved to flourish into a morally autonomous community and culture. The flourishing of the black community, which privacy and separation allow, is central to understanding the narrative's ambivalence—echoing the writing of many feminist theorists—about jettisoning privacy, even when it is the site of violence and injustice.[67] Anita Allen has vigorously defended the positive dimensions of privacy against the traditionalist feminist school. Allen rejects the traditional feminist argument that privacy is the domain of "conservative male ideology," which reinforces subordination and seclusion. In response Allen writes, "Women have had too much of the wrong kinds of privacy: they have home-centered, care-taker's lives, when they have often needed and wanted forms of privacy inside and outside the home that foster personal development, while also making them more fit for participation in social life."[68]

Morrison weaves her own defense of a reconstructed notion of privacy through-out the novel, marking the possibilities and potential of a black community whose integrity is protected. For example, the flourishing of an autonomous black com-munity is exemplified in the narrative's description of how Violet's neighbors came to her family's rescue after her mother suffered a breakdown. These neighbors found them an abandoned house in which to live and gave them food to eat. The care Violet's neighbors provided is unthinkable except in the context of a world in which there are more than passing bonds of affection and concern. The mutual aid of the Vesper County of Violet's youth is similar to the civic associations of Harlem when she is older—organizations such as the Civic Daughters and the National Negro Business League, whose members included the likes of Alice Manfred and whose "clients" continue to be people like Violet Trace. The development of an institutional capacity within the black community capable of responding to need within its borders demonstrates a community that is both independent and able to determine the response to its urgent problems.

Like her ambivalence about the private violence against black women's bodies and sexuality, Alice Manfred also exemplifies the black community's complicated relationship with its cultural production and the autonomy upon which it rests. Black musical expression exists almost as its own character in *Jazz*'s narrative; its presence throughout the novel is central to the creation of the particular cultural community that unfolds. The blues-jazz idiom is perhaps the best example of the constructive possibilities of black cultural autonomy. Alice Manfred, however, attri-butes the violence that leads to her niece's death at the hands of her lover to the disorderly music whose presence is everywhere on the streets of Harlem. The music is disruptive to the orderliness of Manfred's life. The "low down" music made her "aware of flesh and something so free she could smell its blood smell; made her aware of its life below the sash and its red lip rouge."[69] The music makes Manfred aware of her own body and sexuality and the ways in which each has been impris-oned by a black community committed to a politics of respectability that deemed sexual expression and desire as things to be unexpressed.[70] Indeed, even Manfred recognizes the "policing" of her body by her parents: "They spoke to her firmly but carefully about her body: sitting nasty (legs open); sitting womanish (legs crossed) breathing through her mouth; hands on hips; slumping at table; switching when you walked."[71] Manfred's sexuality is not her own; it belongs to the collective, communal trust of the black community,[72] or at best it is the property of her husband—to be put to the (re)productive use of bearing children.[73] The music forces Manfred to confront, as she has never before, that there are women who had not succumbed to being owned by others, but the demands of self-possession for black women necessi-tated the facing of the fact that "power concedes nothing without struggle." It neces-sitated recognition that freedom came with a price, so the women who had chosen not to succumb to the black community's controls and to white domination chose to arm themselves—with ice picks, razor blades, switchblades, packets of lye, or shards of glass. It also forces Manfred to realize that she has allowed herself to be unarmed.

Although the low-down music fosters Manfred's consciousness about how her body and sexuality are controlled by others—by both white and black men alike—and their self-respecting female accomplices, Manfred continues to view the music with dread. Manfred notices the threat of degradation in the presence of "not just ankles, but knees in full view; lip rouge red as hellfire; burnt matchsticks rubbed into eyebrows; fingernails tipped with blood." The cause of this degradation for Manfred is none other than music: "Songs that used to start in the head and fill the heart had dropped on down, down to places below the sash and the bucked belts. Lower and lower, until the music was so lowdown you had to shut your windows and just suffer the summer sweat when men in shirtsleeves propped themselves in window frames, or clustered on rooftops, in alleyways, on stoops and in the apartments of relatives playing the lowdown stuff that signaled Imminent Demise."[74] Indeed, Manfred rejects the sociological explanations of the race riots of the World War I period, believing instead that "the music" was the source of the violence because "it made you do unwise disorderly things."[75] Manfred intends to critique and reject the thorough recklessness of the low-down music because it could only end in the riot that killed her sister and her brother-in-law.

Because *Jazz* juxtaposes the violence aimed at the black, corporate body against violence aimed at the black, female body, it is quite significant that jazz is associated with violence. Alice Manfred frames music as "dangerous" and having the potential to foment violence. She asks rhetorically, "And where there was violence wasn't there also vice? . . . [Including,] of course, race music to urge them on."[76] Race music is the site where "a clarinet coughs and clears its throat waiting for the woman to decide on the key."[77] Indeed, it is the music of longing, hunger, appetite, music of the "barrel hooch"—it is jazz and blues. The words of the "nasty" music are described as not only as "greedy, reckless[,] loose and infuriating, [but also as] hard to dismiss because underneath, holding up the looseness like a palm, are the drums that put Fifth Avenue into focus."[78] *Jazz*'s narrative affirms Manfred's fear of the angry potential and disorderly possibilities of race music. Race music confused the boundaries of private and public, as it provided an outlet, for musician and listener alike, to express their private sorrow and longings in a uniquely public way. This confuses Alice, who has been taught to conform to a racial-gender norm implicit within discourses about privacy.

Manfred attempts to ease her discomfort with the music produced by "fingering horns" by dismissing its import, and she is buffeted by the conclusions of sermons and editorials of the opinion leaders in black America. Nevertheless, Manfred recognizes the seriousness of this "embarrassing" music—"she heard a complicated anger in it; something that disguised itself as flourish and roaring seduction." Manfred declares that the lowdown music moved her beyond hurt and toward anger: "It made her hold her hand in the pocket of her apron to keep from smashing it through the glass pane to snatch the world in her fist and squeeze the life out of it for doing what it did and did and did to her and everybody else she knew or knew about. Better to close the windows and shutters, sweat in the summer heat of a silent Clifton Place apartment than to risk a broken window or yelping that might not know where or how to stop."[79] The low-down music ushers in a new consciousness for Alice Manfred. This consciousness is one that moves her beyond the earliest emotions of fear and hurt and toward anger. The basis of Manfred's anger is not articulated explicitly, but given the fact that she is watching a protest march marking the death of her sister, brother-in-law and others who have met with similar fates, one needn't wonder long as to the basis of Manfred's anger. The object of such anger is similarly ambiguous—aimed only at the world for what it had done to her and those around her. Unlike the earlier expression of Manfred's desire to hurt her husband's lover, this desire for violence warrants neither contempt nor laughter. However, its expression seems as awkward as the trampling of a competitor under a horse's hooves; it is exemplified in the crashing of one's fist through the glass window, and it is as ambiguous as "squeezing the life" out of the world. Manfred's anger is a serious anger, and it is destined to remain so given Manfred's choice to suppress it by shoving the offending hand into her apron pocket or shuttering herself away from the low-down music.

By shining a light on the consequences of the law's failure to protect the integrity of black communities—in their possession of property, or their familial and bodily integrity—*Jazz* calls us to see what a community whose autonomy is not respected looks like. In this sense, we interpret the narrative as calling for a boundary of sorts around the black community, whose history is littered with the incursions against property and bodily integrity by hostile others. The novel also suggests that privatization not only protects against invasions from without but also allows individual and communal flourishing and cultural development from *within*. Such flourishing is exemplified in the rise of black social-aid and business organizations that care for the disadvantaged, the increase in communal attachments that care for children whose mothers have ceased to be caretakers, and the further development of cultural practices that aid in the construction of a critical consciousness of the outside (and inside) world. The creation of authentic community is the ground on which counternarratives and competing normative visions are constructed. It is the competition for alternative meaning, the novel offers, as the source for a reconstructed word that neither belongs to the hostile outside world, or the autonomous inside community. The reconstructed word in a new amalgamation, improvisation—indeed, a new creation.

Jazz and the Reconstruction of the Word

The Failing Word

Jazz challenges the social and legal distinctions that have allowed violence to be perpetrated against vulnerable bodies. Morrison disrupts the private-public distinction that has allowed both race and gender violence to escape the law's censure. More importantly, however, the novel highlights and criticizes the law's role in creating and perpetuating the categorical distinctions that justified its inaction in the face of so-called private terror. It is through such disruption that the narrative reveals the multiplicity of controls over black women's bodies by outside others—be they white male employers or loving parents in search of respectability. The narrative also upsets the dichotomy between reason and emotion as exemplified by the distinction between words and rhythm.[80] The central claim of this section is that *Jazz* destabilizes conventions about the separateness of "word" from "rhythm." For Morrison, challenging the "mind-body split" allows her to articulate the possibility of the rhythm's reconstruction of the word, which leads to a reconstruction of the black community.

As *Jazz* unfolds, Manfred remembers the role music played in the political display against the race riots that had brought Dorcas to New York City. The public, political response to the violence against the black, corporate body is paired in Manfred's memory with the rhythm of the drums that are played as the demonstrators march along Fifth Avenue. Manfred remembers standing there for hours "listening to drums saying what graceful women and the marching men could not."[81] The rhythm of the drums speaks to Manfred, but the narrative suggests that its meaning might be hidden to those beyond the black community. Manfred remembers, "What was possible to *say* was already in print on a banner that repeated a couple of promises from the Declaration of Independence and waved over the head of its bearer. But what was *meant* came from the drums. It was July 1917 and the beautiful faces of the cold and quiet; moving slowly into the space the drums were building for them."[82] Here, Manfred's memory presents a space (and perhaps a dissonance) between what is safe to *declare* on a banner on a public street in New York—"a couple of promises"[83]—and what is known and understood by a black community whose independent integrity and moral agency constitute the ground upon which such promises are criticized as empty as they relate to black life in the United States.[84] Manfred's memory allows us to witness the constant hermeneutic crisis that marks black life in the early twentieth century, which is lived in the space between what is *said* in the hallowed words of our founding documents and what is *lived* in black experiences.[85] Further, Manfred notes, "The drums and freezing faces hurt her, but hurt was better than fear and Alice had been frightened for a long time . . . Now, down Fifth Avenue from curb to curb came a tide of cold black faces, speechless and unblinking because what they meant to say but did not trust themselves to say the drums said for them, and what they had seen with their own eyes and through the eyes of others the drums described to a T. The hurt hurt her, but the fear was gone at last."[86] It is impossible for the reader to miss the fact that this description of the drums is Manfred's second attempt to describe the scene that she witnessed. It is almost identical to the previous description, bearing in it the repetition that is central to its being cemented into our consciousness. In the first description we are told that the drum does for the black community something that it could not do for itself—express a meaning that the community's words cannot. However, the narrative is not content to merely repeat what has been stated before. This "riff" plays upon the same essential theme as the initial impression but varies it in important ways. In Manfred's second memory of the drums, we are faced with a hermeneutic crisis—the unbridgeable gulf between declarations and meanings—but we are met with a hermeneutic harmonization because the drums do not simply remark upon the emptiness of words but carry with them the fulfillment of words that dare not be spoken. Here, rather than show the world of the drums as a pragmatic (and deficient) compromise, as in Manfred's initial depiction, the reader comes to the conclusion that the drums are seen as worthy substitution and alternative, meaning-giving devices.[87] The drums serve as both evidence of the rupture of meanings between black life and the words of the unfulfilled promises—the crisis—and as the potential reparative tool for the breach.

Not only does the narrative suggest a critique of the power of words—the empty promises of the "Declaration of Independence"—but it also suggests the emptiness of the Constitution's language. The choice of the "Declaration of Independence" as an alternative to the Constitution's text is central to the African American constitutional hermeneutic, especially as the Supreme Court has, for most of its history, emptied the Constitution of its commitment to more than merely formal equality.[88] For example, the U.S. Supreme Court's most recent response to the terror of family violence suggests that the days of judicial acquiescence to state impotence are not over. In *Castle Rock v. Gonzalez*, the Court rejected a plaintiff's civil rights suit against a local government and several police officers for their failure to respond to her requests to enforce a permanent restraining order. Jessica Gonzales, who had separated from her husband, received a permanent restraining order, which limited her estranged husband's access to her residence and to their children. After noticing that her children were missing from her front yard, Gonzales reported the children missing and informed the police that she suspected that her husband had taken them, a violation of the restraining order. After several hours of calling and visiting the police department, during which time she was repeatedly told to call again later, her estranged husband arrived at a police precinct and opened fire, where he was subsequently killed. After killing him, the police found Gonzales's three daughters in the cab of his truck, already murdered. Gonzales brought suit alleging that the police's failure to act pursuant to her restraining order constituted a violation of the Due Process Clause of the Fourteenth Amendment.

Gonzales's suit was based on her assertion that the permanent restraining order entitled her to the state's protective services, which required them to act whenever they were under a reasonable belief that the terms of the restraining order were being violated. Here, there was no question that such a reasonable belief existed. At issue was whether the words printed on the back of the restraining order might be construed to have created an entitlement to the aforesaid services.[89] The Court rejected the contention that the language on the restraining order created a mandatory obligation on the part of local police officers to arrest violators. The Court explained that, in light of the long history of police discretion in the decision to make arrests, the order's language must be read as not imposing a mandatory obligation on the police, even in the context of domestic violence.

The Court's ruling also reconstructs a private-public dichotomy that undermines the usefulness of the order's words as effective sources of protection for Mrs. Gonzales and her family. The Court declared that even if the order's words could be read to infer a mandatory duty to arrest a violator, such a conclusion would not translate into an entitlement for Mrs. Gonzales. The Court explained that making the officers' duties, with respect to violators of restraining orders, mandatory served the "public rather than private ends." Hence, Gonzales's concerns for her safety and that of her children are separable from the interest of the state's interest in insuring that its criminal proscriptions are not flouted. Presumably, the protection of Gonzales's safety does not rise to the level of a public concern even where there is a text arguably committed to such a proposition. Here, the Court—like its earlier decisions—continues to rely on a rigid separation of these spheres even where their separation means vulnerability and terror.[90]

The Court's decision also ignores the social and historical contexts that gave rise to mandatory-arrest policies in various states. As Justice Stevens, writing in dissent, notes, the majority gave "short shrift" to mandatory arrest statutes in the particular context of domestic violence. The dissent pointed out that during the 1980s and 1990s, several states passed mandatory arrest statutes in order to eliminate police discretion over arrests in the domestic violence context.[91] Justice Stevens wrote that Colorado's mandatory arrest statute was explicitly aimed at effectively responding to "the crisis of police underenforcement in the domestic violence sphere,"[92] which stemmed, in part, from "the perception by police departments and police officers that domestic violence was a private, 'family' matter and that arrest should be used as a last resort."[93] The dissenters contended that, given the historical context of Colorado's mandatory arrest statute, the dissent rejected the majority's conclusion that there was no clear evidence that Colorado intended to eliminate police discretion in the exercise of its obligations where there was probable cause that a restraining order was being violated.

Like the participants in the march in Alice Manfed's Harlem, the text and the word proved to be powerless for Mrs. Gonzales. It proved to be powerless in prodding action from a police department otherwise occupied, even though she had what she thought (erroneously, said a majority of the Supreme Court) was a "contract" enforceable for the protection of herself and her children against violation by a violent intimate. For her, in reality, the words on the back of the restraining order were not meant for her protection. She possessed no privity of the contract enacted between the violator of the order and the state, as the terror suffered at his hands is deemed a private harm. Like those walking through the New York streets armed with the unfulfilled promises of the Declaration of Independence in the Harlem of the 1920s, the word had proved powerless to protect—indeed, the word had failed.

Reconstructing the Word

This chapter is clearly not the first text to assert that cultural and artistic expressions possess the potential to transform the nature of legal reasoning.[94] Indeed, I am not the first to claim such a central role for jazz.[95] I do assert, however, that jazz—and the cultural and artistic lineage from which it springs—serves as an appropriate metaphor for the way in which the law might be reconstructed to address present day injustices. Christopher Bracey has argued that jazz serves as an appropriate metaphor for rethinking the role of the judge in adjudication that "is self-consciously engaged in the constructive enterprise of giving full meaning and content to minority rights."[96] Jazz's disruption and reconfiguration connect it to the repetitive reworking of the novel's narrative. Jazz, like the novel's narrative, disrupts the many assumptions out of the cultural and political era in which it appears. It serves as a refutation of the assertion of the permanence and naturalness of racial separation (and hence subordination).[97] As a product of the interaction between black "vernacular forms transformed . . . with the tools of Western music,"[98] jazz embodies the cultural mongrelization of American society that racial subordination attempted to deny. Moreover, the transformation of European instruments and rhythmic patterns when fused with West African rhythmic patterns serves to indicate the alchemist quality of cultural experience—that is, that cultural production cannot be sealed off into distinct racialized or privatized space. The very presence of jazz spoke to the possibility of not only a cultural world that transcended racial boundaries but also a social-political-economic order that transcended them as well. As Ralph Ellison writes about the cultural dualisms present in black musical traditions, "You got glimpses, very vague glimpses of a far different world than that assigned by segregation laws, and I was taken very early with a passion to link together all I loved within the Negro community and all those things I felt in the world which lay beyond."[99]

Despite jazz's identity as cultural hybrid, its development as a distinct musical form, suggests Leroi Jones (later Amiri Baraka), is impossible without the rise of a segregated black community in the post-Reconstruction era. He writes, "The Negro could never become white and that was his strength; at some point, always, he could not participate in the dominant tenor of the white man's culture. It was at this juncture that he had to make use of other resources, whether African, subcultural, or hermetic. And it was this boundary, this no man's land, that provided the logic and beauty of his music."[100] Jazz, then, is grounded in the experience of the tightening of the color line against blacks, and it is nurtured by the community that is constructed "behind the veil." Scholars have described jazz music as the artistic expression of "cultural identity and frustration" that are the result of the post-Reconstruction era.[101] Thus, jazz as a cultural form both disrupts the assumption of the hermetically sealed, racially fragmented culture defended by a racially subordinating society and continues to find use in the specificity and particularity of the cultural form that articulates a set of racially dependent experiences that defined reality for blacks in the United States.

Jazz as product of a cultural hybridization also highlights the simultaneous naturalness and unnaturalness of jazz as cultural production. By this, I mean jazz is "natural" to the extent that it is the result of the cultural combinations and adaptations that occur when cultures meet, even on grounds of radical inequality. By "unnatural," I simply mean that there is nothing inevitable about jazz as a cultural production. Jazz is a product of the interactions between diverse cultural material to create something altogether new. As Ellison indicates, "Jazz finds its very life in an endless improvisation upon traditional materials." Ellison goes on to define the "jazz moment" as an individual's challenge that asserts one's independence from, yet connection to, the tradition—"each solo flight, or improvisation represents . . . a definition of his identity as individual, as member of the collectivity and as a link in the chain of tradition."[102] Eric Porter describes jazz's "improvisational spirit" as the simultaneous extension of folk musical forms by black musicians, such as the blues and the spirituals, with the assistance of written composition, yet "escaping the confines of the written score by reaching back into the vernacular" tradition.[103]

At the center of *Jazz*'s narrative sits an incredible improvisation—the relationship that develops between Violet Trace and Alice Manfred—that opens up a world of different possibilities for each character. After violently disrupting Dorcas's funeral by attempting to vandalize the dead girl's corpse, Violet had made attempts to see and speak with Alice Manfred. Understandably, Manfred rejected Violet's overtures, declaring, "I don't have a thing to say to you. Not one thing."[104] Their relationship begins strangely, with Violet not offering an apology for her behavior at the funeral but simply asserting that she needed a place to rest. During Violet's third visit, while Manfred stitches Violet's dress, Manfred and Violet Trace have an exchange that underscores the ways in which their interactions disrupts the ordinary responses of victim and violator:

"At first I thought you came here to harm me. Then I thought you would want to offer condolences. Then I thought you wanted to thank me for not calling the law. But none of that is it, is it?"
  "I had to sit down somewhere. I thought I could do it here. That you would let me and you did."[105]

Violet's visits, which were as irregular as they were unscheduled, became a space of freedom for Manfred—indeed Manfred admits that Violet is the only visitor to whom she looks forward. Manfred, who prided herself on her hospitality and the role of playing host, takes a certain license with Violet's visits because they allow for a lack of pretense. Manfred observes, "The thing was how Alice felt and talked in her company. Not like she did with other people. With Violet she was impolite. Sudden. Frugal. No apology or courtesy seemed required or necessary between them. But something else was—clarity."[106] What makes Manfred and Violet's relationship reminiscent of the improvisation of the jazz moment is its rejection of the standard response to the tragedy that connects these two women. They allow themselves to break from the routine of offering condolences, apologies, and recriminations, but their interaction never denies the legitimacy of any of these feelings; however, their interaction does not allow them to stop there. Here, in this new, complex relationship, upon which each has grown to depend, they are allowed to respond as they feel in the moment. Their interaction stands as a declaration that the "story" need not go according to script.[107] It declares that interactions between individuals need not follow the path worn by others. This is best summed up when the not-so-omniscient narrator, whose words have guided us through the narrative, says,

So I missed it altogether. I was sure one would kill the other. I waited for it so I could describe it. I was so sure it would happen. That the past was an abused record with no choice but to repeat itself at the crack with no power on earth could lift the arm that held the needle. I was so sure, and they danced and walked all over me. Busy, they were, busy being original, complicated, changeable—human, I guess, you'd say, while I was the predictable one, confused in my solicitude into arrogance, thinking my space, my view was the only one that mattered. I got so aroused while meddling, while finger-shaping, I overreached and missed the obvious.[108]

The insistence that things might be other than they are, that the past has no hold on the present or future even as there is recognition of the past's importance, is quite possibly the central meaning of the jazz moment and, indeed, most central to American democracy.[109]

Notes

1. See generally Schur, "Locating Paradise in the Post-Civil Rights Era."
2. West, "Caring for Justice," 197–98; and Ball, *The Word and the Law*, 73–95.
3. See Griffin, *Who Set You Flowin'*?
4. Paquet-Deryis, "Toni Morrison's *Jazz* and the City," 219.
5. See Jones, "Traces in the Cracks"; and O'Reily, "In Search of My Mother's Garden."
6. For an exploration of domestic violence in *Jazz*, see Knadler, "Domestic Violence in the Harlem Renaissance."
7. For a history of the East St. Louis Riot of 1917, see Elliot Redwick, *Race Riot at East St. Louis*.
8. Few other critiques consider Alice Manfred as the focal point in Morrison's critique of racial and gender violence. See Griffin, *Who Set You Flowin'*? 185. I adopt this position because the reader comes to know Manfred's inner thoughts more than other characters. In addition, the narrative constructs Manfred as one who is both self-conscious and self-critical, leading to a certain level of trust in Manfred's self-presentation. Also, by framing Manfred as "normal" (i.e., not mentally unstable like Violet and Joe Trace), the narrative can reveal the extent of the wounds on the black psyche caused by racial and gender violence. Manfred's madness cannot be as easily dismissed as either Violet's or Joe's madness can.
9. See generally Baker, *Betrayal*, 1–15.
10. While I hesitate to make too much of a distinction between "race violence" and "gender violence" for fear that I will be replicating what I seek to reject, it is necessary that one take the world as given, rather than as one wishes it were. For a persuasive critique of this "narrow" conception of gender violence, see Harris, "Gender, Violence, Race and Criminal Justice." By her definition, all of the violence that is projected against the black community, without regard to gender, is gender violence in that it was the projection of white male gender performance against the black community. While I am persuaded by Harris's arguments in this regard, I am not sure what this may mean for women who are the victims of violence at the hands of men in the so-called private sphere. This is to say, I am not sure whether the response to the broader category of gender violence that Harris presses would be structured in ways that reinforce particular gender hierarchies or not, with the gender violence that occurs against black males being accorded more importance than that which occurs against black women at the hands of black males. It is on that ground, then, that I am comfortable with the distinctions—clumsy though they may be—introduced above.
11. On the construction of the black, corporate body as a black, male body, see Anderson, "Abominations of a Million Men: Reflection of a Silent Minority."
12. For a relevant, modern discussion of the contexts that increase the risk of and shape the nature of black women's greater vulnerability to gender violence, see Miller, "Getting Played," 46–47.
13. For a discussion of the normative possibilities of community, see Cover, "Nomos and Narrative."
14. See generally Ball, *The Word and the Law*. See also White, *When Words Lose Their Meaning*, 244.
15. I should be clear here to state that by "reaction" I do not mean a communal violent reaction, or even a necessarily "political" reaction. Rather, black people respond to this violence by including it as a central element in the narratives about their lives. This, then, forces the community to respond—either by migrating, marching, fighting back, or running away. The community in *Jazz*, however, does not "take on" the burden of facing the

pervasive violence against black women. This violence forms part of the ordinary social background, rather than the way that slavery or segregation might serve as the background for social solidarity against which we define ourselves and work to escape.

16. Baker, *Betrayal*, 4–6.

17. Morrison, *Jazz*, 3.

18. Ibid., 7.

19. Ibid., 73.

20. Ibid., 73–74.

21. Ibid., 73–74. While this section does not indicate, explicitly, that these incidents were violence against black women, this conclusion seems to fit best with the language of the section, in which the only descriptive used is "white," used to designate attackers who had been indicted. Moreover, this fits with the next paragraph in the text, which speaks of black women defending themselves as armed and not defenseless, as she takes Dorcas to have been.

22. Ibid., 86. Manfred's bourgeois naivety and her murderous response to the woman who has attracted her husband's attentions are not inconsistent. Such simultaneously held positions of innocence and revenge are key to the discipline imposed on black women's sexual identities and behavior in the northern urban areas. For a broader discussion of this dynamic, see Carby "Policing the Black Woman's Body in an Urban Context." However, such responses, which inevitably let men off the hook, do not go by without critique; Violet, who "does hair," is criticized by her customer, who says, "Now I reckon you going to tell me some old hateful story about how a young girl messed over you and how *he's* not to blame because *he* was just walking down the street minding his own business, when this little twat jumped on his back and dragged him off to bed. Save your breath" (ibid., 14).

23. An alternative interpretation of Violet and Manfred's violence against their respective sexual competitors is that it fits the classic revenge narrative. Such revenge can be seen as an alternative when the law fails to redress a wrong. See generally Posner, *Law and Literature*. In this interpretation, Violet and Manfred's violence can be read as an attempt to protect what the law had attempted to destroy—the integrity of the black family unit and the integrity of black affective commitments. Their resort to violence to keep their households in tact is a rejection of the narrative of the absent black father. See Spillers, *Black, White, and in Color*.

24. I do not mean to suggest here that there is always some response but rather that the sense that some response would be appropriate is always present.

25. The historicized reading of violence against black bodies is certainly a misimpression on the novel's part. The violence that attends black women's lives is perhaps more present than the violence that attends black lives and bodies, but the latter is no less a thing of another place and time, left to the South or to history.

26. Morrison, *Jazz*, 57.

27. This "low-down" is likely blues music, which, as Angela Davis suggests, actually allows black women to publicize and critique the violence that is being committed against them. See Davis, *Blues Legacies and Black Feminism*, 25. Porter notes the absence, or marginalization, of female voices from the early canonization of blues music, as "manhood was often a crucial element in a discussion of aesthetics, culture, race, economics, national identity and other issues. Porter, *What Is This Thing Called Jazz?* 27.

28. Morrison, *Jazz*, 101. Even here, the gendered dimension of racial violence is present. See Harris, "Gender Violence, Race and Criminal Justice."

29. Morrison, *Jazz*, 126.

30. Ibid., 128.

31. Ibid., 57.

32. The courageous mass movement down the Harlem streets is clearly opposed to the reaction that the black community has in the face of violence between men and women. The omniscient narrative describes the interactions with activities on the streets saying, "If a foght breaks out between a man and a woman do they cross in the middle of the block to watch or run to the corner in case it gets messy." Morrison, *Jazz*, 72. The crowds' willingness to confront racial violence, yet flee from "domestic" violence raises the quandary of the black community's disparate response to these different types of violence. On the significance of the law's silence, see Zanita Fenton, *Silence Compounded*.

33. On the law's indifference to the terrorization of blacks in post-Reconstruction America, see Philip Dray, *At the Hand of Persons Unknown*.

34. Carbado, "The Construction of O. J. Simpson as a Racial Victim," 160.

35. Examples that illustrate this include the focus on racial profiling, which, in popular discourse, has been limited to "driving while black," a single subset of racial profiling that largely affects black males and the incarceration rates of black men in prisons. For an insightful discussion of how black political discourse ignores the troubles of black females, see Kelly, "Countering the Conspiracy to Ignore Black Girls."

36. Ibid., 1253.

37. The law's privatization of violence against black bodies historically, including the period about which Morrison writes, occurred in the Supreme Court's decision in *United States v. Harris* (1883). There the Court declared that Congress did not have the power to remedy "private violence." Throughout the 1880s, the Supreme Court effectively undermined many of the Reconstruction era's most significant legislative initiatives, narrowing the scope of the Fourteenth Amendment to remedying only the states' violations of the rights of citizens. See also *United States v. Stanley* (1883) and *United States v. Cruikshank* (1875). More recently, the Supreme Court has recommitted itself to this narrowed reading of the Fourteenth Amendment by invalidating Congress's authority to create a civil penalty to remedy gender-motivated violence in the Violence Against Women Act. See *United States v. Morrison* (2000).

38. See Ford, "Constitutionality of Proposed Federal Anti-Lynching Legislation."

39. On the social construction of the public and private sphere, see Olsen, "Constitutional Law."

40. See generally Williamson, "A Rage for Order." See also Carby, "'On the Threshold of the Women's Era.'"

41. Walter Brundage has estimated that one third of all lynchings involved "mass mobs." See Brundage, *Lynching in the New South*.

42. See generally Kennedy, *Race Crime and the Law* and Kennedy, "The State, Criminal Law, and Racial Discrimination." See also Meares and Kahan, *Urgent Times: Policing and Rights in Inner-City Communities*.

43. Morrison, *Jazz*, 4.

44. Ibid., 55.

45. Ibid., 74

46. Ibid., 199.

47. For an explanation of the positive forms of privacy, see Allen, *Uneasy Access*.

48. Hersch, *Subversive Sounds*, 86–98.

49. See Cone, *The Spirituals and the Blues*, 97–127 (discussing the blues as a "secular spiritual"). In the novel, Joe approaches his upstairs neighbor to rent her spare room to meet with Dorcas, offering to pay her fifty cents a week, Joe says, "You be surprised what you can save if you like me and don't drink, smoke, gamble or tithe." Joe's statement suggests an equivalence among activities that most would view as vices and the

last, which is commonly thought of as virtuous. Here, the equation undercuts efforts to distinguish between worldly vice and sacred addiction; they all seem read like disempowering obsessions. Morrison, *Jazz*, 48.

50. Schneider, *Battered Women and Feminist Lawmaking*, 87.

51. Ibid., 89. Schneider's defenses of privacy emphasize an individualism that is often absent in the community-focused conceptions of black feminist critics.

52. Olsen, "Constitutional Law," 325.

53. Williams, *The Alchemy of Race and Rights*, 164.

54. For a discussion of the ways that the law was used in postemancipation America to undermine the autonomy of the black family, see Davis, *Neglected Stories* and Higginbotham, *Shades of Freedom*. In the novel, Joe Trace's search for a "private" place to which he can bring Dorcas is framed in the language of respectability. Joe's attempt to rent a room from his upstairs neighbor, Malvonne, is based on his search for both respectability and a "respectable lay." When Malvonne initially rejects his offer to rent a room in her home for two dollars a month, he responds, "Come on, girl. You driving me to the street. What I'm asking for is better ain't it? Every now and then I visit with a respectable lady." This in contrast to his response to Malvnonne's suggestion that he would better use his money to engage a prostitute. He responds, "I don't want nobody off the street. Good Lord." Joe Trace's response, even as he asks his neighbor to hide his intentions to cheat on his wife, is one of moral outrage that he would be driven to engage with a woman from the streets or engage her *in* the streets, either of which is read as lacking respect. It is the privacy, and respectability that accompanies it, that justifies Joe Trace's willingness to pay two dollars per month. Morrison, *Jazz*, 46–47.

55. Siegel, "The Rule of Love." Privacy is also sexualized. Lesbians and gay men have often been denied the right of privacy in their most intimate relations. See Harper, *Private Affairs*, 28. See also *Bowers v. Hardwick* (1987).

56. Morrsion, *Jazz*, 126. That blacks were commonly defrauded of their property is further illustrated in the novel, as we see a description of Violet's grandmother's reverse migration to the South after she had migrated to Baltimore. She had left as a slave but had returned as a free woman. Returning to Vesper County, True Belle saw the depths into which her daughter and her grandchildren had sunk (ibid., 138).

57. For an insightful theoretical argument regarding the connection between property ownership—or at the very least, the importance of the state's respect for property ownership—to the social contract, see generally Atuahene, "From Reparation to Restoration."

58. Morrison, *Jazz*, 153.

59. Dorothy Roberts has made this point most forcefully and called for a conception of privacy as a constitutive element of equality. Considering the large disparity in the number of black women who are prosecuted because their infants test positive for crack cocaine, Roberts has pointed out that this disparity results from the disproportionate number of black women who deliver their children in public hospitals, which aggressively perform such tests on poor women. Roberts argues that situation exists "because of the racist attitudes of health care professionals" (Roberts, "Punishing Drug Addicts Who Have Babies," 1432–33). See also Roberts, *Shattered Bonds*.

60. Williams, *Alchemical Notes*, 415.

61. For a discussion of the black community's struggle, as expressed in literary productions, for respectable sexuality that would undergird family integrity and its attendant privilege, yet also for the benefit of achieving the public goal of deserved citizenship, see generally Candice Jenkins, *Private Lives, Proper Relations*, 1–35.

62. See generally Austin, "Sapphire Bound!"

63. For a discussion of how welfare policies incorporate a pro-marriage rhetoric, see Onwuachi-Willig, "The Return of the Ring." The novel conveys Alice Manfred's fraught relationship with marriage in her realization of her critique of her empty attempt to cause violence to her husband's mistress by "galloping . . . on a horse she neither owned nor knew how to ride, over the twitching, pulpy body of a woman who wore white shoes in winter, laughed loud as a child, and who had never seen a marriage license." Morrison, *Jazz*, 86. The breaking of social conventions by wearing white shoes in winter and having never married are conjoined for the reader to get a image of the woman to whom Alice Manfred intended to do harm. But the narrative also recognizes that Manfred's husband had chosen this woman, and in choosing her, had rejected Alice Manfred. Further, after the fun has been had, it is Alice Manfred who is stuck with the wifely task of burying her deserting husband.

64. Morrison, *Jazz*, 76.

65. Ibid., 54–55

66. Ibid., 67; emphasis added.

67. Increasingly, feminist theorists have paid attention to the cultural dilemmas that laws against domestic violence raise for women of color, who are required to separate themselves from their cultural communities in an attempt to leave abusive relationships. See Coker, "Enhancing Autonomy for Battered Women" and Mahoney, "Exit."

68. Allen, "The Proposed Equal Protection Fix for Abortion Law," 441. See also Allen, *Uneasy Access*.

69. Morrison, *Jazz*, 58.

70. See Carby, "Policing the Black Woman's Body in Urban Context." On the importance of a politics of respectability as a civil rights strategy, see Kennedy, *Race, Crime and the Law*, 17–21.

71. Morrison, *Jazz*, 76.

72. One of the surest signs of the black community's vulnerability to the demands of outsiders is the common lament that white men routinely "raped our women." The rape, although perpetrated against a single black woman, is interpreted as a fundamental insult and incursion against the collective black community. Such a communal, collective interpretation of interracial rape is all the more problematic in light of the ways in which the black community has often identified with the black rapist and against his black, female victim, because the trope of the black, male rapist is thought to be another entry point of white domination—often ending with the lynch mob. For an interesting analysis of the way in which Anita Hill's claims of sexual harassment against former Judge Clarence Thomas at his confirmation hearings was interpreted as the ultimate act of racial betrayal, see Kennedy, *Sellout*.

73. Morrison, *Jazz*, 76.

74. Ibid., 56.

75. Ibid., 58.

76. Ibid., 79.

77. Ibid., 64.

78. Ibid., 60.

79. Ibid., 59.

80. See Perry, "Occupying the Universal."

81. Morrison, *Jazz*, 53.

82. Ibid., 54–55.

83. For other examples of promises unkept, see Soifer, "Status, Contract, and Promises Unkept."

84. See Perry, "Occupying the Universal," 102–4.

85. It should be noted that the black experience in America marked a hermeneutic crisis in America itself since its earliest days. See Brandon, *Free in the World*; and Davis, *The Problem of Slavery in the Age of Revolution*.

86. Morrison, *Jazz*, 54.

87. For a discussion of Morrison's *Beloved* and law, see West, *Caring for Justice*, 197–98. See also Ball, *The Word and the Law*, 84–87.

88. On the negotiation of the promises of universal equality in the Declaration of Independence and the Constitution's compromise with, and preservation of, the institution of slavery, see Rael, *Black Identity & Black Protest in the Antebellum North*, 255–57; and Oakes, *The Radical and the Republican*, 34.

89. The text on the back of the restraining order read, "NOTICE TO LAW ENFORCEMENT OFFICIALS." It continued, "YOU SHALL USE EVERY MEANS TO ENFORCE THIS RESTRAINING ORDER. YOU SHALL ARREST, OR, IF AN ARREST WOULD BE IMPRACTICAL UNDER THE CIRCUMSTANCES, SEEK A WARRANT FOR THE ARREST OF THE RESTRAINED PERSON WHEN YOU HAVE INFORMATION AMOUNTING TO PROBABLE CAUSE THAT THE RESTRAINED PERSON HAS VIOLATED OR ATTEMPTED TO VIOLATE ANY PROVISION OF THIS ORDER."

90. Justice Stevens, joined by Justice Ginsburg, challenges with his dissent the ahistorical vision that underlies the Court's easy separation of public and private domains. *Castle Rock*, 778–84.

91. I note here the controversial nature of mandatory arrest statutes, particularly in many communities of color. See Coker, "Shifting Power for Battered Women," 1012–13.

92. *Castle Rock*, 780 (Stevens, J., dissenting).

93. Ibid.

94. See Minow, "Words and the Door to the Land of Change."

95. For examples, see Bracey, "Adjudication, Antisubordination, and the Jazz Connection"; and Beyer, "The Second Line." For my purposes, "jazz" is not merely the specific cultural phenomenon known as jazz, but is also the larger constellation of black cultural forms that are antecedent to jazz.

96. Bracey contends that "free jazz" movement of the late 1950s and 1960s serves as an appropriate metaphor for the transformation of adjudication because it was "deeply oppositional to more traditional forms of jazz." In modeling free jazz's oppositional character, Bracey seeks to highlight the need for judges to reject the impulse to "not reflexively indulge the status quo" when engaged in the adjudication of minority rights.

97. See Hersch, *Subversive Sounds*.

98. Porter, *What Is This Thing Called Jazz?* 6.

99. Ellison, "That Same Pain, That Same Pleasure," 71.

100. Jones, *Blues People*, 80. See also Jones, *Black Music*, 13. While I do not suggest that the description of jazz, and the cultural form that produced it, is "private" or the property of black people exclusively, its status as unknown to a wider culture certainly provided a measure of insulation from certain kinds of intrusions on its development.

101. See Beyer, "The Second Line"; and Calmore, "Critical Race Theory."

102. Ellison, "The Charlie Christian Story," 267.

103. Porter, *What Is This Thing Called Jazz?* 25.

104. Morrison, *Jazz*, 75.

105. Ibid., 82.

106. Ibid., 83.

107. For emphasizing the importance of this aspect of *Jazz*'s narrative, I am grateful to Marc Fajer.

108. Morrison, *Jazz*, 220–21.

109. See Crouch, "A Blues to be Constitutional."

Bibliography

Allen, Anita. "The Proposed Equal Protection Fix for Abortion Law: Reflections on Citizenship, Gender, and the Constitution." *Harvard Journal of Law & Policy* 18 (1995): 419–55.

———. *Uneasy Access: Privacy for Women in a Free Society*. Totowa, NJ: Rowan & Littlefield, 1988.

Anderson, Victor. "Abominations of a Million Men: Reflection of a Silent Minority." In *Black Religion after the Million Man March*, edited by Garth Baker-Fletcher, 19–26. Maryknoll, NY: Orbis, 1998.

Atuahene, Bernadette. "From Reparation to Restoration: Moving Beyond Restoring Property Rights to Restoring Political and Economic Visibility." *Southern Methodist University Law Review* 60 (2007): 1419–70.

Autin, Regina. "Sapphire Bound!" *Wisconsin Law Review* (1989): 539–78.

Baker, Houston A. *How Black Intellectuals Have Abandoned the Ideals of the Civil Rights Era*. New York: Columbia University Press, 2008.

Baker, Katharine. "Dialectics and Domestic Abuse." *Yale Law Journal* 110 (2001): 1459–91.

Ball, Milner. *The Word and the Law*. Chicago: University of Chicago Press, 1993.

Beyer, Jonathan. "The Second Line: Reconstructing the Jazz Metaphor in Critical Race Theory." *Georgetown Law Journal* 88 (2000): 537–63.

Bowers v. Hardwick, 478 U.S. 279 (1987).

Bracey, Christopher. "Adjudication, Antisubordination, and the Jazz Connection." *Alabama Law Review* 54 (2003): 853–67.

Brandon, Mark. *Free in the World: American Slavery and Constitutional Failure*. Princeton, NJ: Princeton University Press, 1998.

Brundage, Walter. *Lynching in the New South*. Chicago: University of Illinois Press, 1993.

Calmore, John. "Critical Race Theory, Archie Shepp, and Fire Music: Securing an Authentic Intellectual Life in a Multicultural World." *South Carolina Law Review* 65 (1992): 2129–2230.

Carbado, Devon. "The Construction of O. J. Simpson as a Racial Victim." In *Black Men on Race Gender and Sexuality: A Critical Reader*, edited by Devon Carbado, 159–93. New York: New York University Press, 1999.

Carby, Hazel. "'On the Threshold of the Women's Era:' Lynching, Empire and Sexuality in Black Feminist Theory." *Critical Inquiry* 12, no. 1 (Autumn 1985): 262–77.

———. "Policing the Black Woman's Body in an Urban Context." *Critical Inquiry* 18, no. 4 (Summer 1992): 738–55.

Castle Rock v. Gonzalez, 545 U.S. 748 (2005).

Coker, Donna. "Enhancing Autonomy for Battered Women: Lessons from Navajo Peacemaking." *University of California at Los Angeles Law Review* 47 (1999): 46–107.

———. "Shifting Power for Battered Women: Law, Material Resources, and Poor Women of Color." *University of California at Davis Law Review* 33 (2000): 1009–55.

Cone, James H. *The Spirituals and the Blues*. Maryknoll, NY: Orbis Books, 1972.

Cover, Robert M. "Nomos and Narrative." *Harvard Law Review* 100 (1983): 4–68.

Crenshaw, Kimberlé. "Mapping the Margins: Intersectionality, Identity Politics, and Violence Against Women of Color." *Stanford Law Review* 43 (1991): 1241–99.

Crouch, Stanley. "A Blues to be Constitutional: A Long Look at the Wild Wherefores of Our Democratic Lives as Symbolized in the Making of Rhythm and Tune." In *The Jazz Cadence of American Culture*, edited by Robert G. O'Meally, 154–65. New York: Columbia University Press, 1998.

Davis, Angela. *Blues Legacies and Black Feminism: Gertrude "Ma" Rainey, Bessie Smith, and Billie Holliday*. New York: Pantheon, 1998.

Davis, David Brion. *The Problem of Slavery in the Age of Revolution, 1770–1823*. Ithaca, NY: Cornell University Press, 1975.

Davis, Peggy Cooper. *Neglected Stories: The Constitution and Family Values*. New York: Hill and Wang, 1997.

Dray, Philip. *The Hands of Persons Unknown: The Lynching of Black America*. New York: Random House, 2002.

Ellison, Ralph. "The Charlie Christian Story." In *The Collected Essays of Ralph Ellison*, edited by John Callahan, 266–72. New York: Modern Library, 2003.

———. "Shadow and Act." In *The Collected Essays of Ralph Ellison*, edited by John Callahan, 302–9. New York: Modern Library, 2003.

———. "That Same Pain, That Same Pleasure: An Interview." In *The Collected Essays of Ralph Ellison*, edited by John Callahan, 63–80. New York: Modern Library, 2003.

Fenton, Zanita E. "Silence Compounded: The Conjunction of Race and Gender Violence." *American University Journal of Gender, Social Policy and the Law* 11 (2003): 271–85.

Ford, William D. "Constitutionality of Proposed Federal Anti-Lynching Legislation." *Virginia Law Review* 34 (1948): 944–53.

Griffin, Farah Jasmine. *"Who Set You Flowin'?" The African American Migration Narrative*. New York: Oxford University Press, 1995.

Harper, Philip Brian. *Private Affairs: Critical Ventures in the Culture of Social Relations*. New York: New York University Press, 1999.

Harris, Angela P. "Gender, Violence, Race and Criminal Justice." *Stanford Law Review* 52 (2000): 777–807.

Hersch, Charles. *Subversive Sounds: Race and the Birth of Jazz in New Orleans*. Chicago: University of Chicago Press, 2008.

Higginbotham, A. Leon. *Shades of Freedom: Racial Politics and Presumptions of the American Legal Process*. New York: Oxford University Press, 1996.

Jenkins, Candice M. *Private Lives, Proper Relations: Regulating Black Intimacy*. Minneapolis, MN: University of Minnesota Press, 2007.

Jones, Carolyn. "Traces in the Cracks: Identity and Narrative in Toni Morrison's *Jazz*," *African American Review* 31, no. 3 (Autumn, 1997): 481–95.

Jones, LeRoi. *Black Music*. New York: Morrow, 1967.

———. *Blues People: Negro Music in White America*. New York: Morrow, 1963.

Kelley, Robin D. G. "Countering the Conspiracy to Ignore Black Girls." In *Faith of Our Fathers: African-American Men Reflect on Fatherhood*, edited by Andre Willis, 157–72. New York: Dutton, 1999.

Kennedy, Randall L. *Race, Crime, and the Law*. New York: Pantheon, 1997.

———. *Sellout: The Politics of Racial Betrayal*. New York: Pantheon, 2008.

———. "The State, Criminal Law, and Racial Discrimination." *Harvard Law Review* 107 (1991): 1255–78.

Mahoney, Martha R. "Exit: Power and the Idea of Leaving in Love, Work, and the Confirmation Hearings." *South Carolina Law Review* 65 (1992): 1283–1319.

Meares, Tracey, and Dan Kahan. *Urgent Times: Policing and Rights in Inner-City Communities*. Boston: Beacon, 1999.

Miller, Jody. *Getting Played: African American Girls, Urban Inequality, and Gendered Violence*. New York: New York University Press, 2008.

Minow, Martha. "Words and the Door to the Land of Change: Law, Language, and Family Violence." *Vanderbilt Law Review* 43 (1990): 1665–99.

Morrison, Toni. *Jazz*. New York: Knopf, 1992.

Oakes, James. *The Radical and the Republican: Frederick Douglass, Abraham Lincoln, and the Triumph of Antislavery Politics*. New York: Norton, 2007.

Olsen, Frances. "Constitutional Law: Feminist Critiques of the Public/Private Distinction." *Constitutional Commentary* 10 (1993): 319–27.

Onwuachi-Willig, Angela. "The Return of the Ring: Welfare Reform's Marriage Cure as the Revival of Post-Bellum Control." *California Law Review* 93 (2005): 1647–96.

O'Reily, Andrea. "In Search of My Mother's Garden, I Found My Own: Mother-Love, Healing, and Identity in Toni Morrison's *Jazz*." *African American Review* 31, no. 3 (Autumn 1996): 367–79.

Paquet-Deyris, Anne-Marie. "Toni Morrison's Jazz and the City." *African American Review* 35 (Summer 2001): 219–31.

Perry, Imani. "Occupying the Universal, Embodying the Subject: African American Literary Jurisprudence." *Cardozo Studies in Law and Literature* 17 (2005): 97–124.

Porter, Eric. *What Is This Thing Called Jazz? African American Musicians as Artists, Critics and Activists*. Berkeley: University of California Press, 2002.

Posner, Richard A. *Law and Literature: A Misunderstood Connection*. Cambridge, MA: Harvard University Press, 1988.

Rael, Patrick. *Black Identity & Black Protest in the Antebellum North*. Chapel Hill: University of North Carolina Press, 2002.

Roberts, Dorothy. "Punishing Drug Addicts Who Have Babies: Women of Color, Equality and the Right of Privacy." *Harvard Law Review* 104 (1991): 1419–82.

———. *Shattered Bonds: The Color of Child Welfare*. New York: Basic, 2001.

Rudwick, Elliot. *Race Riot in East St. Louis: July 2, 1917*. Carbondale, IL: Southern Illinois University Press, 1982.

Schneider, Elizabeth. *Battered Women and Feminist Lawmaking*. New Haven, CT: Yale University Press, 2000.

Schur, Richard. "Locating Paradise in the Post-Civil Rights Era: Toni Morrison and Critical Race Theory." *Contemporary Literature* 45 (2004): 276–99.

Siegel, Reva B. "The Rule of Love: Wife Beating as Prerogative and Privacy." *Yale Law Journal* 105 (1996): 2117–2207.

Soifer, Aviam. "Status, Contract, and Promises Unkept." *Yale Law Journal* 96 (1987): 1916–59.

Spillers, Hortense J. *Black, White, and in Color: Essays on American Literature and Culture* Chicago: Chicago University Press, 2003.

United States v. Cruikshank, 92 U.S. 542 (1875).

United States v. Harris, 106 U.S. 629 (1883).

United States v. Morrison, 529 U.S. 598 (2000).

United States v. Stanley, 109 U.S. 3 (1883).

West, Robin. *Caring for Justice*. New York: New York University Press, 1997.

White, James Boyd. *When Words Lose Their Meaning: Constitutions and Reconstitutions of Language, Character, and Community*. Chicago: University of Chicago Press, 1984.

Williams, Patricia J. *The Alchemy of Race and Rights: Diary of a Law Professor*. Cambridge, MA: Harvard University Press, 1991.

Williamson, Joel. *A Rage for Order: Black/White Relations in the American South since Emancipation*. New York: Oxford University Press, 1986.

9

When Testimony Fails

Law and the Comforts of Intimacy in Gayl Jones's *Corregidora*

Rebecca Wanzo

While cases such as *Plessy v. Ferguson* (1896) infamously illustrate the failure of the U.S. courts to endorse full citizenship for African Americans, the civil rights victories under the Warren court offer the possibility that the law can be an important means by which African Americans can attain justice. However, U.S. history is filled with accounts of the law failing to be a salve for racial injury. Even cases that produce positive outcomes for African Americans can fail to provide truly reparative resolutions. In everyday legal parlance, reparative justice requires that a perpetrator both accept responsibility for causing injury and make restitution. A number of scholars have made arguments about what the enactment of reparations would look like, but I want to focus here on its most expansive meaning. "In the most literal sense," Christopher Kutz explains, "a claim of repair is a claim to be made whole, to have a harm healed or corrected."[1] However, being made "whole" after racial injury—after any trauma—is a challenging and sometimes impossible exercise. Because racially injured subjects cannot return to a point of knowledge before the wound—where they no longer know what it is like to have been wounded—reparative justice is inevitably incomplete. Given the checkered history of the law's efficacy and the impossibility of the law making a racially injured citizen politically or therapeutically whole, African Americans may sometimes decide, or be forced, to abandon the law as the path to reparations for harms perpetrated on black citizenry.

But to what might they turn when they recognize that no legal or institutional redress will *fully* repair the damage done by historical traumas and individual injuries? This question is at the center of Gayl Jones's 1975 novel, *Corregidora. Corregidora* is an allegory about the relationship between the Western black subject and the law and the struggles to find intimacy when the law fails to address state wrongs. In exploring Western black subjects' hope for the law's possibilities and their psychological struggles with the law's failures, the issues raised by this novel resonate far beyond the specific contours of its plot. Jones's neoslave narrative tells the story of Ursa Corregidora, who has been taught to provide testimony about her ancestor, Old man Corregidora. As Ursa explains, he was a "Portuguese slave breeder and whoremonger . . . He fucked his own whores and fathered his own breed. They did the fucking and had to bring him the money they made. My grandmamma was his daughter, but he was fucking her too."[2] A history of racial-sexual injury was essential to the Corregidora women's identities, as they made their testimony about his rape and prostitution of first one woman and then their own daughter into the foundation for their agency. The bodies of Ursa, her mother, grandmother, and great-grandmother all transmit testimony and serve as physical "evidence." In a legal model, their testimony would provide the basis for reparations.

However, Jones *begins* the novel by placing the likelihood of reparative testimony into question. Ursa's evidentiary status is irrevocably altered when she suffers a miscarriage and hysterectomy on the very first page. Jennifer Cognard-Black describes the character's "womb-lack" as the "narrative opening" of the text, and, indeed, this rupture opens up the narrative about transmitting history, not only transforming and expanding Ursa's reading of her life, but also expanding the possibilities for how to read her story about slavery, history, and the failure of reparative justice.[3] The novel is thus not only about slavery's legacy and surviving it but also about living in the shadow of the legal process when subjects are alienated from it as a vehicle for wholeness. African Americans' alienation from the law is built on what might always be a phantasm—that their testimony in some amorphous judicial encounter *could* pave the way to true reparations for social and political oppression as well as wounds on the soul. As a text where a black, sexually violated subject is explicitly told that her body is evidence and that her testimony of painful histories is essential to the survival of her people, the novel allegorically illustrates the law's attractions even as it emphasizes the testimony's inadequacies—legal and otherwise.

The same expectations and challenges of offering testimony of racial injury also face those who have survived sexual injury.[4] Therefore Ursa Corregidora's status as an African American *woman* highlights the specific racial-sexual injury that black women experienced during slavery and beyond.[5] The body is only sometimes evidence of racialized injury, but enslaved black women perpetually represented the threat and outcome of bodily violence. Their children could be evidence of intercourse without consent, and their bodies were tools for enabling further racial injury.[6] As Harriet Jacobs famously writes in *Incidents in the Life of a Slave Girl*, "Slavery is terrible for men, but it is far more terrible for women. Superadded to the burden common to all, they have wrongs, and sufferings, and mortifications peculiarly their own."[7] The "mortification" that is specifically their own is the racial-sexual injury, a layered victimization made explicit through the similar vulnerabilities of such racially and sexually victimized bodies in the legal system. While all scholars should be leery of what Janet Halley calls the "like race," argument, which conflates racial oppression with other kinds of oppression, they should be equally leery of the "like rape" argument, where the word "rape" can be too easily utilized to describe harm; there are structural similarities. Most specifically, certain kinds of bodies (those of people of color and women) are more vulnerable to injury even as their painful, intimate testimony runs the risk of not being believed—a fact that has implications for how others' stories about suffering are read.

Giving legal testimony is an incongruous process, as the testifier can be called to give extraordinarily intimate testimony in an alienating setting. "Intimacy" is usually used to describe a feature of romantic and sexual relationships, but it can be defined more broadly as emotional closeness in a mutual relationship where self-disclosure takes place. Immanuel Kant's understanding of intimacy is useful here. He describes close relationships as connections between people that involve an absence of constraint, an unburdening of the heart, and a complete communion.[8] In giving testimony, an absence of constraint can be demanded, an unburdening of the heart may be desired, and complete communion could be needed to transmit the extent of the trauma. While Ursa delivers testimony to many people, she has a reflexive relationship with the narrative; the self-disclosure leads her not to a closer communion with others but back to her ancestors and the injury. She is raised to understand that her most intimate relationship is with her family history. After her miscarriage, she struggles to understand what the possibilities for intimacy are for herself in the wake of losing this most troubled of intimate attachments—an attachment to her body and to her testimony evidence as a means of procuring justice.

"They burned all the papers": Ambivalence and the Reparative Imagination

Corregidora illuminates the desires and challenges faced by the black subject seeking reparations for racial injury in the United States, but it also has a larger diasporic scope, as Ursa Corregidora's family narrative begins in Brazil. The history of slavery and emancipation in Brazil sets the stage for a very particular kind of racial injury that the Corregidora women endure, an injury inflicted after emancipation.[9] Brazil was the last country to emancipate slaves in the Americas (1888), and this period includes a moment in Brazilian abolitionist history that is pivotal in this novel—the government burning of papers related to slavery in 1890. This moment illustrates the kind of troubled frameworks that often accompany legal attempts to address reparative desire, one that stands between escape and remembrance. When the government called for the burning of papers, they claimed that the intention was to eradicate the history of injustice.[10] It was, as Frances Windance Twine writes, part of a troubling, whitening intervention that has shaped much of Brazilian policy.[11] However, such erasure can also be a grievous injury because it attempts to leave no trace of the injury, and the Corregidora women experience it as such. As they tell it, "when they did away with slavery down there they burned all the papers so it would be like they never had it."[12] This erasure was an act of violence to them, and the burning is an event emphasized in the narrative that the Corregidora women pass down: "My great-grandmama told my grandmama the part she lived through that my grandmama didn't live through and my grandmama told my mama what they both lived through and my mama told me what they all lived through and we were supposed to pass it down like that from generation to generation so we'd never forget. Even though they'd burned everything to play like it didn't never happen."[13] The Corregidora women's reparative desires are thus shaped not only by the initial racial-sexual injuries but also by the destruction of evidence. Destruction of the papers even extends the violence of slavery into the process of liberation. Legislative solutions produce further injury through a gesture that would allegedly lead to a color-blind culture. Color-blind state practices can, as Neil Gotanda and others have argued, fail to address the material realities of race as a constant factor in social and political formation.[14] Ursa and her foremothers therefore emphasize the constant presence of racialized, sexual injury in their lives. For them, justice requires the creation and acknowledgment of a historical record.

With a reproductive imperative, Ursa's foremothers attempt to disrupt a system of justice in which black bodies can be rendered invisible. Such intervention involves emphasizing the visibility made possible through testimony and the assertion that, despite various cultural disavowals, black women's testimony can be evidence. As Kimberlé Williams Crenshaw has argued, "the discrediting of Black women's claims is the consequence of a complex intersection of a gendered sexual system, one that constructs rules for appropriate good and bad women, and a race code that provides images defining the allegedly essential nature of Black women."[15] A partial justification for enslavement argues for the inherent degraded nature of Black women; thus, "if these sexual images form even part of the cultural imagery of Black women, then the very representation of a Black female body at least suggests certain narratives that may make black women's rape either less believable or less important."[16] At age five, Ursa, unwittingly replicating a larger culture of disbelief that greets black women's testimonies of suffering with incredulity, made the mistake of asking her Great Gram if she was telling the truth with her stories. Great Gram slaps her and says, "When I'm telling you something don't you ever ask if I'm lying. Because they didn't want to leave no evidence of what they done—so it couldn't be held against them. And I'm leaving evidence. And when it comes time to hold up the evidence, we got to have evidence to hold up. That's why they burned all the papers, so there wouldn't be no evidence to hold up against them."[17] Asserting the value of their stories of injury as evidence is Great Gram's counternarrative to a culture of disbelief and devaluing. The evidence they can hold up is their own bodies, the products of rape and miscegenation, and while the older generation that experienced the initial injury may be lost, they mandate that there should be at least one generation to fulfill the family role of passing on the family history.

Great Gram never questions the efficacy or presumption of using the body as evidence, even though the issue of what counts as evidence has been tendentious in cases of racial justice and sexual violence. "Evidence," as a category, is subject to cross-examination, but when a person is evidence, interrogation can cause further harm. While the body can function as physical evidence that an event occurred, the event is often not interpreted as forced injury. The wounded body can be read as a result of the injured person's own behavior as opposed to malfeasance on the part of the accused, and the bruised female body can be a sign of rough consensual sex. The mixed-race child is a sign of miscegenation, but the complicated histories sometimes carried in skin pigmentation are not transparent. The unreliability of the body as evidence is why testimony is so essential to making claims about injury. Of course, testimony, too, is tendentious evidence—perhaps even more so than the body.[18] However, Great Gram insists on the integrity of the body-and-testimony combination and that the Corregidora women, in body and speech, can transform themselves into the evidence that Brazilian legislators destroyed.

Unspoken here is that the outcome of delivering evidence is judgment. The theme of judgment undergirds this text; as Melvin Dixon notes, the word "corregi-dore" means "judicial magistrate" in Portuguese, and Ursa acts as a judge who can correct the wrongs done to her family.[19] However, as Corregidora is the name they received from their slave owner, he, too, stands in as a magistrate, structuring the rule of law for his slaves and shaping the testimonial imperative that they would form in response to the abuse that he inflicts upon their bodies and psyches. Slave law enabled the abuse of black bodies and the protection of white ones, thus the Corregidora women began their lives outside of the law's protection and estab-lished their own set of laws for their family. If the Rule of Law, as Lynne Henderson writes, is a set of rules governing and prescribing behavior as well as protecting the rights of citizens, then it is clear that there are laws in place for the Corregidora women, and Ursa broke the primary one: to reproduce.[20] Corregidora women must all know the history, must promise that no romantic relationship take prece-dence over the narrative imperative, and must be prepared to bear witness "when it come time to hold the evidence."[21]

The allusion to that distant time, however, is one of the central cracks in the logic of witnessing within Ursa's family. Where, exactly, will they present the evidence? African Americans often evoke judgment in the afterlife as compensation for the absence of justice on earth; however, there is no allusion to being a witness for a Christian God, who would know assuredly what happened without the papers. The evidence might be presented when making the case for reparations, but there is no plan for these women in Kentucky to leave the country and seek judicial or financial redress in Brazil. Or perhaps the time to bear witness, in a novel that moves fluidly back and forth in time, is any moment when one can educate others about this history. If that is the case, then Ursa's testimony fails repeatedly to pro-duce a good outcome. When she acts as a witness to her great-grandmother's and grandmother's sexual assaults and to her mother's and her own status as products of these rapes, her story does not produce sympathy or justice. No great commu-nion or recognition happens after her delivery of their history.

As it becomes clear in the novel that the testimony will have no literal legal venue, the testimony itself becomes a legal allegory. The allegorical space in which the subject can be a witness to racial-sexual injury and in which judgment occurs is the community. The absence of reparation is made clear not only in terms of thwarted justice from the state but also in terms of whether testimony allows peo-ple to become part of a community. Trauma can destroy interactions between a survivor and a community, and testimony can be an attempt to reconcile the community and the survivor. In Jones's story, this reconciliation does not occur. The fact that the testimony of racial-sexual injury does not cause racial solidarity is often illustrated by the exchanges Ursa and her mother have with men. Because the two of them insist on the significance of the injury done to their family, they have difficulty building loves and lives. In turn, the men in their lives are angered by their traumatized behavior. Ursa's father, Martin, is disgusted by the attach-ment to their maternal history and by the idea that he may have merely been used to "help" in the making of more Corregidora women.[22] Mutt is similarly critical of Ursa's foremothers as an obstruction, asking, "Are you mine, Ursa, or theirs?"[23] In the brief period Martin lived in the Corregidora household, he was unable to have intimacy with Ursa's mother because she felt uncomfortable doing so when her mother and grandmother were in the house; thus, her relationship with them was an obstruction to any intimacy she and Ursa's father might build. He was also a "black bastard" who could have disrupted the physical evidence, as part of what makes the Corregidora women evidence is their clearly mixed-race bodies. When Ursa was initially born bald, Ursa's mother claims that she "knew" that Mama and Gram "hated me then," because the long black hair was a sign of the Corregidora woman. Their bodies are simultaneously a sign of black history and a means of separating them from others of African descent.

Testimony about racial-sexual injury also does not provide an impetus for disrupting the cycle of intimate violence. If anything, Jones blends the language of violence in the text, inviting us to see the violence between black men and women on the same continuum as the acts of violence Old man Corregidora committed. The author recognizes the relationship between state violence and intimate violence, between the violence inflicted upon African Americans under slavery and its ensuing implications for intraracial, interpersonal relationships. Like Martin, Ursa's husbands are verbally or physically abusive. Ursa's "fall" at the beginning of the novel occurred during an argument with Mutt, and the text implies that he caused it. Both husbands refer to her body in violent ways, and she uses similar language to describe herself. The violence of this historical narrative—made more visceral in the text by the violence of the language—informs Ursa's view of intimacy, her body, and the world. Ursa often refers to intercourse as "fucking," her eyes as "tears," and her vagina as her "hole" and "birthmark." The language she can use about herself is overdetermined by her family history. The treatment Ursa receives at the hands of her lovers does not facilitate a healthier vision of herself. Her husbands speak of her in terms of ownership, referring to her "pussy" as "mine" or as "a little gold piece." They replicate a language that blends in with her foremothers' narrative of Old man Corregidora's ownership and abuse. Technically, Ursa is a secondary survivor of the trauma of her foremothers; though she was not a prostituted and raped slave, she has been affected by their narratives. In the depiction of her secondary traumatization, however, Jones foregrounds the institutional nature of sexual violence and the way that history can predetermine victims.

Despite the cyclical violence, Mutt insists during a discussion of what happened to his own ancestors that the two of them are not like their ancestors, injured by a pattern of violence and trauma. Mutt's grandfather had bought freedom for himself and his wife, but when he got into debt, his wife was taken:

"You can imagine how he must have felt."

I nodded but said nothing.

"Don't look like that, Ursa," he said and pulled me toward him. "Whichever way you look at it, we ain't them."

I didn't answer that, because the way I'd been brought up, it was almost as if I was.[24]

The repetition here is not one of simplistic doubling—Mutt and Ursa are not Old man Corregidora and Great Gram, nor are their lives mere continuations of the same kind of violence visited on Mutt's grandparents. However, they are "them"—both

Ursa's ancestors and Mutt's—in that patterns of violence against women, ownership of black bodies, and separation of black couples are conditions that are irrevocably shaped by a history of racial-sexual injury. Tadpole, who eventually becomes Ursa's second husband, asks Ursa if she hates "him," meaning Mutt. In the middle of discussing the testimonial imperative of her family, Ursa replies as if he had asked her about Old man Corregidora. Personal and family narrative blend together so that the violence her slave-owning ancestor caused in the past is inextricably linked to the violence she experiences in the present.

Readers never gain any sense of what outcome the Corregidora women should expect from being—or embodying—evidence, except perhaps the therapeutic value of telling the story. However, the shadowy allusion to an outcome problematizes the idea that their testimonies are productive. Jones not only demonstrates that testifying may be an unfair burden for Ursa but she also questions whether such testimonies of traumatic history constitute an absolute good. Jones does not position testimony as an inefficacious event or project, but she does present the idea that testimony can fail to produce the desired results for the testifier—particularly when the nature of the trauma is so excessive that no response can be appropriate compensation. This acknowledgment invites the reader to think about alternatives that do not rely on testimony as the mechanisms by which victims are healed.

As a genre of communication that blends the legal and the intimate, testimony is a privileged means of forging alternative paths to healing traumatized subjects. And yet even as a purely therapeutic practice, it can further traumatize its speakers. Just as the burning of the papers was a complicated political gesture, the Corregidora women's path to justice produces some traumatic results. The grievous rupture of Ursa's miscarriage illustrates the ambivalence that may accompany the tension between articulating an entirely new path where the mechanism for history's remembrance and redress of the future are eradicated and acknowledging how the remembrance of history might actually be a burden to subjects. The family imperative to make generations and deliver testimony makes it difficult for her to have her "own life," as her personal memories are inescapably intertwined with the Corregidora legacy. Gayl Jones's radical intervention into narratives of reparation is an acknowledgment of the ways in which a cultural history can be a burden rather than merely a much-romanticized strength. Certainly, some conservative and even leftist projects have proposed a distancing from history when articulating political projects and individual agency. For example, Wendy Brown describes an attachment to slavery as a "wounded attachment" to a history that can prevent the subject from proactive political projects that are future focused.[25] More specifically, Brown criticizes the narration of injury and political desire that always begins with the older historical injury. While *Corregidora* is a novel about how the history of slavery shapes the subjectivity of slave descendents, Jones illustrates the possible ambivalence to making such memories central to creating a political community. The history of Ursa Corregidora's foremothers' survival is a source of strength. The record should be remembered not only because it serves as possible grounds for compensation but also because the historical record should reflect the lives of all citizens and not just narratives produced by state agents. However, this record shapes who Ursa is, and a subjectivity grounded in such a traumatic event is not without consequences.

Ursa *becomes* the testimony about this history. Yet as scholars of trauma and testimony have argued, testimony is a slippery, unwieldy representative of historical truth and identity. Even as Ursa and her foremothers become consumed by the narrative, in their telling of it the testimony cannot communicate the reality of the experience. Testimony involves a demand for intimacy, but, even if intimacy is achieved, it depends upon a phantasm of truth transference. When someone begins to narrate a trauma, they are already transforming it by putting it into language. The testifier becomes distant from her own history, and the audience—even a sympathetic one—can only imaginatively reconstruct the story from their own points of understanding. Thus, when Ursa becomes this testimony, she becomes fragmented and alienated from her own self, thus encouraging people to relate to a version of herself that is, in itself, an alienated product.

Unified subjectivity may be a phantasm as well, but Jones calls attention to how profound the alienation can be when the testifier depends on an outcome that may never happen. What is the true restitution for the traumas that Gram and Great Gram endured and that shaped the life possibilities for Ursa and her mother, haunting every act of agency? A common conceit in popular legal fiction is the lawyer's statement that "nothing can bring her back" or "nothing can ever compensate for the loss." Such statements are the preface to the request for some limited compensation, a compensation that is unquestionably not real justice. What haunts the Corregidora women is that they want justice—they want true compensation for what can never be compensated. Thus, even without the amorphous judge or jury to whom they will present evidence because "they burned all the papers," their testimony will inevitably fail. As they have become the testimony they deliver, that failure also impacts their sense of themselves as subjects. An outcome of Ursa's foremothers' testimonial labor was the passing on of their history. Ursa can no longer pass on the testimony, but her identity has become the testimony as she can never become whole through the maternal mandate of generation making. She thus must find other means of fulfillment.

The Impossibility of Free Wombs

As allegory about slavery, memory, and testimony, the story of Ursa's loss of purpose due to the loss of her capacity to reproduce highlights the ways in which testimony about racial injury is deeply entwined not only with the past but also with the future. Testimony delivers information not only about individual or group pasts but also about the possibilities for the community's future. Similar to other cases about injury that are individual but often serve as representative examples of larger institutional treatment, a verdict—if there is one—in the favor of the testifier would be an acknowledgment of communal danger or a warning against the further commission of injury. The burning of the papers is not something that afflicted only Ursa's family. In a conversation with her second husband, Tadpole, she learns that his family was most likely victimized by the destroying of evidence. His father had bought land, and when his mother "went in the courthouse to claim the land, somebody had tore one of the pages out of the book . . . Anyway, they ain't nothing you can do when they tear pages out of the book and they ain't no record of it. They probably burned the pages."[26] Tadpole's approach to the history of racial injury is the antithesis of Ursa's. While she claims that his family's history is the "same" as his own, he denies that and argues that there is "nothing you can do" when they destroy evidence. The women of Ursa's family insist on family memory being evidence of the injury, and thus they refuse to accept the injustice.

However, as is often the case with injury, their own experience leaves them unable to build community with others also scarred by the legacies of slavery. Ursa moves through the world disconnected and has difficulty building relationships with others. This is the most perilous version of the wounded attachment to which Wendy Brown refers—an attachment to the wound so deep that it blinds the speaker to more proactive political engagements. However, Jones does not imagine a world where these attachments could be obliterated when the world and its people are shaped by history. The novel does not offer a model for building intimacy and moving politically or personally forward. Ursa's haunting is simply the most explicit version of this in the novel. Traumatic injuries remain with the descendants of slaves, shaping the possibilities for how such black subjects understand themselves and the possibilities for their futures. Jones asks how a child born of such a legacy can be free of it and, moreover, *should* she be free?

In posing such a question, *Corregidora* evokes another important moment in Brazilian abolition history, an act of ameliorative legislation that interrogated the question of freedom when mothers and foremothers were still bound by slavery's chains. In 1871, the Chamber of Deputies and Senate in Brazil approved the "Law of the Free Womb," which freed the children of enslaved mothers. The law was a response to forces pressing for emancipation, but in many practical ways the child born of a slave mother was still enslaved. As Martha Abreu describes it, slave owners resisted compliance to the law, and few people could make use of the "emancipation fund" established so that the children of slaves could compensate slave owners for the loss of labor. Therefore, such children were fraudulently deprived of funds that would free them, and children often ended up working up on the plantation. Thus, the "free womb" was a meaningless concept in relation to the material circumstances of the enslaved mothers.[27]

The impossibility of a free womb, given the enslavement of the mothers, is an undergirding theme of *Corregidora*. Ursa's womb was never her own—her foremother's enslavement literally and psychologically bound it. The psychological ties were then passed on—albeit in a transformed form—to their descendants. While I will not downplay the material realities of slavery and call Ursa enslaved, the chains of enslavement were passed on to Ursa with a *différance*. Narratives attached to wombs emphasize both possibility and constraint; the womb's allegorical use as a space of creativity masks the ways in which it is always tethered to a variety of things. Wombs were an instrument of enslavement, and a womb shapes the possibility for agency prior to a subject's birth. From class to IQ to religion, the mother's womb has been used to define what the possibilities are for a subject prior to her birth. It is, then, a mechanism for defining and, sometimes, limiting a subject.

The womb is simultaneously private and public, psychological and structural. It illustrates the strange bedfellows of intimacy and law in the makeup of racial injury. But it is the womb that also illustrates what can take the place of the law's inadequate compensations for injury. An irony of the womb functioning as a tool for determining status lies with the fact that it also stands for the ultimate metaphor for creation—creation as an expansive act that offers limited possibilities. Such expansive possibilities for creation are thus the tools for Ursa's salvation. As numerous scholars of *Corregidora* have noted, Ursa's inability to create with the womb is channeled into her blues singing. Singing the blues is an act of creation that lacks the limitations of the act of childbearing in her family. While the blues does not make her whole or fill her hole, as Houston Baker explains in his discussion of the blues, "what emerges is not a filled subject, but an anonymous (nameless) voice issuing from the black (w)hole."[28]

While Ursa was unable to relate to people of African descent with her personal testimony of racial injury, the blues is a means by which she forges connection with others. She can speak about the black hole by speaking to and from the black (w)hole. I would suggest that the blues functions as compensation for the law's failures because of the ways in which it is structurally similar to legal performance. The blues often features a single actor who testifies to personal pain. In the blues and in the law, individual testimony is interpreted and valued in terms of how it functions in relationship to testimonies like it (in terms of other great blues performers and the reasonable-man or reasonable-woman standard often interpellated in legal practice). Yet despite the mandate for generic similarity, the audience values and rewards the exceptional display of authenticity—the voice that can deliver the most extraordinary emotion. The blues audience's judgment of Ursa's singing can be compensation for the absent state judgment. In addition, she can be her own judge. In speaking lyrics that come from the (w)hole, a collective that Ursa cannot experience in her own interpersonal interactions or by solely delivering her testimony in court, she can be part of a collective beyond the family narrative. It is a way of being part of a community that was, in some ways, denied to her by her foremothers' mandate that she be a Corregidora woman.

The blues is not a cure-all in the text, however. Emotionally sustained by her profession as a blues singer, Ursa passes through decades of her life without being able to articulate what she needs to fill the holes left by her thwarted reproduction, her painful family narrative, and her own traumatic history with romantic partners. The blues initially provided some relief to her pain, but it could not completely fill the void left by the unreasonable expectations of reparative judgment and justice. Nonetheless, critics typically read the blues as healing and fulfilling Ursa. Gayl Jones herself has claimed that the blues has a "unifying effect, 'which brings a sense of wholeness not to the individual in solitude . . . but in communion.'"[29] However, Jones sets up a problematic about testimony at the beginning of the tale that is not solved by the blues, even if the blues does some work for the character.

The first time Ursa discovered that people liked her singing, she was a young girl who fought with her mother about "singing Devil music." Her mother dragged her away from the place she was singing because "no Corregidora [could] behave with just telling," an ironic claim given the fact that the "telling" of testimony is the foundation of their identities, and they are expected to behave according to the family narrative. Ursa tells her mother that she was "no Corregidora," indicating that the blues would be a space away from the Corregidora women's legacy, even as Ursa understands that the songs she sings come from her foremothers' pain. When Ursa declares, "let no one pollute my music. I will dig out their temples. I will pluck out their eyes," she gestures to the importance of the blues to her survival, but survival politics typically fall short of transforming oppressive psychological blocks and political oppression.[30] There is much evidence in the text that the music is her sustenance, is a way of communicating her history that is more compelling to people than testimony of her family's history, and is a means of giving voice to her pain. But when asked what the blues do for her, she says, "It helps me explain what I can't explain"; thus, for her the blues is an aid and not a definite solution. The impossibility signified by "I can't explain" alludes to something that should be explained but is still not completely articulated. The blues, which doubles as a pain that one wants to eliminate and a language that one nonetheless often takes pleasure in, often appears masochistic in the novel—just as the attachment to the Corregidora legacy does. While the blues helps Ursa communicate, this kind of communication allows her and her partner, Mutt, to dwell in a rhythm that seduces while failing to move out of a call-and-response routine that never progresses toward true comprehension:

> "What you looking for, anyway, woman?"
> "What we stopped being to each other."
> "I never knew what we was."
> "Something you gave me once, but stopped giving me."
> "I want to fuck you."
> "That's not what I mean."
> "I still want to fuck you."
> "That's not what I mean."
> "I still want to fuck you."
> "What you stopped giving me."[31]

The ways in which the blues functions as an alternative to legal exchanges is again apparent here as the call and response of legal testimony: patterned questions, expected and sometimes repetitive answers, and exchanges that may or may not move participants psychologically forward. In their exchanges, Ursa and Mutt establish what Cathy Caruth would refer to as their respective traumatic histories.[32] These exchanges, however, are not acts of "empathy or understanding." Mutt has "refused" Ursa's "tears," and "the tears of empathy are refused by the man as a kind of misunderstanding."[33] The heart of their link to each other is their misunderstanding of each other and of the impossibility of a romantic connection that involves unconflicted intimacy or the complete unburdening of their hearts. Jones asks what it would take for the pair to hear each other in their exchanges; how, in other words, can they have a revolution in communication where pain is not only articulated but also comprehended and where an appropriate response is provided by the listener? How can they respond appropriately given the impossibility of ever completely understanding what the other is saying? This is similar to the question posed by testimony in the law. The questions evoked by the challenges they share resemble the kinds of questions that arise from the challenges facing legal testimony about trauma. For both cases, intimacy is at the core of the pattern of communication—intimacy that would allow the subjects to find some kind of fulfillment from delivering testimony about their pain. If we acknowledge that complete communion or understanding is impossible, and yet intimacy is demanded for appropriate redress, how do actors compensate for the failure of interpersonal exchange? When we understand how important intimacy is to the affective logic structuring expectations about what the law might provide, we can move closer to understanding what kinds of measures black subjects might turn to as a substitute for the promise of reparations through legal justice.

"I can't explain": The Frontiers of Intimacy

The alternative offered by *Corregidora* is a kind of intimacy that abandons the hope of complete communion. Anthony Giddens has argued that intimacy in the late-twentieth century has often been configured as a "social relation" that "is entered into for its own sake for what can be derived by each person from a sustained association with another; and is continued insofar as it is thought by both parties to deliver enough satisfaction for each individual to stay within it."[34] Instead of a romantic, complete communion, couples develop a tentative, working relationship for purposes of transforming themselves. It is a relationship for personal growth, and this is the kind of relationship into which Ursa and Mutt enter. The text ends with Ursa reuniting—perhaps briefly—with her first husband Mutt after two decades, and their communication is facilitated by a new sexual intimacy and a verbal exchange that breaks through the boundaries Ursa has placed around herself. Her foremothers' stories are still with her in the room; it is, in fact, a story she heard from her great-grandmother that makes her understand the interconnectedness of love and hate that can exist in abusive relationships, and it allows her to find the courage to tell Mutt that she does not want to be hurt. It would be easy to read the ending of this novel as feeble progress—after decades of loneliness Ursa reunites with a man who was verbally and physically abusive toward her. She finally understands that her great-grandmother felt she had some measure of power over Old man Corregidora when she performed fellatio, as the threat of injury is risked because of the desire for pleasure. Ursa then moves beyond her grandmother's history in her final call-and-response exchange in the novel. Mutt repeatedly declares, "I don't want the kind of woman that hurt you," and Ursa replies, "Then you don't want me." In a break of the rhythm, Ursa finally states, "I don't want a kind of man that'll hurt me neither."[35] That is what Ursa had been unable to explain. As a narrative of pain was her background before she was born, the simple act of being able to state a desire that she had previously been unable to articulate is progress for Ursa as a subject. Her response to the impossibility of justice is interpersonal and psychological, not institutional.

Moving forward interpersonally, however, never results in reparations for Ursa or the other women. Those around her do not come to understand the complexity of the racial-sexual injury that shaped her life and that of her foremothers. While the claim that she does not want to be hurt gestures toward how that history shaped her, the novel never provides a way for Ursa to gain justice for her foremothers by presenting evidence and receiving judgment. It is almost a utopian dream or phantasm—a lost object for which Ursa continuously compensates. The novel imprints the readers with this history through the repetition of the visceral narrative, and Jones is in no way suggesting that the narrative is unimportant. The story illustrates that, where the harm is psychological, reparation is a challenging enterprise. It in no way suggests that the Corregidora women's story should not be told or that seeking justice can never be productive. Rather, it asks what can be done while one waits for reparations, or, conversely, what does one do in the twilight of failed reparative aspirations?

Notes

1. Kutz, "Justice in Reparations," 279.
2. Jones, *Corregidora*, 8–9.
3. Cognard-Black, "I Said Nothing," 43.
4. The classic texts in this field include Susan Brownmiller's *Against Our Will: Men, Women, and Rape* (New York: Bantam, 1975); MacKinnon, "Reflections of Sex Equality Under the Law"; and Estrich, "Rape."
5. See Davis, *Women, Race and Class*, 23.
6. I am using consent in the strictest sense here, as slave women literally could not give consent, but I do acknowledge that complex structures of intimacy were possible even during chattel slavery. For one of the most nuanced discussions of this, involving the most famous relationship between a slave owner and slave in history, see Reed, *Sally Hemings and Thomas Jefferson*.
7. Jacobs, *Incidents in the Life of a Slave Girl*, 92.
8. Kant, *Lectures on Ethics*, 203–4.
9. I should mention that *Corregidora* is not the only time that Jones has written a narrative about a black woman dealing with the trauma of Brazilian slavery. In *Song of Anninho*, the narrator Almeyda has also suffered state violence and is the voice of the history of her people—the *quilombos* of Palmares. For more on *Song*, see Harris, "A Spiritual Journey: Gayl Jones's Song for Anninho;" and King, "Resistance, Reappropriation, and Reconciliation: The Blues and Flying Africans in Gayl Jones's *Song for Anninho*."
10. Toplin, *The Abolition of Slavery in Brazil*, 235.
11. Twine, *Racism in a Racial Democracy*, 111.
12. Jones, *Corregidora*, 8–9.
13. Ibid., 9.
14. Gotanda, "A Critique of Our Constitution is Color-Blind."
15. Crenshaw, "Mapping the Margins," 1271.
16. Ibid., 1271.
17. Jones, *Corregidora*, 14.
18. See, for example, Felman and Laub, *Testimony: Crises of Witnessing in Literature, Psychoanalysis, and Literature.*
19. See Dixon, "Language as Evidence in the Novels of Gayl Jones," 239.
20. Lynne Henderson explains that "the Rule of Law is the reification of rules governing rights and duties to which we pay homage; thus, this is a 'government of laws not men": the Rule of Law transcends humans and is superior to them. The virtue of the Rule of Law is that it is ostensibly "neutral" and prevents the abuse of persons. The neutrality and generality of the Rule of Law seek to serve the goals of protecting individuals from arbitrary treatment of and of respecting people as autonomous and equal." Henderson, "Legality and Empathy," 1587.
21. Jones, *Corregidora*, 14.
22. Ibid., 119.
23. Ibid., 45.
24. Ibid., 151.
25. See generally Brown, "Wounded Attachments."
26. Jones, *Corregidora*, 78.
27. Martha Abreu compellingly argues that the free-womb law transformed discourse, opened up the discussion of allowing for the recognition of rights for slave families, and moved the country further toward abolition. I do not disagree with this claim, but

I would follow other historians who argue that it did not transform the lives of the great majority of slaves. See Abreu, "Slave Mothers and Freed Children."
28. Baker, *Blues, Ideology, and Afro-American Literature*, 5.
29. Rushdy, *Remembering Generations*, 65.
30. Jones, *Corregidora*, 77.
31. Ibid., 98.
32. Caruth, *Unclaimed Experience*, 41.
33. Ibid.
34. Giddens, *The Transformation of Intimacy*, 58.
35. Jones, *Corregidora*, 185.

Bibliography

Abreu, Martha. "Slave Mothers and Freed Children: Emancipation and Female Slave Debates on the 'Free Womb' Law Rio de Janeiro, 1871." *Journal of Latin American Studies* 28 (October 1996): 567–80.

Baker, Houston. *Blues, Ideology, and Afro-American Literature: A Vernacular History*. Chicago: University of Chicago Press, 1984.

Brown, Wendy. "Wounded Attachments." *Political Theory* 21, no. 3 (1993): 390–410.

Caruth, Cathy. *Unclaimed Experience: Trauma, Narrative, and History*. Baltimore, MD: Johns Hopkins University Press, 1996.

Cognard-Black, Jennifer. "'I Said Nothing': The Rhetoric of Silence and Gayl Jones's Corregidora." *National Women's Studies Association Journal* 13 (Spring 2001): 40–60.

Crenshaw, Kimberlé. "Mapping the Margins: Intersectionality, Identity Politics, and Violence Against Women of Color." *Stanford Law Review* 43 (July 1991): 1241–99.

Davis, Angela. *Women, Race, and Class*. New York: Vintage, 1981.

Dixon, Melvin. "Language as Evidence in the Novels of Gayl Jones." In *Black Women Writers (1950–1980): A Critical Evaluation*, edited by Mari Evans, 236–48. Garden City, NY: Anchor-Doubleday, 1984.

Estrich, Susan. "Rape." *The Yale Law Journal* 95 (May 1986): 1087–1184.

Felman, Shoshanna, and Dori Laub. *Testimony: Crises of Witnessing in Literature, Psychoanalysis, and Literature*. New York: Routledge, 1992.

Giddens, Anthony. *The Transformation of Intimacy: Sexuality, Love, and Eroticism in Modern Societies*. Stanford, CA: Stanford University Press, 1992.

Gotanda, Neil. "A Critique of Our Constitution is Color-Blind." *Stanford Law Review* 44 (November 1991): 1–68.

Harris, Trudier. "A Spiritual Journey: Gayl Jones's *Song for Anninho*." *Callaloo* 16 (October 1982): 105–11.

Henderson, Lynne N. "Legality and Empathy." *Michigan Law Review* 85 (June 1987): 1574–1653.

Jacobs, Harriet. *Incidents in the Life of a Slave Girl*. Clayton, DE: Prestwick House, 2006.

Jones, Gayl. *Corregidora*. Boston, MA: Beacon Press, 1975.

Kant, Immanuel. *Lectures on Ethics*. Translated by Louis Infield. London: Methuen, 1930.

King, Lovalerie. "Resistance, Reappropriation, and Reconciliation: The Blues and Flying Africans in Gayl Jones's *Song for Anninho*." In *After the Pain: Critical Essays on Gayl Jones*, edited by Fiona Mills and Keith B. Mitchell, 241–57. New York: Peter Lang, 2006.

Kutz, Christopher. "Justice in Reparations: The Cost of Memory and the Value of Talk." *Philosophy & Public Affairs* 32 (July 2004): 277–312.

MacKinnon, Catharine A. "Reflections of Sex Equality Under the Law." *Yale Law Journal* 100 (March 1991): 1281–1328.

Plessy v. Ferguson, 163 U.S. 537 (1896).

Reed, Annette Gordon. *Sally Hemings and Thomas Jefferson: An American Controversy*. Charlottesville: University Press of Virginia, 1997.

Rushdy, Ashraf A. *Remembering Generations: Race and Family in Contemporary American Fiction*. Chapel Hill: University of North Carolina Press, 2001.

Toplin, Robert Brent. *The Abolition of Slavery in Brazil*. New York: Antheneum, 1971.

Twine, Frances Windance. *Racism in a Racial Democracy*. New Brunswick, NJ: Rutgers, 1998.

Part III

Owning Culture

10

Papa's Got a Brand New Bag

James Brown, Innovation, and Copyright Law

K. J. Greene

The music world lost an unparalleled artist with the death of James Brown, the self-proclaimed "Godfather of Soul," in 2006. James Brown achieved the rare musical triumph of "bringing a unique brand of southern black music to the fore-front of American culture—without sanitizing it for a white public."[1] Remarking on Brown's musical legacy, *Rolling Stone* magazine opined that Brown's contribution to popular music and rock and roll exceeded that of the Beatles and Elvis combined.[2] Much like ragtime genius Scott Joplin; jazz giants such as Jelly Roll Morton, Louis Armstrong, and Fats Waller; and blues legend Bessie Smith before him, Brown's artistic innovations permeate popular music, making it difficult to say where Brown's influence ends and that of other artists begins. "Soul Brother Number One," as Brown also proclaimed himself, revolutionized soul music; pio-neered the genres of soul, funk, and disco music; and changed the shape of jazz as well. Highlighting the impact of his work, Princeton University hosted a two-day symposium shortly after Brown's death entitled "Ain't That a Groove: The Genius of James Brown."

James Brown's artistry extended well beyond music and influenced spheres of politics, culture, and law. Brown contributed tirelessly to the civil rights move-ment of the 1960s, often canceling "shows to perform benefit concerts for black political organizations like the Southern Christian Leadership Conference."[3] Dur-ing the height of the civil rights movement, Brown's 1968 song "Say It Loud, I'm Black and I'm Proud" fueled demands for racial and economic equality and was a catalyst for the "black is beautiful" movement. Brown, it was said, was "the one man in America who can stop a race riot in its tracks and send the people home to watch television."[4]

Brown was also fiercely entrepreneurial and independent, so much so that he supported conservative candidates such as Richard Nixon for president. Brown's own personal issues—including drug use, tax problems, and run-ins with the criminal justice system—were legend, as often seems to go with genius.[5] Further, as has often been true in the black musical community, Brown's "unbridled machismo [resulted in] black women . . . [being] simply attached as a postscript to a male-directed message."[6] He sang as much when he declared "It's a Man's, Man's World" in 1966. Ironically, the song was at least cowritten by a woman, as later litigation over the song's ownership would indicate.[7]

Brown was an extremely savvy businessman, being one of the first major black artists "to understand the value of owning the rights to his own recordings and publishing."[8] When Brown's record label refused to support his vision of making recordings from his live performances, Brown financed the recording of his legendary *Live at the Apollo*, 1962 himself.[9] The record became a huge commercial success, and Brown pioneered the market for live performance recordings. Brown recognized that the huge amount of money he generated in the early 1960s—grossing $450,000 on touring alone in 1963—"represented no more than a mere pittance compared to what was his due."[10] Brown refused to record for a full year after a contract dispute with his label at the time, King Records, forcing the label to grant "almost every concession [Brown] had been seeking: his own publishing, a vastly improved royalty rate, a minimum of 25,000 singles and comparable LPs in 'free goods' . . . and expanded . . . artistic control."[11]

Given his impact both on culture and on the legal system, focusing on the work of James Brown from a legal and cultural perspective is germane to applying standards of originality in copyright law to digital sound sampling controversies. From an intellectual property (IP) legal perspective, Brown's music provides two valuable insights on copyright protection. First, it reaffirms the insight that copyright law provides poor protection to truly innovative artists like Louis Armstrong, whose jazz innovations define modern jazz, and Scott Joplin, who pioneered the genre of ragtime. As a great innovator, Brown's signature sound defines modern funk and forms the underlying basis for hip-hop. When an artist is so innovative that his or her idiom becomes a "style," the idea-expression dichotomy of copyright law effectively allows mere imitators to usurp the true innovator. The idea-expression dichotomy provides that copyright law should not protect raw ideas and their analogs but, rather, only their expression. However, innovators such as Armstrong, Joplin, and, now, Brown, have historically found their genius reduced to an idea—so that playing "in the style" of Louis Armstrong or Jimi Hendrix is not copyright infringement but merely imitation, which copyright law permits. Indeed, we can likely identify leading innovators by looking at who is being extensively imitated, if not who is outright copied. The work of true innovators, such as Scott Joplin, serves to "unleash an even greater flood of rivals and imitators."[12]

The second insight arising from James Brown's artistry is that an overly protective copyright law can stifle artistic innovation. Digital sound sampling—the borrowing— (or theft, depending on one's perspective) of small snippets from sound recordings of other artists' music—was essential to the development of hip-hop, now recognized as an art form in itself. It might well be true that rap music could not have existed without James Brown's polyrhythmic innovations. James Brown's influence teaches us that copyright must be strong enough to protect the compensatory interests of artists, but it can not be so strong and inflexible that it stifles the next great innovator. The price of genius in the copyright context may preclude innovators from capitalizing on all the fruits of their creation in exchange for a broader public domain.

Black Music, James Brown, and Innovation

Booker T. Washington famously posited that "no race that has anything to contribute to the markets of the world is long in any way ostracized."[13] African American artists have been at the forefront of musical innovation in the United States, and the music they have created has tremendous global economic wealth. There is great concern today among legal scholars that intellectual property, including copyright, is providing a stifling overprotection to copyright owners at the expense of a broad public domain. IP law has the potential to "silence and deaden our future musical culture."[14] However, copyright law has historically underprotected works by black music artists. There is a disconnect between the structure of copyright law, which protects original works of authorship fixed in a tangible form, and black cultural production arising from African oral traditions.

My scholarship has analyzed how the legal structure of copyright law and the social dynamic of race deeply influenced and affected black cultural production in music.[15] Scholars have recognized the impact of copyright law on cultural production—styles of complex jazz such as bebop, for example, "represented a conscious step toward African and African American music that could not be commercialized by whites."[16] However, until recently, intellectual property law focused almost wholly on doctrine and legal theories such as law and economics but not on the intersection of the dynamics of race (or gender) in the IP context. James Brown, as a black innovator, reflects many of these currents and crosscurrents in the legal and cultural vortex around cultural production.

Music historians agree that the most pivotal names in the new "soul" music that emerged in the 1950s were Ray Charles and James Brown.[17] Recognizing the genius of James Brown, the great jazzman Quincy Jones famously proclaimed that James Brown "is our Elvis . . . our Beatles."[18] It has been said similarly that "by any measure of real musical greatness—endurance, originality, versatility, breath of influence," James Brown "towers" over the greatest performers of his time, including Elvis, the Beatles, Stevie Wonder, and the Rolling Stones.[19]

The revolutionary influence of Brown's musical innovation spanned a broad spectrum of music from major soul stars such as Aretha Franklin to jazz genius Miles Davis.[20] Brown almost single-handedly staved off the decline of indigenous black American music in the face of the "British invasion" of the 1960s.[21] Brown did all this early in his career despite criticism from both sides of the color line. Prominent white critics chastised Brown as "the greatest demagogue in the history of Negro entertainment . . . his whole vast success . . . is based less on talent and skills than on the unique faculty for sizing up the black public and making himself the embodiment of its desires."[22] Brown was similarly branded by some voices in the black community as an "Uncle Tom" because of his support of mainstream politicians, his processed hair, and his willingness to perform for troops during the Vietnam war.[23]

Brown was the main innovator in the creation of the genre of "funk" music.[24] When Brown partnered with legendary bassist Bootsy Collins in 1970, music historians noted that "funk was never to sound the same again."[25] Brown reinvented "funk" music from its origins and as counterpoint to "cool" strands in jazz. Artists such as Sly and the Family Stone, Kool and the Gang, and George Clinton "recycled" Brown's funk innovations.[26] Brown also profoundly influenced rap music, a musical form that might be considered indivisible from Brown's innovations. Music analysts note that "Brown has been called the "Godfather of Soul," but in many ways he is also the "Godfather of Rap.""[27]

Brown's creativity, like that of many blues and jazz artists and the rappers that followed them, poses challenges to many aspects of copyright doctrine. Innovators in creative works are arguably harmed by the standards for copyrightability, which require original works of authorship. Originality in copyright law means little more than producing something with a modicum of creativity that is not precisely copied from a previous work. The U.S. Supreme Court has set the standard for originality so low that almost any work more creative than the arrangement of names and numbers in a phone book likely qualifies for copyright protection.[28]

Emblematic of Brown's musical innovation was his song "Papa's Got a Brand New Bag," which was a number one hit on the rhythm and blues (R&B) charts for eight weeks, fueling the soundtrack of the turbulent year of 1965.[29] Although Brown was a peerless self-promoter, there was more reality than hyperbole when, in discussing "Papa's Got a Brand New Bag," he remarked that "I'm actually fighting the future . . . take any record off your stack and put it on your box, even a James Brown record, and you won't find on that sounds like this one, it's a brand new bag, just like I sang."[30] Music historians agree, noting that the song "truly changed the face of music."[31]

As a primordial innovator, Brown can serve as a kind of metaphor for black musical production, which has always been at the forefront of American music. The founding fathers established copyright law as a means for increasing cultural productivity by giving economic incentives for the creation of artistic works.[32] Analysts note that "in large part, the early music industry [in the United States] was built largely on the creativity and innovation of black composers and artists."[33] One would think, then, that black artists would have been among the prime beneficiaries of copyright law given their astounding contributions to the world of music. However the actual history of black cultural production and the law is one of inequality rooted in racial animosity.[34] The emergence of Brown represents a shift in trends of appropriation because he was able to capture much of the value of his innovation, although clearly not all, as explored below.

The music of James Brown built upon the blues tradition of slaves that, most scholars believe, originated in the Mississippi delta in the 1890s.[35] Ironically, Brown claimed to have little affection for traditional blues, notwithstanding that "the two hits with which Brown announced himself the king of funky soul and modernity in 1965, 'Papa's Got a Brand New Bag' and 'I Got You (I Feel Good),' were both cast in the twelve-bar blues form." [36] The history of African American musical production, as exemplified by Brown, presents challenges to copyright doctrine, which assumes individual rather than communal creation. Early blues giants such as Charlie Patton routinely created in communal fashion "with ideas and songs swapped and guitar patterns exchanged" among blues musicians.[37]

Blues scholars note that "originality in blues . . . is not a question of sitting down and making up songs out of thin air . . . [but rather] consists of combining phrases, lines and verses with compatible emotional resonances into associational clusters that the reflect the singer's own experiences, feelings and moods and those of his listeners."[38] When these structural issues are grafted upon a system of social discrimination, arising from what Thurgood Marshall termed systematic "lawlessness" attendant to being black in America, the whole "incentive" theory of copyright is turned on its head.[39] Given the pervasive appropriation of property from African Americans lasting until recent decades, it is not surprising that blacks would fare poorly under an intellectual property regime. For early black artists, "copyright law failed miserably to protect either economic rights that adhere to a copyright creator . . . [or] their personal interests—known as moral rights—in artistic creation."[40] Scholars such as Keith Aoki have also similarly documented how black inventors fared poorly under the regime of patent law.[41]

We can perhaps extract two benefits from the low standard of copyright originality. First, it encourages imitation and arguably leads to a more prolific production of cultural works, although these typically will be of lower quality than the original innovation. I say "typically" because, when we look at Brown's music, we see it spawns disco, which is generally considered a less potent genre of music than Brown's. But it also spawned funksters, such as George Clinton, who, although derivative, are every bit as inventive as Brown. Secondly, the low standard of creativity set by copyright law allows judges to "avoid making value judgments about qualities of works that they may be unable to comprehend."[42]

On the down side, a minimal standard of originality elevates imitation over innovation. The idea-expression dichotomy, which does not confer copyrights in either "styles" or genre, along with the ability of artists to make "cover" records of any previously released sound recording has the effect of shortchanging innovators under copyright law. Thus Scott Joplin, the great innovator of ragtime, created "the most popular 'pop' style of music of the first two decades [of the twentieth century] [which was] utilized profitably by any number of white composers [such as Irving Berlin]."[43] Joplin, like so many early blues and jazz artists, never came anywhere near to realizing the financial fruits of ragtime music, which was literally the soundtrack of America for many decades. Indeed, Joplin, the "king of ragtime," was "totally forgotten by the general public" until the 1970s blockbuster film "The Sting" repopularized his signature tune, "The Entertainer."[44]

Innovators who are primarily performers, rather than composers, also face disadvantage under copyright law. In idioms such as jazz and blues, the improvisational nature of the music often elevates the importance of performance over that of an original composition.[45] Their performance invariably is deemed a "style" under copyright law, which through "its emphasis on originality . . . tends to place the author or creator at the center of property ownership."[46] While James Brown was known as the "hardest working man in show business" based on his bravura concert performances, copyright law neither rewards hard work like his nor protects pure performance that is not "fixed" in some tangible medium, such as a sound recording.

Furthermore, in the sound recording context, only the composer of a song, not the person who sings on the record, is entitled to performance royalties. So a singer such as Ella Fitzgerald, who clearly was among the greatest of jazz innovators in voice but not known as a composer of music, would have no ability to stop another singer from copying her style of vocalization. Further, copyright law does not typically protect improvisation, which is arguably at the heart of innovation—unless simultaneously "fixed" in some form such as a recording or written notation. Of course, the whole point of improvisation is not to fix one's artistry in writing. Hence, as my earlier work demonstrates, jazz faces a structural disadvantage in connection with the structure of copyright law.[47]

Copyright does not protect performance style—hence artists from Prince to Michael Jackson have copied Brown's distinctive performance style. Performance, like improvisation, is not considered "fixed' for purposes of copyright law, and thus many performances rooted in a black cultural idiom have been readily appropriated by the dominant culture, including the distinctive screams of Little Richard (see the Beatles on "She Loves You, Yeah, Yeah"), dances such as the "cakewalk," which created fortunes early in the twentieth century, and "boogie-woogie" styles of piano playing pioneered by master stylists from Jelly Roll Morton to James P. Johnson and Fats Waller. Perhaps overly broad protection of performances too could squash creativity. But time and time again, it seems to be innovative performers in the black tradition that find themselves unprotected under copyright law structures. Many, if not most, of the great innovators in blues and jazz died either in obscurity or in poverty despite copyright's promise to offer "incentives" for artistic creation. The list would include Scott Joplin, the "King of Ragtime"; Robert Johnson, widely considered to be the greatest bluesman ever; Jelly Roll Morton, who claimed to have invented jazz; Fats Waller, the most underappreciated artist and composer in all of jazz in my mind; and Mamie Smith, whose 1920 recording of "Crazy Blues" was the first mass-selling blues record in history and launched the modern recording industry.[48]

Copyright law, unlike patent law, is not designed to foster innovation. Patent law sets strict standards of novelty and nonobviousness.[49] The minimal-originality standard has some social benefit, but one can question why the burden of genius in innovation has fallen so heavily on black artists. My work has illustrated that the law can be "race neutral" in its wording and still have an adverse effect on groups historically left out of the promise of liberty and justice for all. For example, copyright's compulsory sound recording doctrine, which has been in effect since 1909, provides that once a composer releases a sound recording to the public, any other artist can rerecord that song provided it is a faithful rerecording of the original.

This provision is known as the "cover recording" section of the Copyright Act. IP scholars, such as Lawrence Lessig, recognize that the compulsory-license provision is "another kind of piracy" in that it gives "recording artists a weaker right than it otherwise gives creative authors."[50] However, Lessig concludes that by "limiting the rights musicians have, by partially pirating their creative work, the record producers, and the public, benefit."[51] What this ahistorical analysis ignores is the social dynamic underlying "cover" records, which from Elvis Presley's rerecording of Big Mama Thornton's "Hound Dog" to Pat Boone's redoing of Little Richard's "Tutti Frutti" fostered the devaluation of works in a black musical idiom.

James Brown, unlike many of the blues and jazz innovators before him, will not go down in obscurity. Brown received enormous financial remuneration during his lifetime that will continue long after his death, given the extensive postmortem copyright term of seventy years. The lesson here is that as social discrimination lessened through the 1950s and 1960s, black artists were able to assert control over IP and contract rights that escaped artists such as Jelly Roll Morton, Bessie Smith, and Bo Diddley before them. During his life, Brown "cashed in" on the present value of his copyrights through the device of "Bowie Bonds"—securities based on the future income his copyrights would generate.[52]

Clearly, an innovator such as James Brown would have benefited from patentlike protection. Patent law provides a shorter term of protection—twenty years—but gives far more extensive protection during the term of protection by prohibiting anyone else from making, using, selling, or importing an invention during the term without a license. Rewarding individual artists with such broad protection would not necessarily result in net social gain. While such protection would benefit innovators in music, it would have the negative effect of reducing creativity, as explored below in the area of digital sound sampling.

James Brown and Digital Sound Sampling

The genre of disco was in essence an "outgrowth of both electronic experimentation and James's Brown's rhythmic dictum." It is highly ironic then that the disco movement is thought to have led to the wane of James Brown's musical influence by the mid 1970s.[53] Brown released a 1979 album entitled "The Original Disco Man" that sold poorly, "an ironic comment, perhaps, on his inability to profit from the success of an idiom he helped create."[54] However, the advent of rap/hip-hop music in the late 1970s resurrected Brown's music. The emergence of rap, like the rise of rock and roll before it, reflected social and cultural currents of race. When rock and roll emerged, advocates of segregation attempted to suppress the music, as they abhorred the notion of white youths dancing to the music of black artists. Similarly, some analysts contend that rap music became a cultural battleground "upon which an intolerant and powerful majority—most of whom happened to be white—attempted to enforce its values against a disenfranchised and largely powerless minority—most of whom happened to be black."[55]

In the early evolution of rap, artists digitally sampled James Brown's complex rhythms and distinctive vocalizations more than any other artist; such sampling was second only to the sampling of music by Brown's protégé, funk master George Clinton. The dense wall of sound or sonic war of some brilliant rap artists, such as Public Enemy, would have been impossible without unregulated digital sampling. There is some irony, then, in early sampling lawsuits, such as the one where a songwriter named Ingrid Chavez sued Madonna for copyright infringement over the song "Justify My Love." The rap group Public Enemy has threatened to sue Madonna because "Justify My Love" sampled the group's song "Security of the First World." Ironically, the inspiration for Public Enemy's song was actually a James Brown composition. "Many in the music industry think Public Enemy's threats are ludicrous because they sampled the 'Security' beat from a 1969 James Brown tune called "Funky Drummer."[56]

Digital sound sampling is a process of "recycling sound fragments previously recorded by other musicians for use in new recordings."[57] Sampling began in Jamaica in the 1960s and 1970s. In the 1980s, "MCs" and rappers in the South Bronx, such as DJ Red Alert and Kool Herc, perfected sampling into an art form, thus creating a genre that revolutionized the recording industry.[58] Until the early 1990s, when copyright infringement lawsuits curbed the practice, digital sampling and hip-hop flourished, and Brown's voice and drum beats powered many classic rap songs from Robb Bass and DJ E-Z Rock's "It Takes Two" to KRS-One's "South Bronx." Brown himself harshly condemned the practice of digital sampling, stating unequivocally that "anything they take off my record is mine."[59] Although the modern recording industry was based in large part on white artists appropriating the work of black blues artists, the first sampling lawsuits involved white composers suing black rappers and hardened the notion that hip-hop artists engage in theft outside the mainstream of musical "borrowings" in other contexts. In 1991, Judge Duffy in the Southern District of New York took the extraordinary step of recommending criminal prosecution of the rapper Biz Markie, who had sampled the maudlin 1970s Gilbert O'Sullivan song "Alone Again, Naturally."[60]

In the first published opinion on sampling, Judge Duffy concluded that digital sound sampling constitutes copyright infringement. However, the landmark opinion contains no legal analysis of sampling—only the Biblical admonition that "Though shalt not steal." The federal judge was clearly outraged by the practice of sampling, but he did not acknowledge the irony of the history of rampant appropriation of the works of black artists by white artists. For example, Scott Joplin found his composition from the finale of his opera "Treemonisha" shamefully appropriated by composer Irving Berlin, who earned "an astonishing thirty thousand dollars in royalties" in 1910 for his "Alexander's Ragtime Band."[61] Another early sampling case, involving Roy Orbison's "Pretty Woman," made it all the way to the Supreme Court on the issue of fair use.[62] The controversial rap group Two Live Crew requested permission to use a sample from "Pretty Woman." Orbison's publishing company, Acuff-Rose, refused to grant a license, and the group released the recording anyway with "shocking lyrics" designed to demonstrate the "blandness of the Orbison original."[63] Ultimately, the Supreme Court ruling permitted Two Live Crew to sample Orbison's song because of fair use's protection of parodies. As a result of these and other sampling lawsuits, Brown was subsequently able to force royalty payments and license agreements on record companies that had facilitated the sampling of his music. Brown released his own inimitably brilliant album of rap songs entitled, fittingly, "I'm Real" in 1989.

The music industry currently requires that every sample be licensed and aggressively pursues unauthorized sampling. A federal court decision in recent years set forth the bright-line rule that every digital sound sample, no matter how brief, requires a license.[64] There is irony here, too, in relation to black cultural production. Analysts postulate that in certain subcultures, such as rap music, sampling has "specific traditions of reference and respect, in which the recognizability of a sample operates to provide credit and simultaneously establish the sampling artist's membership in a community."[65] In this sense, the wide sampling of James Brown's music reflected a reverence for it.

The music of James Brown is so distinctive that even a tiny snippet of his voice is recognizable. An example of this is the early 1990s rap song "It Takes Two" by rappers Rob Base and DJ E-Z Rock. Looped throughout the hit song is a James Brown scream of less than two seconds. Although brief, the "scream" makes the song uniquely distinctive. Under copyright law's *de minimis* doctrine, the use of a very small piece of a copyrighted work is typically not actionable as copyright infringement,[66] but this rule disadvantages a truly unique sound such as a James Brown scream.

The *Bridgeport* decision, however, suggests that requiring hip-hop deejays to pay for the samples may not benefit the musicians who created and performed the music. The case involved the music of funk master George Clinton, a genius himself and a true innovator even if his sound is built upon Brown's. However, George Clinton was divested of many of his copyrights by the plaintiff, Bridgeport Music. Bridgeport is a shadowy entity that some analysts contend exists simply to purchase copyrighted works and find entities to sue for copyright infringement.[67] So we have a company, Bridgeport Music, that creates nothing itself but takes a formal ownership position acting as an author and squelching artistic use by others, which seems unconscionable. As a result, the decision favors the rights holder—who might have acted dubiously when contracting with the musician—over the music's creator.

In another sampling case, a federal court validated the rights of the rap group the Beastie Boys to use a flute solo by innovative jazz flautist James Newton.[68] The Beastie Boys obtained a license from the sound recording owner, as usual, the record label, for the recording of Newton's composition "Choir" but not a license from the composer himself. The court held that the rappers used such a small portion of the song that the use was *de minimis*, or legally insignificant, and that, in any event, Newton was really claiming infringement of his distinctive and unique style of playing the flute. Copyright law does not protect artistic performance or style, and so Newton lost his copyright infringement suit. The case underscores the weak protection copyright accords to performance, and perhaps this leads one to wonder—why does it seem that black artists more often than not end up on the losing end of these cases?

Copyright law's strict rules against digital sound sampling result in the artistic stifling of "mash-up" albums. The most famous mash-up is probably DJ Danger Mouse's *Grey Album*, which combined the music of the Beatles' *White Album* with the lyrics of Jay-Z's *Black Album*. Because DJ Danger Mouse (a.k.a. Brian Burton) did not get permissions to use any of the recordings, he was, in theory, liable for massive copyright infringement damages. The record labels did not, in fact, sue DJ Danger Mouse. Instead, they hailed the recording as a breakthrough success of a massive Internet hit without marketing and signed him to a record deal—after he promised not to use unauthorized materials again. The sampling issue brings into relief the stark choices between rewarding artists, such as Brown, and insuring there is a broad public domain from which other artists can draw. Part of the conundrum is, I think, the aggressive enforcement of copyright by distribution entities such as record labels, film studios, and television networks. This overly aggressive stance toward the use of copyrighted material is probably best exemplified by the Recording Industry Association of America (RIAA), which, until recent months, aggressively sued so-called digital downloaders who share music on the Internet.[69]

The RIAA, the lobbying arm of the record industry, says it has engaged in mass litigation against internet downloaders to "protect artists," but a cynical public is well aware that protecting artists is the lowest priority of big entertainment conglomerates—in part because of the dark history of appropriation of the work and undercompensation of black artists. If big companies can sue for any and every use of their copyrighted materials, why not artists? Taking the position that all uses of IP must be paid for would increase the revenues of artists, such as Brown, whose work is much in demand, but the ultimate price for creativity may be too high. While rap music sampling took much from James Brown, it resurrected his artistry and perpetuated it for generations to come. Although a techno song by L.A. Style declared years ago that "James Brown is Dead," the innovator par excellence will live on forever through his music.

Notes

1. Greig, *Icons of Black Music*, 19.
2. Christgau, "The Genius," 46.
3. Maycock, "James Brown: Soul Survivor."
4. Goldman, "Does He Teach us Black the Meaning of 'Black is Beautiful?'" 39.
5. This piece will not focus on the foibles, which are well documented elsewhere. See, for example, Moser and Crawford, *Rock Stars Do the Dumbest Things*.
6. George, *The Death of Rhythm and Blues*, 104.
7. *Newsome v Brown*.
8. Sullivan, *The Hardest Working Man*, 119.
9. Egan, *Defining Moments in Music*, 286.
10. Guralnick, *Sweet Soul Music*, 238.
11. Ibid., 242.
12. Gammond, *Scott Joplin and the Ragtime Era*, 87.
13. Boxill, *Blacks and Social Justice*, 20.
14. Demers, *Steal This Music*, 146.
15. See Greene, "Copyright, Culture and Black Music: A Legacy of Unequal Protection."
16. Calmore, "Critical Race Theory, Archie Shepp, and Fire Music," 317.
17. Haskins, *One Nation Under a Groove*, 38–39.
18. See Carr, *A Century of Jazz*, 188.
19. DeCurtis, Henke, and George-Warren, *Rolling Stone Album Guide*, 85.
20. Ibid.
21. See Gillett, *The Sound of the City*, 233–34.
22. Goldman, "Does He Teach us Black the Meaning of 'Black is Beautiful?'" 40.
23. Brown, *I Feel Good*, 156–57.
24. Gates and West, *The African-American Century*, 284.
25. Carr, *A Century of Jazz*, 190.
26. Keyes, *Rap Music and Street Consciousness*, 40.
27. Haskins, *One Nation Under a Groove*, 41.
28. *Feist Publications, Inc. v. Rural Telephone Service Co* (1991).
29. Whitburn, *The Billboard Book of Top 40 Hits*, 87–88.
30. Sullivan, *The Hardest Working Man*, 102.
31. Shapiro, *Turn the Beat Around*, 95.
32. The U.S. Constitution provided the basis for both copyright and patent protection in Article I, Section 8.
33. See Greene, "'Copynorms,' Black Cultural Production, and the Debate Over African-American Reparations," 1188.
34. Black artists were segregated into "race record" ghettoes, and performance rights organizations, such as ASCAP, excluded black composers. See Reich, *Jelly's Blues*, 145.
35. Oakley, *The Devil's Music*, 46.

36. Wald, *Escaping the Delta*, 218.
37. Oakley, *The Devil's Music*, 58.
38. Palmer, *Deep Blues*, 69.
39. *Regents of the University of California v. Bakke* (1977).
40. See Greene, "What the Treatment of African American Artists Can Teach about Copyright Law," 383.
41. See Aoki, "Distributive and Syncretic Motives," 722.
42. VerSteeg, "Originality and Creativity in Copyright Law," 21.
43. George, *The Death of Rhythm and Blues*, 8.
44. Waldo, *This Is Ragtime*, 3.
45. "Jazz Has Got Copyright Law and that Ain't Good," 1959.
46. Katyal, "Performance, Property, and the Slashing of Gender in Fan Fiction," 477–78.
47. See Greene, "Copyright, Culture, and Black Music."
48. Wolfe and Lornell, *The Life and Legend of Leadbelly*, 81.
49. Miller, "Nonobviousness," 2.
50. Lessig, *Free Culture*, 55, 57.
51. Ibid., 58.
52. Gates and West, *The African-American Century*, 22.
53. Shapiro, *Turn the Beat Around*, 111.
54. Palmer, "James Brown," 147.
55. Stanley, *Rap: The Lyrics*, v.
56. Givens, "Justify My Copyright."
57. See, for example, Bergman, "Into the Grey," 623.
58. See Johnstone, "Underground Appeal," 399–400. The early history of rap is set forth by rapper KRS-One in the 1986 song "South Bronx," which features heavy sampling of James Brown's music and voice.
59. See Brown, "'They Don't Make Music the Way They Used To,'" 1957.
60. *Grand Upright Music Ltd. v. Warner Bros. Records, Inc.* (1991). See also Arewa, "From J. C. Bach to Hip-Hop," 581.
61. See Greene, "Copyright, Culture and Black Music."
62. *Campbell v. Acuff-Rose Music, Inc.* (1994).
63. Barrett, *Intellectual Property*, 632–33.
64. *Bridgeport Music, Inc. v. Dimension Films* (2005).
65. Tushnet, "Payment in Credit," 159.
66. See Cromer, "Harry Potter and the Three-Second Crime," 266.
67. Wu, "Jay-Z Versus the Sample Troll."
68. *Newton v. Diamond* (2003).
69. See Greene, "Copynorms."

Bibliography

Aoki, Keith. "Distributive and Syncretic Motices in Intellectual Property Law." *University of California–Davis Law Review* 40 (2007): 717–801.

Arewa, Olufunmilayo B. "From J. C. Bach to Hip-Hop: Musical Borrowing, Copyright and Cultural Context." *North Carolina Law Review* 84 (2006): 547–645.

Barrett, Margreth. *Intellectual Property: Cases and Materials*. 3rd ed. St. Paul, MN: West Group, 2007.

Bergman, Bryan. "Into the Grey: The Unclear Laws of Digital Sampling." *Hastings Communications and Entertainment Law Journal* 27 (2005): 619–52.

Boxill, Bernard R. *Blacks and Social Justice*. 2nd ed. Lanham, MD: Rowman & Littlefield, 1992.

Bridgeport Music, Inc. v. Dimension Films, 410 F.3d 792 (6th Cir. 2005).

Brown, James. *I Feel Good: A Memoir of a Life of Soul*. New York: New American Library, 2005.

Brown, Jeffrey H. "'They Don't Make Music the Way They Used To': The Legal Implications of 'Sampling' in Contemporary Music." *Wisconsin Law Review* (1992): 1941–91.

Calmore, John O. "Critical Race Theory, Archie Shepp, and Fire Music: Securing an Authentic Intellectual Life in a Multicultural World." In *Critical Race Theory: The Key Writings that Formed the Movement*, edited by Kimberlee Crenshaw, Kendall Thomas, and Gary Peller, 315–28. New York: New Press, 1995.

Campbell v. Acuff-Rose Music, Inc., 510 U.S. 569 (1994).

Carr, Roy. *A Century of Jazz: A Hundred Years of the Greatest Music Ever Made*. London: Hamlyn, 2004.

Christgau, Robert. "The Genius." *Rolling Stone*, January 25, 2007.

Cromer, Julie. "Harry Potter and the Three-Second Crime: Are We Vanishing the De Minimis Defense from Copyright Law?" *New Mexico Law Review* 36 (2006): 261–96.

DeCurtis, Anthony, James Henke, and Holly George-Warren. *Rolling Stone Album Guide*. 3rd ed. New York: Random House, 1992.

Demers, Joanna. *Steal This Music: How Intellectual Property Law Affects Musical Creativity*. Athens: University of Georgia Press, 2006.

Egan, Sean, ed. *Defining Moments in Music: The Greatest Artists, Albums, Songs, Performances and Events that Rocked the Music World*. London: Cassell Illustrated, 2007.

Feist Publications, Inc. v. Rural Telephone Service Co., 499 U.S. 340 (1991).

Gammond, Peter. *Scott Joplin and the Ragtime Era*. New York: St. Martin's, 1975.

Gates, Henry Louis, Jr., and Cornel West. *The African-American Century: How Black Americans Have Shaped Our Country*. New York: Free Press, 2000.

George, Nelson. *The Death of Rhythm and Blues*. New York: Pantheon, 1988.

Gillett, Charlie. *The Sound of the City: The Rise of Rock and Roll*. 2nd ed. New York: Da Capo, 1996.

Givens, Ron. "Justify My Copyright." *Entertainment Weekly*, February 1, 1991. http://www.ew.com/ew/article/0,,313175,00.html (accessed July 20, 2009).

Goldman, Albert. "Does He Teach Us Black the Meaning of 'Black Is Beautiful?'" In *The James Brown Reader: 50 Years of Writing about the Godfather of Soul*, edited by Nelson George and Alan Leeds, 39–42. New York: Plume, 2008.

Grand Upright Music Ltd. v. Warner Bros. Records, Inc., 780 F. Supp. 182 (S.D.NY. 1991).

Greene, K. J. "'Copynorms,' Black Cultural Production, and the Debate Over African-American Reparations." *Cardozo Arts and Entertainment Law Journal* 25 (2008): 1179–1227.

———. "Copyright, Culture and Black Music: A Legacy of Unequal Protection." *Hastings Communications and Entertainment Law Journal* 21 (1999): 339–92.

———. "What the Treatment of African American Artists Can Teach about Copyright Law." In *Intellectual Property and Information Wealth: Issues and Practices in the Digital Age*, Vol. 1, edited by Peter K. Yu, 385–94. Westport, CT: Praeger, 2007.

Greig, Charlotte. *Icons of Black Music: A History in Photographs, 1900–1999*. Berkeley, CA: Thunder Bay, 1999.

Guralnick, Peter. *Sweet Soul Music: Rhythm and Blues and the Southern Dream of Freedom*. New York: Back Bay Books, 1999.

Haskins, James. *One Nation Under a Groove: Rap Music and Its Roots*. New York: Jump at the Sun/Hyperion Books for Children, 2000.

"Jazz Has Got Copyright Law and that Ain't Good." *Harvard Law Review* 118 (2005): 1940–61.

Johnstone, Chris. "Underground Appeal: A Sample of the Chronic Questions in Copyright Law Pertaining to the Transformative Use of Digital Music in a Civil Society." *Southern California Law Review* 77 (2004): 397–432.

Katyal, Sonia K. "Performance, Property, and the Slashing of Gender in Fan Fiction." *American University Journal of Gender, Social Policy and the Law* 14 (2006): 461–518.

Keyes, Cheryl L. *Rap Music and Street Consciousness*. Urbana: University of Illinois Press, 2002.

Lessig, Lawrence. *Free Culture: How Big Media Uses Technology and the Law to Lock Down Culture and Control Creativity*. New York: Penguin, 2004.

Maycock, James. "James Brown: Soul Survivor." *PBS American Masters Series*. http://www .pbs.org/wnet/americanmasters/database/brown_j.html (accessed July 20, 2009).

Moser, Margaret, and Bill Crawford. *Rock Stars Do the Dumbest Things*. New York: Macmillan, 1998.

Newsome v. Brown, U.S. App. LEXIS 30979 (2nd Cir. 2006).

Newton v. Diamond, 349 F.3d 591 (9th Cir. 2003).

Oakley, Giles. *The Devil's Music: A History of the Blues*. New York: Taplinger, 1977.

Palmer, Robert. *Deep Blues: A Musical and Cultural History of the Mississippi Delta*. New York: Penguin, 1981.

Palmer, Robert. "James Brown (excerpts)." In *The James Brown Reader: 50 Years of Writing about the Godfather of Soul*, edited by Nelson George and Alan Leeds, 145–47. New York: Plume, 2008.

Regents of the University of California v. Bakke, 438 U.S. 265 (1977).

Reich, Howard. *Jelly's Blues: The Life, Music, and Redemption of Jelly Roll Morton*. Cambridge, MA: Da Capo, 2003.

Shapiro, Peter. *Turn the Beat Around: The Secret History of Disco*. New York: Faber and Faber, 2005.

Stanley, Lawrence A., ed. *Rap: The Lyrics*. New York: Penguin, 1992.

Sullivan, James. *The Hardest Working Man: How James Brown Saved the Soul of America*. New York: Gotham, 2008.

Tushnet, Rebecca. "Payment in Credit: Copyright Law and Subcultural Creativity." *Law and Contemporary Problems* 70 (2007): 135–74.

VerSteeg, Russ. "Originality and Creativity in Copyright Law." In *Intellectual Property and Information Wealth: Issues and Practices in the Digital Age*, Vol. 1, edited by Peter K. Yu, 1–32. Westport, CT: Praeger, 2007.

Wald, Elijah. *Escaping the Delta: Robert Johnson and the Invention of the Blues*. New York: Amistad, 2004.

Waldo, Terri. *This Is Ragtime*. New York: Hawthorn, 1976.

Whitburn, Joel. *The Billboard Book of Top 40 Hits*. 8th ed. New York: Billboard Books, 2004.

Wolfe, Charles, and Kip Lornell. *The Life and Legend of Leadbelly*. New York: HarperCollins, 1992.

Wu, Timothy. "Jay-Z Versus the Sample Troll: The Shady One-Man Corporation that's Destroying Hip-Hop." *Slate*, November 16, 2006. http://www.slate.com/id/2153961.

11

Legal Fictions

Trademark Discourse and Race

Richard Schur

Fiction
1 a: something invented by the imagination or feigned; specifically: an invented story **b**: fictitious literature (as novels or short stories) **c**: a work of fiction
2 a: an assumption of a possibility as a fact irrespective of the question of its truth "a legal fiction" **b**: a useful illusion or pretense
3: the action of feigning or of creating with the imagination

—*Merriam-Webster's Dictionary*

Culture, whether as ideology or as everyday ritual, is where power inequalities manifest themselves in the behavior and values of ordinary people. This chapter examines how trademark law has enabled the ongoing circulation of racialized images and how its doctrinal building blocks offer striking analogies for understanding how race has operated and continues to function. Circulation of racial imagery is not simply an accidental effect of the current trademark system but a fundamental element of its logic. The entire purpose of trademarks is to rely on catchy slogans, fanciful phrases, and distinctive imagery to serve as proxies for authenticity or quality claims about product and corporate identities. Sometimes, these marks are truly arbitrary without any literal or cultural referent. Other times, marks build on existing but legally unrecognized cultural narratives or metaphors. In other words, trademark law is a key site within legal discourse where stereotypes and assumptions can get transformed into operative and potentially valuable fictions.[1] This chapter invokes I. Bennett Capers's strategy of "reading back" and "reading black" to suggest how much trademark law can teach us, perhaps unintentionally, about the function and operation of race in contemporary life.[2] This approach reveals that the concept of race, as a social fiction that identifies a person, is a key, albeit unspoken, feature of trademark discourse.[3] The slippage between racial and trademark discourse can also be found in unexpected places in American culture, including major civil rights cases such as *Plessy v. Ferguson* (1896) and *Gratz v. Bollinger* (2003).[4]

In the past decade, at least six African Americans, including comedian Damon Wayans, have sought to trademark the "N-word" or a variant of it. Ultimately, the applications were either abandoned or rejected.[5] In at least two instances, the U.S. Patent and Trademark Office (USPTO) refused to recognize the marks because they were deemed "scandalous," the governing legal standard for potentially offensive trademarks. In rejecting the applications, the USPTO relied on a series of cases involving a wide range of topics to define the meaning of "scandalous." The USPTO specially rejected the arguments made by those seeking the trademark for their usages that the petitioners believed were acts of resistance or transgression. For many, the USPTO's rejection of these trademark applications signals a commitment to antiracism.[6] The appeal to the seemingly universal rule prohibiting scandalous trademarks allows the USPTO to avoid entering the contentious debate within African American culture about the "N-word" and apply a more global, or colorblind, doctrine. Such a position, however, cannot easily reconcile the ongoing use of racial (or what might be considered racist) trademarks—such as Aunt Jemima, Uncle Ben, the Cleveland Indians, and the Kansas City Chiefs—throughout American culture. Many of these images originated during Jim Crow segregation after the first federal trademark statute in 1870, and they *continue to provide financially lucrative corporate identities*. Similarly, many trademarks that include white people, such as the Clabber Girl, Mr. Clean, the Morton Salt girl, and the Quaker Oats man, also constitute racialized and potentially racist images. Initially, businessmen deployed these images precisely to represent innocence, purity, and even cultural authority. Even today, race remains a central feature in marketing and promotions. Whether it's Tommy Hilfiger's or Sprite's transformation into hip-hop brands during the 1990s or Disney's efforts to create a putatively "multicultural" set of heroines in recent years to complement its bevy of white princesses from earlier decades, corporations carefully evaluate how racialized images will affect the meaning and use of their products.

The most common way to challenge a trademark is by claiming an infringing use. At issue in a trademark infringement case is whether consumers are confused, mistaken, or deceived about the "real" origin of a product or service.[7] Courts have developed a number of doctrines to help resolve trademark disputes: "false designation of origin," "consumer confusion," "dilution," and "fair use."[8] Few, if any, of these legal concepts have been developed in response to a specific racial dispute. Nonetheless, these doctrines contain a preference for a clear system of identity labels that can stabilize meaning for consumers. Via race, gender, and other stereotypes, corporations have created coherent and stable market identities. Ironically, trademark law protects and promotes the very kind of stereotypes that civil rights and antidiscrimination law seek to prohibit. In other words, trademark law is designed to regulate corporate behavior, maintain a kind of capitalist semiotics—or system of representation—and foster consumer confidence in the commodities being purchased. The statutory language constructs a false-fact binary that omits, neglects, and elides the very fictive or imaginary nature of most trademarks. By using this naturalizing language, legal discourse helps trademark owners transform their marketing and public relation's *hopes* into accepted social *facts*.

"False Designation of Origin"

Any person who, on or in connection with any goods or services, or any container for goods, uses in commerce any word, term, name, symbol, or device, or any combination thereof, or any false designation of origin, false or misleading description of fact, or false or misleading representation of fact.

—15 U.S.C. sec. 1125(a)

Few contemporary consumers probably realize that "Aunt Jemima" began as a song, predating the brand name by over twenty years—if not longer.[9] The song became a staple of minstrel shows, especially those that featured African American performers who "sought to capitalize on America's racism by marketing themselves as 'genuine,' 'real,' or 'bonafide' 'Negroes.'"[10] These minstrel performers needed to make such marketing claims in order to succeed against the numerous competing minstrel shows created and owned by white Americans. Their rhetoric of being the "genuine" article illustrates why trademark law developed to help regulate corporate symbols because consumers, especially white consumers, might be confused about the origin of minstrel performances. African American owners of minstrel shows, the most famous being Billy Kersands, might have had legitimate infringement claims against those white owners, but African Americans lacked any meaningful access to the courts during Jim Crow segregation. The absence of litigation in these instances signals how personal and institutional racism deeply affected legal reasoning of the period and the legal decisions we have inherited from earlier generations. While the minstrel show has virtually disappeared from American culture because of its racist imagery, the name and image of Aunt Jemima has not.

Despite being sung frequently by African American performers, "Aunt Jemima" and other minstrel tunes offered stereotypical depictions of African Americans to the delight of their multiracial audiences. Unlike some church pulpits which allowed African Americans the space to contest racism and white supremacy, the minstrel stage was a capitalist institution to the core. One purpose of this beacon of popular culture and forerunner to much of today's popular imagery in film, television, comics, and video games is to give the audience what it wants—even if that means primarily recirculating outdated racialized imagery. The grand irony of the minstrel show, especially in this discussion of trademark, was that it could not have existed without *false designations of origin and false or misleading representation of fact*. Performers, both white and black, invited the inference that minstrelsy originated in and accurately represented southern plantation life.[11] Its humor and its popularity rested on this false designation of origin.

And it was precisely one of the minstrel shows' more popular "misrepresentations of fact" that become a trademarked property.[12] Charles Rutt, a white business owner from St. Joseph, Missouri, had developed a ready-to-mix pancake batter in 1889. According to several historians, Rutt attended a minstrel show, witnessed a performance of "Aunt Jemima," and "decided to mimic it, using not only the name but the likeness of the Southern mammy emblazoned on the lithographed posters advertising the" show.[13] As luck would have it, Rutt soon encountered business problems and sold his company, including the famous trademark and logo. The subsequent owners decided to transform Aunt Jemima into a "household name" by finding an appropriate individual to "exemplify . . . Southern hospitality" and make it into a national brand.[14] The trademark owners hired a former domestic to appear as Aunt Jemima at the 1893 World's Fair in Chicago. This publicity stunt succeeded in raising the reputation of the Aunt Jemima brand. The Aunt Jemima trademark crafted a racial fiction to accompany a mass-produced good with little connection to either African Americans or the South. Aunt Jemima became quite popular, with dolls, books, and commercials devoted to telling her story and cir-culating her and a particularly (racialized) image of Southern hospitality. Today, the trademark Aunt Jemima is owned by Quaker Oats and is a significant element of their business holdings.

The creation of the Aunt Jemima brand has come to elide the mark's origins in minstrelsy, even if it reconstructs an image of southern hospitality that is deeply intertwined with the history of race and racism. In effect, trademark law allows the owners of such marks, such as the Aunt Jemima trademark, to create a fictive iden-tity for the consuming public by its deployment of a particular symbol or word. Jessica Silbey identifies three reasons why trademark confers this right: (1) to pro-duce a distinctive mark or identity that distinguishes it from others in the market-place; (2) to "reduce consumer search costs by making goods easier to identify and purchase and therefore encourage consistent quality among goods for consumer satisfaction;" and (3) to "protect the producer's investment in good will and the consumer's expectations of quality and consistency."[15] As a proxy for determining a commodity's origin (as opposed to where it is physically produced) and a conve-nient social fiction, the trademark reduces the complexity of mass-industrial pro-cesses and global supply chains to create a supposedly coherent marker of quality in an increasingly competitive world market. The Aunt Jemima trademark, despite the tenor of 15 U.S.C. sec. 1125(a), is not a fact but an elaborate fiction created and promoted by Charles Rutt, Quaker Oats, and others for financial gain.

Ironically, as Alex Johnson has argued, race too has historically operated as a proxy—usually a wildly inaccurate one—for individual worth and quality.[16] If the Aunt Jemima mark historically relied on the image of a southern mammy to obscure the modern web of contractual and manufacturing relations, the act of categorizing a few races based on supposedly biological characteristics encourages scholars and laypeople alike to think of individual races having a clearly defined origin and to "forget" the varied and interwoven historical and cultural factors that shape racial categories.[17] From this premise, Johnson argues that the current racial "trademark" in blackness needs to be destabilized and ultimately abandoned by breaking down established racial stereotypes. Johnson seeks to replace racial identities with ethnic identities and trademarks, which rely much more on his-tory and cultural consciousness as the unifying elements.[18] Any attempt to develop a more accurate system of racial identity must negotiate this necessarily fictive nature and the possibility of social acceptance or rejection. As a form of trademark, racial classifications create the fiction of a coherent origin despite the increasing flow of people, services, and goods. Precisely because globalization is threatening the coherence of assigning stable origins to anything and market competition is greater than ever before, trademarks, even race-based ones, have become essen-tial elements in marketing because they simplify and order the complexities of contemporary capitalism. For example, Quaker Oats updated Aunt Jemima in the late 1980s, but they did so to maintain the brand's commercial power, even after numerous African American artists used her image as a vehicle to criticize the racist nature of American visual culture. The updated version (discussed later) continues to produce race, albeit along the colorblind rules of contemporary society. As a "distinguishing" mark, Aunt Jemima, like existing racial classifications, remains a potent symbol of origin despite the reality it frequently conceals.

"Consumer Confusion"

[A trademark infringes on another trademark when it] is likely to cause confusion, or to cause mistake, or to deceive as to the affiliation, connection, or association of such person with another person, or as to the origin, sponsorship, or approval of his or her goods, services, or commercial activities by another person.

—15 U.S.C. sec. 1125(a)

A trademark cannot be merely a generic or descriptive phrase. Rather it must be arbitrary and fanciful so that it can be truly distinctive in the marketplace. Once a proposed trademark is deemed sufficiently arbitrary or fanciful, a corporation or person can own that particular use of the mark. If a second mark comes along that might confuse consumers, the owners of the original mark can bring suit for trademark infringement. In resolving this dispute, lawyers, judges, and litigants must contemplate the consumer or reader response to an image or text to determine whether it is "likely to cause consumer confusion."

Following trademark's main purpose, the "consumer confusion" cause of action allows a mark owner to imagine how consumers understand competing signs and images and challenge any potential misunderstandings that might harm the public. As is well known, slavery and segregation instituted a race-based caste system that structured how whites interacted with other racial groups. Read through the perspective offered by trademark law, the purpose of race and racial discourse is to avoid consumer/social confusion about a person's identity. Race, by creating or instituting a seemingly stable system of classification, enables the labeling and sorting of people into discrete categories and thus shapes social interaction. Race, like the concept of trademarks, is clearly a modern phenomenon that is "needed" to make sense of a world where people and goods move across the globe with relative ease. Trademarks and racial labels help identify a person or object's place or status in the world, including defining who is free and who is enslaved. Such labels have also proved extremely effective in conferring the kind of status and class privileges, which the American Revolution, at least theoretically, dismantled.

Law only recognizes arbitrary or fanciful marks. At first glance, racial labels appear descriptive in that terms like "black," "white," "Asian," or "Indigenous" seem to lack a fanciful or arbitrary element. However, as many scholars have noted over the past thirty years, racial categories are a curious blend of ancestry, physical appearance, cultural practice, and social consensus.[19] Like the most effective trademarks, the concept of race and racial labels has come to seem "natural" and merely descriptive because European and American thinkers devoted considerable energy—one might even call it a sustained public relations campaign—to persuade people of their value and worth.[20] It takes considerable effort to unlearn racial categories and to see how the complex blend of physical attributes, personal histories, and cultural practices get reduced and pigeonholed into a handful of racial labels.

As both a market brand and a racial stereotype, the figure of Aunt Jemima reveals the overlap between trademark and race discourse's goal of creating stable "brand" identities as a source of economic value in an increasingly complex market economy. The image of Aunt Jemima clearly conveys a distinctive image (although Mrs. Butterworth has offered some competition as another mammy-inspired brand) in the syrup and premade pancake mix aisle of the grocery store. From the view of trademark law, there is nothing descriptive in linking African American women to pancake-related products, even if Charles Rutt's ostensible purpose in appropriating the Aunt Jemima figure was to invoke slavery and the raced divisions of late-nineteenth-century labor and link the leisure provided by the instant pancake mix with that experienced by rich, white southerners. Looking at the trademark through the lens of African American cultural studies, Aunt Jemima helped "clear up" social and cultural confusion about the appropriate "place" of African Americans in the United States. If trademark law assumes that consumer confusion arises only when a second trademark enters the marketplace, cultural studies would point out that the marketplace invites the very consumer confusion about labor, manufacturing, commodity flows, and, ultimately, identity that trademark appears to steady. As a legal fiction that, in turn, is transformed into personal or corporate property, trademark helps consumers navigate the social world by offering a series of familiar and comforting narratives that seek to displace the real and complex social dynamics that produce both the consumer good and the mark's signifying structure. Trademarks, like race discourse itself, seek to reduce confusion in social and market transactions.

While she might relieve some (white) consumers of any remaining confusion they might possess about race relations or their place in the racial hierarchy, Aunt Jemima also causes "consumer confusion" for others. Despite the appeal to a universal subject, trademark law necessarily relies on a vague or unspecified subjectivity to determine the kind of symbols that will produce "consumer confusion." Who exactly are these consumers who get confused by certain trademark imagery? Is Aunt Jemima merely a brand name, or does she support existing racial distinctions and promote white supremacy? Is Aunt Jemima a universal symbol, or is she one aimed at particular individuals or communities? Does the putatively universal subject of law view such imagery through a racialized lens? Like many other legal fictions, trademarks, via their construction in trademark law, ask the American public to engage in an intentional misreading of underlying social and cultural conditions. The Aunt Jemima trademark, in effect, encourages consumers to ignore the complicated history of race relations and just purchase some "premixed" pancake batter and syrup. Of course, precisely what trademarks omit is *who* historically has mixed the batter and how those economic inequalities continue to shape the distribution of income and wealth in American culture.

Defenders of this trademark might argue that Aunt Jemima is nothing more than a distinctive brand identity, which helps consumers identify the product and its history of quality. Critics, however, might point out, in the words of Adrian

Piper, that "racism is primarily a visual pathology" because "it feeds on perceived appearance."[21] The very coherence of many trademarks, especially those that rely on raced beings, invokes racial difference in the service of business profit. For example, the National Basketball Association (NBA) has long denied that Jerry West, a white basketball player from the 1960s, served as the model for their logo, a player dribbling the ball in controlled manner, and rejected suggestions to revise their logo and make it more "racially" representative of the players in and style of the league. By contrast, Nike's Air Jordan features a player soaring through the air with legs akimbo and the ball raised high in anticipation of a slam dunk. The Air Jordan "saved" Nike by linking the company to Michael Jordan's style of play and, by implication, to African American iterations of basketball. For both Nike and the NBA, the social meaning of race affects their marketing choices and has created lucrative ownership interests in racially marked logos. Invoking universal or cosmopolitan consumers to explain the success and value of these marks would be almost unthinkable. However, law resorts precisely to this fiction when creating trademark doctrine. By ignoring race at the doctrinal level, law reinforces the power of race as a social force because it denies *how* these trademarks gain their semiotic value and how capitalism relies on racial fictions for its efficacy.

The consumer confusion doctrine also operates in another way. Race is deeply embedded in our national discourse and helps us order our experiences and perceptions. Efforts to alter the nation's racial taxonomy encounter significant resistance because any changes to our system of racial classification would foster "consumer confusion" between and within racial groups. Because social terms largely shape our own self-understandings, a change in racial terminology can cause individuals to rethink their personal identities and commitments. The turn from "Black" to "African American" in the 1970s caused considerable controversy, some of which still erupts today, about whether a term that features racial solidarity and African origins ("black") or ethnic or cultural solidarity ("African American") is most appropriate, fitting, or desirable.[22] Many outsiders still fail to appreciate the significance of this intragroup debate and refuse to acknowledge the validity of the claims being made. In effect, many who resist these changes in racial terms are, in effect, claiming rightly or wrongly that these new identity labels are causing "consumer confusion." Despite the jarring movement from commercial and racial metaphors, the consumer confusion doctrine helps explain why people and communities assert ownership claims over racial identity labels and why new terms can be viewed as a form of social fraud. Viewing race through the lens of trademark law helps reveal how much many Americans have invested in these racial identities. While law defines racial terms outside the bounds of trademark, race nonetheless functions socially like a trademarked identity as a way to ascribe origin and forestall cultural confusion.

The mammy image, whether in *Gone With the Wind* or as Aunt Jemima, has long been the object of considerable critical analysis by African American artists and cultural critics. During the 1960s and 1970s, numerous artists such as Jeff Donaldson, Joe Overstreet, Murry DePillars, Betye Saar, and Faith Ringgold deployed Aunt Jemima to contest dominant images of African Americans.[23] Art historian Michael Harris argues that these artists "interceded to manipulate them [the Aunt Jemima images] for effect, deconstructing the visual sign, questioning Aunt Jemima's role as a popular trademark, and giving voice and humanity to all the black women aggrieved by the stereotypical representation."[24] For Harris, these images reverse existing stereotypes, "signal the humbling of oppressors, and herald the anticipation of racial transformation."[25] M. M. Manring notes that academics during this same period sought to topple white supremacy by engaging in a revisionist analysis on the mammy figure upon which Aunt Jemima is based.[26] Borrowing trademark's doctrinal tools, I would frame these ironic reversals of Aunt Jemima as attempts to create a sort of "consumer confusion" in the "brand" or "identity" associated with the Aunt Jemima figure, both as a purveyor of pancakes and broader racial stereotypes. Clearly attuned to the social effects of advertising, civil rights- and Black Power–era artists viewed their art as challenging the monopoly in racist imagery owned by corporate America. For these artists, challenging the racialized imagery governed by trademark law constituted a fundamental part of their social justice activities as they sought to reconstruct the "brand identity" of African Americans. In this period, many activists believed that a radical reconstruction of racial identities could eradicate most forms of discrimination and racism. Underlying this logic is the premise that racism relied primarily on conscious motivations for efficacy. In response to the recent shift to marketing strategies that emphasize less conscious methods of persuasion, many activists now favor antiracist actions that focus on the unconscious effects of racism.

"Dilution"

Dilution by Blurring; Dilution by Tarnishment.—
(1) . . . the owner of a famous mark that is distinctive, inherently or through acquired distinctiveness, shall be entitled to an injunction against another person who, at any time after the owner's mark has become famous, commences use of a mark or trade name in commerce that is likely to cause dilution by blurring or dilution by tarnishment of the famous mark . . .

—15 U.S.C. sec. 1125(c)

This shift in trademark doctrine from deception to dilution, especially due to its recent legislative acceptance, provides an interesting point of entry into contemporary discussions of race. Despite its relatively recent vintage, dilution nonetheless retains a foundation of nineteenth-century conceptions of racial identity. First proposed in Frank Schechter's famous article and codified only within the last few decades, dilution offers an alternative understanding of trademark.[27] Challenging the accepted notion that public policy protected trademarks in order to limit consumer deception, Schechter argued that "the *creation and retention of custom*, rather than the designation of source, is the primary purpose of the trademark today, and that the preservation of the uniqueness or individuality of the trademark is of paramount importance to its owner."[28] In explaining why trademark should adopt the dilution framework, Schechter continues on to note that the greatest fear of the trademark owner is "the gradual whittling away or dispersion of the identity and hold upon the public mind of the mark or name by its use upon non-competing goods."[29] Ironically, in explaining the need for this expansion of trademark law, Schechter cites a decision involving competing uses of the Aunt Jemima brand name.[30] In codifying the dilution doctrine, Congress has created a fairly detailed set of potentially relevant factors for determining whether dilution has occurred.[31] The question remains an open one as to whether the dilution cause of action, inspired by Schechter, will be a popular one or whether the statutory framework created by Congress will be effective.

What ought to be striking to contemporary readers about this initial effort to theorize dilution is Schechter's emphasis on culture and identity. Long before the culture wars of the 1980s and even the ban on state-sanctioned segregation, Schechter had the foresight to predict the role of culture—what he terms custom and identity—in shaping consumer and thus corporate behavior. Quite presciently, Schechter recognized how the purveyors of trademarks seek to produce cultural meaning and mark their products with distinctive identities. This insight, based in his legal realism, encourages him to craft legal doctrine around the actual behavior and expectations of early twentieth-century trademark owners. In the era of Jim Crow segregation in the South and de facto segregation in the North, racial identity was deeply linked to cultural behavior and the cultural meaning of products and images. Perhaps inadvertently, Schechter incorporated racialized conceptions of identity into his suggestion for trademark reform precisely because he sought to harmonize corporate expectations—based on their view of early twentieth-century social and cultural relations—with legal doctrine. As noted above, Schechter proposed the dilution doctrine because he believed that the "gradual whittling away or dispersion of the identity" ought to constitute trademark infringement.[32] His dilution doctrine seeks to stabilize and protect ownership rights in identity. In some respects, this effort to guarantee a right to a static meaning of images and words seems to conflict with Schechter's own understanding that trademarks constitute cultural artifacts, which by definition are dynamic objects that will change in both use and meaning over time. Such an approach also ignores the very dynamism (and complexity) of identity, which Jim Crow segregation sought to deny.

Consider, for example, the *Plessy v. Ferguson* decision, which exemplifies the concerns that caused Schechter to develop the dilution doctrine.[33] *Plessy* is most remembered for sanctioning racial segregation in public accommodations and announcing the holding that "separate but equal" is constitutional. While this is an accurate summary of the case, it omits several key facts: Plessy described himself as "of mixed descent, in the proportion of seven eighths Caucasian and one eighth African blood; that the mixture of colored blood was not discernible in him"; and that he "paid for a first class passage."[34] Although Plessy tried to claim that he had been mischaracterized as black and that this form of labeling constituted a theft of his property in whiteness, the Court brushed aside this as being an insignificant issue. Rather, they viewed his concern as a fairly simple contract problem about determining the proper cost of the fare.[35] Plessy also raised the concern "that the enforced separation of the two races stamps the colored race with a badge of inferiority." The court also rejected this argument claiming, "if this be so, it is not by reason of anything found in the act, but solely because the colored race chooses to put that construction upon it."[36] In the language of the dilution doctrine and contemporary discourse on race, Plessy raised concerns that Jim Crow's racial categories would tarnish the self-described identities of people, especially African Americans. The Supreme Court responded by noting that the meaning of words and identities are so plastic that the railroad and the state, in their role of public servants, ought to possess the power to label and identify individuals. The court also made it very clear that the federal government should not interfere if there is an interpretative conflict between the state and particular individuals about the meaning of an identity or brand name.

Viewed through the lens of contemporary trademark discourse, we might translate Plessy's argument into a dilution claim against Jim Crow segregation for tarnishing or blurring his brand/racial identity. Plessy, in effect, claimed that the State of Louisiana and the railroad violated his trademarked identity in its deployment of a binary racial code that stole the good reputation of his name. Moreover, by enforcing a separation of the races, segregation "stamps the colored race with a badge of inferiority," thus "dispersing" the very qualities of identity for which many African Americans had fought and struggled. Contrary to both the "false designation of goods" and "consumer confusion" doctrines, Plessy here is not claiming that the scheme for racial identification performs a deception on the American public. Rather, his argument is focused on the economic harms to African Americans caused by the stigma associated with Jim Crow segregation. The U.S. Supreme Court refuses to acknowledge any dilution of African American racial identity and blames Plessy and African Americans for reading any possible insult in segregation. The *Plessy* decision culminates by expressing its confidence that state schemas for determining racial identity can effectively establish a person's racial origin, much like a trademark designates a product's source. As for any possible remaining inequalities, the Court opined, "If one race be inferior to the other socially, the Constitution of the United States cannot put them upon the same plane."[37] If *Plessy* were a trademark decision, it would have thoroughly rejected Schechter's proposal to create a cause of action for dilution.

The civil rights movement, however, has changed how courts viewed race. Dilution by blurring or tarnishment—as a basis for a civil rights violation, once thoroughly rebuffed—has perhaps become accepted. In *Gratz v. Bollinger*, the petitioners claimed that that the University of Michigan's undergraduate admission's formula violated the Equal Protection clause of the Constitution by discriminating against whites.[38] The University of Michigan desired to create a diverse student body. As part of that effort, the university developed a formula that assigned points for a range of criteria. Applicants were admitted based on the number of points they earned. The formula "automatically distributes 20 points to every single applicant from an 'underrepresented minority' group, as defined by the University. The only consideration that accompanies this distribution of points is a factual review of an application to determine whether an individual is a member of one of these minority groups."[39] Chief Justice Rehnquist, writing for the majority, concluded that this "admissions policy is not narrowly tailored to achieve respondents' asserted compelling interest in diversity; the admissions policy violates the Equal Protection Clause of the Fourteenth Amendment."[40] The Court's primary objection to the plan was that this overbroad use of racial identity failed to consider the nuanced set of factors, including social class and artistic merit, in making admission decisions. They reasoned that racial categories were too broad and might blur the "real" disadvantages a particular applicant has experienced or tarnish, by insufficiently rewarding, the artistic or creative merit of a white applicant.

Obviously, the *Gratz* reasoning is a far cry from that of *Plessy* because it endorses diversity and integration. There is, however, a grand irony in that *Plessy* rejected an African American's request for a more complex racial classification system in order to integrate public accommodations and *Gratz* criticized the University of Michigan for failing to have a more nuanced approach to racial identity to protect the interests of white students. The Supreme Court neither viewed the petitioners as asserting a property claim nor considered the cases through the perspective offered by trademark. Reading these decisions through the dilution doctrine, however, suggests that Schechter's initial concerns about how society creates property interests in customs, and ultimately identity, remain a key legal problem. Both Homer Plessy and Jennifer Gratz viewed the decisions of the East Louisiana Railway and the University of Michigan as assaults on their racial identity. Perhaps, more significantly, both argued that their adversaries misunderstood their identities and thus damaged their property interests in their respective racial identities.

Neither Court seemed overly concerned with how these identities came into being, assuming that racial identities were "merely" facts to be discovered instead of, what Schechter might label, "the creation and retention of custom."[41] As not merely facts, racial labels represent a cultivated identity that blends or balances social expectation and individual agency. Certainly, vigorous debates within the African American community over the appropriate terms for describing racial identity have continued for the past one hundred years, with individuals making considerable "investments" in particular names or identities. Similarly, George Lipsitz has argued that identity politics has caused whites during the post–civil rights era to reconsider their investment in racial identity when buying a home, choosing a school, and numerous other "ordinary" and seemingly "colorblind" decisions.[42] For Lipsitz, contemporary dialogues about race, exemplified by the decision in *Gratz*, perpetuate that investment. *Gratz* and *Plessy* suggest that, despite considerable changes in civil rights law, racial identity continues to be viewed like a trademark, subject to potential dilution resulting from competing marks. Schechter's solution to the dilution problem, however, does not seek an end to the investment in racialized identities. Rather, it affords them greater protection and requires that the government further the regulation of those identities. In his groundbreaking article, the creation and retention of custom is the "primary purpose of the trademark today, and that the preservation of the uniqueness or individuality of the trademark is of paramount importance to its owner."[43] Ironically, both Plessy and Gratz sought to protect their individuality by contesting the social meaning of their ascribed, or adopted, racial identity.[44]

An analysis of Aunt Jemima and other minstrel-era figures reveals the continuing racialized nature of trademark doctrines, including dilution. In 1968, Quaker Oats changed Aunt Jemima's appearance by abandoning the bandana and slimming her figure.[45] Just two decades later, Aunt Jemima had another makeover, transforming her into more of a middle-class woman, with pearl earrings and new hairstyle. Although the company will not reveal exactly why it changed her image, Quaker Oats is clearly struggling to protect its longstanding investment in the distinctive Aunt Jemima brand while conforming to contemporary racial norms.[46] In this instance, it is not a competing brand but shifting cultural norms that threaten to tarnish the "good" will associated with Aunt Jemima and blur the "real" corporate identity behind the product. Arguably, the true "color" of Quaker Oats is green, not white, in that they would likely claim that the only reason they have deployed a racialized trademark is because it has proven a success in the marketplace. From their perspective, Quaker Oats, like any corporation, must negotiate the stereotypes and biases of their consumers in marketing their products. What this description necessarily omits is that the trademark's owners have invested heavily in a racist figure, reaped considerable financial rewards from that figure, and still actively seek to promote this raced trademark to a new generation of consumers. Ironically, it is Schechter's theory of dilution that helps expose the active agency of corporations, such as Quaker Oats, in promoting racial stereotypes through their trademarks. Rather than allow such racial trademarks and stereotypes to get dispersed as cultures change, the concept of dilution and its revised assumptions about the purpose of trademarks provides the doctrinal cover for the continued existence of Aunt Jemima, Uncle Ben, the Morton's Salt girl and other racial trademarks.[47]

Although Quaker Oats updated Aunt Jemima's image, she has remained a powerful symbol for artists. During the early 1990s, a number of African American artists found considerable notoriety for their ironic appropriations of racist imagery. Unlike artists inspired by the Black Arts Movement, Kara Walker and Michael Ray Charles appear to resurrect the stereotypical images without clearly contesting them, offering an ironic or postmodern commentary on them. Echoing a fairly common reaction in the African American community, Michael Harris, an artist and art historian, views their work as merely reviving visual stereotypes.[48] Although they do not typically rely on trademark doctrines to describe their work, Walker and Charles might defend their imagery in language that might sound a lot like Schechter's description of trademark. Walker and Charles would readily acknowledge that Aunt Jemima, the Pillsbury Doughboy, and other trademarked imagery have become key elements of custom and culture. Contesting the more oppositional strategies of the Black Arts Movement, they would not seek to challenge them directly (as Joe Overstreet did when he portrayed Aunt Jemima spraying bullets with a machine gun). Rather, they seek to tarnish them and blur their meaning precisely by remaining faithful to the original imagery. Of course, this produces considerable ambiguity, which probably concerns both members of the Black Arts Movement and the trademark owners alike. For African American activists, their mimicry is insufficiently critical because many viewers might miss or ignore the challenge to racism and wrongly believe the image reinforces the trademark's original racism. For the trademark owners, any racial controversy—including that created by Betye Saar's open letter condemning Charles and Walker—about their products probably hurts their public image significantly.

Percival Everett, a contemporary African American writer who eschews all racial stereotypes, has also suggested that tarnishment or blurring might be the key to transcending race. In his short story, "The Appropriation of Cultures," Everett imagines what might happen if southern African Americans began to adopt the Confederate battle flag rather than contesting it.[49] The story begins when an African American male purchases a used pickup truck but refuses to peel off an old Confederate flag sticker on the rear window. His acceptance of and interest in this image baffles both blacks and whites. The story ends with African Americans successfully blurring or tarnishing this racial symbol's meaning:

Soon, there were several, then many cars and trucks in Columbia, South Carolina, sporting Confederate flags and being driven by black people. Black businessmen and ministers wore rebel flag buttons on their lapels and clips on their ties. The marching band of South Carolina State College, a predominantly black land grant institution in Orangeburg, paraded with the flag during homecoming. Black people all over the state flew the Confederate flag. The symbol began to disappear from the fronts of big rigs and the back windows of jacked-up four-wheelers. And after the emblem was used to dress the yards and mark picnic sites of black family reunions the following Fourth of July, the piece of cloth was quietly dismissed from its station with the U.S. and state flags atop the State Capitol. There was no ceremony, no notice. One day, it was not there.[50]

For Everett, Walker, Charles, and other contemporary African American artists, dilution through tarnishment or blurring offers a potential solution to the continued existence of racialized trademark imagery. While it is unlikely that corporate America would acquiesce to any efforts to appropriate imagery as the story suggests, Everett nonetheless reveals how the very concept of dilution requires its proponents to view the cultural life of trademarks from the owner's perspective rather than that of black consumers who have been offended by a mark. Moreover, Everett's story suggests that some trademarks or symbols need to be tarnished. On this score, the universalist tenor of trademark law tends to ignore how the very customs or identities protected by the dilution doctrine may be too deeply implicated in racism to deserve the protection of federal law.

Conclusion

As commodification proceeds, it is more important than ever for corporations to create and nurture a brand identity that connects potential consumers to their products or services. Race, as a key social marker, offers a potentially effective way to brand products to ethnic specific communities. This is a seemingly benign way in which companies might create linkages between their products with potential consumers. For example, FUBU, an acronym meaning "For Us, By Us," proved pretty popular during the 1990s among African American consumers, as the brand name infused the products with a political meaning. As this commodification and trademark-ification of African American culture has proceeded with all deliberate speed, artists from a wide range of genres and styles have interrogated both the investment in and effect of creating brands heavily associated with African American bodies. Artists, including Kehinde Wiley and Hank Willis Thomas; writers, such as Paul Beatty and Colson Whitehead; and filmmakers, most notably Spike Lee, have all explored the relationships among race, racialization, and trademarked imagery.

This chapter considers how governing trademark doctrines, such as "false designation of origin," "consumer confusion," and "dilution," rely extensively on identity constructs in order to create property interests for trademark owners. Both the need for and the logic behind trademark bears a striking resemblance or similarity to the ongoing maintenance of racial terms. Rather than being disparate or unrelated, racial classification and trademarks appear to constitute mutually enforcing cultural structures and create order amid an increasing complex and globalized exchange of ideas, goods, and services. Trademarks and racial classifications help create stability and market value at a moment when economic forces seem ready to destroy existing distribution of resources and power. Unlike other forms of intellectual property law, a trademark, theoretically, can last forever. While copyrights and patents provide a monopoly for a mere term of years, trademark seeks to create a perpetual regime of (racial) signification.

Trademark law focuses almost exclusively on ensuring that a particular symbol, image, or meaning—including those contained within racialized marks—will retain a potent meaning and protect investments in consumer good will. It is the discursive framework that transforms arbitrary or fanciful fictions into private grants of monopoly power over language and imagery. For their corporate owners, a distinctive identity—no matter how parochial or culturally specific—is necessary to survive and thrive. Arguably, it is precisely the most specific identities, those that explicitly and implicitly refer to ongoing power dynamics, that are the most successful in the marketplace. Trademark ensures that these identities cannot be tarnished or blurred and protects against fraudulent or deceptive uses of names or identities, even if the crafted corporate identities rely on questionable assumptions or stereotypes. Trademark's reliance on and relation to racial discourse exemplifies the continuing challenge for civil rights activists. Can antiracist activists eradicate the scandalous and disparaging nature of racism solely by relying on a universal appeal to human rights but without acknowledging the considerable and ongoing psychic and economic investments in racial identity? Does trademark law have a greater role to play in regulating the use of racist and racialized imagery, especially as corporate America has mobilized racial discourse in its pursuit of profit and wealth?

Notes

1. For an introduction on the relation between trademark law and racism, see Greene, "Trademark Law and Racial Subordination: From Marketing of Stereotypes to Norms of Authorship."
2. See Capers, "Reading Back, Reading Black, and *Buck v. Bell*"; and Capers, "Reading Back."
3. Because this chapter is designed to show the similarities between racial and trademark discourses, I will be defining race through trademark. Trademarks are defined as indicators of origin, markers of identity, and carefully crated social fictions. Like racial classifications, the various components of these definitions do not completely contradict one another. The intellectual underpinning of trademarks, as a result, can lack coherence even as they are essential features of contemporary capitalism.
4. For examples of law scholars using trademark terms to argue why we ought to forgo racial labels, see Johnson, "Destabilizing Racial Classifications"; and Troutt, "A Portrait of the Trademark as a Black Man."
5. See Fears, "Patent Offense," sec. C.
6. See also *Pro-Football v. Harjo* (2003), which stripped the trademark rights to the Redskin logo from the football franchise. While the team still uses the image and mascot, it is no longer protected by trademark law. This is another exception that "proves" how few resources exist within trademark law to challenge racist marks and logos.

7. My argument here is a revisionist one in that trademark has not historically been seen as either a raced area of law or one that specifically addresses racism. Rather, many commentators see it as way of regulating "unfair competition" and of maintaining an efficient and fair marketplace. See McKenna, "The Normative Foundations of Trademark Law," 1860. Given that race established the conditions of the marketplace and the relative "bargaining" positions of its participants during the nineteenth century, trademark, whether intended as a racialized area of law or not, was inevitably caught up in the economic and commercial racism of the day. It is my argument that this racism continues to infect the metaphors deployed by legal discourse to theorize the proper bounds of trademark law.

8. Because I have explored the hidden racial meaning of fair use within my book, I have focused my chapter on rereading other aspects of trademark doctrine. See Schur. *Parodies of Ownership.*

9. Kern-Foxworth, *Aunt Jemima, Uncle Ben, and Rastus,* 64–65.

10. Sotiropoulos, *Staging Race,* 22.

11. Manring observes that Aunt Jemima is a particularly "plastic" figure who has been molded to fit a wide range of political, cultural, and scholarly uses. Manring, *Slave in a Box,* 19.

12. See also Harris, *Colored Pictures,* 90.

13. Kern-Foxworth, *Aunt Jemima, Uncle Ben, and Rastus,* 65.

14. Ibid., 66.

15. Silbey, "The Mythical Beginnings of Intellectual Property Law," 360.

16. Johnson, "Destabilizing Racial Classifications," 911.

17. For an excellent overview of how courts have regulated the meaning of racial identity, see Gross, *What Blood Won't Tell: A History of Race on Trial in America.*

18. Ibid., 931–39.

19. See Winant, "The Theoretical Status of the Concept of Race," 181–90; and Haney Lopez, *White by Law.*

20. See Hannaford, *Race;* and Gossett, *Race.*

21. Piper, *Out of Order,* 2:177.

22. To place this conversation in a broader context, there have been robust intragroup debates about the meaning of "Indian," "Indigenous," "First Nations," and "Native American" and potential categories developed around "Hispanic," "Latino/a," "Chicano/a," and "Mexican American."

23. See Harris, *Colored Pictures,* 86–124.

24. Ibid., 107.

25. Ibid., 116.

26. Manring, *Slave in a Box,* 49.

27. See Schechter, "The Rational Basis for Trademark Protection," 813–33; and 15 U.S.C. sec 1125(c). For an overview of how dilution became part of the statutory trademark scheme, see Bone, "Schechter's Ideas in Historical Context and Dilution's Rocky Road."

28. Schechter, "The Rational Basis for Trademark Protection," 822 (italics in original).

29. Ibid., 825.

30. For the cited case, see *Aunt Jemima Mills v. Rigney & Co.* (1917). Despite its discussion of the competing uses of the Aunt Jemima brand name, the court did not consider the irony of creating a trademark out of a potentially racist stereotype.

31. The United States Code states the following:

   (B) For purposes of paragraph (1), 'dilution by blurring' is association arising from the similarity between a mark or trade name and a famous mark that impairs the distinctiveness of the famous mark. In determining whether a mark or trade name is likely to cause dilution by blurring, the court may consider all relevant factors, including the following:

(i)   The degree of similarity between the mark or trade name and the famous mark.

(ii)   The degree of inherent or acquired distinctiveness of the famous mark.

(iii)   The extent to which the owner of the famous mark is engaging in substantially exclusive use of the mark.

(iv)   The degree of recognition of the famous mark.

(v)   Whether the user of the mark or trade name intended to create an association with the famous mark.

(vi)   Any actual association between the mark or trade name and the famous mark.

(C) For purposes of paragraph (1), 'dilution by tarnishment' is association arising from the similarity between a mark or trade name and a famous mark that harms the reputation of the famous mark.

See 15 U.S.C. sec. 1125.

32. Schechter, "The Rational Basis for Trademark Protection," 825.

33. *Plessy v. Ferguson* (1896).

34. Ibid., 541.

35. Ibid., 549.

36. Ibid., 551.

37. Ibid., 552.

38. *Gratz v. Bollinger* (2003).

39. Ibid., 271–72.

40. Ibid., 275.

41. Schechter, "The Rational Basis for Trademark Protection," 822.

42. See generally Lipsitz, *The Possessive Investment in Whiteness*.

43. Schechter, "The Rational Basis for Trademark Protection," 822.

44. While Plessy questioned whether the government's racial classification was accurate, Gratz readily agreed with being identified as white. Where their claims overlap is that both questioned the social meaning of these identity labels.

45. Kern-Foxworth, *Aunt Jemima, Uncle Ben, and Rastus*, 90–91; and Manring, *Slave in a Box*, 169.

46. Ibid., 176–77.

47. Although this sentence might suggest that it is the mere existence of the dilution doctrine that allows or causes continued corporate investment in raced trademarks, I am too much of a legal realist not to acknowledge that such investment would likely continue even if Schechter had not proposed the dilution doctrine or if it had been roundly rejected by the courts and Congress.

48. Harris, *Colored Pictures*, 219.

49. Everett, "The Appropriation of Cultures," 24–30.

50. Ibid., 30.

Bibliography

15 U.S.C. sec 1125

Aunt Jemima Mills v. Rigney & Co., 247 Fed. 407 (C. C. A. 2d, 1917).

Bone, Robert. "Schechter's Ideas in Historical Context and Dilution's Rocky Road." *Santa Clara Computer and High Technology Law Journal* 24 (2008): 469–506.

Capers, I. Bennett. "Reading Back, Reading Black." *Hofstra Law Review* 35 (Fall 2006): 9–22.

———. "Reading Back, Reading Black, and *Buck v. Bell*." In *Justice Unveiled: African American Culture and Legal Discourse*, edited by Lovalerie King and Richard Schur. New York: Palgrave-Macmillan, 2009.

Everett, Percival. "The Appropriation of Cultures." *Callaloo* 19, no. 1 (Winter 1996): 24–30.

Fears, Darryl. "Patent Offense: Wayan's Hip Hop Line." *Washington Post*, March 15, 2006, sec. C.

Gossett, Thomas. *Race: The History of an Idea in America*. New York: Oxford University Press, 1997.

Gratz v. Bollinger, 539 U.S. 244 (2003).

Greene, K. J. "Trademark Law and Racial Subordination: From Marketing of Stereotypes to Norms of Authorship." *Syracuse Law Review* 58 (2008): 431–45.

Gross, Ariela. *What Blood Won't Tell: A History of Race on Trial in America*. Cambridge, MA: Harvard University Press, 2008.

Haney Lopez, Ian. *White by Law: The Legal Construction of Race*. New York: New York University Press, 1996.

Hannaford, Ivan. *Race: The History of an Idea in the West*. Baltimore, MD: Johns Hopkins University Press, 1997.

Harris, Michael. *Colored Pictures: Race and Visual Representations*. Durham: University of North Carolina Press, 2003.

Johnson, Alex. "Destabilizing Racial Classifications Based on Insights Gleaned from Trademark Law." *California Law Review* 84 (1996): 887–952.

Kern-Foxworth, Marilyn. *Aunt Jemima, Uncle Ben, and Rastus: Blacks in Advertising, Yesterday, Today, and Tomorrow*. Westwood, CT: Greenwood, 1994.

Lipsitz, George. *The Possessive Investment in Whiteness: How White People Benefit from Identity Politics*. Philadelphia: Temple University Press, 1998.

Manring, M. M. *Slave in a Box: The Strange Career of Aunt Jemima*. Charlottesville: University of Virginia Press, 1998.

McKenna, Mark. "The Normative Foundations of Trademark Law." *Notre Dame Law Review* 82 (2007): 1840–1916.

Piper, Adrian. *Out of Order, Out of Sight: Selected Writings in Art Criticism, 1967–1992*. Vol. 1 and 2. Cambridge, MA: MIT Press, 1996.

Plessy v. Ferguson, 163 U.S. 537 (1896).

Pro-Football v. Harjo, 284 F. Supp 2d 96 (D.D.C. 2003).

Schechter, Frank. "The Rational Basis for Trademark Protection." *Harvard Law Review* 40, no. 6 (1927): 813–33.

Schur, Richard. *Parodies of Ownership: Hip Hop Aesthetics and Intellectual Property Law*. Ann Arbor: University of Michigan Press, 2009.

Silbey, Jessica. "The Mythical Beginnings of Intellectual Property Law." *George Mason Law Review* 15 (Winter 2008): 319–79.

Sotiropoulos, Karen. *Staging Race: Black Performers in Turn of the Century America*. Cambridge, MA: Harvard University Press, 2006.

Troutt, David D. "A Portrait of the Trademark as a Black Man: Intellectual Property, Commodification, and Redescription." *U.C. Davis Law Review* 38 (April 2005): 1141–1207.

U.S. Patent and Trademark Office. Serial No. 76639548. Alexandria, VA: 2006.

———. Serial No. 77309301. Alexandria, VA: 2008.

Winant, Howard. "The Theoretical Status of the Concept of Race." In *Theories of Race and Racism: A Reader*, edited by Les Back and John Solomos, 181–90. New York: Routledge, 2000.

12

The Telecommunications Act of 1996 and the Overdevelopment of Gangsta Rap

Akilah N. Folami

This chapter explores how the Telecommunications Act of 1996 has contributed to the proliferation of gangsta rap on broadcast radio and has affected hip-hop by dissuading the voices of more "positive" rappers who might contest gangsta rap. Specifically, the Telecommunications Act of 1996 has contributed to stifling the discourse within the hip-hop community by increasing and solidifying corporate media conglomeration and control of the nation's radio airwaves. Such media conglomeration has been instrumental in creating the dominant gangsta image that has become, for the most part, the de facto voice of contemporary hip-hop culture. Moreover, the Telecommunications Act has contributed to limiting access to the radio airwaves to those that would challenge gangsta rap and the resulting gangsta image, which is steeped in racial and sexist stereotypes.

In addition to revealing the law's role in shaping hip-hop, I also aim to challenge a number of prevailing misconceptions about gangsta rap. Many critics have written off gangsta rap because of its misogyny, violence, and unbridled exhortation to material consumption. I will argue, however, that social commentary and resistance to gangsta rap can still be found within its very commercialized image. Despite the violence and misogyny—largely directed at other black men and black women—contained within gangsta rap, gangsta rap must continue to be considered within the context of hip-hop's origins, the commodification of black cultural expression, and the broader marketplace for American music.

While rappers have relied on the very racialized and stereotyped images that have contributed significantly to their own exclusion and repression in the first place, they have reaped, as a generation, more financial reward than any other generation of black activists, musicians, and artists. Hip-hop as a path to enrichment is not something to be overlooked. Not unlike the originators of rap, today's gangsta rappers are primarily black male youth with limited societal visibility and resources. They have not only achieved more than a modicum of commercial success but also have managed to maneuver in a mass-mediated and corporate-dominated space. Despite the constraining effects of the Telecommunications Act to radio access and visibility, these artists have still managed to provide some seeds of resistance to the mainstream gangsta image. Although such seeds of resistance may not receive as much attention as that of the gangsta image itself, it is evidence of resistance nevertheless. Evidence of such struggle provides a crucial lens through which to view civic and participatory democracy and dialogue that this country highly values. The Telecommunications Act must not inhibit such subversive voices (of either gangsta rappers or others) or the development of a robust dialogue in hip-hop and within the broader black community over the gangsta image and the sexist, racialized, and hypercommodified images that underlie it.

Black American Subversion: Hip-hop to Gangsta Rap in Context

Historically, black Americans have suffered from exclusionary practices, repression, and violence in public spaces throughout the United States, but they have navigated these spaces nevertheless—through music, spectacle, and other subversive forms of cultural expression—in order to challenge dominant public policies of repression. Urban black (and Latino) youth continued these historical practices of subversion with the emergence of hip-hop, developed at a time when they were essentially abandoned and rendered invisible by both white and black politicians alike as well as the dominant public discussion. Soon after the passage of several civil rights acts, federal aid to already-declining industrial cities was significantly decreased. The white dominant class and the bourgeoning black middle class—unconcerned, unable, or unsure of how to fix the poverty problem in America's urban areas—turned their attention to other issues, leaving the poorest urban residents in America's large cities vulnerable.[1]

Although black civil-rights leaders attained positions of political power, with some becoming mayors of cities, many were crippled by the lack of adequate funding of social programs to aid the condition of the urban poor. [2] For example, the South Bronx, which most cite as the birthplace of hip-hop, would suffer a significant downward spiral during this time, soon becoming "the poorest, toughest neighborhood in the whole of New York City."[3] As industry jobs vanished in the South Bronx, youth violence and gangs proliferated, [4] and the city was soon declared a wasteland.[5] Unsure of what to do with the urban poor, politicians and others adopted a policy of abandonment. While the black bourgeoisie sought relief from racial discrimination by turning to educational and economic achievement, its urban counterpart survived with substandard housing, schooling, and social services and, often, turned to drugs and a slow spiritual and physical death.[6] By the late 1970s (when hip-hop emerged), following the death of Malcolm X and the decimation of the Black Panther party—both of which gave public voice to America's urban areas—the political fervor for economic and political equality died down, at least as it related to the black lower and urban class.[7]

Isolated and ignored, in what was categorized by most as a dying city, these youth decided to celebrate and to live—despite the deteriorating conditions around them—through hip-hop, which consisted of deejaying, b-boying (or break dancing), graffiti-writing, and rapping. While these acts were not originally overtly political acts, they were subversive and signaled to the ruling authority that, while the South Bronx had been abandoned and declared a wasteland, the youth were living and claiming their space in the midst of political neglect and the resulting chaos.[8] The message was clear: I am here and here to stay. A culture (of survival) was being born in the South Bronx in the midst of the massive socioeconomic transformation and decline.

By 1979, hip-hop had its first commercial successes with the Sugarhill Gang's "Rapper's Delight,"[9] and then in 1982, it had another with, "The Message," by Grandmaster Flash and the Furious Five, which served as rap's first social commentary on life in the South Bronx ghetto.[10] With the advent of rap groups Run-DMC and Public Enemy, rap would become more defiant, critical, and filled with racial pride. Rap would be declared "black America's CNN,"[11] broadcasting what would otherwise not be "seen" or heard by the dominant discourse.[12] With artists rapping about police brutality, the criminal justice system, inadequate social programs, unemployment, sex, rape, AIDS, poverty and declining living conditions, listeners learned about life in urban spaces, primarily those in the East.[13]

At the same time and diametrically opposed to the confrontational, yet socially conscious, rappers coming from the East, came the fiery sound of the West coast. With the five-member group called Niggaz With Attitude (N.W.A.), America got a glimpse of life on the West coast. This image was filled with police brutality, gang violence, crack, and pure, seething rage.[14] In contestation with "positive" rap, the West coast sound was defined as "gangsta" rap, and was filled with references to black women as "hos" and "bitches" and black men as "gangstas" and "niggas." Their sound and image rejected the Afrocentric and nationalist sounds of East coast rap, while rap music as a whole offered a stark alternative to black, bourgeoisie norms and ethics.

Many formerly taboo and private topics were now open for critique in rap music generally and in gangsta rap in particular. Rappers have challenged the notion that "nigger" is an inherently pejorative word and sought to rework its socially constructed meaning.[15] In addition, rappers have forged a new identity that extends beyond the civil-rights and black-nationalist public spheres. These rappers have adopted the traditional black bourgeois notions of attaining the American dream via capitalism and consumerism, but they have rejected its elitism and belief that one had to assimilate to achieve them. They wanted a piece of the American pie while staying grounded to the urban culture and speaking in their own voice and on their own terms.[16] Gangsta rap has survived calls for censorship on obscenity and indecency grounds and boycotts from black and white middle class communities. Moreover, it would be deemed protected speech under the First Amendment, which gave voice to a historically marginalized segment of the population or that shed light on conditions in America's blighted urban areas.

The gangsta sound remains prominent in contemporary rap lyrics even as some critics argue that life in the 'hood is not as bad as it was in the early 1990s. These critics contend that today's "gangsta" lyrics are merely a corporate creation designed to sell an image that has become popular with a certain buying demographic. They assert that the current state of rap, with the pervasive gangsta rap lyrics, reflects the corporate interest in continuing to sell the commodified gangsta identity and signals the death of hip-hop's subversive nature and its disconnection from the legacy of subversion in the black community. Upon closer inspection, however, subversion can still be found therein despite its commercialization. Such subversion must be acknowledged and room must be made for it in today's consumer oriented society that is replete with media images and symbols.

The Commodified "Gangsta" and Resistance to the Gangsta Image by the "Gangsta" Himself

Despite rap's commercial successes, it must be considered within the context of its hip-hop origins. As commodified as it may be, it still gives voice to what would otherwise be an invisible and marginalized group of black and Latino male youth. Many cultural and critical theorists rightly contend that any concept of resistance must account for the market in such a consumer-driven, mass-mediated society.[17] Scholars have shown that consumers are far from just a "passive receiving structure for media messages, whether they be political, cultural, or advertising," but that everyday social relations and identities can be formulated in complex processes of media mediations.[18]

One such complex process is the subcultural practice of recoding, which, according to Aoki, "differs from the countercultural ('60s student movements) in that it recodes cultural signs rather than poses a revolutionary program of its own."[19] Instead, it must be grasped as a textual activity. Plural and symbolic, its resistance is performed through a spectacular transformation of the whole range of commodities, values, and common-sense attitudes that are contested, confirmed, and customized. In this bricolage, the false nature of these stereotypes is exposed as the arbitrary character of the social lines they define. In that way then, "culture [becomes] political in its role as a forum for the deployment of images that can be reworked for a variety of political ends."[20]

Gangsta rap serves as an example of Aoki's "subcultural practices." Today, rap has become one of the largest music genres in America. Several studies have established that the largest consumer base for sales of rap music is white male suburban youth.[21] Some scholars explain rap's enormous popularity among white consumers by arguing that white audiences partake in a voyeuristic gaze upon black street culture. Their consumption of rap music, then, is premised on preconceived stereotypic notions of the "other," the life of the "other," and what an encounter with the "other" would look like. White voyeuristic rap fans, like other voyeurs, seek exotic locations and lifestyles and what they perceive to be authentic experience, and they seek to experience them in comfort and security.[22] They only find "staged authenticity"[23] though, as corporate media conglomerates entrench these images of black life with negative racial stereotypes.[24]

Samuels contends that the "more rappers were packaged as violent black criminals, the bigger their white audiences became."[25] Ice-T, the self proclaimed OG (original gangsta) rapper from the West coast, who paved the way for N.W.A., Ice Cube, and others, would define this process, as the "niggafication" of white suburban youth and the commodification of the "nigga" persona.[26] Experience no longer mattered and gave way to the commodified effect of creating a consumer culture of rap and, by extension, the perceived underworld. Through gangsta rap lyrics, rap voyeurs are taken to the ghetto, which for listeners is "a place of adventure, unbridled violence, erotic fantasy, and/or an imaginary alternative to suburban boredom."[27] As a result, "where the assimilation of black street culture by whites once required a degree of human contact between the races, the street is now available at the flick of a cable channel [or radio station]—to black and white middle class[es] alike."[28] Some identify these lyrics as a corporately produced "neo-gangsta," which exemplifies the concept of staged authenticity.[29] These neogangsta lyrics are steeped with racial stereotypes about urban black men and women and are in turn marketed and delivered to the consuming white audience.[30] Introduced voyeuristically is the ghetto-centric nigga persona who more often than not is a gangsta, making his money as a pimp, hustler, drug dealer or killer, and the black woman "skeezer," "bitch," or "ho" who is intent on bringing the gangsta down via sexual manipulation or even violence.[31]

To some cultural theorists, this corporate and market-driven imagery offers an appealing fantasy to consumers and a mass voyeuristic consumption of that fantasy (regardless of the harsh reality it might depict) due to the dominant class's control over the media.[32] Pursuant to its access to and ownership of the media, the dominant class exercises a type of cultural control of the media, thereby ensuring that its dominant narratives, beliefs, and interests get represented.[33] Such control does turn, however, to some extent on the consent of the subjugated and on their acceptance and internalization of the dominant norms.[34] Rappers participate, then, in their own subjugation to corporate, cultural-hegemonic ideologies by supplying such rap lyrics and acting out the "staged authenticity," which is at the center of the voyeuristic gaze.[35] On the surface, rap and hip-hop culture's reliance on such exaggerated and negative stereotypes does nothing to subvert these images of black men and women.

Viewing the commodification of gangsta rap through the lens of Aoki's analysis of subcultural practices suggests, however, that "such stereotypical images [can be used to the group's] political advantage, or at the very least, to contest, neutralize and complicate such representations."[36] In essence, such images can be reworked "to 'talk back' to power on multiple . . . levels and in so doing, to transform further iterations of the dominant discourse in an on-going, open-ended series of micro-negotiations."[37] This process of micronegotiations, or talking back (to negative stereotypes, in particular) through the prevailing racist discourses, is by no means simple or easy, especially for subordinate groups. It often requires subordinate groups to, in some degree, consent to their own subjugation and adopt, consciously or unconsciously, a mental state that has been called by some a "contradictory consciousness."[38] Because of political and economic structures, a subordinate group possesses limited opportunities to challenge such stereotypes without appropriating certain aspects of the dominant discourse.[39]

Other scholars have argued that, given these and other examples, contemporary discussions about democratic dialogue must address the role of the market because the market often shapes meanings and effects the forms of communications in civil society, including those of the "autonomous" publics and counterpublics. These scholars posit then that there must be recognition "of a more creative politics of citizenship and a greater creativity in conceiving the political, such that it can at least potentially encompass a greater range of social sites of production and reproduction that will include spheres of commerce and consumption."[40] In the context of gangsta rap, the contribution of gangsta rappers to their own staged authenticity certainly takes on, in some ways, the meanings provided by the dominant class. Such meanings, however, are "not static or guaranteed."[41] Rather, they are "susceptible to varying degrees of negotiation and resistance . . . for recoding and reinterpretation along reconfigured artistic, cultural, economic, political and legal agendas."[42] The recoding of negative racial representations, no matter how small, can even serve as a type of contestation and subversive expression.[43] Hence, with regard to the current affairs of rap and despite the limited space available *within* the market driven mass media for contestation and "acute tension" between the corporate media conglomerates and rappers,[44] rappers such as Jay-Z, Ice Cube, Jadakiss, and even 50 Cent have actualized the potential of which Aoki speaks. They have employed subcultural practices that serve to subvert and dismember the dominant racialized gaze upon the "gangsta" image that predominates rap lyrics played on the radio.

In the movie *Get Rich or Die Tryin'* (2005), viewers get yet another mass-mediated depiction of the life of a gangsta turned rapper, portrayed by real-life rapper 50 Cent. The film includes scenes of hustling in the underground economy (50 Cent selling drugs on the streets of New York), of street violence (his mother's body set ablaze after gasoline was poured on her, his friend betraying him and shooting him in the mouth, and the extraction of another hustler's teeth with pliers), and of him bling-blinging (50 Cent riding down the street in his new, shiny, white BMW that is the envy of the other hustlers on the block). However, the dominant gaze on the gangsta identity is shifted, even if only temporarily. During the movie, the scene shifts from the predominant gangsta melodrama to a humanistic picture of a depressed 50 Cent sitting with his mouth wired shut and drool falling down his face. He sits on the couch in his bathrobe, in a house that has no heat on a cold, snowy, winter day, and laments his inability to provide for his son and his son's mother, while she, wrapped in a coat to keep warm, looks on him with pity.

Rather than taking on the skeezer/ho image or the self-sacrificing black woman/ mother who gives her life for the sake of the black man or race[45] and is incidentally rarely given a scripted part in the staged authenticity of gangsta drama, his son's mother confronts him about his pitiful state and tells him she resents that their son has to see him in this condition. Enraged, 50 Cent tells her to leave and she in turn storms off. In the end, the two embrace, thereby showing the intimacy between a black man and black woman. This example offers another instance of how the film challenges dominant narratives and stereotypes. The dominant gaze is further subverted when the voyeur glimpses a scene with 50 Cent, a black man conspicuously present in the life of his son, not only playing with him on the beach but also apparently enjoying it.

One can even find evidence of contestation of the commodified gangsta image on the rap recordings themselves. Some rappers include on their albums one or two tracks which have the effect of subverting the dominant gaze of listeners. For example, Jadakiss's song, "Why?" takes on a clearly political and serious tone (although it is wedged in between his other songs on the album glorifying the gangsta life), suggesting that former President George W. Bush had information about the September 11th terrorist attack on the New York World Trade Center before it happened.[46] Jay-Z, a multiplatinum rapper who has reaped significant financial reward from his many gangsta antics, asserts in a tract titled "Moments of Clarity" in his album *The Black Album* that while he could rap positive rap like Talib Kweli or Common, he would not make any money if he continued to do so. Given his (and most rappers') former situation as a young black man in urban America who had to hustle to make ends meet, he asserts that he had to make the best of his situation as a rapper by in turn rapping about record industry–endorsed topics that made more money. His lyrics suggest that he is aware that he is being exploited by the music industry and that he has chosen to take on and adapt the corporate-created and consumer-driven public image. The song suggests that he does this to reap some financial rewards and to ultimately help the inner city and its inhabitants.

Moving beyond his recordings, there is other evidence of his efforts to challenge the gangsta image. For example, Jay-Z has invested in small businesses in and throughout Brooklyn[47] and has started the Shawn Carter (Jay-Z's real name) Scholarship Fund for inner city youth interested in attending college.[48] Similarly, rapper 50 Cent has begun negotiations with Steve Jobs, of Apple Computer, to develop a low cost G-Unit computer for sale to inner city schools.[49] Moreover, rappers have pushed the envelope of their former (and, arguably, continued) embrace of the gangsta image to subvert the dominant understandings and representation of that image by taking on different identities and roles that are also within the larger public's view. Rapper Ice Cube produced a reality-based documentary for the HBO network to foster a discourse on race relations and racial stereotypes. Two families, one black and one white, exchanged lives by painting their faces in a way that reflected the racial identity of the other family and then discussed their experiences after living in the other family's skin.[50]

Contemporary rap, even in the face of commodification, cannot be completely equated with co-optation because the rappers' fights were always "fought out within the circuits of the market."[51] Rap and rappers' subcultural practices are examples of Michel Foucault's theory that "there are no relations of power without resistance; the latter are all the more real and effective because they are formed right at the point where relations of power are exercised."[52] So while it may seem that corporate-controlled and market-driven mass media have exclusive control over cultural expression in general and over rap in particular, creating a "frozen homogeneity, the actual effect of such mass media over-saturation may actually be to bring about the proliferation of multiple and hybrid sites of negotiation, contestation, [and] resistance."[53] By subverting the dominant gaze within the commodified realm of the mass media, rappers have managed to maneuver in a tight space and have, as a result, contested such homogeneity.

Given the commodified nature of rap and the spaces that commodification opens for subcultural practices, it is an open question as to how critics should respond to lyrics that degrade black women and promote violence. However, censoring such lyrics and images is still not the answer.[54] According to Aoki, it arguably may not even be possible to get rid of such harmful messages via censorship and regulation—especially given the technological developments of the internet, rap's outlaw nature, and the consumer demand for the forbidden. Rather, more contestation and dialogue (by either the rappers themselves or others) is necessary, especially as these negative lyrics and images become hypercommodified, mass mediated, and contextualized as the cultural by-product of the larger dominant discourse. In fact, the proliferation of gangsta rap has led to some (much needed) discourse within the black community—discourse that explores the underlying issues (often rooted in the larger dominant norms on race, gender, and class) related to the production and distribution of gangsta rap and the image of black women that it presents. For example, *Essence* magazine, as part of its year-long "Take Back the Music" campaign, held a town-hall meeting at Spelman College in 2005 to discuss the misogyny and violence in rap lyrics and videos. The meeting and campaign grew out of a controversial and highly publicized incident in which students rejected rapper Nelly's offer to perform at a Spelman event that was originally held to raise awareness for bone marrow treatment within the black community.[55] The students took particular issue with his misogynistic rap lyrics and one of his videos, "Tip Drill."[56] The "Take Back the Music" campaign included petition drives and a telethon to phone complaints to television networks and radio stations that ran offensive materials.[57]

Another example of how rap has fostered greater dialogue within the black community involved a controversy between Oprah Winfrey and rapper Ludacris. Winfrey, in a momentous event, made a surprise visit to former rapper Ed Lover's live radio show on Power 105.1 located in New York to diffuse the growing controversy between her and the hip-hop community, as she was being labeled "anti-rap."[58] During her visit, Oprah asked Ed Lover why he referred to women as "bitches," to which Ed Lover initially replied that the term was not always used or meant in a demeaning way and that men are also often referred to by that term. After Oprah explained that while rappers may see their use of such word (and the word nigga), primarily for entertainment purpose, some listeners do not get that it is not meant to be taken literally. As a result of the exchange, Ed Lover vowed to Oprah and to his listening audience that he would never use the word "bitch" again on air.[59] As these examples demonstrate, despite the limited access to the nation's airwaves to those who would contest gangsta rap and its imagery, some dialogue has occurred. While gangsta rappers' (and others') acts of contestation may seem small and, hence, perhaps ineffective in challenging the harmful effects of the mass production of rap's lyrics and imagery, such small acts of resistance, still have their place: they subvert the dominant meaning of the gangsta image. Expanding these spaces for contestation and discourse is necessary and possible as long as the law does not stifle this dialogue. The Telecommunications Act, however, has had the effect of limiting access to the nation's radio airwaves, especially for those who would challenge the gangsta image.

The Telecommunications Act's Role in Encouraging Gangsta Rap and Stifling Commentary and Subversion in Hip-hop

The role of the Telecommunications Act of 1996 in the contest over the meaning of, and the challenge to, the gangsta image has been anything but neutral. On its face, the passage and enforcement of the Telecommunications Act is and was steeped with the rhetoric of property rights and market competition. It relaxed local ownership restrictions by allowing one entity to control both a television and radio station in the fifty largest markets. Hence, "one licensee may own two TV and up to six radio stations or one TV and seven radio stations in the same market if that market has at least 20 separately owned broadcast (radio/TV), newspaper and cable voices."[60] Congress believed that in passing the Telecommunications Act a "deregulated marketplace would best serve public interest."[61] The purpose of promoting competition (and hence diversity), on the radio in particular, was not met and was arguably doomed at the outset; immediately following the passage of the Telecommunications Act, large corporate conglomerates went on a buying spree of numerous small, local radio stations.[62] In fact, only one year after passage of the Telecommunications Act, "concentration in ownership mostly resulted from mergers involving the fifty largest owners . . . [namely with] . . . Chancellor Media, Clear Channel, Infinity, and Capstar, owning a majority of stations that play some of the nations' most popular formats." Hence, the "sheer size of the biggest parent companies allow those owners to control radio's content."[63]

Ultimately, as a direct result of such deregulation, "there was a steady narrowing of voices available through the major channels, a decrease in the diversity of sounds, opinions, and ideas, news and art available to mass audiences."[64] And to cultural critic, Mark Anthony Neal, "In the aftermath of the Telecommunications Reform Act, the massive consolidation in radio has left fewer people making the decisions about what music will be played. The ten largest radio conglomerates in the U.S. control more than two thirds of the national radio audience, with Clear Channel and Viacom (which, incidentally owns both MTV and BET) controlling more than 40 percent of that. That these conditions impact what music you hear on the radio and the ability of local groups to get on their local radio station goes without saying."[65] While the Telecommunications Act required the Federal Communications Commission (FCC) to conduct biennial reviews of the ownership regulations and their enforcement to ensure that the public benefitted from this competition, many scholars have found that the FCC's "tendency toward deregulation reduces competition and diversity to the detriment of the public."[66] Moreover, the FCC has, in actuality, historically rejected this kind of deregulation because it has traditionally seen its role as protecting the public by promoting a diversity of interests and voices heard over the nation's radio airwaves, achieved primarily by limiting a concentration in media ownership.

For example, federal regulation of the radio airwaves began with the enactment of the Radio Act of 1927. It created a five-member panel, called the Federal Radio Commission (FRC) that was authorized to assign frequencies, regulate broadcasting hours, and regulate the general use of airwaves.[67] Congress mandated that "the standard for licensing radio stations was that the broadcaster's goals served the 'public interest, convenience, or necessity' of the people in the local broadcast market."[68] The Communications Act of 1934 replaced the FRC with the FCC and required a government agency to grant licenses to stations for a definite and temporary duration and in accordance with the public interest. The underlying belief was that the airwaves were a "scarce public resource"[69] entrusted to broadcasters, who, "in exchange for the free and exclusive right to exploit their licensed channels of the public radio frequency spectrum, were granted a trusteeship of such and were required to air programming that served the 'public convenience, interest or necessity.'"[70] The FCC "interpreted the public trustee doctrine as requiring that broadcast stations 'be operated as if owned by the public . . . as if people of a community should own a station and turn it over to the best man in sight with this injunction: Manage this station in our interest.'"[71] Broadcasters were then "to familiarize themselves with the needs and interests of their communities."[72] Moreover, the "trusteeship model did not equate the public interest with economic competition . . . the FCC [granted] licenses only if there was a 'reasonable expectation that [such] competition may have some beneficial effect.'" Therefore, "economic efficiency could only factor into the equation as a supporting force, not a guiding principal."[73]

In addition, as part of the trusteeship doctrine to protect the public's best interest, the FCC "believed that regulating local and national radio ownership was the best method of promoting competition, diversity, and localism in the radio market." Thus, the FCC began placing limits on radio ownership "to encourage diversity of ownership in order to foster the expression of varied viewpoints and programming and to safeguard against undue concentration of economic power."[74] The FCC established that "local residence compliments the statutory scheme and [its] allocation policy of licensing a large number of stations throughout the country, in order to provide for attention to local interests, and local ownership also generally accord[ed] with the goal of diversifying control of broadcast stations."[75] To the FCC, media consolidation limited the marketplace of ideas: it therefore sought a diversification of ownership, including local ownership, which it presumed would result in an attention to local interests.[76]

However, during the early 1980s, there was an ideological shift about what would best serve and meet the needs of the public over the radio airwaves. "Up until the early 1980s, FCC policy basically aimed to restrict ownership concentration both locally and nationally . . . the presumption was relentlessly against concentration and toward maximizing the number of independent media voices."[77] The trusteeship model was soon replaced with the marketplace model, which was premised on the belief that market forces could best meet the public interest requirement. Marketplace ideology rejected the scarce-airwaves theory under the trusteeship model because this new model viewed all resources, including the airwaves, as scarce. Like other resources, it was assumed that the unregulated operation of the laws of supply and demand would make the most efficient use of airwaves.[78] As a result, most proponents of the marketplace model believed that deregulation, including deregulation of radio media ownership, was the most effective means of ascertaining and meeting public demand. Such demand hinged primarily on consumption habits and the act of treating radio content as a consumer good.[79]

Many scholars have determined that the theory behind the marketplace model is based on erroneous assumptions and ideological flaws and that its adoption has lead to less diversity and competition, not more. Some have also pointed out that the market model assumes that "commercial market forces are pre-political and ideologically neutral; that the marketplace of ideas [as expressed through the media] is open and readily accessible to advocates of diverse or controversial issues of public interest."[80] In a capitalist society, the public debate is "dominated by those who are economically powerful. The market . . . does not assure that all relevant views will be heard, but only those that are advocated by the rich."[81]

Significantly, the marketplace model, which is largely premised on meeting the demands of consumers and on consumption theory, also fails to take into account the ways in which corporate-controlled mass media influences consumer demand. "Consumption is managed by the mass media's capacity to convey imagery and information across vast areas to ensure a production of demand. Goods are increasingly sold by harnessing symbols."[82] While these symbols and "signs seem to come . . . from nowhere—across radio waves, fibers, unseen cables, and invisible microwaves and lasers . . . these images do, however, come from somewhere, and increasingly they come from fewer and fewer places,"[83] due to corporate conglomeration and control of many media outlets.

Although the power of media is widening, the power base has consolidated since the adoption of the marketplace model. In 1981, "twenty corporations controlled most of the business of the country's 11,000 magazines, but only five years later that number had shrunk to six corporations . . . [and] . . . despite 25,000 media outlets in the United States, twenty-nine corporations control most" of them.[84] As a result, "mass media . . . and the corporate restructuring and commodification of urban space have made street corners and their speakers invisible, inaudible and obsolete as forums and agents of political dialogue . . . More of the texts we encounter in everyday life are the products of corporate marketing departments than the creations of individual authors."[85] The model marketplace theory then "relies upon opinions, beliefs, tastes and habits already formed and presumed legitimate . . . It is inherently reactive and conservative."[86]

It was primarily this shift from the trusteeship model to the marketplace model that influenced the drafting of the Telecommunications Act of 1996. Despite the questionable assumptions of the marketplace-model theory, the concern for diversity of ownership and attention to local interest, central to the trusteeship model, were replaced. Economic efficiency and competition, secondary considerations under the trusteeship model, became, and remain, the decisive standard under the new marketplace-model theory. The new model essentially assumed that as long as there is economic competition the rest (i.e., diversity in opinions and ownership) will fall into place. As a result, less focus was placed on diversity in ownership or on viewpoint diversity. In fact, "now as long as competition exists, wide dispersal of ownership is seen as unimportant in itself and possibly inefficient."[87]

Some scholars have argued then that with the passage of the Telecommunications Act of 1996, which "relaxed local ownership restrictions, it is difficult to explain why a single entity owning upwards of eight stations in the largest markets would reach out to the smallest groups without the government telling them to do so."[88] Although "local stations were supposed to be assets to local communities [and] the ownership rules were designed to keep ownership as diverse as possible . . . all that changed in the 1990s [with the passage of the Telecommunications Act]."[89] Prior to the change in the 1990s, "radio companies used to be severely constrained from owning . . . too many stations . . . Local stations were supposed to be assets to local communities."[90] However, as a result of being pressured by a GOP-controlled Congress, President Clinton "signed into law the Telecommunications Act, which essentially did away with ownership restrictions on radio. Now, just a handful of companies control radio in the 100 largest American markets."[91] When media giants like Clear Channel, Cumulus, Citadel, and Viacom were able to purchase multiple radio stations after the Act removed ownership caps on stations, the media companies bought up all of the local stations and consolidated the stations in order to maximize profits.[92]

Media conglomerates abandoned any commitment to the idea of the local interest. They "laid off hundreds, decimated community programming and all but standardized play lists across the country . . . Waves of layoffs left all the Clear Channel radio stations [in particular] with no community affairs department."[93] With individual staff responsibilities doubling, Clear Channel lost its knowledge base about the music industry.[94] Prior to the passage of the Act, when music decisions were made at the local level, "the station's Music Director ha[d] much greater discretion in introducing new artists to his station's play list . . . If the Music Director [wa]s in touch with his market's live music scene and [knew] which bands [we] re creating a local stir and selling out shows, he [could] incorporate them into his station's play list confident that such a move w[ould] attract rather than send away listeners."[95]After the Act's passage, Clear Channel maximized profits by downsizing local stations and hiring regional programmers to oversee radio programming and operations.[96] This change led to further movement away from the local interests of the listening community. Neal elaborates, "In the past, for example, if a particular region had 20 radio stations, 20 different program directors (PDs) would likely decide what would be played. In the current environment playlist decisions are now in the hands of a smaller group of PDs, who often cede some of their decision making power to regional and national program directors."[97]

The changes affected local disc jockeys (DJs) as well. To increase profits, some stations even replaced these live local DJs with prerecorded announcers.[98] The disc jockeys had been the key to the radio industry because they "understood local tastes and intricacies."[99] In the late 1990s, such stations adopted software that allowed DJs to "voice track" or "cyberjock" their shows.[100] Voice tracking or cyberjocking allowed DJs to "spend a few minutes taping their short sound bites."[101] A computer would then patch together their show by combining the prerecorded vocal drops, with listener calls, "songs, promos, sound effects and commercials stored on a hard disk," which would then be sent out to other conglomerate owned stations in other local and regional areas.[102] Randy Dotinga writes, "Thanks to advances in audio technology and pioneering work by Clear Channel Communications, an epidemic of digital fakery has struck the radio industry. Only the listeners are live and local at many radio stations, and Clear Channel is gambling that nobody will notice. Or care."[103] Cyberjocking and voice tracking allowed Clear Channel (and other media conglomerates) to "cut down the total number of disc jockeys and to spotlight its top talents."[104] Hundreds, if not thousands, of DJ positions were eliminated by "simply having one company jock send out his or her show to dozens of sister stations. Thanks to clever digital editing, the shows still often sound[ed] local."[105]

Additionally, Van Alstyne has explored the ways in which radio consolidation allowed the few media conglomerates to generate significant advertising revenue, to enhance a station's ability to control what the public hears on the radio or at a live concert, and to facilitate "more coercive behavior by parent companies [of radio stations] against labels and artists."[106] Specifically, station owners could "exert pressure on labels, and in turn the label's artists, through listener appreciation concerts, . . . [which] . . . showcase the station rather than a particular band . . . [and] . . . usually

involve several play-list acts, each performing only a few songs."[107] Parent companies of the stations also knew that they could "leverage their access to the airwaves
to coerce labels and artists in the form of pay-for-play and play-for-play because
they [the labels and artists] have no comparable means to promote their material."[108]
Lastly, decreased music diversity resulted from consolidation because, "if one owner
holds most of the stations in a particular music format for a region, it is safer for
the station to remain consistent in its play list. By only adding a few new songs, the
station does not risk offending an advertiser."[109] As a result, "with few open slots for
new music on tightly controlled playlists, it is increasingly difficult for new artists to
enter the airwaves . . . Upstart [artists] have difficulty attracting audiences outside
their hometown because they do not get airplay."[110]

As is evident by the narrow range of rap music currently dominating the airwaves, it is obvious that hip-hop and its artists have felt the effects of media conglomeration. According to Jeff Chang, the power shift away from hip-hop culture's
true believers and captains of the industry in favor of the media monopolies
occurred during the mid-1990s.[111] An example of the negative effects of such a shift
in hip-hop culture on the once thriving, pre–corporate (pre-Telecommunications
Act) adulterated, hip-hop scene occurred at KMEL-FM, one of the first leading hip-
hop stations in the country, in the San Francisco Bay Area. During the late 1980s and
early 1990s, as a result of the explosion of hip-hop on shows like *Yo! MTV Raps*, Top
40 radio stations discovered that rap had multicultural appeal. KMEL was one of the
first Top 40 crossover pop stations in the nation to abandon its pop format, embrace
rap, and target young multiracial audiences with hip-hop, dance, and freestyle rapping. KMEL was considered, by the local community, the "people's station" because
it engaged the social issues of the San Francisco community.

KMEL's programs, *Street Knowledge* and *Street Soldiers*, with radio personalities
Davey D and Cameron Paul, were particularly well known for discussing the social
issues that confronted the Bay Area urban community. In addition, it was "located
in an area blessed with one of the strongest campus and community radio networks in the country, as well as one of the most fiercely competitive commercial
markets in the country."[112] The station brought "local California artists and college
and community DJs to the station, and while most were never offered full-time
DJ positions, they brought their listeners with them, and pushed KMEL to play
cutting-edge music and offer community-oriented programming."[113] Although
much smaller than the major cities of Chicago, Miami, and Los Angeles, the Bay
Area station became the number-two music station in the fourth-largest radio
market in the country, commanding the largest radio audience among the highly
coveted eighteen to thirty-four demographic.[114] It thrived with its music and talk
shows, community oriented programming, and its pioneering "Summer Jam"
concerts, which were soon imitated throughout the country.[115] Moreover, in the
Bay Area, competing stations often "deferred to the mix show DJs to break new
artists, resulting in national hits for local artists . . . the result was a massive growth
in the local urban radio audience."[116]

Also during the 1980s, a thriving network of independent labels ("indies") and
regional distributors that were closely connected to the local market and talent
reaped considerable success with rap artists, more so than the further removed
and distant major record companies.[117] In fact, "in 1996, for the first time, and

probably the last, indie record label market share had peaked and taken together actually outsold all the major labels."[118] With the passage of the Telecommunications Act, San Francisco's two most popular radio stations, KMEL and KYLD, were both bought out by the same company and their resources consolidated.[119] These stations, prior to 1996, had competed for listeners by developing and showcasing new talent and by being up to date on local community affairs. When the then-parent company to KMEL, Evergreen Media, purchased KYLD in 1996, it essentially ended the ratings war between KMEL and KYLD. After a series of subsequent corporate mergers, which culminated in a whopping $24 billion deal in 1999, both stations passed from AMFM Inc. into the hands of Clear Channel. This series of changes resulted ultimately in a format change of KMEL to prevent canniblization of sister-station KYLD.

With the national trend being towards fewer songs, KMEL and KYLD's playlists now "looked so similar that, on any given weeknight, more than half of each stations . . . countdowns might be the exact same songs."[120] With conglomeration, "specialty shows were quietly eliminated . . . local personalities got fired . . . community affairs programming was severely reduced . . . [and] . . . with narrowing playlists, local, new and independent [hip-hop] artists—the kind of folks unable to compete with six-figure major label marketing budgets—inevitably got squeezed out."[121] As the tide turned, "even mixshow DJs—once hired to be the tastemakers and to break a record—increasingly found their mixes subjected to executive approval."[122]

For independent labels, the picture was equally grim. After the passage of the Act, they simply were unable to compete with the expensive advertising costs for radio airplay of their talent. Wendy Day of Rap Coalition's Intelligence Program writes, "Radio is a very important component in rap record sales for a major label or distributor. It can mean the difference between being an underground artist hoping to sell units, or an international superstar able to transcend into film, television, and lucrative commercial endorsements and touring opportunities."[123] The Future of Music Coalition (FOM), a nonprofit think tank based in Washington, DC, researched the effect of radio station ownership on musicians and the public. It concluded that "major record labels have large promotional budgets. Because the promotional money is there, radio companies have an incentive to make access to the airwaves more scarce, and thus more expensive."[124] Furthermore, according to Mark Anthony Neal, "among the major-label conglomerates, the competition for the airwaves is fierce, as airplay directly affects sales."[125]

As a result of the steep prices to market their artists on the radio, the sales of independent labels decreased, and they either closed down or were bought out.[126] With the shrinking space available on the radio and with independent labels closing shop, it became increasingly difficult for new artists to be heard.[127] Hence, "with intense consolidation in both the recording industry and commercial radio, artists are squeezed out of a hearing at both the labels and radio stations. While independent labels remain an option for artists, the reality is that the four major label conglomerates—the four industry gatekeepers—are responsible for more than 80 percent of what makes it on commercial radio play lists." [128]

As the previous section of this chapter has established, the corporations that dominate the media perpetuated the gangsta image through their marketing and their emphasis on gangsta rap to the exclusion of other alternative voices that would contest such lyrics or images. The passage of the Telecommunications Act of 1996 has led to the development of huge corporate-media conglomerations in radio, who in turn control the radio airwaves and its content. The Act has made it virtually impossible for alternative voices in rap (either by the gangsta rappers themselves through their alternative "positive" tracks or by other "positive" rap artists) to be heard on the radio, since corporate conglomerates are less concerned with diversity in ideas than in meeting market-created consumer demand for such lyrics.

The songs of rappers considered to be more positive, such as Common, Talib Kweli, Mos Def, The Roots, and Dead Prez, are not played on the radio nearly as much as those of the gangsta rappers. Moreover, rappers who do not fit the gangsta mold, such as Jin, an Asian American rapper who came to the hip-hop forefront after winning several rap contests on BET, are simply squeezed out for lack of promotion.[129] Similarly, former producer-turned-rapper Kanye West struggled to break into the rap industry. Given his overall appearance and style, which contrasted the gangsta image or the stereotypical hip-hop apparel, he was not as easily marketable the way other rappers who fit the mold were.

For producer Buckwild, a Bronx native and producer of numerous successful, commercial and indie songs and artists, the hip-hop game is creatively dying, particularly in New York, because of "[the] one-artist saturation thing: Whoever's hitting it at one time runs the whole game. There's no diversity. The classic time for hip-hop was '94 and '95 when you had ten different artists running the game. You had Wu-Tang, Nas, Mobb Deep, Biggie, Puffy, and a Tribe Called Quest. You had mad different flavors because no two artists were the same."[130] However, now, according to Buckwild, "you have everybody that sounds the same . . . We are definitely missing that artistry, producer and rapper-wise, and a lot of artists haven't been discovered yet . . . when these artists start to surface, we're going to have a renaissance wand, there's going to be a big change in the game."[131]

Some have sought to expose alternative voices in hip-hop and local talent by developing alternate radio stations using low band radio airwaves.[132] According to the Prometheus Radio Project, a nonprofit organization founded by a small group of radio activists in 1998, "a free, diverse, and democratic media is critical to the political and cultural health of our nation, yet we see unprecedented levels of consolidation, homogenization, and restriction in the media landscape." As a result, the organization has committed to working toward "a future characterized by easy access to media outlets and a broad, exciting selection of cultural and informative media resources."[133] Moreover, some rappers have turned to the Internet or satellite radio to distribute some of the music that they would like to have—but that often is not—played on the corporate controlled radio airwaves.[134]

Because the Telecommunications Act of 1996 has led to the corporate conglomeration of radio, it ultimately has led to the limiting of discursive space within the hip-hop community. Rappers and others have attempted to pry open that space by other means and by what some would characterize as "small" acts of resistance. These acts of resistance are important given the limited space in which there is to maneuver. Whether on their albums or in other media outlets, such as television, film, satellite radio or the internet, rappers and others have begun to expand, yet again, the notion of the public sphere and where and how subversive or counterhegemonic discourse may occur. More space, however, must be made for those that have not reaped the same visibility or financial reward as gangsta rappers, given the access provided to them on the radio airwaves. In order to achieve a greater democratization of the nation's radio airwaves, the Telecommunications Act should encourage, rather than limit, such dialogue. The Telecommunications Act has stifled this process of dialogic democracy and has served to further marginalize the alternative or subversive voices of women and rappers (including gangsta rappers) that would serve to challenge the views, beliefs, interests, or cultural meanings inscribed by the corporate media conglomerates.

Notes

1. Rose, *Black Noise*, 127.
2. Dawson, "A Black Counterpublic?" 216.
3. Dick Hebdige, "Rap and Hip-Hop," 223–24.
4. Neal, "Postindustrial Soul," 369.
5. Chang, *Can't Stop, Won't Stop*, 15. Jeff Chang describes how, at one point, South Bronx housing units spanning the equivalent of four square blocks were burned down in a week, leaving thousands of vacant lots and abandoned building throughout the borough. Despite the growing blazes, seven fire companies in the Bronx were closed down along with thousands of firefighters and fire marshals laid off.
6. Neal, *Postindustrial*, 369. Crack served as a temporal escape from the realities of abject poverty, but, unlike other temporal releases of the past like religion or music, it helped to destroy community relationships, to increase black-on-black crime, and, because it was relatively easy and inexpensive to make, to lead many youth to believe that the sale of it was a viable career option that would lead to upward mobility.
7. See *Black Commentator*, "There Needs to be a Movement."
8. Rose, *Black Noise*, 59.
9. Light, "About a Salary or Reality?" 139.
10. While black youth have always suffered high rates of unemployment since the 1960s, more so than any other race, "in 1986, in the middle of the Republican years, black teenage unemployment was officially as high as 43.7 percent . . . [and] six years later . . . remained virtually unchanged." Lusane, "Rap, Race, and Politics," 352.
11. Samuels, "The Rap on Rap," 149.
12. Rose, *Black Noise*, 18.
13. Dyson, "The Culture of Hip-hop," 66. Through other groups like Boogie Down Productions, blacks and other listeners learned about black history, heroes and sheroes, intellectuals, scientists, political theorists—all information that was not readily available (or even acknowledged) by the dominant discussion on blacks and race relations.
14. Light, "About a Salary or Reality?" 142.
15. Although the term "nigga . . . through hip-hop became the embodiment of black defiance," it did "not mean black as much as it mean[t] being a product of the postindustrial ghetto." Baldwin, "Black Empires, White Desires," 166. Indeed, rappers (and hip-hop culture) have arguably reworked the word so that it is now used by, and can refer to, nonblacks (ibid.). However, while rappers and hip-hop culture may have refashioned the meaning and use of the N-word intraracially, it is questionable to what

extent the word has been reshaped when used interracially, particularly when used by a white person when speaking to a black person.

16. Ibid.,168.
17. Coombe and Cohen, "The Law and Late Modern Culture," 1047.
18. Stychin, "Identities, Sexualities, and the Postmodern Subject," 99. See also Collins and Skover, "Commerce and Communication," 699.
19. Aoki, "'Foreign-ness' and Asian American Identities," 59. Stychin uses the term "decoding," to describe to the same practice of cultural resistance. Stychin, "Identities, Sexualities, and the Postmodern Subject," 95–96.
20. Stychin, "Identities, Sexualities, and the Postmodern Subject," 101.
21. Samuels, "The Rap on Rap,"47.
22. Ibid., 153.
23. Ibid. Samuels analogizes white consumption of rap with the staged authenticity of tourists. Staged authenticity is defined as the paradox of the tourists who are searching for the real in their touristic travels, and yet they only see the front of the stage, without recognizing or reacting to the back stage processes of production and commodification.
24. Ibid., 147–48
25. Ibid., 147. See also Davey D, "Hip-hop's Ultimate Battle."
26. Judy, "On the Question of Nigga Authenticity," 113.
27. Kelley, "Looking for the 'Real' Nigga," 130.
28. Samuels, "The Rap on Rap," 153.
29. Coates, "Keepin' It Real."
30. Ibid., 152. See also Baldwin, "Black Empires, White Desires,"166.
31. For his discussion of how Ice Cube's song "You Can't Fade Me" and how this form of voyeurism works, see Light, "About a Salary or Reality?"145.
32. See Collins and Skover, "Commerce and Consumption," 710.
33. Lears, "The Concept of Cultural Hegemony," 571.
34. Ibid., 591.
35. Ibid., 567, 573.
36. Aoki, "Foreign-ness," 1.
37. Ibid., 59.
38. Harris, "Race and Essentialism in Feminist Legal Theory," 614. See also Lears, "The Concept of Cultural Hegemony," 570.
39. Aoki, "Foreign-ness," 58; and Madow, "Private Ownership of Public Image," 140. See also Coombe, "Room for Manoeuver," 69.
40. Coombe, "Reflections," 1052.
41. Coombe, "Tactics of Appropriation," 414.
42. Aoki, "Foreign-ness," 4.
43. Merry asserts that although small acts of subversion are characteristically individual acts of resistance that do not, for the most part, rise to the level of protest movements like that of the 1960s civil rights era, such acts are still very important when power is understood in the context of social relationships and discourses. While these individual acts of resistance may not be inspired by a vision of a more just society and do not generate social movements, they are nonetheless "political activity which does not conform to conventional understandings of politics, yet is engaged in struggles over power." Merry, "Resistance and the Cultural Power of Law," 15–16.
44. Rose, *Black Noise*, 124. Rose argues that resistance often occurs as a hidden transcript in rap, operating within the dominant text, destabilizing dominant meanings, and legitimizing a counterhegemonic one (ibid., 103).

45. See Collins, *Black Feminist Thought*, 174.

46. Jadakiss, "Why."

47. See CNN/Money, "Will Smith, Jay-Z Back Beauty Line."

48. See Shawn Carter Scholarship Foundation Web site, "Company Goals."

49. Strong, "50 Cent Negotiating with Apple for Branded Line of Home Computers."

50. "Families Swap Race on 'Black, White.'"

51. Baldwin, "Black Empires, White Desires," 161. Many cultural critics have argued that rap has always served a dual purpose of giving voice to marginalized black youth (primarily male) *and* of promising financial success. Rap never called for the overthrow of the capitalist system but rather for the opening up of space so that rappers, whether they be considered positive rappers or not, could be made visible and, moreover, could partake in America's riches.

52. Foucault, *Power/Knowledge*, 142.

53. Aoki, "Foreign-ness," 59–60.

54. Even if gangsta rap was silenced, the issues that underpin the lyrics would still be present and problematic, as rappers are products of the misogynistic, violent, and consumerist culture that created them. See Weisstuch, "Sexism in Rap."

55. Willens, "Black College Women Take Aim at Rappers."

56. In the video, several scantily dressed black women simulate sex with each other, and, in one scene, a credit card is swiped through a woman's buttocks. Bailey, "Dilemma."

57. Willens, "Black College Women Take Aim At Rappers."

58. See Richburg and Burke, "Oprah Responds To Hip-hop Criticism."

59. Before the close of the interview, Ed Lover suggested to Oprah that she should have a show exploring these and other issues related to the hip-hop community, to which Oprah declined. Almost a year after her radio appearance, Oprah would explore some of these questions on her show.

60. Wiley, "Communications Law Overview," 405–6.

61. Bednarski, "From Diversity to Duplication," 275.

62. Ibid., 287.

63. Van Alstyne, "Clear Control," 640.

64. Chang, *Can't Stop, Won't Stop*, 445.

65. Neal, "Rhythm and Bullshit?"

66. Van Alstyne, "Clear Control," 628.

67. Prindle, "No Competition," 287.

68. Ibid., 288.

69. Bednarski, "From Diversity to Duplication," 277.

70. Varona, "Out of Thin Air," 151.

71. Ibid., 151.

72. Bednarski, "From Diversity to Duplication," 278.

73. Ibid., 279.

74. Prindle, "No Competition," 272.

75. Ibid., 316.

76. See Mezey and Niles, "Screening the Law," 179–81; Varona, "Out of Thin Air," 61; and Prindle, "No Competition," 287–88.

77. Baker, "Media Concentration," 869.

78. See Rainey and Rehg, "Marketplace of Ideas," 1937.

79. See Drale, "Communication Media in a Democratic Society," 224.

80. See Rainey and Rehg, "Marketplace of Ideas," 1937.

81. Fiss, "Free Speech and Social Structure," 412–13.

82. Coombe, "Objects of Property and Subjects of Politics," 1862–63.

83. Ibid., 1863.
84. Ibid.
85. Coombe, "Reflections," 1038.
86. Drale, "Communication Media in a Democratic Society," 233.
87. Baker, "Media Concentration," 870.
88. Prindle, "No Competition," 299.
89. Boehlert, "Radio's Big Bully."
90. Ibid.
91. Ibid.
92. Chang, *Can't Stop, Won't Stop*, 441–42.
93. Ibid.
94. Ibid., 442.
95. Ortner, "Serving a Different Master," 158.
96. See Boehlert, "Radio's Big Bully."
97. Neal, "Rhythm and Bullshit?"
98. Ibid.
99. Van Alstyne, "Clear Control," 660. See also Folami, "Deliberative Democracy."
100. Dotinga, "'Good Mornin' (Your Town Here)."
101. Ibid.
102. See Chang, *Can't Stop, Won't Stop*, 442; and Dotinga, "'Good Mornin' (Your Town Here)."
103. Dotinga, "'Good Mornin' (Your Town Here)."
104. Ibid.
105. Boehlert, "Radio's Big Bully."
106. Van Alstyne, "Clear Control," 653.
107. Ibid., 645.
108. Ibid., 653.
109. Ibid., 660.
110. Ibid., 659.
111. Chang, *Can't Stop, Won't Stop*, 440.
112. Ibid.
113. Ibid., 441.
114. See Wikipedia.org, "KMEL."
115. See Davey D, "KMEL Announces Summer Jam Line Up."
116. Chang, *Can't Stop, Won't Stop*, 441.
117. Dyson, "The Culture of Hip-hop," 66.
118. Chang, *Can't Stop, Won't Stop*, 444.
119. See Wikipedia.org, "KMEL."
120. Chang, *Can't Stop, Won't Stop*, 442.
121. Ibid., 443.
122. Ibid.
123. Day, "Radio."
124. Futureofmusic.org, "Radio Deregulation."
125. Neal, "Rhythm and Bullshit?"
126. Prindle, "No Competition," 309.
127. Neal, "Rhythm and Bullshit?"
128. Ibid.
129. Strong, "Jin Says Rap Career Is Over, Records."
130. Thomas, "Buckwild: Still Diggin." For a discussion of how female rappers and female R&B groups fit into this diverse conversation within hip-hop, see Pough, *Check It While I Wreck It*, 20.

131. Ibid.
132. Jam, "Pirate Fuckin' Radio."
133. Prometheus Radio, "About Us."
134. See Tardio, "E-40 Gets Down With MySpace.com" and Gregory, "Ludacris Lands Show On XM Satellite Radio."

Bibliography

Aoki, Keith. "'Foreign-ness' & Asian American Identities: Yellowface, World War II, Propaganda, and Bifurcated Racial Stereotypes." *Asian Pacific American Law Journal* 4, no. 1 (1996): 1–60.

Bailey, Moya. "Dilemma." Wiretap, May 24, 2004. http://www.alternet.org/wiretap/18760.

Baker, Edwin C. "Media Concentration: Giving Up On Democracy." *Florida Law Review* 54 (2002): 839–919.

Baldwin, Davarian L. "Black Empires, White Desires: The Spatial Politics of Identity in the Age of Hip-Hop." In *That's the Joint! The Hip-Hop Studies Reader*, edited by Murray Forman and Mark Anthony Neal, 159–76. New York: Routledge, 2004.

Bednarski, Anastasia. "From Diversity to Duplication Mega-Mergers and the Failure of the Marketplace Model under the Telecommunications Act of 1996." *Federal Communications Law Journal* 55 (2003): 237–93.

Black Commentator. "There Needs to be a Movement: Political Action in the Hip Hop Era." June 24, 2004. http://www.blackcommentator.com/96/96_cover_hip_hop.html.

Boehlert, Eric, "Radio's Big Bully," Salon.com Arts & Entertainment, April 30, 2001, http://archive.salon.com/ent/feature/2001/04/30/clear_channel/print.html.

Chang, Jeff. *Can't Stop Won't Stop.* New York: St. Martin's Press, 2005.

CNN/Money. "Will Smith, Jay-Z Back Beauty Line," CNN, March 18, 2005, http://money.cnn.com/2005/05/18/news/newsmakers/cosmetics.

Coates, Ta-Nehisi. "Keepin' It Real: Selling the Myth of Black Male Violence, Long Its Expiration Date." *Village Voice*, June 4, 2003. http://www.villagevoice.com/news/0323,coates,44584,1.html.

Collins, Patricia Hill. *Black Feminist Thought: Knowledge, Consciousness, and the Politics of Empowerment.* New York: Routledge, 2000.

Collins, Ronald K. L., and David M. Skover. "Commerce and Communication." *Texas Law Review* 71 (1993): 697–746.

Coombe, Rosemary J. "Objects of Property and Subjects of Politics: Intellectual Property Laws and Democratic Dialogue." *Texas Law Review* 69 (1991): 1853–80.

———. "Room for Manoeuver: Toward a Theory of Practice in Critical Legal Studies." *Law and Social Inquiry* 14 (1989): 69–121.

———. "Tactics of Appropriation and the Politics of Recognition in Late Modern Democracies." *Political Theory* 21 (1993): 411–33.

Coombe, Rosemary, and Jonathan Cohen. "The Law and Late Modern Culture: Reflections on Between Facts and Norms from the Perspective of Critical Culture Legal Studies." *Denver University Law Review* 76 (1999) 1029–55.

D, Davey. "Hip Hop's Ultimate Battle: Race and the Politics of Divide and Conquer." http://www.daveyd.com/articleultimatebattlerace.html.

———. "KMEL Announces SummerJam Line Up." *Daveyd.com*, November 18, 2008. http://www.daveyd.com/summerjam.html.

Dawson, Michael C. "A Black Counterpublic?: Economic Earthquakes, Racial Agenda(s), and Black Politics." *The Black Public Sphere: A Public Culture Book*, edited by The Black Public Sphere Collective, 199–228. Chicago: University of Chicago Press, 1995.

Day, Wendy. "Radio." Murder Dog, August 25, 2006. http://www.murderdog.com/august%5Frapcointelpro/radio.html.

Dotinga, Randy. "'Good Mornin' (Your Town Here)." *Wired News*, August 6, 2002. http://www.wirEd.com/news/business/1,54037-0.html.

Drale, Christina S. *Communication Media in a Democratic Society*, Communication Law and Policy 9 (2004): 213–34.

Dyson, Michael Eric. "The Culture of Hip Hop." In *That's the Joint! The Hip-Hop Studies Reader*, edited by Murray Forman and Mark Anthony Neal, 61–68. New York: Routledge, 2004.

Fiss, Owen. "Free Speech and Social Structure." *Iowa Law Review* 71 (1986): 1405–25.

Folami, Akilah. "Deliberative Democracy on Air: Reinvigorate Localism—Resuscitate Radio's Subversive Past." *The Federal Communications Law Journal* (forthcoming).

Forman, Murray, and Mark Anthony Neal, eds. *That's the Joint! The Hip-Hop Studies Reader*. New York: Routledge, 2004.

Foucault, Michael. *Power/Knowledge: Selected Interviews and Other Writings 1972–1977*, edited by Colin Gordon. New York: Pantheon Books, 1980.

Futureofmusic.org. "Radio Deregulation: Has It Served Citizens and Musicians?" November 18, 2008. http://www.futureofmusic.org/images/FMCradiostudy.pdf.

Gregory, Eben. "Ludacris Lands Show On XM Satellite Radio." Allhiphop.com, September 29, 2005. http://www.allhiphop.com/Hiphopnews/?ID=4887.

Harris, Angela P. "Race and Essentialism in Feminist Legal Theory." *Stanford Law Review* 42 (1990): 581–616.

Hebdige, Dick. "Rap and Hip-Hop: The New York Connection." In *That's the Joint! The Hip-Hop Studies Reader*, edited by Murray Forman and Mark Anthony Neal, 223–32. New York: Routledge, 2004.

Lears, T. J. "The Concept of Cultural Hegemony: Problems and Possibilities." *The American History Review* 90 (1985): 567–93

Jadakiss. "Why." *Kiss of Death*. June 22, 2004. CD.

Jam, Billy. "Pirate Fuckin' Radio." Hiphopslam.com, November 18, 2008. http://www.hiphopslam.com/scratch/pirate_fuckin_radio.html.

Jay-Z. "Moment of Clarity. *The Black Album*. November 13, 2003. CD.

Judy, R. A. T. "On the Question of Nigga Authenticity." In *That's the Joint! The Hip-Hop Studies Reader*, edited by Murray Forman and Mark Anthony Neal, 105–18. New York: Routledge, 2004.

Kelley, Robin D. G. "Looking for the "Real" Nigga: Social Scientists Construct the Ghetto." In *That's the Joint! The Hip-Hop Studies Reader*, edited by Murray Forman and Mark Anthony Neal, 119–38. New York: Routledge, 2004.

Light, Alan. "About a Salary or Reality?—Rap's Recurrent Conflict." In *That's the Joint! The Hip-Hop Studies Reader*, edited by Murray Forman and Mark Anthony Neal, 137–46. New York: Routledge, 2004.

Lusane, Clarence. "Rap, Race, and Politics." In *That's the Joint! The Hip-Hop Studies Reader*, edited by Murray Forman and Mark Anthony Neal, 351–62. New York: Routledge, 2004.

Madow, Michael. "Private Ownership of Public Image: Popular Culture and Publicity Rights." *California Law Review* 81 (1993): 125–238.

Merry, Sally E. "Resistance and the Cultural Power of Law." *Law and Society Review* 29 (1995): 11–26.

Mezey, Naomi, and Mark C. Niles. "Screening the Law: Ideology and Law in American Popular Culture." *Columbia Journal of Law and the Arts* 28 (2005): 91–185.

MSNBC. "Families Swap Race on 'Black, White.'" February 27, 2006. http://www.msnbc .msn.com/id/11394595/.

Neal, Mark Anthony. "Postindustrial Soul: Black Popular Music at the Crossroads." In *That's the Joint! The Hip-Hop Studies Reader*, edited by Murray Forman and Mark Anthony Neal, 363–88. New York: Routledge, 2004.

Neal, Mark Anthony. "Rhythm and Bullshit? The Slow Decline of R&B, Part Three: Media Conglomeration, Label Consolidation and Payola." Popmatters.com, June 30, 2005. http://popmatters.com/music/features/050630-randb3.shtml.

Ortner, Michael. "Serving a Different Master—The Decline of Diversity and the Public Interest in American Radio in the Wake of the Telecommunications Act of 1996." *Hamline Journal of Public Law and Policy* 22 (2000): 139–73.

Phillips, Chuck. "Wiesenthal Center Denounces Ice Cube's Album." *Los Angeles Times*, November 2, 1991, sec. CA.

Prindle, Gregory M. "No Competition: How Radio Consolidation Has Dismissed Diversity and Sacrificed Localism." *Fordham Intellectual Property, Media and Entertainment Law Journal* 14 (2003): 279–325.

Prometheus Radio. "About Us." November 18, 2008. http://www.prometheusradio.org/about_us.

Rainey, R. Randall, and William Rehg. "Marketplace of Ideas, the Public Interest, and Federal Regulation of the Electronic Media: Implications of Habermas' Theory of Democracy." *Southern California Law Review* 69 (1996): 1923–87.

Richburg, Chris, and Clarence Burke. "Oprah Responds to Hip Hop Criticism." Allhiphop. com, May 12, 2006. http://www.allhiphop.com/hiphopnews/?ID=5667.

Rose, Tricia. *Black Noise: Rap Music and Black Culture in Contemporary America*. Hanover, NH: Wesleyan University Press, 1994.

Samuels, David. "The Rap on Rap: The 'Black Music' That Isn't Either." In *That's the Joint! The Hip-Hop Studies Reader*, edited by Murray Forman and Mark Anthony Neal, 147–54. New York: Routledge, 2004.

Shawn Carter Scholarship Foundation Web site. "Company Goals." November 18, 2007. http://scartersf.org/#.

Sheridan, Jim, director. *Get Rich or Die Tryin'.* DVD. New York: Paramount, 2005.

Strong, Nolan. "50 Cent Negotiating with Apple for Branded Line of Home Computers." AllHipHop.com, June 19, 2006. http://www.allhiphop.com/Hiphopnews/?ID=5798.

Strong, Nolan. "Jin Says Rap Career Is Over, Records 'I Quit.'" Allhiphop.com, August 25, 2006. http://www.karazen.com/news/may05/jin_5_20.php.

Stychin, Carl. "Identities, Sexualities, and the Postmodern Subject: An Analysis of Artistic Funding by the National Endowment for the Arts." *Cardozo Arts and Entertainment Law Journal* 12 (1994): 79–132.

Tardio, Andres. "E-40 Gets Down With MySpace.com." *Hiphopdx.com*, February 21, 2006. http://www.hiphopdx.com/index/news/id.3905/p.all/print.true.

Thomas, Chris. "Buckwild: Still Diggin." Allhiphop.com, August 25, 2006. http://www.allhiphop .com/features/?ID=1434.

Van Alstyne, Adam J. "Clear Control: An Antitrust Analysis Of Clear Channel's Radio And Concert Empire." *Minnesota Law Review* 88 (2004): 627–67.

Varona, Anthony E. "Out of Thin Air: Using First Amendment Public Forum Analysis to Redeem American Broadcasting Regulation." *University of Michigan Journal of Law Reform* 39 (2006): 149–98.

Weisstuch, Liza. "Sexism in Rap Sparks Black Magazine to Say 'Enough!'" *Christian Science Monitor*, January 12, 2005, http://www.csmonitor.com/2005/0112/p11s01-almp.html.

Wikipedia.org. "KMEL." November 18, 2008. http://en.wikipedia.org/wiki/KMEL.

Wiley, Richard E. "Communications Law Overview: Recent Developments in Convergence, Competition and Consolidation." *PLI/Pat* 597 (2000): 395–853.

Willens, Kathy. "Black College Women Take Aim at Rappers." *USA Today*, April 23, 2004. http://www.usatoday.com/life/music/news/2004-04-23-spelman-protest-rappers_x.htm.k.

Afterword

Lovalerie King

> I know what the world has done to my brother and how narrowly he has survived
> it . . . One can be, indeed one must strive to become, tough and philosophical
> concerning destruction and death . . . But it is not permissible that the authors
> of devastation should also be innocent. It is the innocence which constitutes the
> crime.
>
> —James Baldwin, "My Dungeon Shook"

When I was nine years old and living in Blytheville, Arkansas, I watched with mild apprehension as my former sharecropper parents signed a contract for aluminum siding that would end up costing us our home. Someone had taught my father to write his name, but he had never learned anything more about reading and writing. My mother had as much knowledge of reading and writing as four or five years of schooling in a one-room country schoolhouse could provide. In other words, my parents neither read what they were signing nor understood that signing it would lead to the loss of their ramshackle but, nevertheless cherished, property. I learned later that my mother had wanted to have someone read the contract for them, but she did not want to inconvenience the salesman. The year was probably 1961, and in 1961 I had no intimate or firsthand relationships with black people who would actually challenge white male authority, which is how my mother felt her request to have someone read the contract would be taken.

No one I knew ever challenged the white man who owned and ran the small grocery store in our otherwise all-black neighborhood and who seemed to feel it was his right to molest any adolescent girl who made the mistake of coming within close proximity to him or to sexually exploit one particularly pitiful older black man who had effectively been broken during his time on a penal farm. I remember that once I had told my own parents that the storeowner touched my eleven-year-old breasts and tried to rub a certain part of his anatomy against a certain part of mine, and they looked more fearful than angry. To my knowledge, they did nothing, and many years passed before I understood why.

I share this aspect of my personal American story in order to signal the perspective I bring to this project and also to explain how and why I first became interested in the law and legal discourse. Obviously, the loss of that ramshackle house made a permanent impression on me for several reasons: it revealed my parents' relative impotence, it caused more than the usual discord within the household, and it necessitated the displacement of our cousins down the street because we would be buying and they could only afford to rent. Our "new" home was located next to the sexual-predator grocer's store; he owned the house and was willing to sell it to us on some kind of special contract arrangement. I was horrified because I knew what everyone else in the neighborhood knew: that the house was filled with rats (not mice, rats!), rats that had one night attacked my infant cousin in his crib and eaten part of his hand and arm before his parents awoke to his screams and rescued him.

Such experiences did nothing to foster healthy self-esteem, but I suspect they drove my desire for knowledge, for information, and for reading everything I could find in an effort to understand why things were the way they were. Long before I encountered James Baldwin, I saw the law as a corrupt power that seemed bent on stealing back the fragile and precarious freedom that had been extended to African Americans through Constitutional amendment. I witnessed my male siblings' loss of freedom to jail and prison sentences. It was as if their prison cells had been waiting for them since birth. Thus, Quentin Miller's chapter in this volume and in his larger, forthcoming work on James Baldwin's treatment of black male imprisonment bears peculiar resonance for me.

In my first job after high school, I worked with a woman who had grown up in Birmingham, Alabama, during the civil rights movement. She gave me a copy of Anne Moody's *Coming of Age in Mississippi* (1968), and I became fascinated with civil rights law and the movement in general. I read everything I could find in the libraries in downtown Lansing, Michigan. My engagement with legal discourse continued when, in 1978, I joined the secretarial staff of the Michigan Attorney General's office and remained there for some fifteen years working in several divisions: Commerce, Education, and, finally, Agriculture, Lottery and Racing (which later became Lottery and Racing). Part of my initial responsibility in that final position was to maintain a small law library for the lawyers who worked in our building. Of course, I spent as much time reading as I could, and I acquired a wealth of additional knowledge working on briefs and other legal documents. Amazingly, in all that time, I never developed the desire become a lawyer.

After my mother died broke and disappointed—having survived my dad by seven years—I took an early retirement so that I could attend school full time. I had transferred from the local community college to Michigan State University in 1991, but I had seldom been able to attend full time. At Michigan State, my undergraduate mentor, Larry Landrum, suggested that I consider a reading of Toni Morrison's *Beloved* (1987) through the lens of Foucault's *Discipline and Punish* (1977). That reading became the basis for my exploration of property, race, and the law in my subsequent dissertation and in the resulting monograph, *Race, Theft, and Ethics: Property Matters in African American Literature* (2007). I had come full circle from my experience in 1961.

* * *

In 2008, this country elected a man to be its president who identifies as African American. Like so many others, I think I must be dreaming, and I don't want to wake up. The cynicism that had been building in me since I was a child is beginning to give way to hope that America might someday move substantially beyond the effects of its paradoxical birth in slavery and freedom and realize its promise of true democracy. I chastise myself for the cynical response I gave to Erica, the young white student who, even before President Barack Obama became the nominee, dared to say to me that she was going to help him get elected—that he was going to win! I told her that members of the white majority culture were only attracted to him because he in no way threatened them or their sense of who they are—that he was seen as "safe," that he was not African American in the way that I am African American. She became quiet, and thinking that she was backing away from the discussion, I assured her that I welcomed the exchange and would not punish her for disagreeing with me. I was that certain of my position. Now, I wonder if that look in her eyes was pity—for my lack of hope, for my cynicism, for how I had allowed my American experiences to shape me. The truth is that two years ago I could not conceive of an African American First Family—not in my lifetime (as they say). Now, that image serves as my computer screen's background. My young students (almost all white at Penn State) showed me that the country had made progress (or at least the younger generations were making progress), and I was especially happy to be in a university setting when the announcement came that Barack Obama was our new President because nowhere do you find more hope and enthusiasm than among college students. Certainly, President Obama understood that and used his knowledge for political advantage.

While some will suggest (and have suggested) that Obama's victory signaled the end of law's engagement with race, the President actually owes a good deal of his success to the fact that he was able to cultivate a public persona that downplayed fundamental racial conflicts within American society and culture. He did his best not to run as the *black* candidate—even when he waxed eloquent about America's racialized history—and his competitors were all too willing to remind us that he *was* the black candidate. Barack Obama became President of the United States because he is well qualified and because he ran an almost flawless campaign during a combined primary and election season that favored the Democratic candidate. He is a thinker and a pragmatist, and certainly the fact of his good looks did not work against him. Perhaps most importantly, he is also an expert in Constitutional law. The statements surrounding his nomination of Judge Sonia Sotomayor to the Supreme Court, along with conservative white male senators' insistence during her confirmation hearings that she *take back* her statement about the benefits of being a *wise Latina*, suggest to me that this volume can contribute to a more honest dialogue about the American justice system.

The results of a single election will not significantly impact the many ways that courts and legislators have encoded (and continue to encode) race, racism, and racial hierarchy within legal discourse. As Karla F. C. Holloway points out in her analysis of the "perp walk" and privacy law, the twentieth-century emphasis on individual rights just might be premised on a notion of privacy that relies on an uncritical application of an upper-class, white male vision of domestic boundaries. Holloway demonstrates that the current emphasis on civil rights as the preeminent legal strategy for achieving racial equality can obscure the ways that legal doctrines relating to sovereignty and property have long captured the attention of African American writers, intellectuals, and artists, and these legal doctrines could play important roles in the continuing struggle for freedom and equality. Thus, while Obama's election is in fact a watershed moment in America's political and cultural history, Holloway's chapter and the others in this book provide evidence that the key building blocks of American jurisprudence retain both hidden and overt traces of the country's racist and racialized past.

Several chapters reveal the extent to which many aspects of law surrounding matters of disability, privacy, trademark, communication, and so on continue to rely on and thus produce racial distinctions that can support white-supremacist policies. Other chapters, like Sharon Harris's work on Lucy Terry, and William Gleason's analysis of Charles Johnson's short story serve as crucial reminders that African American literature has long been engaged in legal critique—a thesis I explore at length in the *Race, Theft, and Ethics*. Akilah Folami's discussion of the fate of message rap under the Telecommunications Act of 1996 illustrates how efforts to offer salient critiques often encounter structural and legal barriers that limit or close off audience access.

Contributors to this volume also interrogate a number of common assumptions about justice, including the image of a blindfolded or veiled Lady Justice holding a scale. Our guiding concern for this project—unveiling justice—is reflected in the opening epigraph taken from John Williams' *The Man Who Cried I Am* (1967): "Was this what so many places in America were going to be like until the law, *justice*, took off her goddamn blindfold and saw what she had been doing with it *on*?" *African American Culture and Legal Discourse* encourages Americans to unpack the visual and literary metaphors that influence our understanding of what it means to be just. While the image of the scale—equally weighing one side against the other—is meant to invoke balance as a key legal value, such a representation wrongly advocates an ahistorical perspective that does not consider the asymmetry that often exists between the two positions. It also assumes that only two positions need to be considered. As the several chapters referencing sovereignty suggest, rarely do legal conflicts involve a neat symmetry of positions. Returning briefly to the 1961 event that helped to shape my engagement with race, property, and legal discourse, even if my former sharecropper parents had been able and willing to initiate a legal action in order to avoid losing our home, the odds against their success were overwhelming. The asymmetry between legal actors typically determines the structure of legal conflicts and race (and, in my family's case, class) is encoded in the crafting of America's legal doctrines and legal structures that disproportionately harm African Americans.

Still, American race relations are much too complex to view through the black-white binary, as Matthew Fletcher's "On Black Freedman" and Sharon Harris's "On Lucy Terry" reveal. Their work examines how hierarchical structures based on race combined with a doctrine of white supremacy can pit racial and ethnic groups against one another. Thus, while the idea of veiled justice is meant to suggest neutrality and objectivity, the chapters herein suggest that a colorblind jurisprudence will necessarily be partial and incomplete because such an ideal encourages legal actors to neglect the very real ways that racial, cultural, gender, class, and other categories shape the very conflicts that law must resolve. Those of us who are interested in justice for all Americans must continue in the project of unveiling it.

Bibliography

Baldwin, James. "My Dungeon Shook." *James Baldwin: Collected Essays*, edited by Toni Morrison, 292. 1963. Reprint, New York: Library of America, 1998.

Foucault, Michel. *Discipline and Punish: The Birth of the Prison*. 1977. Reprint, New York: Vintage, 1995.

King, Lovalerie. *Race, Theft, and Ethics: Property Matters in African American Literature*. Baton Rouge: Louisiana State University Press, 2007.

Moody, Anne. *Coming of Age in Mississippi*. New York: Dell, 1968.

Morrison, Toni. *Beloved*. New York: Knopf, 1987.

Williams, John A. *The Man Who Cried I Am*. 1967. Reprint, New York: Thunder's Mouth, 1965.

Contributors

I. Bennett Capers is an associate professor of law at Hofstra Law School where he specializes in criminal law and procedure, race and the law, law and literature, and gender and the law. His articles have appeared in *Harvard Civil Rights-Civil Liberties Law Review, Yale Journal of Law and the Humanities, Indiana Law Journal, Hofstra Law Review, Michigan Journal of Race and the Law, New York University Review of Law and Social Change, California Law Review, Howard Law Journal,* and *Columbia Law Review.* He is currently a visiting professor at Fordham Law School.

Charlton Copeland is an associate professor at the University of Miami Law School. His teaching and research interests include administrative law, federalism, civil procedure, constitutional law, law and religion, and race and the law. His publications include "Private Pathologies and Public Policies: Race, Class and the Failure of Child Welfare" in *Yale Law & Policy Review.* He is currently working on several articles, including "Federalism Beyond Power: Judicial Mediation of the Federal-State Relationship," "Anti-Constitutional: The Legitimacy and Limits of Judicial Invalidation of Constitutional Amendments," and "Then There Were Two: The Supreme Court's Section Five Jurisprudence and the Political Isolation of Race and Gender."

Matthew L. M. Fletcher is an associate professor at Michigan State University College of Law and director of the Indigenous Law and Policy Center, sits as an appellate judge for the Pokagon Band of Potawatomi Indians and the Hoopa Valley Tribe, and is a consultant to the Seneca Nation of Indians Court of Appeals. He is an enrolled member of the Grand Traverse Band of Ottawa and Chippewa Indians located in Peshawbestown, Michigan. He will coauthor the sixth edition of *Cases on Federal Indian Law* (Thomson West) with David Getches, Charles Wilkinson, and Robert Williams. He recently published *American Indian Education: Counternarratives in Racism, Struggle, and the Law* (Routledge). His articles have appeared in the *Harvard Journal on Legislation, Houston Law Review, Hastings Law Journal,* and *Tulane Law Review,* and he is currently writing a book on the history of the Grand Traverse Band. He has worked as a staff attorney for the Pascua Yaqui Tribe, the Hoopa Valley Tribe, the Suquamish Tribe, and the Grand Traverse Band, and he has litigated over twenty tribal court cases. He is married to Wenona Singel and they have a son named Owen.

Akilah Folami is an associate professor at Hofstra University School of Law. She has written on media consolidation in broadcast radio and its effect on music and American youth, particularly in hip-hop culture, and has testified before the Federal Communications Commission regarding her findings. Professor Folami's scholarly interests include the intersection of communications law, popular culture, and the regulation of speech. Prior to joining Hofstra, she clerked for

Honorable Constance Baker Motley of the U.S. District Court for the Southern District of New York and practiced in intellectual property and other Internet-related issues at two major New York law firms.

William Gleason is an associate professor of English at Princeton University, where he specializes in nineteeth and twentieth-century American literature, American popular writing, and American social and cultural history. He is the author of *The Leisure Ethic: Work and Play in American Literature, 1840–1940* (1999) as well as essays on such figures as Frederick Douglass, Charles Chesnutt, Edith Wharton, Edgar Rice Burroughs, Thomas Pynchon, and Louise Erdrich. "It Falls to You" is his third essay on the work of Charles Johnson. Gleason is currently completing a study of race, architecture, and American literature.

K. J. Greene is a native New Yorker, a graduate of the Yale Law School, and a tenured law professor on the faculty of Thomas Jefferson School of Law in San Diego, California, where he teaches contracts, intellectual property, music law, and entertainment law. He was recently selected by peers in the San Diego intellectual property bar as one of the top ten intellectual property (IP) attorneys in San Diego County, and he has developed a national reputation as an IP scholar and a leading expert on the subject of African American music and copyright law. As an attorney in leading New York law firms, Greene represented clients such as Time-Warner/HBO, film producer Spike Lee, pop singer Bobby Brown, television star Geraldo Rivera, and the ground-breaking rap group Public Enemy. Before attending law school, he served with honor in the U.S. Marine Corps.

Sharon M. Harris is a professor of English at the University of Connecticut, Storrs and the author or editor of ten books, including critical studies such as *Executing Race: Early American Women's Narratives of Race, Class, and Society* (2005); collections of critical essays, including *Periodical Literature of Eighteenth-Century America* (2005); and scholarly editions, including *Writing Cultural Autobiography: Rebecca Harding Davis's Autobiographical Narratives*. She is also a series editor for the University of Nebraska Press's Legacies of Nineteenth-Century U.S. Women's Writings. In addition, Professor Harris was a founding officer of the Society of Early Americanists (1992–99) and founding president of the Society for the Study of American Women Writers (1998–2003). In 2005 and 2007, respectively, Professor Harris was awarded a National Endowment of the Humanities Fellowship and a University of Connecticut Humanities Institute Fellowship. Professor Harris currently has several projects in press: *Dr. Mary Walker: An American Radical* (Rutgers), *The Selected Letters of Mercy Otis Warren* (Georgia), *A Feminist Reader: From Sappho to the Gorilla Grrrls* (3 volumes, Cambridge), and *Rebecca Harding Davis: The Civil War Years* (Georgia).

Karla F. C. Holloway is James B. Duke Professor of English and professor of law at Duke University. Her research and teaching focus on African American studies, biocultural studies, ethics, and law. Her board memberships, including the Greenwall Foundation's Board in Bioethics; Princeton University's Council for the Program in the Study of Women and Gender; and her faculty affiliation with the Trent Center for Bioethics, Medical Humanities, and the History of Medicine reflect her scholarly interests. Since the publication of her book, *Passed On—African*

American Mourning Stories (2002), she has led national discussions urging end-of-life care conversations in African American communities. Her public essays on death and dying, featured on National Public Radio, include the well-received "Giving a Name to the Pain of Losing a Child." Professor Holloway's recent essays indicate her scholarship's interdisciplinarity and include "Cruel Enough to Stop the Blood: Global Feminisms and the U.S. Body Politic, or: 'They Done Taken My Blues and Gone'" (*Meridians* 6, no. 5); the controversial "Accidental Communities: Race, Emergency Medicine and the Problem of Polyheme" in *The American Journal of Bioethics*; and "Private Bodies/Public Texts: Literature, Science, and States of Surveillance" in *Literature and Medicine* (2007). Her current work-in-progress, a book on bioethics and law with a focus on race and gender, is under contract with Johns Hopkins University Press. She is the recipient of national awards and foundation fellowships, most recently the Rockefeller Foundation's Bellagio Residency Fellowship and the Sheila Biddle Ford Foundation fellowship at Harvard University's Du Bois Institute.

Gerald Horne holds the John J. and Rebecca Moores Chair of History and African American Studies at the University of Houston. His research has addressed issues of race in a variety of relations involving labor, politics, civil rights, and war. He is the author of more than seventeen books and one hundred scholarly articles and reviews. His recent publications include *The End of Empires: African-Americans and India* (Temple, 2008), *The Deepest South: The U.S., Brazil and the African Slave Trade* (New York University Press, 2007), *The White Pacific: U.S. Imperialism and Black Slavery in the South Seas after the Civil War* (Hawaii, 2007), *Cold War in a Hot Zone: The U.S. Confronts Labor and Independence Struggles in the British West Indies* (Temple, 2007), *Black & Brown: Africans and the Mexican Revolution, 1910–1920* (New York University Press, 2005), *Race War! White Supremacy & the Japanese Attack on the British Empire* (New York University Press, 2003), *Powell v. Alabama: The Scottsboro Boys and American Justice* (Franklin Watts, 1997), and others. His forthcoming books are *Mau Mau in Harlem? The U.S. and the Liberation of Kenya* (Palgrave, 2009), *Reds in Paradise? Radical Labor and Racism in the Making of Modern Hawaii* (Hawaii, 2009), and *Negroes with Guns? African-Americans and the British Empire Confront the U.S. Before the Civil War.*

Lovalerie King is an associate professor of English, affiliate faculty in Women's Studies, and director of the Africana Research Center at Penn State-University Park. She specializes in African American literary history. Her publications include *Race, Theft, and Ethics: Property Matters in African Literature* (2007); *The Cambridge Introduction to Zora Neale Hurston* (2008); and two coedited volumes: *James Baldwin and Toni Morrison: Comparative Critical and Theoretical Essays* (2006), and *New Essays on the African American Novel: from Hurston and Ellison to Morrison and Whitehead* (2008).

D. Quentin Miller is an associate professor of English at Suffolk University and has published or edited three books: *Re-Viewing James Baldwin: Things Not Seen*, *John Updike and the Cold War: Drawing the Iron Curtain*, and *Prose and Cons: New Essays on U.S. Prison Literature*. He is editor of the composition textbook *The Generation of Ideas*, the literature textbook *Connections*, and one of the coeditors of the *Heath Anthology of American Literature*. His essays have appeared in such journals as *American Literature, Legacy, Forum for Modern Language Studies, English Language Notes,* and *American Literary Realism.* He is developing a book-length study of James Baldwin.

Richard Schur is an associate professor and director of Interdisciplinary Studies at Drury University. His articles and essays on African American literature, hip-hop studies, African American art, critical race theory, and intellectual property law have appeared in journals such as *Contemporary Literature, American Studies, African American Review, Biography,* and *Law & Inequality,* and in several edited collections. He is the author of *Parodies of Ownership: Hip-Hop Aesthetics and Intellectual Property Law* (2009).

Rebecca Wanzo is an associate professor of English and Women's Studies at Ohio State University. Her book, *The Suffering Will Not Be Televised: African American Women and Sentimental Political Storytelling* (SUNY) examines how African American women make claims about their pain legible in the political logic of storytelling about suffering in the United States. Her research interests include African American literature and culture, cultural studies, critical race theory, feminist theory, graphic storytelling, and theories of affect.

Rochelle Raineri Zuck is an assistant professor of English at the University of Minnesota-Duluth. Her research and teaching interests include eighteenth- and nineteenth-century American literatures, African American and American Indian literatures, and print culture. She has published an essay entitled "Cultivation, Commerce, and Cupidity: Late-Jacksonian Virtue in James Fenimore Cooper's *The Crater*" in *Literature in the Early American Republic.* She is currently working on her first book project, tentatively titled *Imagined Citizens: Ethnic Nationalisms and Crises of Culture, 1816–1856.*

Index